Study Guide Plus

for

Essentials of Sociology
A Down-to-Earth Approach
Third Edition

Study Guide Plus

for

Henslin
Essentials of Sociology
A Down-to-Earth Approach
Third Edition

Prepared by

Gwendolyn E. Nyden
Oakton Community College

Allyn and Bacon
Boston   London   Toronto   Sydney   Tokyo   Singapore

ISBN 0-205-29986-5

Printed in the United States of America

10 9 8 7 6 5 4 3 2 1   03 02 01 00 99

TABLE OF CONTENTS

Study Guide Plus

for

Essentials of Sociology
A Down-to-Earth Approach
Third Edition

SUCCESSFUL STUDY STRATEGIES

Welcome to Sociology! You are about to embark on a fascinating journey in which you will discover new and interesting information about yourself and the world around you. This study guide has been prepared to accompany the textbook <u>Sociology: A Down-to-Earth Approach</u> by James M. Henslin. In this introductory chapter you will learn about some preliminary steps to take, strategies for success, and hints for taking different kinds of tests in order to achieve academic success..

BECOMING A BETTER STUDENT

Whether you are a seasoned college student or just starting out, there are some preliminary steps you can take that will make you a better student.

Be Familiar with Campus Resources

One key to student success is becoming familiar -- or more familiar -- with resources on your college campus. The following are just a few that may be available to you:

- **Student services:** At student services centers you will find academic, personal and career counseling, seminars and workshops on issues of special concern to you as a student.
- **Services for special populations:** If you are a student returning to college after many years, a student with disabilities, a minority student, or an international student, there may be a center to assist you in meeting your specific academic goals.
- **Instructional support services:** Your college may offer instructional support services, sometimes through a learning lab or a tutoring center, where you can get help in developing the study, reading, and writing skills essential to your success in college.

Working Out Your Own Strengths and Weaknesses

Give thought to your own strengths and weaknesses as a student. Consider these questions:

- Do you remember material best when you've heard it or when you've read it for yourself?
- Do you need to be actively involved with the material in order to learn it?
- Do you learn best when you cover everything at once or when you study smaller units?

Besides understanding how you learn, evaluate your current study habits and assess areas that may need improvement. Do you study better when you're alone or in a group? Do you study best when you set a beginning and ending time and tasks are clearly outlined? Consider these questions:

- Do you feel as if there is never enough time to spend on school work?
- Do you have a hard time managing possible conflicts to your study time?
- Do you have trouble concentrating on your school work?
- Do you have trouble taking notes and identifying which information is important?

If you answered "YES" to any or all of these questions, you may want to seek the assistance of student services or a learning center. Someone there will be able to help you in developing better study habits.

Managing Your Time Efficiently

The next step towards college success is learning to manage your time more productively. We must all learn to work within the constraints of the 24-hour day. As a college student you must decide how to divide your time between school, family and/or friends, and most probably work. Take a few minutes and jot down your "typical" day--noting tasks to be accomplished and the time each takes.

WEEKLY SCHEDULE FOR FALL SEMESTER							
	Sunday	Monday	Tuesday	Wednesday	Thursday	Friday	Saturday
7:00 am		wake up	wake up	wake up	wake up	wake up	
8:00		breakfast/ school	breakfast/ school	breakfast/ school	breakfast/ school	breakfast/ school	
9:00		class--SOC	class--BIO	class--SOC	class--BIO	class--SOC	wake up
10:00	wake up	class--ART	class--LIT	class--ART	BIO lab	class--ART	
11:00							
12:00 pm		lunch		lunch		lunch	work
1:00	volunteer-- ecology ctr.	class--HIS	lunch	class--HIS	lunch--HIS	class	
2:00		work	work	work	work	work	
3:00							
4:00							
5:00	work-out	work-out	work-out	work-out	work-out	work-out	work-out
6:00	dinner	dinner	dinner	dinner	dinner	dinner	dinner
7:00	study	study	study	study	study	party with friends	party with friends
8:00							
9:00	study break	study break	study break	study break	study break		
10:00	study	study	study	study	study		
11:00	bed	bed	bed	bed	bed		
12:00 am						bed	bed

Figure 1: AN EXAMPLE OF A TYPICAL SEMESTER SCHEDULE

From this you can develop a schedule for the entire semester similar to the one in Figure 1. List the days of the week across the top and the hours of the day down the side. Within the boxes write down activities that you do regularly -- sleep, meals, job, classes, exercise, and volunteering. The blank boxes represent your "free time." What you do during these times will change from week to week. For instance, one week you may decide to work extra hours, another week you may spend more time with friends, and yet another week, you may devote those hours to studying. By mapping your semester early, you will be able to maximize your use of time.

It would also be helpful for you to have a schedule of all of your assignments for the entire semester. Figure 2 illustrates this schedule; to make one of your own, list the courses across the top and

ASSIGNMENT SCHEDULE--FALL SEMESTER					
	Sociology	Art	History	Biology	Literature
WK 1					
WK 2	essay on culture	charcoal project due	proposal on research topic	quiz--Ch 1-2 lab assign. 1	
WK 3				quiz--Ch 3-4	review Pride & Prejudice
WK 4	observation at day care ctr.			quiz--Ch 5-6 lab assign. 2	
WK 5		watercolor project due	preliminary bibliography	quiz--Ch 7-8	
WK 6	evaluation of trip to county jail			quiz--Ch 9-11 lab assign. 3	review Emma
MID TERM					
WK 7	tst--Ch 1-8	NO MID-TERM	tst--Ch 1-10	tst--Ch 1-11	
WK 8	review of major sociology bk		Outline of research paper	quiz--Ch 12 lab assign. 4	
WK 9		pastels project due		quiz--Ch 13-14	
WK 10	family history due			quiz--Ch 15-16; lab assign. 5	review Sense & Sensibility
WK 11		acrylic project due	annotated bibliography due	quiz--Ch 17-18	
WK 12	observation of political rally			quiz--Ch 19; lab assign. 6	
WK 13		oil painting due		quiz--Ch 20	review Persuasion
WK 14			research paper due	quiz--Ch 21; lab assign. 7	Final paper on Austen
FINALS WK	tst--Ch 9-15	Final project due	tst--Ch 11-18	tst-Ch 12-21	NO FINAL

Figure 2: AN EXAMPLE OF A TYPICAL ASSIGNMENT SCHEDULE

the weeks of the semester down the side. Within the boxes list tasks that must be completed for each class in a specific week, noting tests, paper assignments, as well as other course work that has a deadline. This will help you in planning how you will divide your time among each of your courses over the semester.

In addition to these semester-based schedules, that can be posted in a highly visible location like a bulletin board above your desk or inside your assignment book, get into the habit of using a daily schedule. This is a list of the day's tasks and the time frame in which you plan to accomplish each. A good time to make up this daily schedule is the evening before; spend a few minutes thinking about and then writing down all the things that you need to do the next day. Not only will this free your mind of thinking about what lies ahead so that you will sleep more easily, but when you get up in the morning you will be prepared to begin the day and not have to waste time organizing at the last minute. Although this daily schedule reflects all the tasks that need to be done during the course of the day, some things are more important than others; get into the habit of prioritizing your list so that the most important are at the top and are guaranteed to get done first.

While making and using schedules is important to your success in college, so is learning to take advantage of spare moments in the day that are otherwise wasted; once you become aware of them you can begin to use them for impromptu study periods. Here are some ideas to consider:

- Most of us spend some time each day just waiting -- for a bus or train, for an appointment with a doctor or professor, or for service in a bank or store. Bring something along to occupy yourself while you wait. It could be a book or article you've been assigned to read, a notebook with notes, or flash cards with formulas or vocabulary on them.
- While you're driving in the car, exercising, or cleaning house, listen to recorded tapes of vocabulary, passages from text, or series of questions and answers on course material.
- Use the time immediately before class begins to recall main points from the previous class lecture, think about questions you have on the material that was covered in the last class or that will be covered in this class, or glance through notes.
- Keep a small notebook of ideas, questions, or thoughts you have about course material; whenever one of these comes to mind you can write it down and think about the answers later.

Finally, don't forget to devote some time each day to study breaks; these are rewards for hard work. Schedule them into your day and then stick to them. They are not only something to look forward to as you are studying hard, but they actually enhance your overall learning. After taking a jog or walk, having coffee with friends, watching a TV show, or reading the newspaper you will return to the task of studying with a mind that is once again ready to tackle important course material.

Developing better concentration

Concentration is a skill that you need to develop if you are going to get the most out of your study periods. When you concentrate you are focusing all of your attention on the task in front of you. If you are able to eliminate distractions you will find this easier to do. But how do you go about doing this? Begin by finding a space that is suitable for studying, one that you associate first and foremost with that activity and not some other. For instance, trying to study on you bed or in the snack bar of the student union is not a good idea, because those areas are not associated primarily with studying.

Many students choose to study in their college library. There are a number of advantages to using the library: it is unlikely that you could find any quieter space in which to concentrate on your school work, the lighting in the library is designed for study, and you can usually claim adequate space in which to spread out your materials. It is also easier at the library to eliminate visual and auditory distractions, as well as telephone and social interruptions. Finally, many libraries have lounges for students to use for periodic breaks. Remember, while we can never completely eliminate all distractions in our world, finding a quiet place away from the hustle and bustle of our everyday lives will help enormously when it comes to studying.

Because concentration is enhanced when we are able to eliminate distractions, here are some additional measures you can take to achieve better concentration:

- **Use lists.** One list is a reminder of what you have to do during the study period; as you accomplish a task, check it off and move on to the next. A second list is for things you have to do later. Many times you find yourself preoccupied with some problem in your life and your mind continues to return to this problem time and time again. While you are trying to study, your concentration is broken by these other thoughts that pop randomly into your mind; if you keep a second list, you can write these interruptions down on it, promising yourself that you will return to the list <u>after</u> you finish studying.
- **Take regular breaks.** Use a timer to keep track of your study time; when the alarm goes off, get up and take a break. This way, you will not be tempted to look at your watch every fifteen minutes, wondering how long you've studied and when your next break time is due.
- **Set a goal for each study session** -- so many pages read or vocabulary words mastered, etc. When you've reached the session goal, close your books and notes until the next time.

DEVELOPING SUCCESSFUL LEARNING STRATEGIES

Using campus resources, assessing your strengths and weaknesses, managing your time, and learning to concentrate better are the first steps to college success. In addition, there are some strategies for acquiring course-specific skills and knowledge. Begin by figuring out what's important and what's not and learning how make the most of the course materials, and then work on achieving mastery over the course contents.

Figuring out what's important in the course

The first place to look for information about what's important in any course is the course syllabus that the professor hands out in the first day, or few days, of class. This document should provide you with an outline of the topics that will be covered over the semester and information on the course work expected of you as a student: how many tests and quizzes there are, the nature of these tests and quizzes and when they are scheduled throughout the semester, as well as deadlines and due dates for written assignments and other class projects. You can use this information when organizing you different time schedules. The syllabus should also include information on how the professor calculates your final grade; you should be able to determine which course work he or she places most emphasis on by looking at how much each component in the course counts towards that final grade.

Making the most of course materials

You will be expected to purchase the required text or texts for the course; often the professor also includes some recommended reading--it's up to you whether or not you read these additional texts. Increasingly in courses such as the one you're taking in sociology there are study guides like this one that accompany the text. This particular study guide includes that following:

- a **Chapter Summary** that summarizes the main ideas found in the chapter.
- a set of **Learning Objectives** that provides statements concerning the main ideas of the chapter. If you want to check your responses, refer back to the page numbers listed with each question.
- a listing of **Key Terms** that contains all of the sociological concepts that are introduced within the chapter.
- a listing of **Key People** that includes some of the major sociologists whose work is discussed within the chapter. In some cases, these are early sociologists who contributed theoretical understanding and research insights to the discipline; in other cases, they are contemporary sociologists who are doing research and developing theory on the subject.
- a **Self-Test** that provides you with an opportunity to see how much of the information you have retained. Each self-test includes multiple choice, true-false, fill-in, and matching questions.
- a section entitled **Down-to-Earth Sociology** that asks questions about the material you have read so that you can relate it to your own life and the world with which you are familiar. Remember there is not necessary a right and wrong answer for these; rather, they are designed to get your opinion, based on your understanding of the facts you have read.
- an **Chapter-by-Chapter Answer Key** that provides answers for all of the questions in the self-test. Check your answers against this; if you got the question wrong, refer back to the pages in the textbook and read those again.
- a **Glossary of Words to Know** that includes some of the words that may be unfamiliar, along with their meanings. It is designed to be a resource for you to use as you read the textbook. If there are words that you don't know that are not included in this glossary, be sure to look them up in a dictionary. Your comprehension of the material is based on the assumption that you understand the words that are used.

The study guide is intended to be used together with the text to maximize your mastery of the material. Here are some suggestions for making the best use of the resources in both the text and the study guide:

- Before reading each chapter, **refer to the Chapter Summary and Learning Objectives** that are found in the Study Guide. The Summary will provide you with a capsule statement of what the chapter is about, and the Learning Objectives will tell you how you should be focusing your attention. Then read the textbook.
- Rather than plunging headlong into the chapter, **take a few minutes and orient yourself**. Start with the chapter title. This tells you what broad area of sociology will be discussed. Keep the title in mind as you read through the chapter and try to create a mental picture of how the various parts of the chapter fit together within this broad area.
- **Approach each chapter one section at time.** Use the section headings to pose questions that you can ask yourself when you finish reading the section. As you finish a section, go back to the Learning Objectives in the Study Guide and try to answer the statement(s) that apply. If you can provide an answer, then proceed to the next section; if you can't, go back to the textbook and review the section you've just read.
- **Remember to read the boxed text**; these pertain to the material in the body of the textbook and are included to give you insights into U.S. society as well as societies around the world. They are designed to bring sociology alive for you.

Achieving mastery over the material

In general, mastery is facilitated by good organization. Students who succeed are generally those who are able to stay on top of the course because they have developed a system for keeping track of all the materials. One suggestion is to purchase a loose-leaf notebook for each course, with the syllabus, handouts, assignments, and notes from your readings and lectures in separate tabbed sections. In this way it will be easier to keep up with all the work and the studying because everything is together in one place.

Many students think that sociology will be an "easy" course; because they are part of the society and thus intimately familiar with it, they believe they have nothing new to learn. This is their first mistake because sociology, like every other discipline, has a vocabulary of its own that must be learned if the student wants to be successful in the course. Here are some ideas to help you in mastering vocabulary:

- **Identify the concepts.** As you are reading the text pay attention to the concepts that are in bold-face type. The definition is provided for you; refer back to that definition as you read.
- **Think of examples.** Try to think of some examples of your own; if you can relate the material to the world with which you are most familiar, you are more likely to remember it.
- **Make up flash cards.** Many times it helps to make up flash cards, with the word on one side and the definition and an example on the other side. Keep these with you and review them while you're waiting in line or stopped at a red light. As you move through your day, get into the practice of looking for examples of those concepts you are presently learning and applying them to situations around you.

All of these strategies will guarantee that you will incorporate new and unfamiliar concepts into your framework and will remember them when the time comes for a test.

Achieving mastery over the material requires more than just learning key concepts. As a general rule, it is best to read the assigned material <u>prior</u> to class. As you read, get into the habit of taking notes, making notes in the margin of the text or in a separate section of your notebook. These should include summaries of the main points of the section you've read, connections between what you're reading now and what you read earlier in the semester, and examples to illustrate these ideas, as well as any questions that were raised in your mind in connection with the reading.

If you have taken the time to read the material in advance, when you go to class you should be prepared for what the professor is going to cover. If you have questions from the reading, now is the time to raise them. Before class begins, divide the pages of your notebook vertically into two columns--a narrower one to the left, representing about one-third the width of the page, and a wider one on the right representing the remaining two-thirds of the page. As you take notes, use the wider column to record what the professor says. Later, as you review what you've written down, use the narrower column in the same way that you would use the margins of your text--for making connections, writing down main ideas, and noting any questions you might have. You can also use this space to make reference to textbook pages that correspond to what the professor has said; this will come in handy when you are studying for exams.

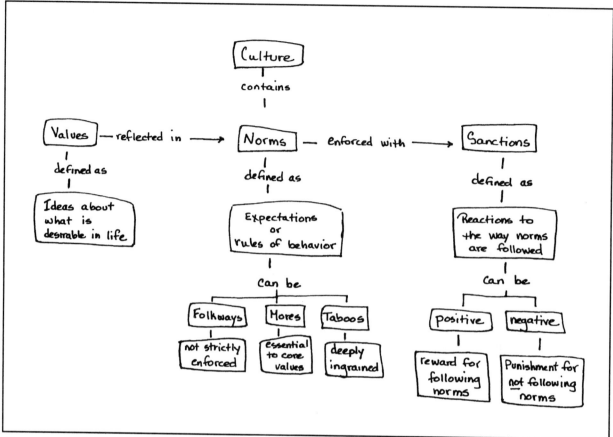

Figure 3: AN EXAMPLE OF A CONCEPT MAP, Illustrating p. 44 of the Henslin text

Sometimes students find in easier to master new and unfamiliar material by drawing a concept map, which presents relationships between ideas and concepts in a visual format. Figure 3 provides an illustration of such a concept map. Concept maps can be drawn for separate sections or topics found within a chapter and then combined into a map for each chapter. The key to mapping successfully is to be able to identify the key concepts that relate to the section or topic and then linking other concepts or ideas to each of these key concepts. Concept maps are helpful because they create a "picture" of the material that summarizes what must be mastered, showing the links between ideas.

Remember, if you miss a class for any reason, it is still your responsibility to find out what was covered. If you know in advance that you will be absent, make arrangements with another student to pick up any handouts that are distributed; you should also make sure that you can get the class notes from the student. It is also a good idea to talk with the professor about making up any class assignments. If the absence is unexpected, you should make a point of getting the notes from another student and talk with the professor about any missed work; don't wait until the end of the semester to do this, do it as soon as you return to school.

Once you feel you have achieved some familiarity with the material, go back to the study guide and follow these steps:

- **Check the list of Key Terms to Define.** Try and define each word and think of an example. Then check the definitions that are provided within each chapter of the Study Guide to see if you are correct. If you need help thinking of an example, refer back to the textbook chapter.
- **Check the list of Key People.** See how many you know and whether or not you can identify their contribution to sociology. If you can't, go back to the textbook and locate them within the chapter. (A quick way to do this is to refer to the Index at the back of the textbook, and then go directly to the page listed.)
- **Take the Self-test.** Mark those questions that you got wrong, and go back to the text to find the correct answer. Then a few days later try them again to see if you've now mastered the material. Use the self-test to review the material just before a test.

All of these aid in your review of the information You might also want to once again review the chapter outline. This provides you with a broad understanding of the ideas that were covered in the chapter. If there is information in the outline that is still unfamiliar to you, go back to the textbook and reread that section. The outline and the self-test can also be used in reviewing material for a test.

SCORING HIGH MARKS ON TESTS

If you have made good use of the suggestions and strategies in the preceding pages, you should be well prepared when it comes time to take tests. Some students also find it helpful to organize study groups prior to major tests. Whether or not this is a help or a hindrance depends on your own personal study style, as well as the character of the group; you will need to assess both before making a decision about getting involved with such an activity. Whatever your decision, keeping up with the reading assignments, learning how to organize your time and your notes, having a place to study that is quiet and free of distractions are all important for mastering the material and demonstrating to the professor that you have learned your lessons by doing well on the test. In addition, there are some specific ideas for approaching tests, including understanding the different types of tests and developing strategies for taking different types of tests.

Strategies for taking objective tests

Most of you reading this guide are quite familiar with objective tests--multiple choice, true/false, matching, and fill-in the blank questions. In fact, the self-tests contained in the chapters that follow include questions of this nature. These types of questions focus on more detailed information and on your ability to recognize the correct answer. In general, when studying for objective tests you will want to focus on details--definitions of key concepts, accomplishments of key figures, specific facts, etc. Here are some strategies that will help you do well on tests of this nature:

- **Read instructions carefully.** Many students, anxious to begin the test, do not take enough time to reading the instructions carefully. Consequently, they often end up making mistakes when it comes to selecting and recording the correct answers.
- **Take time to read each question.** Likewise, students read questions and answers too quickly, often missing important clues that would help them to select the correct answer.

- **Pace yourself.** Perhaps students rush because they are afraid they will not have enough time to complete the exam. If you want to avoid this problem and improve your chances of getting high marks, start by finding out in advance how many questions will be on the test and use this information to calculate about how much time per item you will have. Then, during the test you can pace yourself so that you don't run out of time and rush at the end.
- **Learn to recognize qualifiers.** In writing the questions, the professor will use qualifying words to change the meaning of seemingly straightforward statements; *all, always, only,* most, usually, some, sometimes, *none,* and *never* are frequently used in this way. You will notice that these range along a continuum from positive to negative--those italicized words on each end set up a qualification that applies 100 percent of the time, while the ones in the middle mean that sometimes the condition exists and sometimes it doesn't. If you see an absolute qualifier and you know that condition occurs only some of the time, then you can eliminate that choice; likewise, you can rule out statements that contain variable qualifiers if you are certain that the condition occurs all of the time.

For instance, the following multiple choice question makes use of qualifiers:

- Sanctions:
    a.   are *always* material.
    b.   can be positive or negative.
    c.   have *very little* impact on *most* people today.
    d.   All of the above.

In approaching the question, ask yourself whether or not there are sanctions that are non-material. Since there are non-material sanctions--a smile, a frown, a compliment or a reprimand--then "a" is incorrect. Likewise, since sanctions do have an impact on most people, then "c" is incorrect. The correct answer is "b."

- **Watch for negatives.** In addition to qualifiers, you must learn to notice negatives. Obvious negatives are words like *not, no,* and *never;* negatives can also be created by adding prefixes like "un-" to words like "important." When students read a question too quickly they may overlook these negatives and end up answering incorrectly.

Another common use of the negative is to ask students to identify which of the following is not, as is illustrated by the following question:

- All of the following are ways of neutralizing deviance, <u>except:</u>
    a.   appeal to higher loyalties.
    b.   denial of responsibility.
    c.   denial of deviant labels.
    d.   denial of injury and of a victim.

In answering this question, you need to identify which *are* ways of neutralizing deviance; three of the four are. The correct answer would be "c;" "denial of deviant labels" is <u>not</u> one of the ways in which people neutralize deviance.

Besides these general guidelines, here are some hints about each type of question that is likely to be found on the typical objective test:

- **Multiple Choice questions:** Begin by reading all the answer choices and ruling out those options that you know are incorrect. You may discover that only one option is left. If more than one option remains, and you have been instructed to choose only one, then you need to give some further thought to the answers. Are there any qualifiers that you need to consider? Are there grammatical clues--subject/verb agreement issues, correct fit between the stem and the answer, etc? Is there an option "all of the above" or "A and C;" it may very well be that there is more than one correct answer, but unless you have been given such an option, you need to rule out all but one choice.

- **True/False questions:** Remember you have a 50-50 chance of being correct regardless of what answer you choose. It is easier to write a true statement than a false one, and most professors want to make sure that students leave the course remembering what is true rather than being confused about what is false. Therefore, you are likely to find more true statements than false ones. For this reason, when you really don't know the answer, it is better to choose "true" than "false." Again, pay attention to the use of qualifying words and negatives.

- **Matching questions:** One of the biggest problems with matching questions, especially if there is a long list to match, is becoming confused about which options you've already chosen and which you haven't. If you're recording your answers on a separate answer sheet, ask the professor if it is okay to mark on the test; if the answer is affirmative, get into the habit of marking which ones you've chosen as you go along. Match those that are most familiar first; by the process of elimination you will end up only with those you don't know and you can then make the best possible guess among what is left.

- **Fill-in-the-Blank questions:** Perhaps these are the most difficult--and dreaded--questions on objective tests because the answers are usually not provided. Sometimes the question is worded in such a way that it is unclear to you what type of answer is being sought; if you run across such questions, ask the professor for some clarification. Sometimes a sentence will contain one blank, other times more than one blank; don't automatically assume that a single blank means the professor is looking for a single word, because he or she may use a single blank but want you to supply a string of words or a complete name. If you see only one blank, but suspect the answer may encompass more than one word, as the professor for clarification.

Here are two examples that illustrate the preceding discussion:

- *One blank--only one word expected:*
  A _____ system is a form of social stratification in which individual status is determined by birth and is lifelong. [The correct term to use here is *caste*.]

- *One blank--two (or more) words expected:*
  _____ is a particular form of violence directed exclusively against women. [The sentence is making reference to *female circumcision*.]

Sometimes you may find more than one blank in a statement, indicating that the professor wants you to provide more than one response. If this is the case, think about concepts or ideas that are linked together in some way and see if they'll fit.

Here are two examples of multiple blanks:

- *More than one blank in a sequence:*
  According to Max Weber, the three dimensions of social class are: (1)_____;
  (2)_____; and (3)_____. [To complete this sentence, you need to three of three concepts that are linked together in Weber's work; the correct answers are: *wealth, power,* and *prestige.*]

- *More than one blank separated in the sentence:*
  A _____ allows its owners to purchase goods but to be billed later while a _____ allows its owner to charge purchases against his or her bank account. [The first statement is referring to a *credit card*, while the second is talking about a *debit card.*]

Strategies for taking essay tests

While the previous tips may help you get through the objective test, they are not suited to essay tests, which are written to maximize your recall of the material and your ability to synthesize and summarize what you have learned. When studying for essay tests you will want to review more global information--trends, theories, and perspectives.

Just as there are strategies for managing the objective test, so too are there ways of managing an essay test in order to maximize your results.

- Once again **read the directions carefully.** Ascertain how many essay questions you are expected to answer and whether they are to be drawn from separate parts of the test--for instance, the professor may want you to answer two from section A and one from section B or one each from sections A, B, and C.
- Once you have gone over the directions, **plan how you will divide the allotted time** among the questions; you want to be able to have enough time to answer all the questions fully. Ask the professor if it makes any difference what order you answer the questions. If it doesn't matter, then decide for yourself the sequence in which to answer them; many students find that getting the easiest question(s) out of the way first allows them to spend more time on those that are more difficult.
- Make sure you **understand what the question is asking** you to do. Essay questions may ask you to compare (show similarities); contrast, differentiate, or distinguish (discuss differences); discuss, evaluate, or criticize (present strengths and weaknesses); demonstrate, justify, prove, show, or support (give evidence that supports an idea or statement); list, identify, enumerate, or state (list with or without a brief discussion or example). As you can see, each is asking you to do something different and you need to understand exactly what the professor wants you to do before you begin.
- In answering an essay question **start with a rough outline**, jotting down ideas that you want to cover. Include both the main ideas and the supporting evidence in your quick outline. By taking a few minutes in the beginning to do this you are assured that your information will be organized carefully and completely.
- In your response **get right to the point**; your introduction should contain a statement of what position you will be taking in trying to answer the question. The paragraphs that follow should

provide supporting statements linked to theories, research and key concepts that you have learned in the course of the semester.

- **Avoid using personal opinions in your essays**, unless otherwise asked to. Remember even when asked to take a position, you should support your position with facts, not personal opinions. Your concluding paragraph should summarize what you have stated, perhaps connecting your argument with some body of knowledge within the particular discipline.
- In general, **stay focused on the subject** and avoid bringing in irrelevant facts simply to pad your essay. Likewise, don't try to stretch a short essay by restating the same thesis several times. A professor will conclude that you really don't have anything to say and will give you the same grade he or she would have if you had written the thesis only once in a briefer essay.
- You should also take care to **write neatly** so the professor can read what you've written. By the time you get to college you are well aware of whether or not your handwriting is legible. If it is not, try printing your response. An essay that is illegible, regardless of how good the ideas and organization are, will most likely not be read or graded by the professor.

Overcoming test anxiety

For many students, taking a test is guaranteed to generate a high level of anxiety. No matter how much preparation you do, when the time for the test rolls around, you are consumed with anxiety. If you're one of those students, check out student services or the learning lab to see if your school offers workshops on overcoming such fears. At the same time, here are a few things you can try for yourself to see if any help to reduce these feelings:

- **Learn to relax.** When you're relaxed you can think more clearly about the task ahead. One way to relax is to learn to do slow, deep breathing--inhaling through your nose and drawing the air up into your lungs and then exhaling through your mouth; yoga is sometimes recommended as an excellent way to become more relaxed.
- **Give yourself pep talks**. Counter negative thoughts that pop into your head with positive ones. You'll feel more confident when your head is filled with positive thoughts than negative ones, and that confidence could make a difference.
- **Visualize**. Try to picture yourself being successful at taking the test. While there is no guarantee that this will produce a successful outcome, it's another strategy for boosting your confidence. This may be all you need to do a great job when the test rolls around.
- **Take control.** Most importantly, you need to feel in control of the situation. When you feel powerless to do anything, the result is often to panic; on the other hand, if you feel powerful, you will be able to master whatever task confronts you.

I hope you have found the preceding tips useful. If you incorporate some of them into your regular routines and use the resources in the Study Guide you should finish the semester with good grades and a better understanding not only of sociology, but of yourself and your social world. I hope that you will enjoy your adventure and find that this subject opens new vistas of understanding to you. Good Luck!

Gwen Nyden, Ph.D.
Oakton Community College
Des Plaines, Illinois

Sources:

Jalongo, Mary Ranck, Twiest, Megan Mahoney, and Gail J. Gerlach. *The College Learner: How to Survive and Thrive in an Academic Environment.* Englewood Cliffs, NJ: Prentice-Hall, 1996.

Lenier, Minnette, and Janet Maker. *Keys to College Success*, 4th edition. Upper Saddle River, NJ: Prentice-Hall, 1998.

Pauk, Walter. *How to Study in College*, 6th edition. Boston: Houghton Mifflin Company, 1997.

CHAPTER 1
THE SOCIOLOGICAL PERSPECTIVE

CHAPTER SUMMARY

- Sociology offers a perspective--a view of the world--which stresses that people's social experiences underlie their behavior.

- Sociology emerged in the mid-1800s in western Europe, during the upheavals of the Industrial Revolution. Early sociologists were Auguste Comte, Herbert Spencer, Karl Marx, Emile Durkheim, and Max Weber. In the early years few women received the advanced education required to become a sociologist and women like Harriet Martineau, who did become sociologists, were largely ignored.

- Sociology became established in North America by the end of the 19th century. Within U.S. sociology there has always been a tension between basic sociology and attempts to reform society. Two early sociologists who combined sociology with social reform were Jane Addams and W.E.B. DuBois.

- A theory is a statement about how facts are related to one another. Because no one theory encompasses all of reality, sociologists use three primary theoretical frameworks: (1) symbolic interactionism--which concentrates on the meanings that underlie people's lives--usually focuses on the micro level; (2) functional analysis--which stresses that society is made up of various parts which, when working properly, contribute to the stability of society--focuses on the macro level; and (3) conflict theory--which stresses inequalities and sees the basis of social life as a competitive struggle to gain control over scarce resources--also focuses on the macro level.

- Research and theory must work together because without theory research is of little value, and if theory is unconnected to research it is unlikely to represent the way life really is.

- Sociological research is needed because common sense is highly limited and often incorrect.

- Eight basic steps are included in scientific research: (1) selecting a topic, (2) defining the problem, (3) reviewing the literature, (4) formulating a hypothesis, (5) choosing a research method, (6) collecting the data, (7) analyzing the results, and (8) sharing the results.

- Sociologists use six research methods (or research designs) for gathering data: surveys, participant observations, secondary analysis, documents, unobtrusive measures, and experiments.

- Ethics are of concern to sociologists, who are committed to openness, honesty, truth, and protecting subjects; sociologists are not supposed to misrepresent themselves or their research.

- Sociologists agree that social research should be value free, but recognize that, at any point in time, sociologists are members of a particular society and are infused with values of all sorts. One of the dilemmas for sociologists is deciding whether the goal of research should be only to advance understanding of human behavior or to reform harmful social arrangements.

LEARNING OBJECTIVES

As you read Chapter 1, use these learning objectives to organize your notes. After completing your reading, briefly state an answer to each of the objectives, and review the text pages in parentheses.

1. Explain the sociological perspective and discuss the contribution that it makes to our understanding of human behavior. (4-5)
2. Discuss why sociology emerged as a science in the middle of the 19th century in Europe. (5)
3. Identify and explain the contribution each of the following made to the development of sociology: Auguste Comte, Herbert Spencer, Karl Marx, Emile Durkheim, and Max Weber. (5-8)

4. Explain how rigidly defined sex roles affected women's involvement in early sociology, using the experience of Harriet Martineau. (8-9)
5. Trace the development of sociology in the United States and explain the tension between social reform and sociological analysis and how applied sociology addresses this tension. (9-13)
6. Explain the chief differences in the three major theoretical perspectives: symbolic interactionism, functional analysis, and conflict theory. (13-18)
7. Compare micro-level and macro-level analysis and state which level of analysis is utilized by each of the major theoretical perspectives. (18-19)
8. Discuss how research and theory work together. (19)
9. Explain why common sense is an inadequate source of knowledge about human behavior. (19-20)
10. Identify the eight steps in a research model. (20-22)
11. List and describe each of the six research methods. (23-27)
12. Describe the major ethical issues involved in sociological research; demonstrate these issues by using the Brajuha, Scarce, and Humphreys research as examples. (28-29)
13. State the key issues in the debate about the proper role of values in sociology. (30)

CHAPTER OUTLINE

I. **The Sociological Perspective**
    A. This perspective is important because it provides a different way of looking at life; and it contribute to our understanding of why people are the way they are.
    B. Sociology stresses the broader social context of behavior.
        1. At the center is the question of how people are influenced by their society.
        2. Sociologists look at the social location--culture, social class, gender, religion, age, and education--of people.
        3. Sociologists consider external influences--people's experiences--which are internalized and become part of a person's thinking and motivations.

II. **The Development of Sociology**
    A. Sociology developed in the middle of the 19th century when social observers began to use scientific methods to test ideas about social life.
        1. Throughout history people have tried to figure out social life, asking questions and forming answers based on superstition or myth.
        2. Sociology emerged as a result of changes in European societies that were taking place at that time: the Industrial Revolution, in which traditional society and culture were transformed; the American and French revolutions, out of which new ideas about the rights of individuals within society were accepted; and the application of scientific methods to find answers for the questions about the natural order and our social world.
    B. Auguste Comte coined the term "sociology" and suggested the use of positivism--applying the scientific approach to the social world--but he did not utilize this approach himself.
    C. Herbert Spencer, another social philosopher, viewed societies as evolutionary, coined the term "the survival of the fittest," and became known for social Darwinism.
    D. Karl Marx, founder of the conflict perspective, believed that class conflict--the struggle between the proletariat and the bourgeoisie--was the key to human history.
    E. Emile Durkheim studied the social factors which underline suicide and found that the level of social integration, the degree to which people are tied to their social group, was a key social factor in suicide. Central to his studies was the idea that human behavior cannot be

understood simply in individual terms, but must be understood within the larger social context in which it occurs.

F.   Max Weber defined religion as a central force in social change, i.e. Protestantism encourages greater economic development and was the central factor in the rise of capitalism in some countries.

III.   **Sexism and Early Sociology**

A.   In the 1800s women were assigned the roles of wife and mother; few were able to acquire the education required to become sociologists and those who did were ignored.

B.   Harriet Martineau was exceptional; she studied social life in Great Britain and the United States and eventually published *Society in America* two to three decades before Max Weber or Emile Durkheim were even born.

IV.   **Sociology in North America**

A.   Sociology was transplanted to the United States in the late 19th century, first taking hold at the University of Chicago, the University of Kansas, and Atlanta University.

B.   Jane Addams was active in promoting social reform. In 1889 she founded Hull House, a settlement house that served the needs of Chicago's urban poor. Sociologists from nearby University of Chicago were frequent visitors.

C.   W. E. B. Du Bois, an African American, created a sociology laboratory at Atlanta University in 1897, conducted extensive research on race relations in the U.S., and helped found the NAACP.

D.   During the 1940s, the focus shifted from reform to theory; Talcott Parsons developed abstract models of society to show how the parts of society harmoniously work together. In the 1950s, C. Wright Mills urged sociologists to get back to social reform; he saw imminent danger in the emergence of a power elite within the United States.

E.   Recently there has been attempts to blend sociological knowledge with practical results through the development of applied sociology.

1.   The role of applied sociologists is to recommend changes.

2.   Clinical sociologists become directly involved in bringing about social change through their work in various social settings.

3.   Applied sociology is not the same as social reform because the goal is not to rebuild society but to bring about change in a limited setting.

V.   **Theoretical Perspectives in Sociology**

A.   Theory is defined as a "general statement about how some parts of the world fit together and how they work." There are three major theoretical perspectives in sociology.

B.   Symbolic interactionism views society as composed of symbols that people use to establish meaning, develop their views of the world, and communicate with one another. A symbolic interactionist studying divorce would focus on the changing meanings of marriage, divorce, and family to explain the increase.

C.   Functional analysis sees society as composed of various parts, each with a function, which contributes to society's equilibrium. Auguste Comte, Herbert Spencer, and Emile Durkheim all contributed to the development of functionalism.

1.   Robert Merton used the term functions to refer to the beneficial consequences of people's actions, and dysfunction to refer to consequences that undermine a system's equilibrium.

2.   In trying to explain divorce, a functionalist would look how industrialization and urbanization both contributed to the changing function of marriage and the family.

D.   According to conflict theory, society is viewed as composed of groups competing for scarce resources. Divorce is seen as the outcome of the shifting balance of power within the family; as women have gained power and try to address inequalities in the relationship, men resist.

E. The perspectives differ in their level of analysis.
   1. Macro level analysis--"an examination of large-scale patterns of society"--is the focus of analysis for functionalists and conflict theorists.
   2. Micro level analysis--"an examination of small-scale patterns of society"--is the focus for symbolic interactionists.

F. Each perspective provides a different and often sharply contrasting picture of the world; sociologists use all three perspectives because no one theory or level of analysis encompasses all of reality.

G. Research without theory is of little value: it becomes a collection of meaningless "facts." Theory that is unconnected to research is abstract and empty, unlikely to represent the way life really is. Sociologists combine research and theory in different ways. Theory is used to interpret data (i.e. functionalism, symbolic interaction and conflict theory provide frameworks for interpreting research findings) and it generates research. Research helps to generate theory.

VI. **Doing Sociological Research**

A. Common sense cannot be relied on as a source of knowledge because it is highly limited and its insights often are incorrect.

B. To move beyond common sense and understand what is really going on, it is necessary to do sociological research.

VII. **A Research Model**

A. Selecting a topic is guided by sociological curiosity, interest in a particular topic, research funding from governmental or private source, and pressing social issues.

B. Defining the problem involves specifying exactly what the researcher wants to learn about the topic.

C. Reviewing the literature uncovers existing knowledge about the problem.

D. Formulating a hypothesis involves stating the expected relationship between variables, based on a theory. Hypotheses need operational definitions--precise ways to measure the variables.

E. Choosing a research method is influenced by the research topic.

F. Collecting the data involves concerns over validity, the extent to which operational definitions measure what was intended, and reliability, the extent to which data produce consistent results.

G. Analyzing the results involves the use of a range of techniques, from statistical tests to content analysis, to analyze data. Computers have become powerful tools in data analysis because they reduce large amounts of data to basic patterns in much less time than it used to take.

H. Sharing the results by writing a report and publishing the results makes the findings available for replication.

VIII. **Six Research Methods**

A. Surveys involve collecting data by having people answer a series of questions.
   1. The first step is to determine a population, the target group to be studied, and selecting a sample, individuals from among the target population who are intended to represent the population to be studied.
   2. In a random sample everyone in the target population has the same chance of

being included in the study. A stratified random sample is a sample of specific subgroups (e.g. freshmen, sophomores, juniors) of the target population (a college or university) in which everyone in the subgroup has an equal chance or being included in the study.

3.   The respondents (people who respond to a survey) must be allowed to express their own ideas so that the findings will not be biased.

4.   Sociologists must decide between asking closed-ended questions in which the respondent selects one from a list of possible answers and open-ended questions in which respondents answer the question in their own words.

5.   It is important to establish rapport--a feeling or trust between researchers and subjects.

B.   In participant observation, the researcher participates in a research setting while observing what is happening in that setting.

C.   Secondary analysis is the analysis of data already collected by other researchers.

D.   Documents--written sources--may be obtained from many sources, including books, newspapers, police reports, and records kept by various organizations.

E.   Unobtrusive measures involve observing social behavior of people who do not know they are being studied.

F.   Experiments are especially useful to determine causal relationships.

1.   Experiments involve independent (factors that cause a change in something) and dependent variables (factors that are changed).

2.   Experiments require an experimental group--the group of subjects exposed to the independent variable--and a control group--the group of subjects not exposed to the independent variable.

IX.   **Issues and Ethics In Sociological Research**

A.   Ethics are of fundamental concern to sociologists when it comes to doing research.

B.   Ethical considerations include being open, honest, and truthful, not falsifying results or stealing someone else's work, not harming the subject in the course of conducting the research, protecting the anonymity of the research subjects, and not misrepresenting themselves to the research subjects.

C.   Efforts by Mario Brajuha and Rik Scarce to honor their research ethics reflect the seriousness with which sociologists view ethical considerations. Research by Laud Humphreys raised questions about how researchers represent themselves to subjects.

X.   **The Dilemma of Values in Sociological Research**

A.   Weber advocated that sociological research should be value free--personal values or biases should not influence social research--and objective--totally neutral.

1.   Sociologists agree that objectivity is a proper goal but acknowledge that no one can escape values entirely.

2.   Replication--repeating a study to see if the same results are round--is one means to avoid the distortions that values can cause.

B.   The proper purposes and uses of sociology are argued among sociologists.

1.   Some lean towards basic sociological research that has no goal beyond understanding social life and testing social theory.

2.   Others feel that the knowledge should be used to reform society.

KEY TERMS

After studying the chapter, review each of the following terms.

applied sociology: sociology that is used to solve social problems--from the micro level of family relationships to the macro level of war and pollution (12)

authority: power that people consider legitimate; also called legitimate power (17)

basic (or pure) sociology: sociological research whose only purpose is to make discoveries about life in human groups, not to make changes in those groups (30)

class conflict: Karl Marx's term for the struggle between owners (the bourgeoisie) and workers (the proletariat) (7)

clinical sociology: a type of applied sociology in which sociologists become directly involved in bringing about social change (12)

conflict theory: a theoretical framework in which society is viewed as composed of groups competing for scarce resources (17)

functional analysis: a theoretical framework in which society is viewed as a whole unit, composed of interrelated parts, each with a function that, when fulfilled, contributes to society's equilibrium; also known as functionalism and structural functionalism (15)

macro level analysis: an examination of large-scale patterns of society (18)

micro level analysis: an examination of small-scale patterns of society (18)

nonverbal interaction: communication without words through gestures, space, silence, and so on (18)

positivism: the application of the scientific approach to the social world (5)

social integration: the degree to which people feel a part of social groups (8)

social interaction: what people do when they are in one another's presence (18)

social location: the groups people belong to because of their location in history and society (5)

society: a group of people who share a culture and a territory (5)

sociological perspective: an approach that seeks to understand human behavior by placing it within its broader social context (4)

sociology: the scientific study of society and human behavior (6)

symbolic interaction: a theoretical perspective in which society is viewed as composed of symbols that people use to establish meaning, develop their views of the world, and communicate with one another (13)

theory: a general statement about how some parts of the world fit together and how they work; an explanation of how two or more facts are related to one another (13)

KEY PEOPLE

The following are key people in the development of socioloogy.

Jane Addams: Addams was the founder of Hull House--a settlement house in the immigrant community of Chicago. She invited sociologists from nearby University of Chicago to visit. In 1931 she was a winner of the Nobel Peace Prize. (9-10)

Mario Brajuha: During an investigation into a restaurant fire, officials subpoenaed notes taken by this sociologist in connection with his participant observation research on restaurant work. He was threatened with jail but would not turn over his notes. (28)

Auguste Comte: Comte is often credited with being the founder of sociology, because he was the first to suggest that the scientific method be applied to the study of the social world. (5-6)

Lewis Coser: Coser pointed out that conflict is likely to develop among people in close relationships because they are connected by a network of responsibilities, power and rewards. (17)

Ralf Dahrendorf: Dahrendorf's work is associated with the conflict perspective; he suggested that conflict is inherent in all relations that have authority. (17)

W.E.B. Du Bois: Du Bois was the first African American to earn at doctorate at Harvard University. For most of his career he taught sociology at Atlanta University. He was concerned about social injustice, wrote about race relations, and was one of the founders of the National Association for the Advancement of Colored People. (10-12)

Emile Durkheim: Durkheim was responsible for getting sociology recognized as a separate discipline. He was interested in studying how individual behavior is shaped by social forces and in finding remedies for social ills. He stressed that sociologists should use social facts--patterns of behavior that reflect some underlying condition of society. (7-8, 16)

Laud Humphreys: This sociologist carried out doctoral research on homosexual activity, but ran into problems when he misrepresented himself to his research subjects. Although he earned his doctorate degree, he was fired from his position because of his questionable ethics. (29)

Harriet Martineau: An Englishwoman who studied British and U.S. social life and published *Society in America* decades before either Durkheim or Weber were born. (9)

Karl Marx: Marx believed that social development grew out of conflict between social classes; under capitalism, this conflict was between the *bourgeoisie*--those who own the means to produce wealth--and the *proletariat*--the mass of workers. His work is associated with the conflict perspective. (6-7, 17)

George Herbert Mead: Mead was one of the founders of symbolic interactionism, a major theoretical perspective in sociology. (14)

Robert Merton: Merton contributed the terms *manifest and latent functions* and *dysfunctions* to the functionalist perspective. (16)

C. Wright Mills: Mills suggested that external influences--or a person's experiences--become part of his or her thinking and motivations and explain social behavior. In the 1950s he urged U.S. sociologists to get back to social reform. He argued that research without theory is of little value, simply a collection of unrelated "facts", and theory that is unconnected to research is abstract and empty, unlikely to represent the way life really is.(5, 12, 19)

Talcott Parsons: Parsons' work dominated sociology in the 1940s-1950s. He developed abstract models of how the parts of society harmoniously work together. (12)

Rik Scarce: Scarce was a graduate student doing research on animal rights groups when there was a break-in and vandalism in one of his university's research lab. He become famous because he refused to turn over research information that he had collected to authorities investigating the crime. He was imprisoned for 159 days on contempt charges. (28-29)

Herbert Spencer: Another early sociologist, Spencer believed that societies evolve from barbarian to civilized forms. The first to use the expression "the survival of the fittest" to reflect his belief that social evolution depended on the survival of the most capable and intelligent and the extinction of the less capable. His views became known as *social darwinism*. (6)

Max Weber: Weber's most important contribution to sociology was his study of the relationship between the emergence of Protestant belief system and the rise of capitalism. He believed that sociologists should not allow their personal values affect their social research; objectivity should become the hallmark of sociology. (8, 30)

SELF-TEST

After completing this self-test, check your answers against the Answer Key beginning on page 223 of this Study Guide and against the text on the pages) indicated in parentheses.

MULTIPLE CHOICE QUESTIONS

1. A group of people who share a culture or territory are referred to as: (5)
    a.   a tribe.
    b.   a cultural grouping.
    c.   a society.
    d.   a nation.

2. Income, education, gender and race all reflect a person's _____. (5)
    a.   personality
    b.   social placement
    c.   social location
    d.   perspective

3. According to the sociological perspective, people do what they do because of: (5)
    a.   internal mechanisms like instincts.
    b.   external influences which become internalized. *by socialization*
    c.   a combination of internal and external forces.
    d.   external forces which are shaped by internal mechanisms.

4. The application of the scientific approach to the social world is known as: (5)
    a.   ethnomethodology.
    b.   sociobiology.
    c.   natural science.
    d.   positivism.

5. The principle of "the survival of the fittest" was first stated by: (6)
    a.   Herbert Spencer.
    b.   Charles Darwin.
    c.   Auguste Comte.
    d.   Karl Marx.

6. According to Karl Marx, capitalists, who own the means of production, exploit the: (6)
    a.   bourgeoisie.
    b.   proletariat.
    c.   masses.
    d.   peasants.

7. According to Emile Durkheim, suicide rates can be explained by: (8)
    a.   social factors.
    b.   common sense.
    c.   the oppression of the proletariat by the bourgeoisie.
    d.   the survival of the fittest.

8. According to Max Weber, the central force in social change is: (8)
    a.   technology.
    b.   economics.
    — c.   religion.
    d.   immigration.

9. Which of the following early sociologists studied social life in England and the United States? (9)
    a.   Emile Durkheim
    b.   Karl Marx
    — c.   Harriet Martineau
    d.   W.E.B. Du Bois

10. One of the first U.S. sociologists to study race relations was: (10)
    a.   Jane Addams
    — b.   W.E.B. Du Bois
    c.   Albion Small
    d.   George Herbert Mead

11. The branch of sociology that focuses on using sociology to solve problems is (12):
    a.   social reform.
    b.   social activism.
    — c.   applied sociology.
    d.   practical sociology.

12. Symbolic In _____ study the symbols people use to establish meaning and communicate. (14)
    a.   Functionalists.
    b.   Symbolic interactionists.
    c.   Dramaturgical theorists.
    d.   Conflict theorists.

13. In explaining the high U.S. divorce rate, the _____C_____ perspective would focus on explanations such as emotional satisfaction, the meaning of children, and the meaning of parenthood. (14-15)
    a.   conflict
    b.   functional
    c.   symbolic interaction
    d.   exchange

14. According to Robert Merton, an action intended to help a system's equilibrium is a: (16)
    — a.   manifest function.
    b.   latent function.
    c.   dysfunction.
    d.   latent dysfunction.

15. _____d._____ sees industrialization and urbanization undermining traditional family tasks. (16)
   a. Conflict theorists
   b. Exchange theorists
   c. Symbolic interactionists
   d. Functionalists

16. The idea that conflict is inherent in all relations that have authority was first asserted by: (17)
   a. Karl Marx.
   b. Auguste Comte.
   —c. Ralf Dahrendorf.
   d. Emile Durkheim.

17. Conflict theorists might explain the high rate of divorce by looking at: (17-18)
   a. the changing meanings associated with marriage and divorce.
   b. society's basic inequalities between males and females.
   c. changes which have weakened the family unit.
   d. the loss of family functions which held a husband and wife together.

18. According to your text, which theoretical perspective is best for studying human behavior? (19)
   a. the functionalist perspective.
   b. the symbolic interactionist perspective.
   c. the conflict perspective.
   d. A combination of all of the above.

19. Sociologists believe that research is necessary because: (19)
   a. common sense ideas may or may not be true.
   b. they want to move beyond guesswork.
   c. researchers want to know what really is going on.
   d. All of the above.

20. _____ steps are involved in scientific research. (20-22)
   a. Four
   b. Six
   c. Eight
   d. Ten

21. A relationship between or among variables is predicted: (20)
   a. by a hypothesis.
   b. by use of operational definitions.
   c. when the researcher selects the topic to be studied.
   d. when the researcher is analyzing the results.

22. Reliability refers to: (21)
   a. the extent to which operational definitions measure what they are intended to measure.
   b. the extent to which data produce consistent results.
   c. the integrity of the researcher.
   d. the ways in which the variables in a hypothesis are measured.

23. Based on the table in your text, all of the following are ways to measure "average" except: (23)
    a. medial.
    b. mean.
    c. median.
    d. mode.

24. All of the following are research methods for gathering data, except: (23-27)
    a. ethnomethodology.
    b. surveys.
    c. unobtrusive measures.
    d. secondary analysis.

25. A sample is defined as: (23)
    a. a selection from the larger population.
    b. a partial representation of the target group.
    c. the individuals intended to represent the population to be studied.
    d. subgroups of the population in which every member has an equal chance of selection.

26. George is interested in doing research on autoworkers. He decides to move to a working class community and get a job on the assembly line of an auto plant so he can experience what it is like to be an autoworker while he is collecting his data. This type of research is: (26)
    a. secondary analysis.
    b. experiment.
    c. unobtrusive measures.
    d. participant observation.

27. The analysis of data already collected by other researchers is referred to as: (26)
    a. surveying the literature.
    b. use of documents.
    c. secondary analysis.
    d. replication.

28. In an experiment, the group not exposed to the independent variable in the study is: (27)
    a. the guinea pig group.
    b. the control group.
    c. the experimental group.
    d. the maintenance group.

29. Research ethics require: (28)
    a. openness.
    b. that a researcher not falsify results or plagiarize someone else's work.
    c. that research subjects should not be harmed by the research.
    d. All of the above.

30.   Research which makes discoveries about life human groups rather than make changes in those groups is: (30)
  a.   pure or basic sociology.
  b.   applied sociology.
  c.   clinical sociology.
  d.   None of the above.

TRUE-FALSE QUESTIONS

T F 1.   The sociological perspective helps us to understand that people's social experiences underlie what they feel and what they do. (4)

T F 2.   Sociologists believe that internal mechanisms are very important in explaining an individual's thinking and motivations. (5)

T F 3.   C. Wright Mills stressed that the sociological perspective enables us to understand how broad social characteristics shape the experiences of individuals. (5)

T F 4.   Historically, the success of the natural sciences led to the search for answers to the social world as well. (6)

T F 5.   Herbert Spencer believed that human societies evolve like those of animal species. (7)

T F 6.   Karl Marx thought that a classless society eventually would exist. (7)

T F 7.   Marxism is the same thing as communism. (7)

T F 8.   According to Durkheim, social integration is the degree to which people feel that they are a part of a social group. (8)

T F 9.   The ideas of Max Weber and Karl Marx are almost identical. (9)

T F 10. Harriet Martineau's work on social life in Great Britain and the United States was largely ignored within the field of sociology. (9)

T F 11. W.E.B. DuBois was the first African American to earn a doctorate at Harvard. (10)

T F 12. Symbolic interactionists primarily analyze how our definitions of ourselves and others underlie our behaviors. (14)

T F 13. According to functionalists, the functions which families fulfill have been largely untouched by industrialization and urbanization. (16)

T F 14. All conflict theorists focus on conflict between the bourgeoisie and the proletariat. (17)

T F 15. Micro level analysis focuses on social interaction. (18)

T F 16. Research generally confirms common sense. (19)

T F 17. After selecting a topic, the next step in the research model is defining the problem. (20)

T F 18. Sociologists have developed six basic research methods. (21)

T F 19. Validity is the extent to which a researcher's operational definitions measure what they are intended to measure. (21)

T F 20. One of the first steps in conducting survey research is to determine a population. (23)

T F 21. In survey research, it is undesirable for respondents to express their own ideas. (24)

T F 22. The wording of questionnaires can affect research results. (24)

T F 23. Secondary analysis and use of documents mean the same thing in terms of research methods. (26-27)

T F 24. In an experiment, the experimental group is not exposed to the independent variable in the study. (27)

T F 25. It is always unethical to observe social behavior in people when they do not know they are being studied. (28)

FILL-IN QUESTIONS

1. The _Sociolog perspective_ stresses the social contexts in which people are immersed and which influence their lives. (4)
2. The use of objective systematic observation to test theories is _scientific method_ (6)
3. The idea of applying the scientific method to the social world is _positivism_. (6)
4. Durkheim used the term _social integration_ to refer to the degree to which people are tied to their social group. (8)
5. The sociology that is used to solve social problems--from the micro level of family relationships to the macro level of war and pollution is called _applied sociology_. (12)
6. _Clinical soc._ is a type of applied sociology in which sociologists become directly involved in bringing about social change. (12)
7. A _thesis/theory_ is a general statement about how some parts of the world fit together and how they work. (13)
8. The theoretical perspective in which society is viewed as composed of symbols that people use to establish meaning, develop their views of the world, and communicate with one another is _Symbolic interacti_. (14) _interactionism_
9. _Functional_ analysis is a theoretical framework in which society is viewed as composed of various parts, each with a function that contributes to society's equilibrium. (15)
10. Karl Marx believed that the key to all human history is class struggle between the _bourgoise_, a small group of capitalists who own the means to produce wealth, and the _proletariat_, the mass of workers who are exploited by the capitalists. (17)
11. Power that people consider legitimate is known as _authority_. (17)
12. _Macro-level_ analysis examines large-scale patterns of society, while _micro-level_ analysis examines small-scale patterns of society. (18)
13. Hypotheses need _operational def._ -- precise ways to measure variables. (20)
14. _Reliability_ is the extent to which data produce consistent results. (21)
15. The six research methods are: (1) _survey_, (2) _participant observation_, (3) _secondary analysis_ (4) _documents_, (5) _experiment_, and (6) _unobtrusive measures_. (22-28)
16. _Rapport_ is a feeling of trust between researchers and subjects. (26)
17. To conduct an experiment, the researcher has two groups: (1) _control_ and (2) _experimental_. (27)
18. Research _ethics_ require openness, honesty, and truth. (28)
19. _Basic_ sociology makes discoveries about life in human groups, not to make changes in those groups. (30)
20. Max Weber argued that sociology should be _value free_, by which he meant that sociologists' personal beliefs about what is good or worthwhile should not affect his or her research. (30)

MATCH THESE SOCIAL SCIENTISTS WITH THEIR CONTRIBUTIONS

c 1. Auguste Comte
a 2. Herbert Spencer
f 3. Karl Marx
d 4. C. Wright Mills
d 5. Emile Durkheim
h 6. Harriet Martineau
i 7. Mario Brajuha
b 8. W.E.B. Du Bois
e 9. Max Weber
l 10. Rik Scarce
j 11. Robert K. Merton
k 12. Laud Humphreys

a. *coined the phrase "survival of the fittest"*
b. *was an early African American sociologist*
c. *proposed the use of positivism*
d. *stressed how individual behavior is shaped by social factors*
e. *believed religion was a central force in social change*
f. *believed the key to human history was class struggle*
g. *encouraged the use of the sociological perspective*
h. *published Society in America and translated Comte's work into English*
i. *refused to turn over notes on his research on restaurant work*
j. *used the terms functions and dysfunctions*
k. *his research reflected questionable ethics*
l. *imprisoned for 159 days on contempt charges*

ESSAY QUESTIONS

1. Explain what the sociological perspective encompasses and then, using the perspective, discuss the forces that shaped the discipline of sociology.
2. Explain each of the theoretical perspectives that are used in sociology and describe how a sociologist affiliated with one or another of the perspectives might undertake a study of gangs. Discuss how all three can be used in research.
3. Choose a topic and explain how you would go through the different steps in the research model.
4. Explain why ethical guidelines are necessary in social science research.

"DOWN-TO-EARTH SOCIOLOGY"

1. In what ways did the life and career of W.E.B. Du Bois reflect the tensions between social reform and sociological analysis? Max Weber argued that sociologists should keep their personal beliefs out of their research, yet Du Bois's work challenges this. What do you think is the proper role for sociologists to take?
2. After reading "Sociologists at Work," (p.13) can you think of other ways in which sociological knowledge and the sociological perspective would be useful in the working world?
3. Take the sociology quiz on page 19 and then compare your answers to those on page 20. Were you surprised by the correct answers? What does this suggest to you about the role of social science research in understanding human behavior?
4. Can you give examples similar to those in your text (on page 24) where researchers have loaded the dice to enhance the qualities of a product or a political candidate?
5. The author provides examples of three different research projects that involved some ethical considerations. In each of these cases, did you agree or disagree with the position taken by the researcher?
6. If you were to become a sociologist, what research topics would you find interesting? What methods would you use? What ethical constraints do you think you might face?

CHAPTER 2
CULTURE

CHAPTER SUMMARY

- Culture refers to the language, beliefs, values, norms, and material objects passed from one generation to the next. Culture is both material (buildings, clothing, tools) and nonmaterial (ways of thinking and patterns of behavior). Ideal culture refers to a group's values, norms, and goals; real culture refers to its actual behavior. People are naturally ethnocentric, using their own culture to judge others; cultural relativism is the attempt to understand other cultures in their own terms.

- Components of culture include symbols, language, gestures, values. norms, sanctions, folkways and mores. Language is essential for culture because it allows us to move beyond the present, sharing with others our past experiences and our future plans. According to the Sapir-Whorf hypothesis, language not only allows us to express our thinking and perceptions but it actually shapes them. All groups have values, standards by which they define what is desirable and undesirable, and norms, rules about appropriate behavior. Socially imposed sanctions maximize conformity to social norms.

- A subculture is a group whose values and related behaviors distinguish its members from the general culture. A counterculture is a subculture which subscribes to values that set its members in opposition to the dominant culture.

- Core values in U.S. society emphasize personal achievement and success, hard work, and moral orientation. Value clusters are interrelated individual values that together form a larger whole; Sometimes individual values contradict one another; these contradictions reflect areas of social tension and potential points for social change. Values that are emerging as core values today within U.S. culture include leisure, physical fitness, self-fulfillment, and the environment. Changes in a society's values often generate opposition.

- Ogburn used the term cultural lag to refer to situations in which a society's nonmaterial culture lags behind its changing technology. Today the technology in travel and communication makes cultural diffusion around the globe occur more rapidly than in the past, resulting in some degree of cultural leveling, a process by which cultures become similar to one another.

LEARNING OBJECTIVES

As you read Chapter 2, use these learning objectives to organize your notes. After completing your reading, briefly state an answer to each of the objectives, and review the text pages in parentheses.

1. Define culture and explain its material and nonmaterial components. (36-37)
2. Explain the relationship between culture shock and ethnocentrism. (37)
3. Discuss the practice of cultural relativism and evaluate some of the criticisms of this approach to understanding culture. (38-39)
4. Discuss the symbolic components of culture, including gestures and language. (39-43)
5. State the Sapir-Whorf hypothesis and discuss its implications for understanding the relationship between language and perceptions. (43)
6. Define the following terms: values, norms, sanctions, folkways, mores, and taboos. (44)
7. Compare and contrast subcultures and countercultures. (45-46)
8. List the core values in U.S. society as identified by Robin Williams and James Henslin. (46-47)
9. Explain what is meant by value clusters and value contradictions. (47-48)
10. Discuss the emergent values in U.S. society and analyze why core values do not change without

meeting strong resistance. (48-49)
11. Demonstrate how values act as blinders. (50)
12. Explain the difference between "ideal" and "real" cultures. (50)
13. State the sociological significance of technology. (50-52)
14. Discuss what William Ogburn meant by the term cultural lag. (52)
15. Define cultural diffusion and cultural leveling and explain the role of technology in both processes. (52-53)

CHAPTER OUTLINE

I. **What is Culture?**
    A. Culture is defined as the language, beliefs, values, norms, behaviors, and even material objects passed from one generation to the next.
        1. Material culture is things such as jewelry, art, buildings, weapons, machines, clothing, hairstyles, etc.
        2. Nonmaterial culture is a group's ways of thinking (beliefs, values, and assumptions) and common patterns of behavior (language, gestures, and other forms of interaction).
    B. Culture provides a taken-for-granted orientation to life.
        1. We assume that our own culture is normal or natural; in fact, it is not natural, but rather is learned. It penetrates our lives so deeply that it is taken for granted and provides the lens through which we evaluate things.
        2. It provides implicit instructions that tell us what we ought to do and a moral imperative that defines what we think is right and wrong.
        3. Coming into contact with a radically different culture produces "culture shock," challenging our basic assumptions about life.
        4. A consequence of internalizing culture is ethnocentrism, using our own culture (and assuming it to be good, right, and superior) to judge other cultures. It is functional when it creates in-group solidarity, but can be dysfunctional if it leads to harmful discrimination.
    C. Cultural relativism consists of trying to appreciate other groups' ways of life in the context in which they exist, without judging them as superior or inferior to our own.
        1. This view attempts to refocus the "lens" in order to help us appreciate other cultures.
        2. Robert Edgerton argues that we should develop a scale to evaluate cultures on their "quality of life" and that those cultural practices that result in exploitation *should* be judged morally inferior to those that enhance people's lives.
II. **Components of Symbolic Culture**
    A. Sociologists sometimes refer to nonmaterial culture as symbolic culture because a central component are the symbols.
        1. Symbols are something to which people attach meaning--that people use to communicate.
        2. Symbols include language, gestures, values, norms, sanctions, folkways, and mores.
    B. Gestures, using one's body to communicate with others, are shorthand means of communication.
        1. Gestures are used by people in every culture, although the gestures and the

meanings differ; confusion or offense can result because of misunderstandings over the meaning of a gesture or misuse of a gesture.

    2.   Gestures, which vary remarkably around the world, can create strong emotions.

C.   Language consists of a system of symbols that can be put together in an infinite number of ways in order to communicate abstract thought. Each word is a symbol, a sound to which a culture attaches a particular meaning. It is important because it is the primary means of communication between people.

    1.   It allows human experiences to be cumulative; each generation builds on the body of significant experiences that is passed on to it by the previous generation, thus freeing people to move beyond immediate experiences.

    2.   It extends time back into the past, enabling us to share our past experiences, and forward into the future, allowing us to share our future plans. It expands connections beyond our immediate, face-to-face groups.

    3.   It allows shared perspectives or understandings and complex, goal-directed behavior.

D.   The Sapir-Whorf hypothesis states that our thinking and perception not only are expressed by language but actually are shaped by language because we are taught not only words but also a particular way of thinking and perceiving. Rather than objects and events forcing themselves onto our consciousness, our very language determines our consciousness.

E.   Values, norms, and sanctions are also components of culture.

    1.   Values are the standards by which people define good and bad, beautiful and ugly. Every group develops both values and expectations regarding the right way to reflect them.

    2.   Norms are expectations, or rules of behavior, that reflect a group's values.

    3.   Sanctions are the positive or negative reactions to the way in which people follow norms. Positive sanctions (a money reward, a prize, a smile, or even a handshake) are expressions of approval; negative sanctions (a fine, a frown, or harsh words) denote disapproval for breaking a norm.

F.   Folkways and mores are different types of norms.

    1.   Folkways are norms that are not strictly enforced, such as passing on the left side of the sidewalk. They may result in a person getting a dirty look.

    2.   Mores are norms that are believed to be essential to core values and we insist on conformity. A person who steals, rapes, and kills has violated some of society's most important mores and will be formally sanctioned.

    3.   One group's folkways may constitute another group's mores. A male walking down the street with the upper half of his body uncovered may be violating a folkway; a female doing the same thing may be violating accepted mores.

    4.   Taboos are norms so strongly ingrained that even the thought of them is greeted with revulsion. Eating human flesh and having sex with one's parents are examples of such behavior.

III.   **Many Cultural Worlds: Subcultures and Countercultures**

A.   Subcultures are groups whose values and related behaviors are so distinct that they set their members off from the dominant culture.

    1.   Each subculture is a world within the larger world of the dominant culture. Each has distinctive way of looking at life, but remains compatible with the dominant culture.

    2.   U.S. society contains tens of thousands of subcultures, some as broad as the way

of life we associate with teenagers, others as narrow as body builders or philosophers. Ethnic groups often form subcultures with their own language, distinctive food, religious practices and other customs. Occupational groups also form subcultures.

B. Countercultures are groups whose values set their members in opposition to the dominant culture.

   1. Countercultures challenge the culture's core values.
   2. While usually associated with negative behavior--heavy metal adherents who glorify Satanism, hatred, cruelty, rebellion, sexism, violence, and death, are an example of a such a negative counterculture--some countercultures are not--the Mormons would be an example of a counterculture because they challenged the core value of monogamy, and yet they were not seen as negative.
   3. Often threatened by a counterculture, members of the broader culture sometimes move against it in order to affirm their own values.

IV. Values in U.S. Society

A. Identifying core values in U.S. society is difficult, due to the many different religious, racial, ethnic, and special interest groups that are found in this pluralistic society.

   1. Sociologist Robin Williams identified achievement and success (especially, doing better than others); individualism (success due to individual effort); activity and work; efficiency and practicality; science and technology (using science to control nature); progress; material comfort; humanitarianism (helpfulness, personal kindness, philanthropy); freedom; democracy; equality (especially of opportunity); and racism and group superiority.
   2. Henslin updated Williams's list by adding education; religiosity (belief in a Supreme Being and following some set of matching precepts); and romantic love (as the basis for marriage) and monogamy (no more than one spouse at a time).

B. Values are not independent units; value clusters are made up of related core values that come together to form a larger whole. In the value cluster surrounding success, for example, we find hard work, education, efficiency, material comfort, and individualism all bound together.

C. Some values conflict with each other. There cannot be full expressions of democracy, equality, racism, and sexism at the same time. These are value contradictions and as society changes some values are challenged and undergo modification.

D. As society changes over time, new core values emerge that reflect changed social conditions. Examples of emergent values in the United States today are: leisure; physical fitness; self-fulfillment; and concern for the environment.

E. Core values do not change without meeting strong resistance. Today's clash in values is so severe that it is referred to as a "culture war."

F. Values and their supporting beliefs may blind people to other social circumstances. The emphasis on individualism is so high that many people in the U.S. believe that everyone is free to pursue the goal of success, thereby blinding them to the dire consequences of family poverty, lack of education, and dead-end jobs.

G. Ideal culture refers to the ideal values and norms of a people. What people actually do usually falls short of this ideal, and sociologists refer to the norms and values that people actually follow as real culture.

V.   **Technology in the Global Village**

    A.   Central to material culture is its technology; in its simplest sense, this refers to tools, in its broadest sense it includes the skills or procedures to make and use those tools.

        1.   New technologies refers to the emerging technologies of an era which have a major impact on human life. Today, new technologies would include computers, satellites, and various forms of electronic media.

        2.   The sociological significance of technology is that it sets a framework for a group's nonmaterial culture, influencing the way people think and how they relate to one another.

    B.   William Ogburn first used the term cultural lag to refer to situations where not all parts of a culture change at the same pace; when some part of culture changes, other parts lag behind.

        1.   A group's material culture usually changes first, with the nonmaterial culture lagging behind.

        2.   Sometimes nonmaterial culture never catches up to the changes; we hold on to some outdated form which was once needed but now has been bypassed by new technology.

    C.   For most of human history cultures had little contact with one another; however, there was always some contact with other groups, resulting in groups learning from one another.

        1.   Social scientists refer to this transmission of cultural characteristics as cultural diffusion.

        2.   Material culture is more likely than the nonmaterial culture to change as a result of cultural diffusion.

        3.   Cultural diffusion occurs more rapidly today, given the changes in travel and communications..

        4.   The world is being united by travel and communication to such an extent that there is almost no "other side of the world." Japan, for example, no longer is a purely Eastern culture, having adopted not only Western economic production, but also Western forms of dress, music, and so on. This is cultural leveling, the process in which cultures become similar to one another.

KEY TERMS

After studying the chapter, review each of the following terms.

counterculture: a subculture whose values place its members in opposition to the values of the broader culture (45)

cultural diffusion: the spread of cultural characteristics from one group to another (52)

cultural lag: William Ogburn's term for a situation in which nonmaterial culture lags behind changes in the material culture (52)

cultural leveling: the process by which cultures become similar to one another; especially by which Western industrial culture is imported and diffused into the Least Industrialized Nations (53)

cultural relativism: understanding a people from the framework of their own culture (38)

culture: the language, beliefs, values, norms, behaviors, and even material objects that are passed from one generation to the next (36)

culture contact: when people from different cultures come in contact with one another (41)

culture shock: the disorientation that people experience when they come in contact with a fundamentally different culture and can no longer depend on their taken-for-granted assumptions about life (37)

ethnocentrism: the use of one's own culture as a yardstick for judging the ways of other individuals and societies, generally leading to a negative evaluation of their values, norms, and behaviors (37)

folkways: norms that are not strictly enforced (44)

gestures: the ways in which people use their bodies to communicate with one another (40)

ideal culture: the ideal values and norms of a people, the goals held out for them (50)

language: a system of symbols that can be combined in an infinite number of ways to communicate abstract thought (41)

material culture: the material objects that distinguish a group of people, such as their art, buildings, weapons, utensils, machines, hairstyles, clothing, and jewelry (37)

mores: norms strictly enforced because they are thought essential to core values (44)

negative sanction: an expression of disapproval for breaking a norm; ranging from a mild, informal reaction such as a frown to a formal prison sentence, banishment, or death (44)

new technology: a technology introduced into a society that has a significant impact on that society (50)

nonmaterial culture (also called *symbolic culture*): a group's ways of thinking (including its beliefs, values, and other assumptions about the world) and doing (its common patterns or behavior, including language and other forms of interaction) (37)

norms: the expectations, or rules of behavior, that develop out of values (44)

pluralistic society: a society made up of many different groups (46)

positive sanction: a reward or positive reaction for following norms, ranging from a smile to a prize (44)

real culture: the norms and values that people actually follow (50)

sanction: an expression of approval or disapproval given to people for upholding or violating norms (44)

Sapir-Whorf hypothesis: Edward Sapir's and Benjamin Whorf's hypothesis that language creates ways of thinking and perceiving (43)

social construction of technology: the view (opposed to *technological determinism*) that culture (people's values and special interests) shape the development and use of technology (51)

subculture: the values and related behaviors of a group that distinguish its members from the larger culture; a world within a world (45)

symbol: something to which people attach meaning and then use to communicate with others (39)

symbolic culture: another term for nonmaterial culture (39)

taboo: a norm so strong that it brings revulsion if it is violated (44)

technological determinism: the view that technology is the driving force behind culture; in its extreme form, technology is seen as taking on a life of its own, forcing human behavior to follow (51)

technology: in its narrow sense, tools; in its broader sense, the skills or procedures necessary to make and use those tools (50)

value cluster: a series of interrelated values that together form a larger whole (48)

value contradiction: values that contradict one another; to follow the one means to come into conflict with the other (48)

values: the standards by which people define what is desirable or undesirable, good or bad, beautiful or ugly (44)

KEY PEOPLE

Review the major theoretical contributions or research findings of these people.

Robert Edgerton: Edgerton attacks the concept of cultural relativism, suggesting that because some cultures endanger their people's health, happiness, or survival, there should be a scale to evaluate cultures on their "quality of life." (39)

Jacques Ellul: This French sociologist was a critic of the impact that technology has on society. (51)

Douglas Massey: This sociologist has studied what happens in urban areas when immigration rates exceed the speed with which new residents can learn English and the proportion of non-English speakers increases. (43)

Marshall McLuhan: An optimist about technology, McLuhan tried to understand the impact of electronic media on people's ideas, values, and way of life. (51)

William Ogburn: Ogburn coined the term "cultural lag." (52)

Neil Postman: Postman has argued that television's emphasis on immediate gratification and quick responses has ruined children's attention spans. (51)

Edward Sapir and Benjamin Whorf: These anthropologists argued that language not only reflects thoughts and perceptions, but that it actually shapes the way a people perceive the world. (43)

JoEllen Shively: Shively researched the reasons why both Anglo and Native American movie-goers identify more with the cowboys than the Indians. (46-47)

William Sumner: Sumner developed the concept of ethnocentrism. (37)

Robin Williams: He identified twelve core U.S. values. (46-47)

SELF-TEST

After completing this self-test, check your answers against the Answer Key beginning on page 227 of this Study Guide and against the text on page(s) indicated in parentheses.

MULTIPLE CHOICE QUESTIONS

1.   A group's ways of thinking and doing, including language and other forms of interaction is: (37)
    a.   material culture.
    b.   nonmaterial culture.
    c.   ideological culture.
    d.   values.

2.   Material culture includes: (37)
    a.   weapons and machines.
    b.   eating utensils.
    c.   jewelry, hairstyles, and clothing.
    d.   All of the above.

3.   All of these statements are true regarding culture, except: (37)
    a.   people generally are aware of the effects of their own culture.
    b.   culture touches almost every aspect of who and what a person is.
    c.   at birth, people do not possess culture.
    d.   culture becomes the lens through which we perceive and evaluate our social world.

4.   The disorientation people experience when coming in contact with a radically different culture and no longer can depend on their taken-for-granted assumptions about life is known as: (37)
    a.   cultural diffusion.
    b.   cultural leveling.
    c.   cultural relativism.
    d.   cultural shock.

5.   An American who thinks bullfights are barbaric is demonstrating: (37)
    a.   cultural shock.
    b.   cultural relativism.
    c.   ethnocentrism.
    d.   ethnomethodology.

6.   Gestures: (40)
    a.   are studied by anthropologists but not sociologists.
    b.   are universal.
    c.   always facilitate communication between people.
    d.   can lead to misunderstandings and embarrassment.

7.   It is possible for human experiences to be cumulative and shared because of: (41-42)
    a.   language.
    b.   cultural universals.
    c.   gestures.
    d.   computers.

8.   The sociological theory that language creates a particular way of thinking and perceiving is: (43)
    a.   sociobiology.
    b.   the Davis-Moore theory.
    c.   the Sapir-Whorf hypothesis.
    d.   the Linguistic perspective.

9.   Sanctions: (44)
    a.   are always material.
    b.   can be either positive or negative.
    c.   have very little impact on most people today.
    d.   All of the above.

10.   Norms that are not strictly enforced are: (44)
    a.   taboos.
    b.   mores.
    c.   values.
    d.   folkways.

11.   Mores: (44)
    a.   are essential to our core values and require conformity.
    b.   are norms that are not strictly enforced.
    c.   state that a person should not try to pass you on the left side of the sidewalk.
    d.   are less important in contemporary societies.

12.   Subcultures: (45)
    a.   are a world within a world.
    b.   have values and related behaviors that set its members apart from the larger culture.
    c.   include ethnic groups.
    d.   All of the above.

13.   Heavy metal adherents who glorify Satanism, hatred, and sexism are examples of: (45)
       a.   ethnocentrists.
       b.   perverted people.
    _c.   countercultures.
       d.   subcultures.

14.   A pluralistic society: (46)
    — a.   is made up of many different groups.
       b.   tends to discourage subcultures.
       c.   does not share core values.
       d.   no longer exists in the world.

15.   Value contradictions occur when: (48)
    — a.   a value, such as the one that stresses group superiority, comes into direct conflict with other values, such as democracy and equality.
       b.   societies have very little social change.
       c.   a series of interrelated values bind together to form a larger whole.
       d.   None of the above.

16.   Ideal culture is: (49-50)
       a.   a value, norm, or other cultural trait that is found in every group.
    — b.   the ideal values and norms of a people, the goals held out for them.
       c.   the norms and values that people follow when they know they are being watched.
       d.   not a sociological concept.

17.   In our society, the custom is for the school year to be nine months long, with students having a three-month summer break. Today, this pattern would an example of: (52)
       a.   a core value.
    — b.   real culture.
       c.   cultural lag.
       d.   value contradiction.

18.   Copying aspects of another group's culture is: (52)
    — a.   cultural diffusion.
       b.   ethnocentrism.
       c.   cultural relativism.
       d.   cultural filching.

19.   According to _____, machines have become an independent force that is out of human control. (51)
       a.   sociologists
       b.   social constructionists
       c.   cultural anthropologists
    — d.   technological determinists

20.   The Golden Arches of McDonald's in Tokyo, Paris, and London are examples of: (53)
       a.   cultural shock.
       b.   cultural contradictions.
       c.   cultural universals.
    — d.   cultural leveling.

TRUE-FALSE QUESTIONS

T F   1.   Most people regularly question the basic assumptions of their daily lives. (37)
T F   2.   No one can be entirely successful at practicing cultural relativism. (38)
T F   3.   Gestures are ways in which people use their bodies to communicate with others. (40)
T F   4.   Without language, human culture would be little more advanced than that of the lower primates. (41)
T F   5.   Without language, humans could still successfully plan future events. (42)
T F   6.   Sanctions are positive or negative reactions to the ways people follow norms. (44)
T F   7.   What norms are considered folkways and mores are pretty much the same around the globe. (44)
T F   8.   Subcultures remain compatible with the dominant culture while countercultures are in opposition to the dominant culture. (45)
T F   9.   Racism and group superiority are core values in U.S. society. (47)
T F   10.   The value cluster surrounding success includes hard work, education, efficiency, and individualism. (48)
T F   11.   Some values conflict with one another. (48)
T F   12.   Concern for the environment has always been a core value in U.S. society. (49)
T F   13.   Core values do not change without meeting strong resistance. (49)
T F   14.   Real culture refers to the values, norms, and goals of a group. (50)
T F   15.   Technology is only used to refer to the tools a culture uses. (50)
T F   16.   New technologies is a term that refers to all technologies that emerge within a society, whether minor or major. (50)
T F   17.   According to social constructionists, values and special interests shape the development and use of technology. (51)
T F   18.   Ogburn referred to the condition of uneven cultural change as "cultural lag." (52)
T F   19.   Most "borrowing" between cultures has involved material culture. (52)
T F   20.   Japan is no longer a purely Eastern culture because of cultural leveling. (53)

FILL-IN QUESTIONS

1.   The material objects that distinguish a group of people, such as their art, buildings, weapons, utensils, machines, hairstyles, clothing, and jewelry are known as _____; their ways of thinking and doing are _____. (37)
2.   The disorientation that people experience when they come in contact with a fundamentally different culture and can no longer depend on their taken-for-granted assumptions about life is _____. (37)
3.   The tendency to use our own group's way of doing things as a yardstick for judging others is known as _____. (37)
4.   A _____ is something to which people attach meaning and then use to communicate with others. (39)

5. The ways in which people use their bodies to communicate with one another are _____. (40)

6. _____ is a system of symbols that can be combined in an infinite number of ways and can represent not only objects but also abstract thought. (41)

7. _____ are ideas of what is desirable in life. (44)

8. The expectations or rules or behavior that develop out of values are referred to as _____. (44)

9. A _____ is a norm so strongly ingrained that even the thought of its violation is greeted with revulsion. (44)

10. The United States is a _____ society, meaning that it is made up of many different groups. (46)

11. _____ are a series of interrelated values that together form a larger whole. (48)

12. Sociologists call the norms and values that people actually follow _____. (49)

13. William Ogburn used the term _____ to refer to a situation in which nonmaterial culture takes a period of time to adjust to changes in the material culture. (52)

14. Air travel and rapid communications have contributed to _____. (52)

15. When Western industrial culture is imported and diffused into the Least Industrialized Nations, the process is called _____. (53)

MATCH THESE SOCIAL SCIENTISTS WITH THEIR CONTRIBUTIONS

___ 1. Edward Sapir and Benjamin Whorf
___ 2. Robin Williams
___ 3. Marshall McLuhan
___ 4. William Ogburn
___ 5. Robert Edgerton
___ 6. JoEllen Shively
___ 7. William Sumner
___ 8. Jacques Ellul

a. *coined the term "cultural lag"*
b. *coined the term a "global village"*
c. *claimed that technology now dominates civilization*
d. *stated that language shapes perceptions of reality*
e. *studied Anglos' and Native Americans' views of westerns*
f. *critiqued the cultural relativism approach*
g. *noted core values of U.S. society*
h. *developed the concept of ethnocentrism*

ESSAY QUESTIONS

1. Explain cultural relativism and discuss both the advantages and disadvantages of practicing it.

2. Consider the degree to which the real culture of the United States falls short of the ideal culture. Provide concrete examples to support your essay.

3. Evaluate what is gained and what is lost as technology advances in a culture.

"DOWN-TO-EARTH SOCIOLOGY"

1. Today Miami is an ethnically diverse city characterized by two language, English and Spanish (p. 42) What problems are created when people live together but speak different languages? Can you think of experiences of your own that are similar? Do you think it is important for Americans to learn another language?

2. Were you surprised to learn that Native Americans like Westerns (p. 46-47)? Why do you think the image of the cowboy has been so positively portrayed, while Native Americans have been so negatively portrayed in U.S. books and movies? What would the reaction be if Native Americans were portrayed with the same traits as we generally associate with cowboys?

3. Do you find yourself agreeing with those who feel that technology transforms culture or those who believe that culture gives shape to technology (p. 51)? What do you think--are we able to control technology or does it control us?

CHAPTER 3
SOCIALIZATION

CHAPTER SUMMARY

- Scientists have attempted to determine how much of people's characteristics come from heredity and how much from the social environment. Observations of isolated and institutionalized children help to answer this question. These studies have concluded that language and intimate interaction are essential to the development of human characteristics.

- Charles Horton Cooley, George Herbert Mead, Jean Piaget, and Sigmund Freud provide insights into the social development of human beings. Cooley and Mead demonstrated that the self is created through our interactions with others. Piaget identified four stages in the development of our ability to reason: (1) sensorimotor; (2) pre-operational; (3) concrete operational; and (4) formal operational. Freud defined the personality in terms of the id, ego, and superego; personality developed as the inborn desires (id) clashed with social constraints (superego).

- Socialization into emotions is one way societies produce conformity; not only do we learn how to express our emotions, but also what emotions to feel.

- Gender socialization is a primary means of controlling human behavior, and a society's ideals of sex-linked behaviors are reinforced by its social institutions.

- The main agents of socialization--family, religion, child care, school, peer groups, and the workplace--each contribute to the socialization of people to become full-fledged members of society.

- Resocialization is the process of learning new norms, values, attitudes and behaviors. Intense resocialization takes place in total institutions. Most resocialization is voluntary, but some is involuntary.

- Socialization, which begins at birth, continues throughout the life course; at each stage the individual must adjust to a new set of social expectations.

- Although socialization lays down the basic self and is modified by our social location, humans are not robots but rational beings who consider options and make choices.

LEARNING OBJECTIVES

As you read Chapter 3, use these learning objectives to organize your notes. After completing your reading, briefly state an answer to each of the objectives, and review the text pages in parentheses.

1. Discuss major studies of isolated and institutionalized children, as well as studies of deprived animals, and state what they demonstrate about the importance of early contact with other humans for the social development of children. (58-61)

2. Define socialization. (61)

3. Explain the contributions of Charles Horton Cooley and George Herbert Mead to our understanding of the development of the self. (61-62)

4. Discuss Jean Piaget's theory of the development of reasoning ability and consider how cultural variations in what we learn through socialization would impact on Piaget's theory of cognitive development. (63-64)

5. Discuss Sigmund Freud's theory of personality and the sociological critique of this theory. (64)

6. Explain what Henslin means when he says that we are socialized into emotions and analyze the relationship between socialization into emotions and social control in society. (64-65)

7. Describe ways in which gender socialization channels human behavior and reinforces cultural stereotypes of men and women. (65-67)
8. List and describe the influence of each agent of socialization on individuals. (68-69)
9. Define the term resocialization and discuss the process of resocialization that takes places within total institutions. (70-71)
10. Discuss socialization through the life course by summarizing each of its stages. (71-75)
11. Explain why human beings are not prisoners of socialization. (75)

CHAPTER OUTLINE

I. **What Is Human Nature?**
A. Isolated children show what humans might be like if secluded from society at an early age. Isabelle, raised in isolation, appeared severely retarded. Without companionship, she had been unable to develop into an intelligent human. Subsequent interaction with others at a fairly early age allowed her to reach normal intellectual levels.
B. Studies of institutionalized children show that characteristics we think of as human traits (intelligence, cooperative behavior, and friendliness) result from early close relations with other humans.
1. When infants in orphanages received little adult interaction, they appeared mentally retarded. When some were placed in the care of adult women--even though the women were mentally retarded--one-on-one relationships developed, and the infants gained intelligence.
2. Genie, who was locked in a small room from infancy until she was found at age 13, demonstrates the importance of early interaction. Intensive training was required for her to learn to walk, speak simple sentences, and chew correctly, yet even so she remained severely retarded.
C. Studies of monkeys raised in isolation have reached similar results. The longer and more severe the isolation, the more difficult adjustment becomes.
D. Babies do not "naturally" develop into human adults; although their bodies grow, human interaction is required for them to acquire the traits considered normal for human beings.
II. **Socialization into the Self, Mind, and Emotions**
A. Charles Horton Cooley (1864-1929) concluded that human development is socially created--that our sense of self develops from interaction with others. He coined the term "looking-glass self" to describe this process.
1. According to Cooley, this process contains three steps: (1) we imagine how we look to others; (2) we interpret others' reactions (how they evaluate us); and (3) we develop a self-concept.
2. A favorable reflection in the "social mirror" leads to a positive self-concept, while a negative reflection leads to a negative self-concept.
3. Even the misjudgments of others' reactions become part of our self-concept.
4. This development process is an ongoing, lifelong process.
B. George Herbert Mead (1863-1931) agreed with Cooley, but added that play is critical to the development of a self. In play, we learn to take the role of others: to understand and anticipate how others feel and think.
1. Mead concluded that children first take only the role of significant others (parents or siblings, for example); as the self develops, children internalize first the expectations of significant others, and then eventually the entire group. The

norms, values, attitudes and expectations of people "in general" are the generalized other.

2. According to Mead, the development of the self goes through stages: (1) ~~imitation~~ (children initially can only mimic the gestures and words of others); (2) play (beginning at age three, children play the roles of specific people, such as a firefighter or the Lone Ranger); and (3) games (in the first years of school, children become involved in organized team games and must learn the role of each member of the team).

3. He distinguished between the "I" and the "me" in development of the self: The "I" component is the subjective, active, spontaneous, creative part of the social self (for instance, "I shoved him"), while the "me" component is the objective part-- attitudes internalized from interactions with others (for instance, "He shoved me").

4. Mead concluded that not only the self but also the human mind is a social product. The symbols which we use in thinking originate in the language of our society.

C. Jean Piaget (1896-1980) noted that when young children take intelligence tests, they consistently give wrong answers while older children are able to give the expected answer. To understand why, he studied the stages a child goes through in learning to reason.

1. The sensorimotor stage (ages 0-2): Understanding is limited to direct contact with the environment (touching, listening, seeing).

2. The preoperational stage (ages 2-7): Children develop the ability to use symbols which allow them to experience things without direct contact.

3. The concrete operational stage (ages 7-12): Reasoning abilities become much more developed. Children now can understand numbers, causation, and speed, but have difficulty with abstract concepts such as truth.

4. The formal operational stage (ages 12+): Children become capable of abstract thinking, and can use rules to solve abstract problems ("If X is true, why doesn't Y follow?").

D. While the work of Cooley and Mead appears to have universal application, there is less agreement that Piaget's four stages are globally true.

1. Child development specialists suggest that the stages are less distinct and that children develop reasoning skills more gradually than Piaget outlined.

2. The content of what children learn varies from one culture to the next; because childhood activities are different, the development of thinking processes will be different.

E. Sigmund Freud (1856-1939) believed that personality consists of three elements.

1. The id (inherited drives for self-gratification) demands fulfillment of basic needs such as attention, safety, food, and sex.

2. The ego balances between the needs of the id and the demands or society.

3. The superego (the social conscience we have internalized from social groups) gives us feelings of guilt or shame when we break rules, and feelings or pride and self-satisfaction when we follow them.

4. Sociologists object to Freud's view that inborn and unconscious motivations are the primary reasons for human behavior, for this view denies the central tenet of sociology that social factors shape people's behaviors.

F. Emotions are not simply the result of biology; they also depend on socialization within a particular society. We learn how to express emotions as well as what emotions to feel.

1. Americans may shake hands with each other to express pleasure in meeting

someone, while Japanese may bow, and Arabs may kiss.

     2.   Society has trained us to give different reactions depending on the situation and our social location; there are even cultural differences in terms of the emotions that are experienced.

    G.   Most socialization is meant to turn us into conforming members of society. We do some things and not others as a result of socialization. When we contemplate an action, we know the emotion (good or bad) that would result; thus, society sets up controls on our behavior.

III. Socialization Into Gender

    A.   Society also channels our behavior through gender socialization. By expecting different behaviors from people because they are male or female, society nudges boys and girls in separate directions from an early age, and this foundation carries over into adulthood.

    B.   Parents begin the process.

     1.   Studies conclude that in U.S. society, mothers unconsciously reward female children for being passive and dependent and male children for being active and independent.

     2.   In general, parents teach their children gender roles in subtle ways--with the toys they buy, the rules they set, and the expectations they have.

    C.   The mass media reinforce society's expectations of gender in many ways.

     1.   On TV, male characters outnumber females and are more likely to be portrayed in higher status positions.

     2.   There are some notable exceptions to the stereotypes, which are a sign that things are changing.

     3.   Although young people spend countless hours playing video games, there are no studies yet showing how these games affect players ideas of gender.

IV. Agents of Socialization

    A.   Our socialization experiences in the family are influenced by social class.

     1.   Research by Melvin Kohn suggests social class differences in child-rearing. Often the main concern of working-class parents is their children's outward conformity (be neat and clean, and follow the rules); they are more likely to use physical punishment to encourage conformity. Middle-class parents show greater concern for the motivations for their children's behavior; they are less likely to use physical punishment and more likely to withdraw privileges and affection.

     2.   Kohn found that over and above social class, the type of job held by the parent is a factor: the more closely supervised the job is, the more likely the parent is to insist on outward conformity.

    B.   Religion plays a major role in the socialization of most Americans, even if they are not raised in a religious family. Religion especially influences morality, but also ideas about the dress, speech, and manners that are appropriate.

    C.   With more mothers working outside the home today, day care has become a significant agent of socialization.

     1.   Researchers find that the effects of day care largely depend on the child's background, with children from poor households or dysfunctional families benefiting from day care.

     2.   Much depends upon the quality of the day care--high-quality day care is beneficial while low-quality day care has negative effects.

     3.   At this point it is difficult to say exactly how day care affects children's social development. Research findings are preliminary and many are contradictory.

D. It school children are placed outside the direct control of the family and learn to be part of a large group of people of similar age--a peer group. Peer groups, linked by common interests, are a powerful socializing force.

1. Research by Patricia Adler, Steven Kless, and Peter Adler demonstrates how peer groups influence behavior. For boys, norms that make them popular are athletic ability, coolness, and toughness. For girls, the norms are family background, physical appearance, and interest in more mature concerns such as the ability to attract boys.

2. It is almost impossible to go against peer groups; those who do, become labeled as "outsiders," "nonmembers," or "outcasts."

E. The workplace is a significant agent of socialization in later life.

1. The part-time jobs we fill during high school and college provide opportunities for anticipatory socialization--learning to play an occupational role before actually entering it.

2. There is a tendency for the work we do to become part of our self-image; we identify ourselves in terms of our occupations.

V. **Resocialization**

A. Resocialization refers to the process of learning new norms, values, attitudes and behaviors.

1. Resocialization in its most common form occurs each time we learn something contrary to our previous experiences, such as going to work in a new job.

2. Most resocialization is mild, but it can be intense.

B. Erving Goffman coined the term total institution to refer to a place--such as boot camps, prisons, concentration camps, or some mental hospitals, religious cults, and boarding schools --in which people are cut off from the rest of society and are under almost total control of agents of the institution.

1. A person entering the institution is greeted with a degradation ceremony by which current identity is stripped away and replaced (e.g. fingerprinting, shaving the head, banning personal items, and being forced to strip and wear a uniform).

2. Total institutions are quite effective because they isolate people from outside influences and information; supervise their activities; suppress previous roles, statuses, and norms and replace them with new rules and values; and control rewards and punishments.

VI. **Socialization Through the Life Course**

A. Socialization occurs throughout a person's entire lifetime.

B. A general outline of the different stages in the life course would include:

1. Childhood (birth to age 12): In earlier times, children were considered miniature adults, who served an apprenticeship in which they learned and performed tasks. To keep them in line, they were beaten and subjected to psychological torture. The current view is that children are tender and innocent, and parents should guide the physical, emotional, and social development of their children, while providing them with care, comfort, and protection.

2. Adolescence (ages 13 to 17): Economic changes resulting from the Industrial Revolution brought about material surpluses that allowed millions of teenagers to remain outside the labor force, while at the same time the demand for education increased. Biologically equipped for both work and marriage but denied both, adolescents suffer inner turmoil and develop their own standards of clothing,

hairstyles, language, music, and other claims to separate identities.

3. Young Adulthood (ages 18-29): Adult responsibilities are postponed through extended education. At some point during this period, young adults gradually ease into adult responsibilities--finishing school, getting a job, getting married.

4. The Middle Years (ages 30-65): People are surer of themselves and their goals in life than before, but severe jolts such as divorce or being fired can occur. For U.S. women, it can be a trying period due to trying to "have it all"--job, family, and everything. Later adulthood results in a different view of life--trying to evaluate the past and to come to terms with what lies ahead. Individuals may feel they are not likely to get much farther in life, while health and mortality become concerns. However, for most people it is the most comfortable period in their entire lives.

5. Older years (age 65 and beyond): People today live longer and there has been an improvement in general health. At the same time, people in this stage become more concerned with death--that their time is "closing in" on them.

VII. **Are We Prisoners of Socialization?**

A. Sociologists do not think of people as little robots who simply are the result of their exposure to socializing agents. Although socialization is powerful, and profoundly affects us all, we have a self, and the self is dynamic. Each of us uses his or her own mind to reason and make choices.

B. In this way, each of us is actively involved even in the social construction of the self. Our experiences have an impact on us, but we are not doomed to keep our orientations if we do not like them.

KEY TERMS

After studying the chapter, review each of the following terms.

agents of socialization: people and groups that influence our self-concept, emotions, attitudes and behavior (68)

anticipatory socialization: learning to play a role before entering it (69)

degradation ceremony: the term coined by Harold Garfinkel to describe rituals that are designed to strip an individual of his or her identity as a group member; for example, a court martial or the defrocking of a priest (71)

ego: Freud's term for a balancing force between the id and the demands of society (64)

gender roles: the roles we play based on what is considered proper for us because we are a male or female; these sex-linked behaviors, based on a society's ideals, are reinforced by social institutions (65)

gender socialization: the ways in which society sets children onto different courses for life because they are male or female (65)

generalized other: taking the role of a large number of people (62)

id: Freud's term for the individual's inborn basic drives (64)

life course: the stages of our life as we go from birth to death (71)

looking-glass self: a term coined by Charles Horton Cooley to refer to the process by which our self develops through internalizing others' reactions to us (61)

mass media: forms of communication directed to huge audiences (66)

peer group: a group of individuals roughly the same age who are linked by common interests (69)

resocialization: process of learning new norms, values, attitudes, and behaviors (70)

self: the concept, unique to humans, of being able to see ourselves "from the outside;" our internalized perceptions of how others see us (62)

significant other: an individual who significantly influences someone else's life (62)

social environment: the entire human environment, including direct contact with others (58)

socialization: the process by which people learn the characteristics of their group--the attitudes, values, and actions thought appropriate for them (61)

superego: Freud's term for the conscience, which consists of the internalized norms and values of our social groups (64)

taking the role of the other: putting oneself in someone else's shoes; understanding how someone else feels and thinks and thus anticipating how that person will act (61)

total institution: a place in which people are cut off from the rest of society and are almost totally controlled by the officials who run the place (71)

KEY PEOPLE
Review the major theoretical contributions or research findings of these people.

Patricia Adler, Steven Kless, and Peter Adler: These sociologists have documented how peer groups socialize children into gender-appropriate behavior. (69)

Philippe Ariès: Ariès studied paintings from the Middle Ages to learn more about past notions of childhood. (72)

Charles H. Cooley: Cooley studied the development of the self, coining the term "the looking-glass self." (61)

Sigmund Freud: Freud developed a theory of personality development that took into consideration inborn drives (id), the internalized norms and values of one's society (superego), and the individual's ability to balance the two competing forces (ego). (64)

Erving Goffman: Goffman studied the process of resocialization within total institutions. (71)

Susan Goldberg and Michael Lewis: Two psychologists studied how parents' unconscious expectations about gender behavior are communicated to their young children. (65)

Harry and Margaret Harlow: These psychologists studied the behavior of monkeys raised in isolation and found that the length of time they were in isolation affected their ability to overcome the effects of isolation. (60)

Kenneth Keniston: Keniston noted that industrial societies seem to be adding a period of prolonged youth to the life course, in which adult responsibilities are postponed. (74)

Melvin Kohn: Kohn has done extensive research on the social class differences in child-rearing patterns. (68)

George Herbert Mead: Mead emphasized the importance of play in the development of the self, noting that children learn to take on the role of the other and eventually learn to perceive themselves as others do. (65)

Jean Piaget: Piaget studied the development of reasoning skills in children. (63)

H.M. Skeels and H.B. Dye: These two psychologists studied the impact that close social interaction had on the social and intellectual development of institutionalized children. (58)

SELF-TEST

After completing this self-test, check your answers against the Answer Key beginning on page 230 of this Study Guide and against the text on page(s) indicated in parentheses.

<u>MULTIPLE CHOICE QUESTIONS</u>

1. From the case of Isabelle, it is possible to conclude that: (58)
    a. humans have no natural language.
    b. she was retarded.
    c. it is impossible for a person who has been isolated to progress through normal learning stages.
    d. All of the above.

2. Research by H. M. Skeels and H. B. Dye demonstrates: (58-60)
    a. the importance of institutional environment for the development of intelligence.
    b. the importance of the caregiver's intelligence for the development of intelligence in young children.
    c. the importance of human contact in the development of intelligence.
    d. the ability of an individual to rise above early deprivation and gain intelligence in later year.

3. Studies of rhesus monkeys demonstrated that monkeys isolated for six months or more: (60)
    a. were still able to adjust to monkey life.
    b. instinctively knew how to enter into "monkey interaction" with other monkeys.
    c. were eventually accepted by other monkeys.
    d. None of the above.

4. The term "looking-glass self" was coined by: (61)
    a. George H. Mead.
    b. Jean Piaget.
    c. Erving Goffman.
    d. Charles H. Cooley.

5. All of the following statements about Cooley's theory of the development of self are correct, <u>except:</u> (61)
    a. the development of self is an ongoing, lifelong process.
    b. we move beyond the looking-glass self as we mature.
    c. the process of the looking-glass self applies to old age.
    d. the self is always in process.

6. According to Mead's theory, children pretend to take the roles of specific people--such as the Lone Ranger, Supergirl, or Batman--during the _____ stage. (62)
    a. imitation
    b. game
    c. play
    d. generalized other

7.   To George Mead, the "I" is the: (62)
     a.   self as subject.
     b.   self as object.
     c.   same as the id.
     d.   passive robot aspect of human behavior.

8.   According to Jean Piaget, children develop the ability to use symbols during the _____ stage. (63)
     a.   sensorimotor
     b.   preoperational
     c.   concrete operational
     d.   formal operational

9.   Freud's term for a balancing force between the inborn drives for self-gratification and the demands of society is the: (64)
     a.   id.
     b.   superego.
     c.   ego.
     d.   libido.

10. According to this chapter, society sets up effective controls over our behavior by: (65)
     a.   hiring police officers and other law enforcement officials.
     b.   defining those who do not abide by the rules as "deviants."
     c.   socializing us into emotions.
     d.   None of the above.

11. The ways in which society sets children onto different courses for life purely because they are male or female is called: (65)
     a.   sex socialization.
     b.   gender socialization
     c.   masculinization and feminization.
     d.   brainwashing.

12. We begin the lifelong process of defining ourselves as female or male in: (65)
     a.   the family.
     b.   school.
     c.   the hospital where we are born
     d.   church.

13. Psychologists Susan Goldberg and Michael Lewis observed mothers with their six-month-old infants in a laboratory setting and concluded that the mothers: (65-66)
     a.   kept their male children closer to them.
     b.   kept their male and female children about the same distance from them.
     c.   touched and spoke more to their sons.
     d.   unconsciously rewarded daughters for being passive and dependent.

14.   According to sociologist Melvin Kohn, middle-class parents try to develop their children's: (68)
        a.   outward conformity
        b.   level of obedience, neatness, and cleanliness.
        c.   curiosity, self-expression, and self-control.
        d.   All of the above.

15.   Melvin Kohn found that social class differences in early socialization were influenced by: (68)
        a.   the educational level of the parents.
        b.   the type of jobs the parents held.
        c.   the age of the parents.
        d.   the parents' income.

16.   Participation in religious services teaches us: (68)
        a.   beliefs about the hereafter.
        b.   ideas about dress.
        c.   speech and manners appropriate for formal occasions.
        d.   All of the above.

17.   According to researchers, which children seem to benefit most from day care? (69)
        a.   middle class children
        b.   poor children
        c.   children from dysfunctional families
        d.   both "b" and "c" above.

18.   A person's musical preferences, clothing styles, and dating standards typically are most influenced by: (69)
        a.   one's parents.
        b.   one's brothers and/or sisters.
        c.   one's peers.
        d.   mass media.

19.   Being able to try out different occupations while working part-time during high school and college contributes to: (69)
        a.   reverse socialization.
        b.   anticipatory socialization.
        c.   both "a" and "b."
        d.   neither "a" nor "b."

20.   The process of learning new norms, values, attitudes or behaviors to match new life situations is referred to as: (70)
        a.   workplace socialization.
        b.   resocialization.
        c.   expectant socialization.
        d.   mature socialization.

21. Resocialization occurs when a person: (70-71)
   a. takes a new job.
   b. joins a cult.
   c. goes to boot camp.
   d. all of the above.

22. Total institutions: (71)
   a. is a term coined by Harold Garfinkel.
   b. exist primarily in societies with totalitarian governments.
   c. are places in which people are cut off from the rest of society and are almost totally controlled by the officials who run the place.
   d. All of the above.

23. As a consequence of the Industrial Revolution, the stage of the life course known as _____ was invented. (73)
   a. childhood
   b. adolescence
   c. adulthood
   d. senior status

24. Given recent social changes that have taken place within the United States, which of the following groups are particularly challenged by the early middle years stage of the life course? (74)
   a. Generation X
   b. women
   c. Baby boomers
   d. men

25. What is it that prevents us from being prisoners of socialization? (75)
   a. our culture
   b. our education
   c. our self
   d. our families

TRUE-FALSE QUESTIONS

T F 1. Studies of institutionalized children demonstrate that some of the characteristics that we take for granted as being "human" traits result from our basic instincts. (58)

T F 2. Because monkeys and humans are so similar, it is possible to reach conclusions about human behavior from animal studies. (60)

T F 3. Charles H. Cooley concluded that our sense of self develops out of our interaction with others. (61)

T F 4. George H. Mead introduced the concept of the generalized other to sociology. (62)

T F 5. Piaget used the term "operational" to mean the ability to reason. (63)

T F 6. Since emotions are natural human responses, socialization has very little to do with how we feel. (64-65)

T F 7. Most socialization is intended to turn us into conforming members of society. (65)

T F 8. Males outnumber females by two to one on television shows. (66)

T F   9.   Sociologist Melvin Kohn found that the main concern of middle-class parents is their children's outward conformity. (68)

T F   10.   Participation in religious services teaches an individual about the dress, speech, and manners appropriate for formal occasions. (68)

T F   11.   Research findings prove that day care doesn't really benefit children. (69)

T F   12.   Next to the family, the peer group is the most powerful socializing force in society. (69)

T F   13,   According to research by Adler, Kless, and Adler, the norms that contribute to a boy's popularity are athletic ability, coolness, and toughness. (69)

T F   14.   Anticipatory socialization involves learning to play a role before actually taking that role on. (69)

T F   15.   Resocialization always requires learning a radically different perspective. (70)

T F   16.   Total institutions are very effective in stripping away people's personal freedom. (71)

T F   17.   Adolescence is a social creation in industrialized societies. (73)

T F   18.   During the later middle years, many people become part of the "sandwich generation," caring for their own children and their aging parents simultaneously. (74)

T F   19.   Industrialization brought with it a delay in the onset of old age. (75)

T F   20.   Most sociologists view humans as little robots: the socialization goes in and the expected behavior comes out. (75)

FILL-IN QUESTIONS

1.   The entire human environment, including all contact with others, is the _____. (58)

2.   _____ is the process by which people learn the characteristics of their group--the attitudes, values, and actions thought appropriate for them. (61)

3.   Charles H. Cooley coined the term _____ to describe the process by which a sense of self develops. (61)

4.   According to George Herbert Mead, the development of the self through role-taking goes through three stages: (1) _____ ; (2) _____ ; and (3) _____ . (63)

5.   _____ is the term used to describe someone, such as a parent and/or a sibling, who plays a major role in our social development. (62)

6.   The idea that personality consists of the id, ego, and superego was developed by _____ . (64)

7.   The different ways in which a society sets children onto different courses for life because they are male or female is _____ . (65)

8.   _____ include the family, religion, day care, schools, peers, and the workplace. (68)

9.   _____ are groups of individuals roughly the same age linked by common interests. (69)

10.   The process of learning new norms, values, attitudes, and behaviors to match new life situations is _____ . (70)

11.   Resocialization generally takes place in _____ such as boot camps, prisons, and concentration camps. (71)

12.   _____ is a term coined by Harold Garfinkel to describe an attempt to remake the self by stripping away an individual's self-identity and stamping a new identity in its place. (71)

13.   The first stage in the life course, which takes place between birth and age twelve, is referred to by sociologists as _____ . (72)

14.   The stage of the life course which poses a special challenge for U.S. women is _____ . (74)

15.   People in the later middle years are sometimes called the _____ because they are often caught between providing care for their elderly parents while they are still raising their own children. (74)

MATCH THESE SOCIAL SCIENTISTS WITH THEIR CONTRIBUTIONS

___1. Melvin Kohn   a. *coined the term "looking-glass self"*
___2. Erving Goffman   b. *conducted studies of isolated rhesus monkeys*
___3. George Herbert Mead   c. *coined the term "generalized other"*
___4. Charles H. Cooley   d. *studied total institutions*
___5. Jean Piaget   e. *found social class differences in child rearing*
___6. Harry and Margaret Harlow   f. *asserted that human behavior is based on unconscious drives*
___7. Sigmund Freud   g. *four stages in the development of reasoning ability*
___8. Philippe Ariès   h. *analyzed images of childhood in the Middle Ages*

ESSAY QUESTIONS

1.   Explain what is necessary in order for us to develop into full human beings.

2.   Why do sociologists ague that socialization is a process and not a product?

3.   How would you answer the question, "Are We Prisoners of Socialization?"

"DOWN-TO-EARTH SOCIOLOGY"

1.   What do studies like the one of identical twins Oskar and Jack (p. 59), tell us about heredity and environment? Have you ever known a set of identical twins? If you are an identical twin, in what ways are you like your sibling? In what ways are you different?

2.   Think about learning what emotions are appropriate for you because or your age, race or ethnicity, gender, and social class background. How were you socialized into emotions; for example, "little boys don't cry" and "little girls don't fight!"?

3.   What are some of the different ways in which boot camp achieves the goal of resocialization (p. 70)? What are some of the pressures exerted on the recruited to conform? Have you ever been a member of a total institution? How did your experiences fit with those contained in this "Down-to-Earth Sociology" box?

4.   Why is it problematic to be caught between two worlds like Richard Rodriguez was (p. 72)? Do you think many people today are in a similar situation? Do you consider yourself to be caught between two worlds?

CHAPTER 4
SOCIAL STRUCTURE AND SOCIAL INTERACTION

CHAPTER SUMMARY

- There are two levels of sociological analysis; macrosociology investigates the large-scale features of social structure, while microsociology focuses on social interaction. Functional and conflict theorists tend to use a macrosociological approach while symbolic interactionists are more likely to use a microsociological approach.

- The term social structure refers to a society's framework. Culture, social class, social status, roles, groups, and institutions are the major components of the social structure. The individual's location in the social structure affects his or her perceptions, attitudes, and behaviors.

- Social institutions are the organized and standard means that a society develops to meet its basic needs. Sociologists have identified nine institutions--the family, religion, law, politics, economics, education, medicine, science, and the military. A tenth -- the mass media -- is emerging.

- Over time, social structure undergoes changes; sweeping changes have followed each of the four social revolutions--the *first* is associated with the domestication of animals and plants, the *second* the invention of the plow, the *third* the invention of the steam engine, and the *fourth* the invention of the microchip. Both Durkheim's concepts of mechanical and organic solidarity, and Tönnies' constructs of *Gemeinschaft and Gesellschaft* focus on the social transformations of agricultural societies to industrial societies.

- Symbolic interactionists examine how people use physical space, noting that each of us is surrounded by a "personal bubble" that we carefully protect. The dramaturgical analysis provided by Erving Goffman analyzes everyday life in terms of the stage, while the ethnomethodologists try to uncover our background assumptions which provide the basic core of our reality.

- Both macrosociology and microsociology are needed to understand human behavior because we must grasp both social structure and social interaction.

LEARNING OBJECTIVES

As you read Chapter 4, use these learning objectives to organize your notes. After completing your reading, briefly state an answer to each of the objectives, and review the text pages in parentheses.

1. Differentiate between macro- and microsociology and indicate which levels of analysis are most likely to be used by functionalists, conflict theorists, and symbolic interactionists. (80-81)
2. Discuss social structure and explain why one's location in this structure affects that person's perceptions, attitudes, and behaviors. (881-82)
3. Define the following concepts: culture, social class, social status, roles, groups, social institutions, and societies. (82-87)
4. Identify the nine social institutions common to all societies and summarize the basic features of each. (86)
5. Distinguish between the five types of societies, listing the characteristics of each society and identifying the technological innovations that produced social revolutions (87-89)
6. Use Durkheim's concepts of mechanical and organic solidarity and Tönnies' typologies of *Gemeinschaft* and *Gesellschaft* to explain what holds societies together. (90)
8. Explain the concept of personal space and discuss how it is defined in different cultures. (92)
9. Outline the key components of both the dramaturgical view of everyday life and ethnomethodology. (92-96)

10.   Explain the Thomas theorem and the social construction of reality. (96-97)
11.   Indicate why both macrosociology and microsociology are necessary for a full understanding of social life. (97-98)

CHAPTER OUTLINE

I.   **Levels of Sociological Analysis**
    A.   Macrosociology places the focus on large-scale features of social structure. It investigates large-scale social forces and the effects they have on entire societies and the groups within them. It is utilized by functionalist and conflict theorists.
    B.   Microsociology places the emphasis on social interaction, or what people do when they come together. Symbolic interaction is an example.

II.   **The Macrosociological Perspective: Social Structure**
    A.   Social structure is defined as the patterned relationships between people that persist over time; it is sociologically significant because it guides our behavior.
        1.   Personal feelings and desires tend to be overridden by social structure. An individual's behaviors and attitudes are determined by that person's location in the social structure.
        2.   Major components or social structure are culture, social class, social status, roles, groups, social institutions, and societies.
    B.   Culture refers to a group's language, beliefs, values, behaviors, and gestures and the material objects used by a group. It determines what kind of people we will become.
    C.   Social class in U.S. society generally is based on income, education, and occupational prestige; a large number of people who have similar amounts of income and education and who work at jobs that are roughly comparable in prestige make up a social class.
    D.   Social status refers to the positions that an individual occupies. Each status provides guidelines for how people are to act and to feel.
        1.   Status set refers to all the statuses or positions that an individual occupies.
        2.   Ascribed statuses are positions an individual either inherits at birth or receives involuntarily later in life. Achieved statuses are positions that are earned, accomplished, or involve at least some effort or activity on the individual's part.
        3.   Status symbols are signs that identify a status.
        4.   A master status--such as being male or female--cuts across the other statuses that an individual occupies. Status inconsistency is a contradiction or mismatch between statuses.
    E.   Roles are the behaviors, obligations, and privileges attached to a status.
        1.   The individual occupies a status, but plays a role.
        2.   Roles are an essential component of culture because they lay out what is expected of people, and as individuals perform their roles, those roles mesh together to form the society.
    F.   A group consists of people who regularly and consciously interact with one another and typically share similar values, norms, and expectations.
    G.   Social institutions are society's organized means of meeting its basic needs.
        1.   The family, religion, law, politics, economics, education, science, medicine, and the military all are social institutions.
        2.   Each institution has its own set of roles, values, and norms that set limits and provide guidelines for behavior.

H.   Society, which consists of people who share a culture and a territory, is the largest and most complex group that sociologists study.

1.   The first societies were hunting and gathering societies; small in size and nomadic, the group moved elsewhere when the supply of food ran out. There were no opportunities to accumulate possessions; therefore these were the most egalitarian of all societies, with social divisions based primarily on the family.

2.   Hunting and gathering societies were transformed into pastoral (characterized by the pasturing of animals) and horticultural (characterized by the growing of plants) societies as a result of the domestication revolution, called the first social revolution. Food surpluses emerged, which led to larger populations and some specialized division of labor. As trade developed, people began to accumulate objects they considered valuable, with leaders accumulating more of these possessions than others. Simple equality began to give way to inequality.

3.   The agricultural revolution (the second social revolution) occurred with the invention of the plow and pastoral and horticultural societies were transformed. A much larger food surplus was produced and more people engaged in activities other than farming. Sometimes referred to as the dawn of civilization, this period also produced the wheel, writing, and numbers. Cities developed, and groups began to be distinguished by their greater or lesser possessions. An elite gained control of the surplus resources. Social inequalities became more complex, and females became subjugated to males.

4.   The Industrial Revolution (the third social revolution) began in 1765, when the steam engine first was used to run machinery. Agricultural society gave way to industrial society. Initially social inequality increased greatly, as the individuals who first utilized the new technology accumulated great wealth, controlling the means of production and dictating the conditions under which people could work for them. A huge surplus of labor developed, as masses of people were thrown off the land their ancestors had farmed; these new industrial workers eventually won their demands for better living conditions. The consequence was that wealth spread to larger segments of society. As industrialization continued, the pattern of growing inequality was reversed.

5.   Industrial societies are being transformed into postindustrial societies, suggesting a fourth social revolution, the information revolution, the basic component of which is information and the primary technological change involved is the microchip. Postindustrial societies are moving away from production and manufacturing to service industries. The U.S. was the first country to have more than 50 percent of its work force employed in service industries. Australia, New Zealand, western Europe, and Japan soon followed.

I.   Sociologists have tried to find an answer to the question of what holds society together.

1.   For Durkheim, mechanical solidarity--based on a collective consciousness that people experience as a result of performing the same or similar tasks--and organic solidarity--a collective consciousness based on the interdependence brought about by how tasks are divided among a populace--explained social cohesion, or the degree to which members of a society feel united by shared values and other social bonds.

2.   For Tönnies, the answer lay in the type of society that existed. *Gemeinschaft* is a society in which life is intimate; a community in which everyone knows everyone

else and people share a sense of togetherness; *Gesellschaft* is a society dominated by impersonal relationships, individual accomplishments, and self interest.

III. **The Microsociological Perspective: Social Interaction in Everyday Life**
   A. The microsociological approach places its emphasis on face-to-face social interaction, or what people do when they are in the presence of one another.
   B. Symbolic interactionists study personal space and how people surround themselves with a "personal bubble," regulating who we let in (intimates) and who we keep out (strangers).
     1. The amount or personal space people prefer varies from one culture to another.
     2. Anthropologist Edward Hall found that Americans use four different distance zones: (1) Intimate distance--about 18 inches from the body--for lovemaking, wrestling, comforting and protecting. (2) Personal distance--from 18 inches to 4 feet--for friends, acquaintances, and ordinary conversations. (3) Social distance--from 4 feet to 12 feet--for impersonal or formal relationships such as job interviews. (4) Public distance--beyond 12 feet--for even more formal relationships such as separating dignitaries and public speakers from the general public.
   C. Dramaturgy is an analysis of how we present ourselves in everyday life. Dramaturgy is the name given to an approach, pioneered by Erving Goffman, for analyzing social life in terms of drama or the stage.
     1. According to Goffman, socialization prepares people for learning to perform on the stage of everyday life.
     2. Impression management is the person's efforts to manage the impressions that others receive of her or him.
     3. Front stage is where performances are given (wherever a person delivers his or her lines). Back stage is where people rest from their performances, discuss their presentations, and plan future performances.
     4. Role performance is the particular emphasis or interpretation that an individual gives a role, the person's "style". Role conflict occurs when the expectations of one role are incompatible with those of another role--in other words, conflict between roles. Role strain refers to conflicts that someone feels within a role.
     5. Teamwork, when two or more players work together to make sure a performance goes off as planned, show that we are adept players.
     6. When a performance doesn't come off, we engage in face-saving behavior--ignoring flaws in someone's performance.
   D. Ethnomethodology involves the discovery of basic rules concerning our views of the world and how people ought to act.
     1. Ethnomethodologists try to undercover people's background assumptions, which form the basic core of one's reality, and provide basic rules concerning our view of the world and of how people ought to act.
     2. Harold Garfinkel founded the ethnomethodological approach.
   E. The social construction of reality refers to what people define as real because of their background assumptions and life experiences.
     1. The Thomas theorem (by sociologist W. I. Thomas) states, "If people define situations as real, they are real in their consequences."
     2. Symbolic interactionists believe that people define their own reality and then live within those definitions.

IV. **The Need for Both Macrosociology and Microsociology**
   A. To understand human behavior, it is necessary to grasp both social structure

(macrosociology) and social interaction (microsociology).
B.   Both are necessary for us to understand social life fully because each in its own way adds to our knowledge of human experience.

KEY TERMS
After studying the chapter, review each of the following terms.

achieved statuses: positions that are earned, accomplished, or involve at least some effort or activity on the individual's part (83)

ascribed statuses: positions an individual either inherits at birth or receives involuntarily later in life (83)

background assumptions: deeply embedded common understandings, or basic rules, concerning our view of the world and how people ought to act (95)

division of labor: how work is divided among the members of a group (90)

dramaturgy: an approach, pioneered by Erving Goffman, analyzing social life in terms of drama and the stage (93)

ethnomethodology: the study of how people use background assumptions to make sense of life (95)

face-saving behavior: techniques used to salvage a performance that is going sour (94)

Gemeinschaft: a type of society in which life is intimate; a community in which everyone knows everyone else and people share a sense of togetherness (90)

Gesellschaft: a type of society dominated by impersonal relationships, individual accomplishments, and self-interest (90)

group: people who regularly and consciously interact with one another; in a general sense, people who have something in common and who believe that what they have in common is significant (85)

horticultural society: a society based on the cultivation of plants by the use of hand tools (87)

hunting and gathering society: a society dependent on hunting and gathering for survival (87)

impression management: the term used by Erving Goffman to describe people's efforts to control the impressions that others receive of them (93)

Industrial Revolution: the third social revolution; it occurred when machines powered by fuels replaced most animal and human power (88)

macrosociology: analysis of social life that focuses on broad features of social structure, such as social class and the relationships of groups to one another; an approach usually used by functionalist and conflict theorists (80)

master status: a status that cuts across the other statuses that an individual occupies (84)

mechanical solidarity: Durkheim's term for the unity or shared consciousness that comes from being involved in similar occupations or activities (90)

microsociology: analysis of social life that focuses on social interaction; an approach usually used by symbolic interactionists (80)

organic solidarity: Durkheim's term for the interdependence that results from people needing the skills, work and products of one another; the solidarity based on the division of labor (90)

pastoral society: a society based on the pasturing of animals (87)

role: the behaviors, obligations, and privileges attached to a status (85)

role conflict: conflict that someone feels *between* roles because the expectations attached to one role are incompatible with the expectations of another role (93)

role strain: conflicts that someone feels *within* a role (93)

social class: a large number of people with similar amounts of income and education who work at jobs that are roughly comparable in prestige (82)

social cohesion: the degree to which members of a group or a society feel united by shared values and other social bonds (90)

social construction of reality: the use of background assumptions and life experiences to define what is real (96)

social institution: the organized, usual, or standard ways by which society meets its basic needs (85)

social interaction: what people do when they are in one another's presence (80)

social structure: the relationship of people and groups to one another (81)

society: a group of people who share a culture and a territory (87)

status: the position that someone occupies; one's social ranking (83)

status inconsistency: a contradiction or mismatch between statuses; a condition in which a person ranks high on some dimensions of social class and low on others (84)

status symbols: items used to identify a status (84)

teamwork: the collaboration of two or more persons who, interested in the success of a performance, manage impressions jointly (93)

Thomas theorem: basically, that people live in socially constructed world; that is, people jointly build their own realities; as summarized by William I. Thomas's statement: "If people define situations as real, they are real in their consequences." (96)

KEY PEOPLE

Review the major theoretical contributions or research findings of these people.

William Chambliss: Chambliss used macro and microsociology to study high school gangs and found that social structure and interaction explained the patterns of behavior in these groups. groups. (98)

Emile Durkheim: Durkheim identified mechanical and organic solidarity as the keys to social cohesion. (90)

Harold Garfinkel: Garfinkel is the founder of ethnomethodology; he conducted experiments in order to uncover people's background assumptions. (95)

Erving Goffman: Goffman developed dramaturgy, the perspective within symbolic interactionism that views social life as a drama on the stage. (93)

Edward Hall: This anthropologist found that personal space varied from one culture to another and that North Americans use four different "distance zones." (92)

Karen Honeycutt: Honeycutt studied television talk shows that feature women and weight themes and identified three categories reflecting how obese women feel about themselves and how audiences react to them. (94)

W. I. Thomas: This sociologist was known for his statement, "If people define situations as real, they are real in their consequences." (96)

Ferdinand Tönnies: Tönnies analyzed different types of societies that existed before and after industrialization. He used the terms *Gemeinschaft* and *Gesellschaft* to describe the two types of societies. (90)

SELF-TEST

After completing this self-test, check your answers against the Answer Key beginning on page 233 of this Study Guide and against the text on page(s) indicated in parentheses.

MULTIPLE CHOICE QUESTIONS

1. Microsociology: (80)
    a. places the focus on social interaction.
    b. investigates large-scale social forces.
    c. places the focus on broad features of social structure.
    d. is used by functionalists and conflict theorists.

2. Sociologists who study social class and how groups are related to one another are using: (80)
    a. dramaturgy.
    b. ethnomethodology.
    c. macrosociology.
    d. microsociology.

3. According to sociologists, differences among individuals in behavior and attitudes is due to: (81)
    a. biology.
    b. location in the social structure.
    c. conceptions of personal space.
    d. different styles of impression management.

4. Culture: (82)
    a. is only the material objects used by a group.
    b. is less important in modern societies.
    c. is the social inheritance, learned from other people.
    d. All of the above.

5. One component of social structure which strongly influences our attitudes and behavior is: (82-83)
    a. social class.
    b. status sets.
    c. normative clusters.
    d. master status.

6. Social class is based on: (82)
    a. income.
    b. education.
    c. occupational prestige.
    d. all of the above.

7. A person is simultaneously a daughter, a lawyer, and a wife. Together these represent her: (83)
    a. social status.
    b. social class.
    c. status position.
    d. status set.

8.   One's race, sex, and the social class of his or her parents are examples of: (83)
        a.   ascribed statuses.
        b.   achieved statuses.
        c.   status inconsistencies.
        d.   status incongruities.

9.   All of the following are correct regarding status symbols, <u>except:</u> (84)
        a.   status symbols are signs that identify a status.
        b.   status symbols often are used to show that people have "made it."
        c.   status symbols are always positive signs or people would not wear them.
        d.   status symbols are used by people to announce their statuses to others.

10.   A master status is: (84)
        a.   always ascribed.
        b.   one that cuts across the other statuses that a person holds.
        c.   fairly easily changed.
        d.   All of the above.

11.   Status inconsistency is most likely to occur when: (84)
        a.   a contradiction or mismatch between statuses exists.
        b.   we know what to expect of other people.
        c.   a person wears too many status symbols at once.
        d.   a society has few clearly defined master statuses.

12.   The behaviors, obligations, and privileges attached to statuses are called: (85)
        a.   status sets.
        b.   master statuses.
        c.   status differentiations.
        d.   roles.

13.   Sociologically, roles are significant because: (85)
        a.   sociologists need something concrete to study.
        b.   they lay out what is expected of people by society.
        c.   most deviant behavior occurs in roles.
        d.   None of the above.

14.   People who regularly and consciously interact with one another: (85)
        a.   develop compatible roles.
        b.   are considered a group, according to the sociological definition.
        c.   make up a social institution.
        d.   all of the above.

15.   Religion, politics, education, and the military are examples of: (86)
        a.   involuntary groups.
        b.   voluntary associations.
        c.   social institutions.
        d.   social fixtures.

16. The simplest societies are the: (82)
    a. horticultural societies.
    b. pastoral societies.
    c. hunting and gathering societies.
    d. primitive societies.

17. Of all types of societies, the most egalitarian is: (87)
    a. hunting and gathering societies.
    b. horticultural societies.
    c. agricultural societies.
    d. industrial societies.

18. Pastoral societies are based on: (87)
    a. the cultivation of plants.
    b. the pasturing of animals.
    c. the invention of the plow.
    d. large-scale agriculture.

19. The domestication revolution led to: (87)
    a. the human group becoming larger.
    b. the creation of a food surplus.
    c. a more specialized division of labor.
    d. All of the above.

20. A society based on large-scale agriculture, using plows drawn by animals is known as a(n): (88)
    a. pastoral society.
    b. farming society.
    c. agricultural society.
    d. horticultural society.

21. In agricultural societies, social inequality: (88)
    a. largely was non existent.
    b. was developing slowly, but social stratification remained limited.
    c. became more extensive than that found in earlier societies.
    d. None of the above.

22. Postindustrial society is based on: (89)
    a. information, services, and high technology.
    b. emphasis on raw materials.
    c. the production of new products.
    d. All of the above.

23. Organic solidarity refers to a society: (90)
    a. with a highly specialized division of labor.
    b. whose members who are interdependent on one another.
    c. with a high degree of impersonal relationships.
    d. All of the above.

24.   Personal space might be a research topic for a sociologist using: (92)
    a.   macrolevel analysis.
    b.   functional analysis.
    c.   symbolic interactionism.
    d.   the conflict perspective.

25.   The Thomas theorem is based on: (98)
    a.   functionalism.
    b.   conflict theory.
    c.   symbolic interactionism.
    d.   exchange theory.

TRUE-FALSE QUESTIONS

T F   1.   Social structure has little impact on the typical individual. (81)
T F   2.   A person's ideas, attitudes, and behaviors largely depend on social class. (82-83)
T F   3.   To sociologists, the terms "social class" and "social status" mean the same thing. (82-83)
T F   4.   Being a student is an example of an achieved status. (83)
T F   5.   Being male or female is a master status. (84)
T F   6.   You occupy a status, but you play a role. (85)
T F   7.   Sociologists have identified five basic social institutions in contemporary societies. (86)
T F   8.   Society is the largest and most complex group that sociologists study. (87)
T F   9.   The simplest societies are called horticultural societies. (87)
T F   10. Hunting-and-gathering societies have been called the "dawn of civilization." (87)
T F   11. The domestication of animals and plants was the first social revolution. (87)
T F   12. Industrial societies were brought about by the invention of the plow. (88)
T F   13. Japan was the first country to have more than 50 percent of its work force employed in service industries. (89)
T F   14. According to Emile Durkheim, with industrialization the basis for social cohesion shifts from organic to mechanical solidarity. (90)
T F   15. *Gemeinschaft* society is characterized by impersonal, short-term relationships. (90)
T F   16. The amount or personal space people prefer varies from one culture to another. (92)
T F   17. According to Erving Goffman, back stages are where we can let our hair down. (93)
T F   18. Role conflict is a conflict that someone feels within a role. (93)
T F   19. A face-saving technique, in which people give the impression that they are unaware of a flaw in someone's performance, is known as impression management. (93)
T F   20. Symbolic interactionists assume that reality has an objective existence, and people must deal with it. (96)

FILL-IN QUESTIONS

1.   _____ investigates such things as social class and how groups are related to one another. (80)
2.   The level of sociological analysis used by symbolic interactionists is _____ . (80)
3.   _____ are signs used to identify a status. (84)
4.   Sociologists refer to the condition in which a person ranks high on some dimensions of social class but low on others as _____ . (84)

5. The simplest societies are called _hunting gathering_ societies. (87)

6. A society based on information, services, and high technology is called the _postindustrial_ society. (87)

7. The degree to which members of a group or society feel united by shared values and other social bonds is referred to as _social cohesion_ (90)

8. Durkheim referred to a collective consciousness that people experience due to performing the same or similar tasks as _mechanical_. (90)

9. Ferdinand Tönnies used the term _Gesellschaft_ to refer to societies dominated by impersonal relationships, individual accomplishments, and self-interest. (90)

10. Erving Goffman used the term _impression management_ to describe people's efforts to control the impressions that others receive of them. (93)

11. _Role conflict_ occurs when the expectations of one role are incompatible with those of another role. (93)

12. Sometimes the same role has conflicting expectations built into it, which is known as _role_. (93)

13. Goffman called the techniques that we use to try and salvage a performance that is going bad as _face-saving_. (93-94)

14. The _Thomas theorem_ states, "If people define situations as real, they are real in their consequences." (96)

15. What people define as real because of their background assumptions and life experiences is the _social construction of reality_. (96)

MATCH THESE SOCIAL SCIENTISTS WITH THEIR CONTRIBUTIONS

b 1. Emile Durkheim   a. *described **Gemeinschaft** and **Gesellschaft** societies*

a 2. Ferdinand Tönnies   b. *wrote about mechanical and organic solidarity*

d 3. Edward Hall   c. *analyzed everyday life in terms of dramaturgy*

c 4. Erving Goffman   d. *found of ethnomethodolgy*

f 5. W. I. Thomas   e. *studied the concept of personal space*

f 6. Harold Garfinkel   f. *wrote a theorem about the nature of social reality*

ESSAY QUESTIONS

1. Choose a research topic and discuss how you would approach this topic using both macrosociology and microsociology.

2. Today we see many examples of people wanting to re-create a simpler way of life. Using Tönnies' framework, analyze this tendency.

3. Assume that you have been asked to give a presentation in your sociology class on Goffman's dramaturgy approach. Describe what information you would want to include in such a presentation.

"DOWN-TO-EARTH SOCIOLOGY"

1. Analyze the statuses and roles in your own life. How does the time and place of your birth affect your life? Have you ever experienced role conflict or role strain? What were the social conditions that produced this?

2. After reading about the social structure of college football (p. 82), describe the social structure of a group to which you belong, identifying the statuses, roles and role expectations.

3. Were you aware of the Amish before reading this chapter (p. 91)? If you had the opportunity to live in one of the Amish communities, would you be comfortable doing so? Why or why not?

4. Are you aware of your own sense of personal space? Have you ever met someone from a different culture and thought that they stood too close too far from you? How does our sense of space depend upon the social environment, e.g. at a party versus on public transportation?

CHAPTER 5
SOCIAL GROUPS AND FORMAL ORGANIZATIONS

CHAPTER SUMMARY

- Groups are the essence of life in society. An essential feature of a group is that its members have something in common and that they believe what they have in common is significant. Society is the largest and most complex group that sociologists study.

- The following types of groups exist within society: primary groups, secondary groups, in-groups and out-groups, reference groups, and social networks. The new technology has given birth to a new type of group, the electronic community.

- Robert Michels noted that formal organizations tend to be controlled by a small group; this elite bypasses members and limits leadership roles to its own inner circle. Michels called this tendency the "iron law of oligarchy."

- A bureaucracy is a hierarchical organization with a division of labor, written rules, written communications, and impersonality of positions. These allow bureaucracies to be efficient and enduring. Bureaucracies endure because of goal displacement. They tend to become a central feature of societies, taking over more and more of everyday tasks.

- The concept of corporate culture refers to the organization's traditions, values, and norms. Much of this culture is invisible. It can affect its members, either negatively or positively depending upon the members' available opportunities to achieve.

- The Japanese corporate model provides a contrast to the U.S. corporate model in terms of hiring and promotion practices, guarantees of lifetime security, worker involvement outside the work setting, the broad training of workers, and the collective decision-making.

- Group dynamics refer to the ways in which individuals and groups influence one another. Size affects the dynamics of a group. Different types of leaders serve different functions in the group; instrumental leaders are task-oriented, while expressive leaders focus on maintaining harmony. Authoritarian leaders give orders, democratic leaders lead by consensus, and laissez-faire leaders are highly permissive.

- The Asch experiment illustrates the power of peer pressure, while the Milgram experiment demonstrates the influence of authority. Both show how easily we succumb to "groupthink," a kind of collective tunnel vision.

LEARNING OBJECTIVES

As you read Chapter 5, use these learning objectives to organize your notes. After completing your reading, briefly state an answer to each of the objectives, and review the text pages in parentheses.

1. Distinguish between groups, aggregates, and categories and explain why they are important to individuals and societies. (104)
2. Define primary groups and explain the role they play in our lives. (104)
3. Compare secondary groups to primary groups in terms of the characteristics of each. (104-105)
4. Describe voluntary associations and explain why there is a tendency for an oligarchy to control these types of secondary groups, especially in socially diverse societies. (105-106)
5. Distinguish between in-groups and out-groups. (106-107)
6. Explain what the purpose of reference groups is and why, within a socially diverse society, we often receive contradictory messages from reference groups. (107-108)

7. Explain the relationship between cliques and social networks. Discuss how "networking" addresses some of the social barriers within a socially diverse society. (108)
8. Show why many of the newsgroups that exist on the Internet can be considered groups in the sociological sense. (108-109)
9. State the definition of bureaucracy, list its essential characteristics, and explain why it has a tendency to endure over time. (110-112)
10. Explain what is meant by the "rationalization of society." (112)
11. Discuss the dark side of bureaucracies, and give examples of each type of problem. (112-114)
12. Identify the consequences of hidden values in the corporate culture, especially noting their impact on women and minority participants. (114)
13. Compare and contrast the Japanese and United States corporate organizational models. (115-117)
14. Explain the concept of group dynamics and indicate how group size affects interaction. (117-119)
15. Describe the two types of leaders in groups, and the three basic styles of leadership. (119-120)
16. Demonstrate the importance of peer pressure to conformity by analyzing the Asch and Milgram experiments. (120-122)
17. Discuss groupthink and explain how it can be dangerous for a society. (121-124)

CHAPTER OUTLINE

I. **Social Groups**
    A. Groups are the essence of life in society. An essential element of a social group is that its members have something in common and that they believe what they have in common makes a difference.
        1. An aggregate consists of individuals who temporarily share the same physical space but do not see themselves as belonging together.
        2. A category consists of people who share similar characteristics, but do not interact with one another or take one another into account.
    B. Primary groups refer to groups characterized by cooperative, intimate, long-term, face-to-face relationships.
        1. The group becomes part of the individual's identity and the lens through which to view life.
        2. They are essential to an individual's psychological well-being, since humans have an intense need for associations that provide feelings of self-esteem.
    C. Secondary groups are larger, more anonymous, formal, and impersonal than are primary groups, and are based on some interest or activity.
        1. Members are likely to interact on the basis of specific roles, such as president, manager, worker, or student.
        2. Secondary groups tend to break down into primary groups, such as friendship cliques at school or work. The primary group serves as a buffer between the individual and the needs of the secondary group.
    D. Voluntary associations are secondary groups made up of volunteers who have organized on the basis of some mutual interest.
        1. Within voluntary associations is an inner core of individuals who stand firmly behind the group's goals and are firmly committed to maintaining the organization. Robert Michels used the term "iron law of oligarchy" to refer to the tendency of this inner core to dominate the organization by becoming a small, self-perpetuating elite.

2. Within a socially diverse society, people who do not represent the appearances, values, or background of the inner circle may be excluded from leadership.

E. Groups toward which individuals feel loyalty are called in-groups, while those toward which they feel antagonisms are called out-groups.

1. The division is significant sociologically because in-groups provide a sense of identification or belonging, give feelings of superiority, and command loyalty, thus exercising a high degree of control over their members. The antagonisms that out-groups produce help reinforce the loyalty of members of the in-group.

2. According to Robert K. Merton, the behaviors of an in-group's members are seen as virtues, while the same behaviors by members of an out-group are viewed as vices. This double standard can pose a danger for pluralistic societies, when out-groups come to symbolize some evil, arousing hatred and motivating members of the in-group to strike out against the out-group.

F. Reference groups are the groups we use as standards to evaluate ourselves, whether or not we actually belong to those groups.

1. They exert great influence over our behavior; people may change their clothing, hair style, speech, and other characteristics to match reference group expectations.

2. Having two reference groups that clearly conflict with each other can produce intense internal conflict.

G. Social networks consist of people linked by various social ties; cliques are a kind of social network.

1. The interactions that take place within social networks connect us to the larger society.

2. Social networks tend to perpetuate social inequality; who you know may be more important than what you know. The "old boy" network, for instance, tends to keep the best positions available to men only, rather than women. The term networking refers to the conscious use or even cultivation of contacts people think will be helpful to them, for instance by joining and belonging to clubs.

H. In the 1990s there is a new type of human group--electronic communities--created through the technology of the Internet.

1. People communicate with one another through thousands of newsgroups.

2. These newsgroups meet the sociological definition of a group because the participants interact with one another and they share a sense of belonging.

II. Bureaucracies

A. Almost 100 years ago, Max Weber noted the emergence of bureaucracies, a new type of organization whose goal was to maximize efficiency and results.

B. The essential characteristics of bureaucracies are: (1) a hierarchy with assignments flowing downward and accountability flowing upward; (2) a division of labor; (3) written rules; (4) written communications and records; and (5) impersonality.

C. Once bureaucracies come into existence, they tend to perpetuate themselves by replacing old goals for new ones.

D. Weber predicted that bureaucracies would dominate social life because they are a powerful form of social organization. He called this process the "rationalization of society."

E. Bureaucracies also have a dark side.

1. Sometimes the rules that govern bureaucratic activity can become too detailed or too cumbersome, such that procedures are no longer carried out efficiently.

2.   Bureaucratic alienation, a feeling of powerlessness and normlessness, occurs when workers are assigned to repetitive tasks in order for the corporation to achieve efficient production, thereby cutting them off from the product of one's labor. To resist alienation, workers form primary groups within the larger secondary organization.

III.   Corporate Culture

A.   Rosabeth Moss Kanter's organizational research demonstrates that the corporate elite maintains hidden values--to keep itself in power and provide better access to information, networking, and "fast tracks" for workers like themselves, usually white and male.

    1.   Workers who fit in are given opportunities to advance; they outperform others and are more committed. Those who are judged outsiders and experience few opportunities think poorly of themselves, are less committed, and work below their potential.

    2.   The hidden values that created this self-fulfilling prophecy remain largely invisible. Because if this, the inner circle reproduces itself, thereby contributing to the iron law of oligarchy.

    3.   Females and minorities do not match the hidden values of the corporate culture and may by treated differently. They may experience "showcasing"--being put in highly visible positions with little power so that the company is in compliance with affirmative action and "slow-track" positions--jobs where promotions are slow because accomplishments in these areas seldom come to the attention of top management.

B.   The Japanese have become a giant in today's global economy because they developed a different form of corporate model.

    1.   In Japan, newly-hired college graduates are viewed as a team working towards the same goal of success for the organization; in the United Sates, employees try to outperform one another and are loyal to himself or herself, not the company.

    2.   In Japan, lifetime security is taken for granted, with employees and firms maintaining mutual loyalties; in the United States, lifetime security is unusual, with companies routinely laying workers off in slow times and workers looking out for "number one."

    3.   In Japan, work is like a marriage, company and employee are mutually committed; in the United States, the work relationship is highly specific.

    4.   In Japan, workers move from one job to another within the corporation; in the United States, workers are expected to perform one job only, and if they do it well they may be promoted up the ladder to the next level.

    5.   In Japan, decision making is a lengthy process, with everyone affected by the decision being given an opportunity to have input; in the United States, decisions are made without necessarily consulting with those who will be affected.

    6.   In reality, most Japanese workers do not work in corporations that reflect the model and in recent years, Japan has turned to the United States for clues on how to be more efficient.

IV.   Group Dynamics

A.   How individuals affect groups and groups affect individuals is known as group dynamics.

B.   The size of the group is significant for its dynamics.

    1.   Sociologist Georg Simmel (1858-1918) noted the significance of group size, making distinctions between a dyad, the smallest and most fragile of all human

groupings containing only two members, and a triad, stronger than dyads because there are three members but still are extremely unstable. It is not uncommon for the bonds between two members to seem stronger, with the third person feeling hurt and excluded.

    2.   As more members are added to a group, intensity decreases and stability increases, for there are more linkages between more people within the group. The groups develop a more formal structure to accomplish their goals, for instance by having a president, treasurer, etc.

C.   Group size also influences our attitudes and behaviors.

    1.   As the size of the group increases, the members of the group feel a diffusion of responsibility.

    2.   As the size increases, the group loses its sense of intimacy.

    3.   As the size increases, the group tends to divide itself into smaller groups.

D.   A leader may be defined as someone who influences the behavior of others.

    1.   There are two types of group leaders. Instrumental (task-oriented) leaders are those who try to keep the group moving toward its goals, reminding the members of what they are trying to accomplish. Expressive (socioemotional) leaders are those who are less likely to be recognized as leaders but help with the group's morale. These leaders may have to minimize the friction that instrumental leaders necessarily create.

    2.   There are three types of leadership styles. Authoritarian leaders are those who give orders and frequently do not explain why they praise or condemn a person's work. Democratic leaders are those who try to gain a consensus by explaining proposed actions, suggesting alternative approaches, and giving "facts" as the basis for their evaluation of the members' work. Laissez-faire leaders are those who are very passive and give the group almost total freedom to do as it wishes.

    3.   Psychologists Ronald Lippitt and Ralph White discovered that the leadership styles produced different results when used on small groups of young boys. Under authoritarian leaders the boys became either aggressive or apathetic; under democratic leaders they were more personal and friendly; and under laissez-faire leaders they asked more questions, made fewer decisions, and were notable for their lack of achievement.

    4.   Different situations require different styles of leadership.

    5.   People who become leaders are seen as strongly representing the group's values or as able to lead a group out of a crisis; they tend to be more talkative and to express determination and self-confidence. Taller people and those judged better looking are more likely to become leaders.

E.   A study by Dr. Solomon Asch indicates that people are strongly influenced by peer pressure. Asch was interested in seeing whether individuals would resist the temptation to change a correct response to an incorrect response because of peer pressure.

    1.   Asch held cards up in front of small groups of people and asked them which sets of cards matched; one at a time, they were supposed to respond aloud. All but one of the group members was a confederate, having been told in advance by the researcher how to answer the question.

    2.   After two trials in which everyone answered correctly, the confederates intentionally answered incorrectly, as they had been previously instructed to do.

3.   Of the fifty people tested, 33 percent gave the incorrect answers at least half of the time because of peer pressure, even though they knew the answers were wrong; only 25 percent always gave the right answer despite the peer pressure.

F.   Sociologist Irving Janis coined the word "groupthink" to refer to situations in which a group of people think alike and any suggestion of alternatives becomes a sign of disloyalty. Even moral judgments are put aside for the perceived welfare of the group.

1.   The Asch and Milgram experiments demonstrate how groupthink can develop.

2.   U.S. history provides examples of governmental groupthink: presidents and their inner circles have committed themselves to a single course of action (refusal to believe the Japanese might attack Pearl Harbor; continuing and expanding the war in Vietnam) even when objective evidence showed the course to be wrong. The leaders became cut off from information that did not coincide with their own opinions.

3.   Groupthink can be prevented only by insuring that leaders regularly are exposed to individuals who have views conflicting with those of the inner circle.

KEY TERMS

After studying the chapter, review each of the following terms.

aggregate: people who temporarily share the same physical space but do not see themselves as belonging together (104)

alienation: Marx's term for the experience of being cut off from the product of one's labor, which results in a sense of powerlessness and normlessness (112)

authoritarian leader: a leader who leads by giving orders (119)

bureaucracies: a formal organization with a hierarchy of authority, a clear division of labor, impersonality of positions, and emphasis on written rules, communications, and records (110)

category: people who have similar characteristics (104)

clique: within a larger group, a cluster of people who choose to interact with one another; an internal faction (108)

coalition: the alignment of some members of a group against others (118)

corporate culture: the orientations that characterize corporate work settings (114)

democratic leader: a leader who leads by trying to reach a consensus (119)

dyad: the smallest possible group, consisting of two persons (117)

electronic community: people who more or less regularly interact with one another on the Internet (108)

expressive leader: an individual who increases harmony and minimizes conflict in a group; also known as a *socioemotional leader* (119)

goal displacement: a process in which a goal is displaced by another, such as when an organization adopts new goals (111)

group: people who think of themselves as belonging together and who interact with one another (104)

group dynamics: the ways in which individuals affect groups and the ways in which groups influence individuals (117)

groupthink: Irving Janis's term for a narrowing of thought by a group of people, leading to the perception that there is only one correct answer; in groupthink the suggestion of alternatives becomes a sign of disloyalty (121)

in-groups: groups toward which one feels loyalty (106)

instrumental leader: an individual who tries to keep the group moving toward its goals; also known as a *task-oriented leader* (119)

the iron law of oligarchy: Robert Michels's phrase for the tendency of formal organizations to be dominated by a small, self-perpetuating elite (106)

laissez-faire leader: an individual who leads by being highly permissive (119)

leader: someone who influences other people (119)

leadership styles: ways in which people express their leadership (119)

networking: the process of consciously using or cultivating networks for some gain (108)

out-groups: groups toward which one feels antagonisms (106)

primary group: a group characterized by intimate, long-term, face-to-face association and cooperation (104)

(the) rationalization of society: the increasing influence of bureaucracies in society, which makes the "bottom line" of results dominant in social life (112)

reference group: Herbert Hyman's term for a group whose standards we consider as we evaluate ourselves (107)

secondary group: compared with a primary group, a larger, relatively temporary, more anonymous, formal, and impersonal group based on some interest or activity (104)

small group: a group small enough so everyone can interact directly with all the other members (117)

social networks: the social ties radiating outward from the self, that link people together (108)

triad: a group of three persons (117)

voluntary association: a group made up of volunteers who have organized on the basis of some mutual interest; the Girl Scouts, Baptists, and Alcoholics Anonymous are examples (105)

KEY PEOPLE

Review the major theoretical contributions or research findings of these people.

George Arquitt and Elaine Fox: These sociologists studied local posts of the VFW and found three types of members and evidence of the iron law of oligarchy. (105)

Solomon Asch: Asch is famous for his research on conformity to group pressure. (120-121)

Charles H. Cooley: It was Cooley who noted the central role of primary groups in the development of one's sense of self. (104)

John Darley and Bibb Latané: These researchers investigated what impact the size of the group has on individual members' attitudes and behaviors. They found that as the group grew in size, individuals' sense of responsibility diminished, their interactions became more formal, and the larger group tends to break down into small ones. (118-119)

Lloyd Howells and Selwyn Becker: These social psychologists found that factors such as location within a group underlie people's choices of leaders. (120)

Irving Janis: Janis coined the term "groupthink" to refer to the tunnel vision that a group of people sometimes develop. (121-124)

Rosabeth Moss Kanter: Kanter studied the "invisible" corporate culture for the most part continually reproduces itself by promoting those workers who fit the elite's stereotypical views. (114)

Ronald Lippitt and Ralph White: These social psychologists carried out a class study on leadership styles and found that the style of leadership affected the behavior of group members. (118-119)

Robert K. Merton: Merton observed that the traits of in-groups become viewed as virtues, while those same traits in out-groups are seen as vices. (106)

Joshua Meyrowitz: This sociologist stresses that the media should not be considered as passible channels of information, but rather, they shape our lives. (109)

Robert Michels: Michels first used the term "the iron law of oligarchy" to describe the tendency for the leaders of an organization to become entrenched. (106)

Stanley Milgram: Milgram's research has contributed greatly to sociological knowledge of group life. He did research on social networks as well as individual conformity to group pressure. (108, 122)

William Ouchi: Ouchi studied the Japanese corporation and identified defining qualities of this corporate model. (115-116)

George Ritzer: Ritzer coined the term the "McDonaldization" of society to describe the increasing rationalization of modern social life. (113)

Georg Simmel: This early sociologist was one of the first to mote the significance of group size; he used the terms dyad and triad to describe small groups. (117-118)

Max Weber: Weber studied the rationalization of society but investigating the link between Protestantism and capitalism and identifying the characteristics of bureaucracy. (110, 112)

SELF-TEST

After completing this self-test, check your answers against the Answer Key beginning on page 237 of this Study Guide and against the text on page(s) indicated in parentheses.

MULTIPLE CHOICE QUESTIONS

1. People who have something in common and who believe that what they have in common is significant are called a(n): (104)
    a.   society.
    b.   aggregate.
    c.   category.
    d.   group.

2. _____ groups are essential to an individual's psychological well-being. (104)
    a.   Primary
    b.   Secondary
    c.   Therapy
    d.   Interpersonal

3. Secondary groups: (104-105)
    a.   have members who are likely to interact on the basis of specific roles.
    b.   are characteristic of industrial societies.
    c.   are essential to the functioning of contemporary societies.
    d.   All of the above.

4. Voluntary associations: (105)
    a.   are groups made up of volunteers who organize on the basis of some mutual interest.
    b.   include political parties, unions, professional associations, and churches.
    c.   have been an important part of American life.
    d.   All of the above.

5. The tendency for organizations to be dominated by a small, self-perpetuating elite is called: (106)
    a.   the Peter Principle.
    b.   bureaucratic engorgement.
    c.   the iron law of oligarchy.
    d.   the corporate power struggle.

6. Sociologists refer to groups which provide a sense of identification or belonging as: (106)
    a. personal groups.
    b. in-groups.
    c. my-group.
    d. homeboys' groups.

7. The groups we use as a standard to evaluate ourselves are: (107)
    a. primary groups.
    b. secondary groups.
    c. reference groups.
    d. evaluation groups.

8. Sociologists refer to social ties radiating outward from the self, linking people together as: (108)
    a. social networks.
    b. reference groups.
    c. cliques.
    d. inner-circles.

9. Sociologists refer to the process of using or cultivating networks for some gain as: (108)
    a. networking.
    b. group dynamics.
    c. social climbing.
    d. being a user.

10. All of the following are characteristics of bureaucracy, except: (110-111)
    a. a division of labor.
    b. a hierarchy with assignments flowing upward and accountability flowing downward.
    c. written rules, communications and records.
    d. impersonality.

11. Goal displacement occurs when: (111)
    a. a bureaucrat is unable to function as a cooperative, integrated part of the whole.
    b. goals conflict with one another.
    c. an organization has achieved its original goals and then adopts new goals.
    d. members of an organization are promoted until they reach their level of incompetence.

12. The term "rationalization of society" was coined by: (112)
    a. Karl Marx.
    b. Emile Durkheim.
    c. Max Weber.
    d. Robert Michels.

13. George Ritzer used the term "the McDonaldization of society" to refer to: (113)
    a. the preference for McDonald's over Burger King.
    b. the spread of McDonald's world-wide.
    c. the increasing rationalization of daily living.
    d. All of the above.

14. We usually refer to the "correct procedures" of bureaucracies as: (112)
    a. a pain in the neck.
    b. red tape.
    c. guidelines.
    d. goal displacement.

15. A feeling of separation from work and from work environments is referred to as: (112)
    a. bureaucratic dysfunction.
    b. alienation.
    c. goal displacement.
    d. goal frustration.

16. Workers resist alienation by: (114)
    a. forming primary groups.
    b. praising each other and expressing sympathy when something goes wrong.
    c. putting pictures and personal items in their work areas.
    d. All of the above.

17. According to Rosabeth Moss Kanter, in a large corporation: (114)
    a. the corporate culture creates a self-fulfilling prophecy that affects an individual's corporate fate.
    b. the people with the best qualifications typically will rise to the top of an organization.
    c. those who work the hardest have the greatest likelihood of being promoted.
    d. All of the above.

18. In which type of corporate model is lifetime security taken for granted? (115)
    a. the United States model.
    b. the Japanese model.
    c. both the United States and Japanese models.
    d. It is not taken for granted in either the United States or Japanese models.

19. Which of the following statements about lifetime security is _correct_? (116-117)
    a. In Japan, the majority of workers enjoy lifetime job security.
    b. In the U.S., more and more corporations are adopting the Japanese model.
    c. During the recessions of the 1990s, it became clear that only about one-third of Japanese workers have lifetime job security.
    d. In the U.S., corporations once provided lifetime security but eliminated such programs with the growing pressures to cut costs in order to compete globally.

20. Small groups: (117)
   a.   are primary groups.
   b.   are secondary groups.
   c.   can be either primary or secondary groups.
   d.   neither primary nor secondary groups, but fall between these two types of groups.

21. Dyads: (117)
   a.   are the most intense or intimate of human groups.
   b.   require continuing active participation and commitment of both members.
   c.   are the most unstable of social groups.
   d.   All of the above.

22. An expressive leader: (119)
   a.   tries to keep the group moving toward its goals.
   b.   is also known as a task-oriented leader.
   c.   increases harmony and minimizes conflict in a group.
   d.   is the director of the drama club.

23. According to sociologists, leaders tend to have certain characteristics which may include: (120)
   a.   they are seen as strongly representing the group's values.
   b.   they tend to be taller and are judged better-looking than others.
   c.   where they sit in a group.
   d.   All of the above.

24. In the Asch experiments, about _____ percent always gave the correct answer, even when that meant going against the sentiments of the groups. (121)
   a.   10
   b.   25
   c.   33
   d.   40

25. The Milgram experiment demonstrates: (122)
   a.   that people who know they are being studied will behave differently as a result.
   b.   the awesome influence of peer groups over their members.
   c.   how strongly people are influenced by authority.
   d.   how isolated political leaders can become.

TRUE-FALSE QUESTIONS

T F   1.   Members of primary groups are likely to interact on the basis of specific roles. (104)
T F   2.   Voluntary associations are a special type of primary group. (104)
T F   3.   Voluntary associations are made up of volunteers who have organized on the basis of some mutual interest. (105)
T F   4.   The iron law of oligarchy was defined by Robert Michels. (106)
T F   5.   Tensions between in-groups and out-groups disappear in socially diverse societies. (106)
T F   6.   Reference groups are the groups we use as standards to evaluate ourselves. (107)

T F   7.   A person has to be a member of his or her reference groups in order to use them as a yardstick. (107)

T F   8.   Networks tend to limit social inequality by giving more people access to opportunities. (108)

T F   9.   Networking refers to the conscious use or even cultivation of networks. (108)

T F   10.   Electronic communities, whose members communicate over the Internet, are not groups because the members of these entities are not involved in face-to-face interactions. (108)

T F   11.   Weber identified five essential characteristics of bureaucracy. (110-111)

T F   12.   In a bureaucracy, each worker is a replaceable unit. (111)

T F   13.   Bureaucracies are likely to disappear as our dominant form of social organization in the near future. (112)

T F   14.   Marx coined the term alienation. (112)

T F   15.   Workers can prevent becoming alienated if they work at it. (114)

T F   16.   The Japanese corporate model emphasizes teamwork and lifetime security. (115)

T F   17.   As a small group grows larger, its intensity decreases and its stability increases. (118)

T F   18.   A leader is one who is officially appointed or elected to be the "leader." (119)

T F   19.   The study of Lippitt and White regarding leadership style concluded that the authoritarian leader got the best results. (120)

T F   20.   The Asch Experiment used fake shocks to demonstrate that people would do anything for authority figures. (122-123)

FILL-IN QUESTIONS

1.   People who have similar characteristics make up a _____. (104)

2.   A _____ group is characterized by more anonymous, formal, and impersonal relationships. (104)

3.   A group made up of volunteers who have organized on the basis of some mutual interest is called a(n) _____. (105)

4.   _____ refers to the tendency of formal organizations to be dominated by a small, self-perpetuating elite. (106)

5.   _____ provide a sense of identification or belonging while producing feelings of antagonisms towards _____. (106)

6.   The groups we use as standards to evaluate ourselves are _____. (107)

7.   The social ties radiating outward from the self, that link people together are known as _____. (108)

8.   _____ occurs when new goals are adopted by an organization to replace previous goals which may have been fulfilled. (111)

9.   The phrase _____ refers to the increasing influence of bureaucracies in society. (112)

10.   _____ is a feeling of powerlessness and normlessness; the experience of being cut off from the product of one's labor. (112)

11.   The smallest possible group is a(n) _____. (117)

12.   A _____ is formed when some members of a group align themselves against other members. (118)

13.   Someone who influences the behavior of others is a(n) _____. (119)

14.   An individual who tries to keep the group moving toward its goals is a(n) _____ leader. An individual who increases harmony and minimizes conflict is a(n) _____ leader. (119)

15. _____ is a narrowing of thought by a group of people, which results in overconfidence and tunnel vision. (121)

MATCH THESE SOCIAL SCIENTISTS WITH THEIR CONTRIBUTIONS

___1. Irving Janis

___2. Georg Simmel

___3. Robert Michels

___4. Stanley Milgram

___5. Solomon Asch

___6. Charles H. Cooley

a. *primary groups*

b. *obedience to authority*

c. *dyads*

d. *the iron law of oligarchy*

e. *groupthink*

f. *conformity to peer pressure*

ESSAY QUESTIONS

1. Define the iron law of oligarchy and discuss why this problem occurs in voluntary associations.
2. Identify the advantages and disadvantages of bureaucracy and discuss some ways in which the problems can be addressed.
3. Explain the three different leadership styles and suggest reasons why the democratic leader is the best style of leader for most situations.

"DOWN-TO-EARTH SOCIOLOGY"

1. Acquire a copy of the organizational chart for your own college or university. Compare it with Figure 5.1 (p. 110) to determine ways in which the charts are similar and ways in which they differ. If you were able to do so, what would you change?

2. What was your reaction to the "Down-to-Earth Sociology" box on p. 113? Can you see evidence in your own life of McDonaldization? What do you see as the advantages of this trend? What do you see as the disadvantages?

3. Read "Managing Diversity in the Workplace" beginning on page 115. Do you think that such programs benefit workers or divide workers? Do you agree or disagree with Roosevelt Thomas that people can work together without assimilation?

4. After reading about the Milgram experiments (pages 122-123), consider how you would have reacted if you had been selected to participate. Under what conditions would you have carried out the orders or disobeyed? Were these methods justified?

CHAPTER 6
DEVIANCE AND SOCIAL CONTROL

CHAPTER SUMMARY

- Deviance, which refers to violations of social norms, is relative; what people consider deviant varies from one culture to another and from group to group within a society. It is not the act itself, but the reaction to the act, that makes something deviant. To explain deviance, biologists and psychologists look for reasons within people, such as genetic predisposition's or personality disorders, while sociologists look for explanations in social relationships.

- Symbolic interactionists have developed several theories to explain criminal activity, one form of deviance. They use differential association theory, control theory, and labeling theory to analyze the extent to explain deviance such as crime. Many people succeed in neutralizing the norms of society and are able to commit deviant acts while thinking of themselves as conformists. Although most people resist being labeled deviant, there are those who embrace deviance.

- Functionalists state that deviance is functional, because it affirms norms and promotes social unity and social change. Strain theory suggests that while people are socialized to accept the norms of material success, many are unable to achieve this goal in socially acceptable ways so they turn to deviance as a means to the goal. According to illegitimate opportunity theory, some people have easier access to illegal means of achieving goals than others do.

- Conflict theorists argue that the group in power imposes its definitions on other groups--the ruling class directs the criminal justice system against members of the working class, who commit highly visible property crimes, while it diverts its own criminal activities out of the criminal justice system. Imprisonment is motivated by the goals of retribution, deterrence, rehabilitation and incapacitation.

- There is a growing tendency towards the medicalization of deviance; according to this view, deviant acts are external symptoms of internal disorders. Thomas Szasz argues that mental illnesses are neither mental nor illnesses, but are simply problem behaviors.

- With deviance inevitable, the larger issues are how to protect people from deviant behaviors that are harmful to their welfare, to tolerate those that are not, and to develop systems of fairer treatment for deviants.

LEARNING OBJECTIVES

As you read Chapter 6, use these learning objectives to organize your notes. After completing your reading, briefly state an answer to each of the objectives, and review the text pages in parentheses.

1. Explain how sociologists study deviance. (130-131)
2. State what Erving Goffman meant by the term stigma. (131)
3. Discuss why norms are essential for social life and the role of sanctions. (131-132)
4. Compare and contrast biological, psychological, and sociological views on deviance. (133)
5. State the key components of the symbolic interaction perspective on deviance, and briefly explain differential association theory, control theory, and labeling theory. (134-137)
6. Discuss the major reasons why functionalists view deviance as functional for society. (139)
7. Describe Merton's strain theory, and list and briefly explain the four types of responses to anomie. (139-140)
8. Identify the relationship between social class and crime by using the illegitimate opportunity theory and perspectives on white-collar crime. (141-142)

9.   Explain the conflict view of the relationship between class, crime, and the criminal justice system. (143-144)
10.   List the four primary reasons for imprisonment. (144-147)
11.   Explain what is meant by the medicalization of deviance. (147-148)
12.   Discuss the approach that our society should take in dealing with deviance. (148)

CHAPTER OUTLINE

I.   **What is Deviance?**
    A.   Sociologists use the term deviance to refer to a violation of norms.
        1.   According to sociologist Howard S. Becker, it is not the act itself that makes an action deviant, but rather how society reacts to it.
        2.   Because different groups have different norms, what is deviant to some is not deviant to others.
        3.   Crime is the violation of rules that have been written into law.
        4.   Sociologists use the term deviance nonjudgementally to refer to any act to which people respond negatively. To sociologists, all people are deviants because everyone violates rules from time to time.
        5.   Erving Goffman used "stigma" to refer to attributes that discredit one's claim to a "normal" identity; a stigma (e.g. physical deformities, skin color) defines a person's master status, superseding all other statuses the person occupies.
    B.   Norms allow social order--a group's customary social arrangements--because they lay out the basic guidelines for how we play our roles and how we interact with others.
        1.   Deviance is often seen as threatening because it violates a group's customary social arrangements and undermines the predictability that is the foundation of social life.
        2.   Human groups develop a system of social control, formal and informal means of enforcing the norms.
    C.   Society's disapproval of deviance takes the form of negative sanctions and ranges from frowns and gossip to imprisonment and capital punishment, although most negative sanctions are informal. Positive sanctions are used to reward people for conforming to norms.
    D.   The sociological explanations of deviance differ from biological and psychological ones.
        1.   Psychologists and sociobiologists explain deviance by looking within individuals; sociologists look outside the individual.
        2.   Biological explanations focus on genetic predisposition--factors such as intelligence, "XYY" theory (an extra Y chromosome in men leads to crime), or body type (squarish, muscular persons more likely to commit street crimes). 3. Psychological explanations focus on personality disorders (e.g., "bad toilet training," "suffocating mothers," etc.). Yet these do not necessarily result in the presence or absence of specific forms of deviance in a person.
        4.   Sociological explanations search outside the individual; social influences--such as socialization, subcultural group memberships, or social class (people's relative standing in terms of education, occupation, income and wealth)--account for why some people break norms.
II.   **The Symbolic Interaction Perspective**
    A.   Edwin Sutherland used the term differential association to suggest that we learn to deviate

from or to conform to society's norms mostly by the people with whom we associate.

    1.   The key to differential association is the learning of ideas and attitudes favorable to following the law or favorable to breaking it. Because we learn both from the various people we associate with, the end result is an imbalance; we conform or deviate depending on which set of messages is stronger.

    2.   Studies have demonstrated that families do teach their members to violate the norms of society; families involved in crime tend to set their children on a lawbreaking path.

    3.   The neighborhood is also likely to be influential; sociologists have found that delinquents tend to come from neighborhoods in which their peers are involved in crime.

    4.   Symbolic interactionists stress that we are not mere pawns, but help produce our orientation to life; our choice of associates helps to shape our sense of self.

B.   According to Walter Reckless, who developed control theory, everyone is propelled towards deviance, but that two control systems work against these motivations to deviate.

    1.   Inner controls are one's capacity to withstand temptations toward deviance, and include internalized morality, integrity, fear of punishment, and desire to be good, while outer controls involve groups (e.g. family, friends, the police) that influence a person to stay away from crime.

    2.   Sociologist Travis Hirschi noted that strong bonds to society lead to more effective inner controls; bonds are based on attachments, commitments, involvements, and beliefs.

    3.   The likelihood that we will deviate from social norms is related to the strength of our control systems--if the systems are strong we are less likely to deviate than if they are weak.

C.   Labeling theory is the view that the labels people are given affect their own and others' perceptions of them, thus channeling their behavior either into deviance or into conformity.

    1.   Most people resist being labeled as deviant, even when engaging in deviant behavior. There are five different techniques of neutralization: (1) denial of responsibility ("I didn't do it"); (2) denial of injury ("Who really got hurt?"); (3) denial of a victim ("She deserved it"); (4) condemnation of the condemners ("Who are you to talk?"); and (5) appeal to higher loyalty ("I had to help my friends").

    2.   Some people invite a deviant label (e.g. motorcycle gangs may pride themselves on getting into trouble, laughing at death, etc.).

    3.   William J. Chambliss's study of law-breaking activities among two groups--the Saints (boys from respectable middle class families) and the Roughnecks (boys from working class families who hang out on the streets)--provides an excellent illustration of labeling theory. There were social class differences not only in terms of the visibility of the law-breaking behavior, but also the styles of interaction with those in authority. These influenced the ways in which teachers and the police saw them and treated them. The study showed how labels open and close door of opportunity for the individuals involved.

III.   **The Functionalist Perspective**

A.   Emile Durkheim stated that deviance is functional, for it contributes to social order.

    1.   Deviance clarifies moral boundaries (a group's ideas about how people should act and think) and affirms norms.

2.   Deviance promotes social unity.

3.   Deviance promotes social change (if boundary violations gain enough support, they become new, acceptable behaviors).

B.   Robert Merton developed strain theory to analyze what happens when people are socialized to desire a cultural goal but denied the institutionalized (i.e., legitimate) means to reach it.

1.   Merton used "anomie" (Durkheim's term) to refer to the strain people experience when they are blocked in their attempts to achieve those goals. He identified five reactions to cultural goals and institutionalized means.

2.   The first reaction is conformity (using acceptable means to seek goals society sets), which is the most common. The other four types of responses are deviant: innovation (using illegitimate means to achieve them); ritualism (giving up on achieving cultural goals but clinging to conventional rules of conduct); retreatism (rejecting cultural goals, dropping out); and rebellion (seeking to replace society's goals).

3.   According to strain theory, deviants are products of their society.

C.   According to illegitimate opportunity theory social classes have distinct styles of crime due to differential access to institutionalized means of achieving socially acceptable goals.

1.   Many poor children in industrialized societies, who are socialized into wanting to own things, end up dropping out of school because of educational failure, thereby closing the door on many legitimate avenues to financial success.

2.   Richard Cloward and Lloyd Ohlin suggest that opportunities for remunerative crime are woven into the texture of life and may result when legitimate structures fail. In this way the poor may be drawn into certain crimes in unequal numbers.

3.   Illegal income-producing activities, such as robbery, drug dealing, prostitution, pimping, gambling, and other "hustles," are functional for those who want to make money, but whose access to legitimate activities is blocked.

4.   Gangs offer disadvantaged youth an illegitimate opportunity structure. Research by Martín Sánchez Jankowski demonstrated that young men joined gangs because they provided them with access to steady money, recreation, anonymity in criminal activities, protection, and a way to help the neighborhood.

5.   White-collar crime refers to crimes that people of respectable and high social status commit in the course of their occupations. Such crimes exist in greater numbers than commonly perceived, and can be very costly--may total about $200 billion a year. They can involve physical harm and sometimes death (concealing information that silicone breast implants might leak, for example).

IV.   **The Conflict Perspective**

A.   Conflict theorists address the issue of why the legal system is inconsistent in terms of providing "justice for all." This inequality is central to their analysis of crime and the criminal justice system--the police, courts, and prisons.

B.   The state's machinery of social control represents the interests of the wealthy and powerful--a power elite; this group determines the basic laws whose enforcement is essential to the preservation of its power.

C.   According to conflict theory, the law is an instrument of repression, a tool designed to maintain the powerful in privileged positions and keep the powerless from rebelling and overthrowing the social order. When members of the working class get out of line, they are arrested, tried and imprisoned in the criminal justice system.

1.   While the criminal justice system tends to overlook the harm done by the corporations, flagrant violations are prosecuted. The publicity given to white collar criminals helps to stabilize the system by providing evidence of fairness.

2.   Usually the powerful bypass the courts altogether, appearing instead before some agency whose members are people from the same wealthy background. Given this, it is not surprising that the usual sanction is a token fine.

3.   Property crimes of the masses are handled by the courts; these crimes not only threaten the sanctity of private property, but ultimately, the positions of the powerful.

D.   Imprisonment is an increasingly popular reaction to crime but fails to teach inmates to stay away from crime.

    1.   The recidivism rate (the proportion of persons who are reasserted) in the United States runs as high as 85-90 percent, and those given probation do no better.

    2.   There is disagreement within U.S. society as to why criminals should be imprisoned. Different reasons include retribution (righting a wrong by making the offender suffer), deterrence (creating fear so others won't break the law), rehabilitation (resocializing offenders to becoming conforming citizens), and incapacitation (removing offenders from circulation).

V.   **The Medicalization of Deviance: Mental Illness**

A.   Medicalization of deviance is the view of deviance as a symptom of some underlying illness that needs to be treated by physicians.

    1.   Thomas Szasz argues that mental illness is simply problem behaviors: some forms of "mental" illnesses have organic causes (e.g. depression caused by a chemical imbalance in the brain); while others are responses to troubles with various coping devices.

    2.   Some sociologists find Szasz's analysis refreshing because it indicates that social experiences, and not some illness of the mind, underlie bizarre behaviors.

B.   In considering the homeless mentally ill, the experience of being homeless can cause mental illness. Because you are on the streets and often have no place to wash yourself or your clothes, you are stared at or ignored, resulting in withdrawal. Homelessness and mental illness can be reciprocal: just as "mental illness" can cause homelessness, so the trials of being homeless, of living on the streets, can lead to unusual and unacceptable thinking and behaviors.

VI.   **The Need for a More Humane Approach**

A.   With deviance inevitable, one measure of a society is how it treats its deviants

B.   The larger issues are how to protect people from deviant behaviors that are harmful to their welfare, to tolerate those that are not, and to develop systems of fairer treatment for deviants.

KEY TERMS

After studying the chapter, review each of the following terms.

capitalist class: the wealthy who own the means of production and buy the labor of the working class (143)

control theory: the idea that two control systems--inner controls and outer controls--work against our tendencies to deviate (135)

crime: the violation of norms that are written into law (131)

criminal justice system: the system of police, courts, and prisons set up to deal with people who are accused of having committed a crime (143)

cultural goals: the legitimate objectives held out to the members of a society (140)

deterrence: creating fear so people will refrain from breaking the law (145)

deviance: the violation of rules or norms (130)

differential association: Edwin Sutherland's term to indicate that associating with some groups results in learning an "excess of definitions" of deviance (attitudes favorable to committing deviant acts), and, by extension, in a greater likelihood that their members will become deviant (134)

genetic predispositions: inborn tendencies (133)

illegitimate opportunity structures: opportunities for crimes woven into the texture of life (141)

incapacitation: the removal of offenders from "normal" society; taking them "off the streets," thereby removing their capacity to commit crimes against the public (146)

institutionalized means: approved ways of reaching cultural goals (140)

labeling theory: the view, developed by symbolic interactionists, that the labels people are given affect their own and others' perceptions of them, thus channeling their behavior either into deviance or into conformity (135)

marginal working class: the most desperate members of the working class, who have few skills, have little job security, and are often unemployed (143)

medicalization of deviance: to make some deviance a medical matter, a symptom of some underlying illness that needs to be treated by physicians (147)

negative sanction: an expression of disapproval for breaking a norm; ranging from a mild, informal reaction such as a frown to a formal prison sentence or even capital punishment (132)

personality disorders: as a theory of deviance, the view that a personality disturbance of some sort causes an individual to violate social norms (133)

positive sanction: reward or positive reaction for following norms, ranging from a smile to a prize (132)

recidivism rate: the proportion of persons who are rearrested (145)

rehabilitation: the resocialization of offenders so that they can become conforming citizens (145)

retribution: the punishment of offenders in order to restore the moral balance upset by the offense (145)

social control: formal and informal means of enforcing norms (131)

social order: a group's usual and customary social arrangements (131)

stigma: "blemishes" that discredit a person's claim to a "normal" identity (131)

strain theory: Robert Merton's term for the strain engendered when a society socializes large numbers of people to desire a cultural goal (such as success) but withholds from many the approved means to reach that goal; one adaptation to the strain is deviance, including crime, the choice of an innovative means (one outside the approved system) to attain the cultural goal (140)

street crime: crimes such as mugging, rape, and burglary (133)

techniques of neutralization: ways of thinking or rationalizing that help people deflect society's norms (135)

white-collar crime: Edwin Sutherland's term for crimes committed by people of respectable and high social status in the course of their occupations (142)

working class: those who sell their labor to the capitalist class (143)

KEY PEOPLE

Review the major theoretical contributions or research findings of these people.

Howard Becker: Becker observed that an act is not deviant in and of itself, but only when there is a reaction to it. (130)

William Chambliss: Chambliss demonstrated the power of the label in his study of two youth gangs--the Saints and the Roughnecks. (136-136)

Richard Cloward and Lloyd Ohlin: These sociologists identified the illegitimate opportunity structures that a woven into the texture of life in urban slums and provide an alternative set of opportunities for slum residents when legitimate ones are blocked. (141)

Emile Durkheim: Durkheim noted the functions that deviance has for social life. (139)

Robert Edgerton: This anthropologist's studies document how different human groups react to similar behaviors, demonstrating that what is deviant in one context is not in another. (130)

Harold Garfinkel: Garfinkel used the term degradation ceremonies to describe formal attempts to mark an individual with the status of an outsider. (131)

Erving Goffman: Goffman wrote about the role of stigma in the definition of who and what is deviant.

Travis Hirschi: Hirschi studied the strength of the bonds an individual has to society in order to understand the effectiveness of inner controls. (135)

Ruth Horowitz: Horowitz did participant observation in a lower-class Chicano neighborhood in Chicago and discovered how associating with people who have a certain concept of "honor" can propel young men to deviance. (134)

Martin Sánchez Jankowski: Jankowski studied gangs and identified traits that characterize gang members and identifying the function that gangs play in urban neighborhoods. (141)

David Matza: Matza noted that the stronger our bonds are with society, the more effective our inner controls are; bonds are based on attachments, commitments, involvments, and beliefs. (135)

Robert Merton: Merton developed strain theory to explain patterns of deviance within a society. (140)

Walter Reckless: Reckless developed control theory, suggesting that our behavior is controlled by two different systems, one external (outer controls like the police, family and friends) and the other internal (inner controls like our conscience, religious principles, and ideas of right and wrong). (135)

Edwin Sutherland: Sutherland not only developed differential association theory, but was the first to study and give a name to crimes that occur among the middle class in the course of their work-- white collar crime.(134, 142)

Gresham Sykes and David Matza: These sociologists studied the different strategies delinquent boys use to deflect society's norms--techniques of neutralization. (135)

Thomas Szasz: Szasz argued that mental illness represents the medicalization of deviance. (147)

Ernest van den Haag: This sociologist is a chief proponent of deterrence and believes that the criminal justice system is too soft. He advocates that juveniles who commit adult crimes be tried as adults, that parole boards be abolished, and that prisoners be forced to work. (145)

Mark Watson: Watson studied motorcycle gangs and found that these people actively embraced the deviant label. (136)

SELF-TEST

After completing this self-test, check your answers against the Answer Key beginning on page 240 of this Study Guide and against the text on page(s) indicated in parentheses.

MULTIPLE CHOICE QUESTIONS

1.   In sociology, the term deviance: (130)
      a.   refers to behavior that is bad enough for those engaged in it to be punished by society.
      b.   refers to all violations of social rules.
      c.   refers to the violation of serious rules.
      d.   refers to crime.

2.   Because norms lay out the basic guidelines for how we play our roles and how we interact with others, they : (131)
      a.   create predictability.
      b.   allow for social order.
      c.   represent the foundation for social life.
      d.   all of the above.

3.   Erving Goffman used the term _____ to refer to attributes, such as blindness, deafness, physical deformities and obesity, that society uses to discredit people. (131)
      a.   master status
      b.   mismanaged impression
      c.   stigma
      d.   deviance

4.   Frowns, gossip, and crossing people off guest lists are examples of: (132)
      a.   retribution.
      b.   degradation ceremonies.
      c.   negative sanctions.
      d.   institutionalized means to achieve goals.

5.   Which of the following attempts to understand deviance in terms of factors that lie outside the individual? (133)
      a.   psychological
      b.   biological
      c.   sociological
      d.   genetic

6.   Differential association theory is based on the: (134)
      a.   functionalist perspective.
      b.   conflict perspective.
      c.   symbolic interactionist perspective.
      d.   psychological perspective.

7.   The idea that two systems--our internalized morality and our network of friends and family who influence us not to deviate--work against our tendencies toward deviance is called: (135)
      a.   conflict theory.
      b.   differential association theory.
      c.   control theory.
      d.   strain theory.

8.   All of the following are ways of neutralizing deviance, except: (135-136)
      a.   appeal to higher loyalties.
      b.   denial of responsibility.
      c.   denial of deviant labels.
      d.   denial of injury and of a victim.

9.   William Chambliss's study of the Saints and the Roughnecks suggests that: (136-137)
      a.   labels are easy to cast off once a person gets away from the group doing the labeling.
      b.   people often live up to the labels that a community gives them.
      c.   people often rebel against the labels given them and lead a completely different life.
      d.   sociological research on labeling has produced few conclusions.

10.   According to sociologist William Chambliss, factors which influence whether or not people will
      be seen as deviant include: (136)
      a.   social class.
      b.   the visibility of offenders.
      c.   styles of interaction.
      d.   All of the above.

11.   According to the _____ perspective, deviance promotes social unity and social change. (139)
      a.   functionalist
      b.   conflict
      c.   symbolic interactionist
      d.   differential association

12.   All of the following are responses to anomie as identified by Robert Merton, except: (140)
      a.   ritualism.
      b.   rebellion.
      c.   retreatism.
      d.   recidivism.

13.   According to Merton's strain theory, people who drop out of the pursuit of success by abusing
      alcohol or drug abuse: (140)
      a.   rebels.
      b.   retreatists.
      c.   neurotics.
      d.   ritualists.

14.   The illegitimate opportunity structures theory is based on: (141)
      a.   the conflict perspective.
      b.   the symbolic interactionist perspective.
      c.   the exchange perspective.
      d.   the functionalist perspective.

15.   According to Martín Sánchez Jankowski, who researched street gangs for more than ten years, the
      motive for joining a gang is: (141-142)
      a.   to escape from broken homes.
      b.   because gangs are seen as an economic alternative to the dead-end jobs held by parents.
      c.   to seek a substitute family.
      d.   to prove their masculinity not only to themselves but more importantly to other males in
            the community.

16.   Crimes committed by people of respectable and high social status in the course of their occupations are called: (142)
        a.   upper-class crime.
        b.   crimes of respectability.
        c.   white-collar crime.
        d.   tuxedo crime.

17.   The criminal justice system is made up of: (143)
        a.   the police.
        b.   the courts.
        c.   the prisons.
        d.   All of the above.

18.   The marginal working class: (143)
        a.   includes people with few skills.
        b.   holds low-paying, part-time, seasonal jobs.
        c.   consists of the most desperate members of the working class.
        d.   All of the above.

19.   According to Henslin, a severe problem associated with the policy of imprisonment is: (145)
        a.   overcrowding.
        b.   recidivism.
        c.   violence in jails.
        d.   being too soft on the prisoners.

20.   The purpose of deterrence is to: (145)
        a.   right a wrong by making the offender suffer so he will become a conformist.
        b.   resocialize the offender so he becomes a conformist.
        c.   remove the offender from circulation.
        d.   create fear in others.

21.   Halfway houses: (145)
        a.   are community support facilities where ex-prisoners supervise aspects of their own lives.
        b.   are examples of deterrence.
        c.   do not require residents to report to authorities.
        d.   All of the above.

22.   _____ switches the focus from punishing offenders to resocializing them so that they can become conforming citizens. (145)
        a.   deterrence
        b.   retribution
        c.   rehabilitation
        d.   incapacitation

23. The removal of offenders from "normal" society, taking them "off the streets," is called: (146)
    a. retribution.
    b. incapacitation.
    c. rehabilitation.
    d. deterrence.

24. The medicalization of deviance refers to: (147)
    a. the castration of sex offenders.
    b. use of lethal injections for the death penalty.
    c. viewing deviance as a medical matter.
    d. All of the above.

25. Which of the following sociologists was critical of the approach of medicalizing deviance? (148)
    a. Emile Durkheim
    b. Robert Merton
    c. Thomas Szasz
    d. Edwin Sutherland

TRUE-FALSE QUESTIONS

T F 1. In sociology, the term deviance refers to all violations of social rules. (130)

T F 2. Across cultures, certain acts are considered to be deviant by everyone. (130)

T F 3. According to differential association theory, the source of deviant behavior may be found in a person's socialization, or social learning. (134)

T F 4. Symbolic interactionists stress that we are involved in producing our own orientations to life through the choices we make about with whom to associate. (145)

T F 5. Travis Hirschi suggested that the stronger our ties to society, the more effective our inner controls will be. (135)

T F 6. No one embraces deviance or wants to be labeled with a deviant identity. (136)

T F 7. Outlaw bikers hold the conventional world in contempt and take pride in getting into trouble. (136)

T F 8. In the study by Chambliss, the Saints and the Roughnecks both turned out largely as their labels would have predicted. (137)

T F 9. The functionalist perspective states that deviance contributes to the social order. (139)

T F 10. According to strain theory, everyone has a chance to get ahead in society, but some people prefer to use illegal means to achieve their goals. (140)

T F 11. All of Merton's modes of adaptation involve illegal behavior. (140)

T F 12. Illegitimate opportunity structures are readily available in urban slums. (141)

T F 13. In his study of gangs, Martín Sánchez Jankowski found that more gang members came from broken homes than from stable homes. (141)

T F 14. White-collar crime is not as costly as street crime. (142)

T F 15. Both functionalists and conflict theorists agree that the criminal justice system functions for the well-being of all citizens. (143)

T F 16. According to conflict theorists, most of those who are imprisoned in the United States come from the working class. (144)

T F 17. Some researchers have found that the recidivism rate in the United States runs as high as 85 to 90 percent. (145)

T F   18.   The purpose of retribution is to create fear so that others won't break the law. (145)
T F   19.   According to Thomas Szasz, mental illness is a myth. (147)
T F   20.   For Durkheim, deviance is inevitable, even among a group of saints. (148)

FILL-IN QUESTIONS

1.   _____ is the violation of rules or norms. (130)
2.   _____ is the violation of norms that are written into law. (131)
3.   Erving Goffman used the term _____ to refer to attributes that discredit people. (131)
4.   _____ is a group's usual and customary social arrangements, on which its members depend and on which they base their lives. (131)
5.   _____ range from mild, informal reactions such as frowns to formal prison sentences or even capital punishment. (132)
6.   Inborn tendencies towards deviances such as juvenile delinquency and crime are called _____. (133)
7.   Crimes such as muggings, rape and burglary are referred to as _____. (133)
8.   The term differential association was coined by _____. (134)
9.   By influencing a person to stay away from crime, friends, family, and the police are all examples of _____ system. (135)
10.   When a deviant reacts by saying "Who are *you* to talk?" he/she is practicing one of the _____. (135)
11.   Strain theory is based on the idea that large number of people are socialized into desiring _____ (the legitimate objects held out to everyone) but many do not have access to _____ in order to achieve those goals. (140)
12.   Embezzlers, robbers, and con artists are all examples of what Robert Merton called _____. (140)
13.   The most desperate members of the working class, who have few skills, little job security, and are often unemployed, are referred to as the _____. (143)
14.   The _____ refers to the proportion of people who are rearrested. (145)
15.   Creating fear so people will refrain from committing a deviant act is the goal of _____. (145)

MATCH THESE SOCIAL SCIENTISTS WITH THEIR CONTRIBUTIONS

___1. Edwin Sutherland   a. *strain theory*
___2. Robert Merton   b. *control theory*
___3. Erving Goffman   c. *white-collar crime*
___4. Thomas Szasz   d. *functions of deviance*
___5. Emile Durkheim   e. *effects of labeling*
___6. William Chambliss   f. *importance of stigma*
___7. Gresham Sykes & David Matza   g. *techniques of neutralization*
___8. Walter Reckless   h. *myth of mental illness*

ESSAY QUESTIONS

1.   Discuss how the different sociological perspectives could be combined in order to provide a more complete picture of deviance.

2. In light of the different explanations for deviance, evaluate the effectiveness of various reactions to deviance.

3. Explain what the author means when he says that "homelessness and mental illness are reciprocal."

"DOWN-TO-EARTH SOCIOLOGY"

1. What can we learn about deviance by looking at it from a cross-cultural perspective? (p. 130) What would happen in the United States if a wife gathered her friends around her husband's bed to beat him because he had not satisfied her sexually? As the example of the Zapotec Indians demonstrates, societies often have covert norms, which contradict the real ones but which should be followed anyway. Can you think of some examples of covert norms that represent the "real" norms in our own society?

2. After reading about when cultures clash on page 132, think what the proper reaction should be when cultural values collide. Should the full force of the law be applied in such cases?

3. What kinds of things have you done that are considered deviant? What kinds of techniques of neutralization did you use in order to help deflect being labeled deviant?

4. How do you feel about pornography on the Internet (p. 138)? Do you think it should be censored? Why or why not?

CHAPTER 7
SOCIAL STRATIFICATION IN GLOBAL PERSPECTIVE

CHAPTER SUMMARY

- Social stratification is a hierarchy of relative privilege based on power, property, and prestige. Every society stratifies its members.

- The major systems of social stratification include: (1) slavery--owning other people; (2) caste--lifelong status determined by birth; and (3) class--based on possession of money or material possessions. Class systems are characteristic of industrialized societies. Gender discrimination cuts across all systems of social stratification.

- Early sociologists disagreed about the meaning of social class in industrialized nations. Karl Marx argued that a person's relationship to the means of production was the only factor determining social class. Max Weber argued that three elements--property, prestige, and power--dictate an individual's standing in society.

- Various arguments have been developed to explain the universal presence of stratification. Functionalist sociologists Kingsley Davis and Wilbert Moore argued that society must offer rewards in order to assure that important social positions are filled by the most competent people. Conflict theorists see that stratification was the consequence of group struggles for scarce resources. Gaetano Mosca believed that leadership perpetuates inequality. Gerhard Lenski combined different views to explain the historical evolution of stratification systems.

- To maintain stratification within a nation, the ruling class controls ideas and information, depends on social networks, controls new technologies and relies on force.

- In Britain, the most striking features of the class system are differences in speech and accent, and differences in education. In the former Soviet Union, the 1917 Revolution resulted in one set of social classes being replaced by another.

- The most common model of global stratification divides nations into three groups: the Most Industrialized, the Industrializing, and the Least Industrialized.

- Four theories explaining the origins of global stratification are colonialism, world system theory, dependency theory, and a culture of poverty. International stratification is maintained both through neocolonialism, the ongoing dominance of the Least Industrialized Nations by the Most Industrialized Nations, and multinational corporations, which operate across national boundaries.

LEARNING OBJECTIVES
As you read Chapter 7, use these learning objectives to organize your notes. After completing your reading, briefly state an answer to each of the objectives, and review the text pages in parentheses.

1. Define social stratification. (154)
2. Describe the characteristics of slavery and note the uses of slavery in the New World. (155-156)
3. Identify the features of caste systems. Give examples of different ones. (156-157)
4. List the characteristics of a class system. (157-158)
5. Identify the basic assumptions of Karl Marx regarding what determines social class. (158-159)
6. Explain why Max Weber was critical of Marx's perspective, and summarize Weber's views regarding social class position. (159)
7. State the basic assumptions of functionalists like Davis and Moore, and present Tumin's criticisms of this viewpoint. (160-161)

95

8. Discuss Mosca's perspective on the universality of social stratification and explain why he is considered to be a forerunner of the conflict view. (161)
9. Compare Marx's early conflict-oriented perspective with that or later conflict theorists. (161-162)
10. Explain how Lenski's views represent a synthesis of the functionalist and conflict views. (162)
11. Explain the mechanisms by which the elite maintains stratification. (162-163)
12. Compare and contrast social stratification in Great Britain and the former Soviet Union. (163-165)
13. Describe the major characteristics of Most Industrialized, Industrializing, and Least Industrialized Nations, and name at least three countries which fit in each category. (165-168)
14. Outline the major theories of how the world's nations became stratified. (168-171)
15. Explain how global stratification has been maintained. (171-173)

CHAPTER OUTLINE

I. **An Overview of Social Stratification**
    A. Social stratification is a system in which people are divided into layers according to their relative power, property, and prestige.
    B. Social stratification refers to the ranking of large groups of people, rather than individuals.
    C. Every society stratifies its members, although some have greater inequality than others.
    D. No matter what system a society may use to divide people into different layers, gender is always an essential part of those distinctions within each layer. On the basis of gender, people are sorted into categories and given differential access to rewards. Social distinctions have usually favored males.
    E. Slavery is a form of social stratification in which some people own other people.
        1. Initially, slavery was based on debt, punishment for violation of the law, or defeat in battle. Given this last practice, many of the first slaves were women, captured after the defeat of their village.
        2. Slavery could be temporary or permanent and was not necessarily passed on to one's children. Typically, slaves owned no property and had no power; however, this was not universally true.
        3. American colonists first tried to enslave Indians and then turned to Africans, who were being brought to North and South America by the British, Dutch, English, Portuguese, and Spanish. When American slave owners found it was profitable to own slaves for life, they developed beliefs to justify what they wanted and to make slavery inheritable.
        4. Slavery still exists in places like the Sudan and Mauritania; apparently villages are raided, the men killed, and the women children captured and sold.
    F. In a caste system, status is determined by birth and is lifelong.
        1. Ascribed status is the basis of a caste system. Societies with caste systems try to make certain that boundaries between castes remain firm by practicing endogamy (marriage within their own group) and developing rules about ritual pollution--teaching that contact with inferior castes contaminates the superior caste.
        2. Although abolished by the Indian government in 1949, the caste system remains part of everyday life, as it has for almost three thousand years. Based on religion, it is made up of four main castes, or varnas, which are subdivided into thousands of specialized subcastes or *jati*. The lowest caste is considered to be "untouchable," and ablution--washing rituals--are required to restore purity for those contaminated by individuals from this group. India's caste system is finally

               breaking down because of industrialization and urbanization.

       3.   An American racial caste system developed in the United States when slavery ended. Even in the earlier parts of this century, all whites were considered higher than all African Americans and separate accommodations were maintained for the races in the South.

   G.   A class system is a form of social stratification based primarily on the possession of money or material possessions.

       1.   An individual's initial social class position is based on that of her or his parents (ascribed status).

       2.   A class system allows for social mobility--movement up or down the social class ladder--based on achieved status.

II.   What Determines Social Class?

   A.   According to Karl Marx, social class is determined by one's relationship to the means of production--the tools, factories, land, and investment capital used to produce wealth.

       1.   The bourgeoisie (capitalists) own the means of production; the proletariat (workers) are the people who work for those who own the means of production.

       2.   As capital becomes more concentrated, the two classes will become increasingly more hostile to one another.

       3.   Class consciousness--awareness of a common identity based on position in the means of production--will develop; it is the essential basis of the unity of workers, according to Marx.

       4.   Marx believed that the workers would revolt against the capitalists, take control of the means of production, and usher in a classless society. However, the workers' unity and revolution are held back by false consciousness--the mistaken identification of workers with the interests of capitalists.

   B.   Unlike Marx, Max Weber did not believe that property was the sole basis of a person's position in the stratification system, but rather that property, prestige, and power determine social class.

       1.   Property is an essential element; however, powerful people, like managers of corporations, control the means of production although they do not own them.

       2.   Prestige may be derived from ownership of property; however, it also may be based on other factors such as athletic skills.

       3.   Power is the ability to control others, even over their objections.

III.   Why is Social Stratification Universal?

   A.   According to the functionalist view expressed by Kingsley Davis and Wilbert Moore, stratification is inevitable.

       1.   Society must make certain that its important positions are filled; to guarantee that the more important positions are filled by the more qualified people, society must offer them greater rewards.

       2.   Davis and Moore argued that society offers greater rewards for its more responsible, demanding, and accountable positions.

   B.   Melvin Tumin offered a critique of the functionalist position.

       1.   He argued that the importance of a position can not be measured by the rewards; such an argument is circular. There must be an independent indicator of importance.

       2.   He noted that if stratification worked as Davis and Moore describe it, society would be a meritocracy--a form of social stratification in which all positions are

awarded on the basis of merit--but it does not work this way (e.g. the best predictor of college entrance is family income, not ability). He also argued that money and fringe benefits are not the only reasons people take jobs.

3.   Finally, he noted that stratification is dysfunctional to many people, not functional.

C.   Conflict theorists stress that conflict, not function, is the basis of social stratification.

1.   Every society has only limited resources to go around, and in every society groups struggle with one another for those resources.

2.   Whenever a group gains power, it uses that power to extract what it can from the groups beneath it. The dominant group takes control of the social institutions, using them to keep other groups weak and to preserve the best resources for itself. Ruling classes develop an ideology to justify people's relative positions.

D.   Gaetano Mosca argued that every society will be stratified by power. According to Mosca, stratification is inevitable; the ruling class is well organized and enjoys easy communication among its relatively few members; it is extremely difficult for the majority they govern to resist.

1.   Society cannot exist unless it is organized, thus, there must be politics to get the work of society done.

2.   Politics results in inequalities of power because some people take leadership positions and others follow.

3.   It is human nature to be self-centered, thus, people in positions of power use their positions to bring greater rewards to themselves.

E.   Marx argued that the bourgeoisie are in power because they control society's resources, using those resources to benefit themselves.

F.   Modern conflict theorists such as C. Wright Mills, Ralf Dahrendorf, and Randall Collins stress that conflict between capitalists and workers is not the only important conflict in contemporary society; the competition for scarce resources results in conflict not only between groups from different classes but also between groups within the same social class (e.g. young vs. old; women vs. men).

G.   Gerhard Lenski offered a synthesis between functionalist and conflict theories.

1.   Functionalists are right when it comes to societies that have only basic resources and do not accumulate wealth, such as hunting and gathering societies.

2.   Conflict theorists are right when it comes to societies with a surplus. In such societies humans pursue self-interests and struggle to control those surpluses. This leads to the emergence of a small elite who then builds inequality into the society, resulting in a full-blown system of social stratification.

IV.   **How do Elites Maintain Stratification?**

A.   Social stratification is maintained within a nation because elites control ideas and information, maintain social networks, and use force.

B.   Ideology can be remarkably more effective than the use of brute force in maintaining inequality.

1.   The control of ideas is used by elites everywhere to maintain their positions of power--whether in dictatorships or in democracies. To the degree that their ideologies are accepted by the masses, political arrangements are stable.

2.   Elites also try to control information through the threat of force, as in a dictatorship, or through the manipulation of the media by the selective release of information, as in a democracy.

3.   Technology aids the elite in its desire to preserve its position. Technology enables

elites to monitor citizens' activities without their even being aware that they are being shadowed.

    4.   Social networks provide valuable information and tend to perpetuate inequality.

V.   Comparative Social Stratification

A.   Great Britain's class system can be divided into upper, middle, and lower classes.

    1.   A little over half of the population is in the lower or working class. Half of the population is in the middle class. About 1 percent is in the upper class.

    2.   The British are extremely class conscious. Language and speech patterns are important class indicators. Education is the primary way the class system is perpetuated from one generation to the next.

B.   The ideal of communism--a classless society--was never realized in the Soviet Union.

    1.   The major basis for stratification was membership in the Communist Party, which consisted of top party officials, a relatively small middle class, and a massive lower class of peasants and unskilled workers.

    2.   Frustrated with the system's inability to be economically successful, Soviet leaders initiated capitalistic reforms in the hopes of turning things around.

    3.   The transition to capitalism has taken bizarre twists, with some Russians organizing into criminal groups, stealing vast amounts of state property, amassing wealth, and intimidating business people.

VI.   Global Stratification: The Three Worlds of Development

A.   The Most Industrialized Nations are the U.S., Canada, Great Britain, France, Germany, Switzerland and other industrialized nations of western Europe, as well as Japan, Australia, New Zealand; they are capitalistic, although variations exist in economic systems. Their wealth is enormous and the poor in these countries live better/longer than the average citizens in the Least Industrialized Nations.

B.   The Industrializing Nations include the former Soviet Union and its former satellites in eastern Europe. People living in these countries have considerably lower income and a poorer standard of living than people in the Most Industrialized Nations, but better than those living in the Least Industrialized Nations.

C.   The Least Industrialized Nations are those where most people live on farms or in villages with low standards of living. These nations account for 68 percent of the world's population.

VII.   How the World's Nations became Stratified

A.   Colonialism occurred when industrialized nations made colonies of weaker nations and exploited their labor/natural resources. European nations tended to focus on Africa, while the U.S. concentrated on Central and South America.

    1.   The more powerful European nations planted their national flags in a colony and sent representatives to run the government. The U.S. planted corporate flags in the particular colony, letting corporations dominate the territory's government.

    2.   Western imperialism and colonialism shaped the Least Industrialized Nations, drawing lines across a map to divide up their spoils, thereby creating states without regard for tribal or cultural considerations. The legacy of European conquests still erupts in tribal violence because tribes with no history of national identity were arbitrarily incorporated into the same political boundaries.

B.   According to world system theory (as espoused by Immanuel Wallerstein) countries are politically and economically tied together.

    1.   There are four groups of interconnected nations: (1) core nations, where

capitalism first developed; (2) semi-periphery (Mediterranean area), highly dependent on trade with core nations; (3) periphery (eastern Europe), mainly limited to selling cash crops to core nations, with limited economic development; (4) external area (most of Africa/Asia) left out of growth of capitalism, with few economic ties to core nations.

2.   A capitalist world economy (capitalist dominance) results from relentless expansion; even external area nations are drawn into commercial web.

3.   Globalization (the extensive interconnections among nations resulting from the expansion of capitalism) has speeded up because of new forms of communication and transportation. The consequence is that no nation is able to live in isolation.

C.   Dependency theory attributes lack of economic development in the Least Industrialized Nations to dominance of world economy by the Most Industrialized Nations.

1.   It asserts that those nations that industrialized first turned other nations into their plantations and mines, taking whatever they needed; as a result, many of the Least Industrialized Nations began to specialize in a single cash crop.

2.   By becoming dependent on the Most Industrialized Nations, these other countries did not develop independent economies of their own.

D.   John Kenneth Galbraith argued that some nations remain poor because they are crippled by a culture of poverty, a way of life based on traditional values and religious beliefs that perpetuates poverty from one generation to the next and keeps some of the Least Industrialized Nations from developing.

E.   Most sociologists find colonialism/world system/dependency theory explanations preferable to the culture of poverty theory because the last places the blame on the victim, but each theory only partially explains global stratification.

VIII.   **Maintaining Global Stratification**

A.   Neocolonialism is the economic and political dominance of Least Industrialized Nations by the Most Industrialized Nations. Michael Harrington assets that the Most Industrialized Nations control the Least Industrialized Nations because they control markets, set prices, etc. They move hazardous industries to the Least Industrialized Nations and sell weapons and manufactured goods to the Least Industrialized Nations, preventing them from developing their own industrial capacity.

B.   Multinational corporations contribute to exploitation of the Least Industrialized Nations.

1.   Some exploit these nations directly by controlling national and local politics, running them as a fiefdom. Multinational corporations work closely with the elites of the Least Industrialized Nations, funneling investments to this small circle of power in exchange for its cooperation.

2.   The Most Industrialized Nations are primary beneficiaries of profits made in the Least Industrialized Nations.

3.   In some situations, multinational corporations may bring prosperity to the Least Industrialized Nations because new factories provide salaries and opportunities which otherwise would not exist for workers in those countries.

C.   In the quest to maintain global domination, the new technologies create even more advantages for the Most Industrialized Nations. The profits generated by multinationals allow the Most Industrialized Nations to invest huge sums in the latest technologies.

KEY TERMS

After studying the chapter, review each of the following terms.

bourgeoisie: Karl Marx's term for capitalists, those who own the means of production (159)

capitalist world economy: the dominance of capitalism in the world, along with the interdependence of the world's nations capitalism has created (170)

caste system: a form of social stratification in which one's status is determined by birth and is lifelong (156)

class consciousness: Karl Marx's term for awareness of a common identity based on one's position in the means of production (159)

class system: a form of social stratification based primarily on the possession of money or material possessions (158)

colonialism: the process by which one nation takes over another nation, usually for the purpose of exploiting its labor and natural resources (168)

culture of poverty: the values and behaviors of the poor that are assumed to make them fundamentally different from other people (171)

dependency theory: the view that the Least Industrialized Nations have been unable to develop their economies because they grew dependent on the Most Industrialized Nations (171)

divine right of kings: the idea that the king's authority comes directly from God (162)

endogamy: the practice of marrying within one's own group (156)

false consciousness: Karl Marx's term to refer to workers identifying with the interests of capitalists (159)

globalization: the extensive interconnections among nations due to the expansion of capitalism (170)

ideology: beliefs about the way things ought to be that justify social arrangements (156)

means of production: the tools, factories, land, and investment capital used to produce wealth (159)

meritocracy: a form of social stratification in which all positions are awarded on the basis of merit (161)

multinational corporations: companies that operate across many national boundaries (172)

neocolonialism: the economic and political dominance of the Least Industrialized Nations by the Most Industrialized Nations (171)

proletariat: Karl Marx's term for the people who work for those who own the means of production (159)

slavery: a form of social stratification in which some people own other people (155)

social class: a large number of people with similar amounts of income and education who work at jobs that are roughly comparable in prestige (159)

social mobility: movement up or down the social class ladder (158)

social stratification: the division of people into layers according to their relative power, property, and prestige; applies to both a society and to nations (154)

world system: economic and political connections that tie the world's countries together (170)

KEY PEOPLE

Review the major theoretical contributions or research findings of these people.

Randall Collins: Collins is a contemporary conflict theorist who has broadened conflict theory to include analysis of competition between groups within the same class for scarce resources. (162)

Ralf Dahrendorf: Dahrendorf is another contemporary conflict theorist who has argued that conflict over scarce resources is not just limited to class conflict. (162)

Kingsley Davis and Wilbert Moore: These functionalists developed a theory of stratification that suggests inequality is universal because it helps societies survive by motivating the most qualified members of society to strive to feel the most important social positions. (160)

William Domhoff: Domhoff has studied the social networks of the elite and documented how members of this group move in a circle of power that multiplies their opportunities. (163)

John Kenneth Galbraith: This economist argued that the Least Industrialized nations remain poor because their own culture holds them back. (171)

Michael Harrington: Harrington saw that colonialism has been replaced by neocolonialism. (171)

Martha Huggins: Huggins has studied poverty in the Least Industrialized Nations. (169)

Gerhard Lenski: Lenski offered a synthesis of functionalist and conflict views of stratification. (162)

Gerda Lerner: This historian has noted that the first people who were enslaved as a result of war and conquest were women. (155)

Oscar Lewis: Lewis is the anthropologist who first suggested the reason some people are poor is because they live in a culture of poverty. (171)

Karl Marx: Marx concluded that social class depended exclusively on the means of production; an individual's social class was determined by whether or not he owned the means of production. (158)

C. Wright Mills: Mills is one of the 20th century conflict theorists who has broadened Marx's original theory to recognize other bases for conflict besides social class. (162)

Gaetano Mosca: Mosca argued that every society is inevitably stratified by power. (161)

James Schellenberg: Schellenberg is a contemporary conflict theorist. (162)

Melvin Tumin: Tumin was the first to offer a criticism of the functionalist view on stratification. (161)

Immanuel Wallerstein: This historian proposed a world system theory to explain global stratification. (170)

Max Weber: Weber argued social class was based on three components--class, status, and power. (159)

SELF-TEST

After completing this self-test, check your answers against the Answer Key beginning on page 244 of this Study Guide and against the text on page(s) indicated in parentheses.

MULTIPLE CHOICE QUESTIONS

1.   The division of people into layers according to their relative power, property, and prestige is: (154)
    a.   social distinction.
    b.   social stratification.
    c.   social distance
    d.   social diversification.

2.   A form of social stratification in which some people own other people is: (155)
    a.   a caste system.
    b.   slavery.
    c.   a class system.
    d.   apartheid.

3.   All of the following were initial bases for slavery except: (155)
    a.   racism.
    b.   debt.
    c.   violation of the law.
    d.   war and conquest.

4.   Slavery in the United States: (156)
   a.   was attempted with Native Americans before turning to Africans.
   b.   was based on an ideology of racial inferiority.
   c.   became inheritable.
   d.   All of the above.

5.   The practice of endogamy is most likely to found in: (156)
   a.   class system.
   b.   caste system.
   c.   meritocracy.
   d.   socialist system.

6.   The best example of a caste system is: (156)
   a.   the contemporary United States.
   b.   South America.
   c.   India.
   d.   none or the above.

7.   Class systems are characterized by: (158)
   a.   social mobility
   b.   geographic mobility
   c.   distribution of social standings belonging to an extended network of relatives
   d.   all of the above

8.   Marx concluded that social class depends on: (159)
   a.   wealth, power, and prestige.
   b.   the means of production.
   c.   where one is born in the social stratification system.
   d.   what a person achieves during his or her lifetime.

9.   According to Max Weber, social class is determined by: (159)
   a.   one's property, prestige, and power.
   b.   one's relationship to the means of production.
   c.   one's tasks and how important they are to society.
   d.   one's political power.

10.   The functionalist view of social stratification was developed by: (160)
   a.   Gaetano Mosca.
   b.   John Kenneth Galbraith.
   c.   Melvin Tumin.
   d.   Kingsley Davis and Wilbert Moore.

11.   Which of the following is not one of the criticisms of the functionalist view which was provided by Melvin Tumin? (161)
    a.   The functionalists do not provide an adequate method for measuring the social importance of the position.
    b.   The functionalists assume that social stratification is beneficial to everyone, which it is not.
    c.   The functionalists consider that stratification is the same everywhere and at all points in history.
    d.   The functionalists view society as a meritocracy in which positions are awarded on the basis of merit, when in reality other factors such as income and gender influence one's placement in the system of stratification.

12.   A form of social stratification in which positions are awarded based on merit is called a(n): (161)
    a.   meritocratic system.
    b.   egalitarian system.
    c.   socialistic system.
    d.   democratic system.

13.   According to conflict theorists, the basis of social stratification is: (161)
    a.   functional necessity in society.
    b.   conflict over limited resources.
    c.   ascribed statuses.
    d.   the way in which individuals perceive their social class position.

14.   Gaetano Mosca argued that every society will be stratified by: (161)
    a.   wealth.
    b.   class.
    c.   individuals' relation to the mean of production.
    d.   power.

15.   The key to maintaining national stratification is control of: (162-163)
    a.   ideas and information.
    b.   social networks
    c.   technology.
    d.   All of the above.

16.   The British perpetuate their class system between generations by: (164)
    a.   emphasis on material possessions such as clothes and cars.
    b.   religion.
    c.   education.
    d.   encouraging persons in all class to marry others within their own class.

17.   In the former Soviet Union, the system of stratification was based on: (164)
    a.   occupation.
    b.   trade union membership.
    c.   Communist party membership.
    d.   education.

18.   The United States, Canada, Great Britain, and France are examples of: (165)
      a.   the Most Industrialized Nations.
      b.   Industrializing Nations.
      c.   the Least Industrialized Nations.
      d.   None of the above.

19.   Most people in the Least Industrialized Nations live on less than _____ a year. (168)
      a. $1,000
      b. $5,000
      c. $8,000
      d. $10,000

20.   _____ is the control of weak nations' labor and natural resources by powerful nations. (168)
      a.   communism.
      b.   colonialism.
      c.   globalism.
      d.   a banana republic.

21.   According to world system theory, all of the following are groups of interconnected nations, except: (170)
      a.   core nations.
      b.   nations on the semiperiphery.
      c.   nations on the periphery.
      d.   nations on the internal area which have extensive connections with the core nations.

22.   The term "banana republic" reflects which of the following theories about global stratification? (171)
      a.   world system theory
      b.   dependency theory
      c.   culture of poverty theory
      d.   neocolonialism

23.   The culture of poverty theory was used to analyze global stratification by: (171)
      a.   Immanuel Wallerstein.
      b.   Max Weber.
      c.   John Kenneth Galbraith.
      d.   Karl Marx.

24.   Multinational corporations: (172-173)
      a.   are companies that operate across many national boundaries.
      b.   always exploit the Least Industrialized Nations directly.
      c.   benefit the Least Industrialized Nations as much as the Most Industrialized Nations.
      d.   All of the above.

25.   According to Henslin, today what is a key to the continued global dominance by the Most Industrialized Nations? (173)
   a.   military strength
   b.   atomic weapons
   c.   development of new technologies
   d.   all of the above

TRUE-FALSE QUESTIONS

T F   1.   According to sociologists, your location in the system of social stratification has a profound effect on your chances in life. (154)

T F   2.   Gender discrimination cuts across all systems of social stratification. (165)

T F   3.   Throughout history, slavery has always been based on racism. (155)

T F   4.   One of the first groups in the New World to be enslaved were Native Americans. (156)

T F   5.   A caste system is a form of social stratification in which individual status is determined by birth and is lifelong. (156)

T F   6.   India provides the only known example of a caste system. (156)

T F   7.   According to Karl Marx, the means of production is the only factor in determining social class. (159)

T F   8.   Marx believed that the tendency for workers to mistakingly identify with the interests of capitalists hindered their unity and impeded revolution. (159)

T F   9.   Max Weber agreed with Karl Marx that property was the basis for social class. (159)

T F   10.   Functionalists believe that people should be rewarded for their unique abilities and the type of position they hold in society is not important. (160)

T F   11.   According to conflict theorists, the oppressed often support laws which operate against their own interests. (161)

T F   12.   Gerhard Lenski said that the functionalist view of stratification was most appropriate when studying societies with a surplus of wealth. (162)

T F   13.   In maintaining stratification, elites find that brute force is more effective than the control of ideas. (162)

T F   14.   The idea of the divine right of kings is an example of how the ruling elite uses ideas to maintain stratification. (162)

T F   15.   Under the leadership of Lenin and Trotsky, the former Soviet Union was able to create a classless society. (164)

T F   16.   The terms "Most Industrialized Nations," "Industrializing Nations," and "Least Industrialized Nations" are used in order to depict stratification among nations along the lines of property, power, and prestige. (165)

T F   17.   The U.S. has generally practiced "economic imperialism." (170)

T F   18.   The expansion of capitalism resulted in a capitalist world economy dominated by the core nations. (170)

T F   19.   The culture of poverty thesis is generally preferred by sociologists as an explanation of global stratification. (171)

T F   20.   Neocolonialism is the economic and political dominance of the Least Industrialized Nations by the Most Industrialized Nations. (171)

FILL-IN QUESTIONS

1.   _____ is a system in which people are divided into layers according to their relative power, property, and prestige. (154)
2.   A form of social stratification in which some people own other people is _____. (155)
3.   A(n) _____ system is a form of social stratification in which individual status is determined by birth and is lifelong. (156)
4.   Caste societies use the practice of _____ to make certain that boundaries between castes remain firm. (156)
5.   According to Marx, the tools, factories, land, and investment capital used to produce wealth is _____. (158)
6.   According to Marx, the awareness of a common identity based on one's position in the means of production is _____. (159)
7.   Karl Marx's term for the mistaken identification of workers with the interests of capitalists was _____. (159)
8.   If stratification was truly organized as the functionalists describe it, society would be a _____, with positions awarded on the basis of merit. (161)
9.   The _____ is the idea that the king's authority comes directly from God. (162)
10.   _____ is the process in which one nation takes over another nation, usually for the purpose of exploiting its labor and natural resources. (168)
11.   World system theory was developed by _____. (170)
12.   _____ is the extensive interconnections among world nations resulting from the expansion of capitalism. (170)
13.   _____ is a culture that perpetuates poverty from one generation to the next. (171)
14.   _____ is the political and economic dominance of the Least Industrialized Nations by the Most Industrialized Nations. (171)
15.   Companies that operate across many national boundaries are _____. (172)

MATCH THESE SOCIAL SCIENTISTS WITH THEIR CONTRIBUTIONS

___1. Karl Marx   a. *world system theory*
___2. Kingsley Davis & Wilbert Moore   b. *criticism of functional view of stratification*
___3. Gaetano Mosca   c. *stressed culture of poverty*
___4. Immanuel Wallerstein   d. *false consciousness*
___5. Michael Harrington   e. *stated functionalist view of stratification*
___6. John Kenneth Galbraith   f. *forerunner of conflict view of stratification*
___7. Max Weber   g. *neocolonialism*
___8. Melvin Tumin   h. *class based on property, prestige and power*

ESSAY QUESTIONS

1.   Compare Marx's theory of stratification with Weber's theory. Discuss why Weber's theory is more widely accepted by sociologists.

2.   Consider why ideology is a more effective way of maintaining stratification than brute force.

3.   In the 1960s, most former colonies around the globe won their political independence. Since that time the position of these countries has remained largely unchanged within the global system of stratification. Provide some evidence as to why political independence alone was not enough to alter their status.

"DOWN-TO-EARTH SOCIOLOGY"

1.   Look at the maps and accompanying tables on pages 166-167. Why do you think the income per person is so much higher in the Most Industrialized Nations? Does money just "go a lot farther" in the rest of the world or do people in these countries have much lower standards of living than people in the Most Industrialized Nations? Do you think you would be able to live on an annual incomes of $1,000?

2.   What was your reaction after reading about children in the Least Industrialized Nations who are growing up in poverty? (p. 169) How does the image of life in the slums compare with your image of life in U.S. inner-city ghettos? What do you think that the Most Industrialized Nations should do about this situation?

3.   Read "Sex Tourism and the Patriotic Prostitute" on page 172. What do you think would happen if the United States government encouraged prostitution as a service to one's country? What would happen if the President of the United States suggested that a way to cut the federal debt would be for young women to prostitute themselves to earn money and contribute to the country to cut this nation's debt? Why do women's groups protest the international sex trade such as that described in this article?

CHAPTER 8
SOCIAL CLASS IN THE UNITED STATES

CHAPTER SUMMARY

- Most sociologists have adopted Weber's definition of social class as a large group of people who rank closely to one another in terms of wealth, power, and prestige. Wealth, consisting of property and income, is concentrated in the upper class. Power is the ability to carry out one's will despite the resistance of others; C. Wright Mills used the term "power elite" to refer to a small group that holds the reins of power in business, government, and the military. Prestige is the regard or respect accorded an individual or social position.

- Status is social ranking. Most people are status consistent, meaning that they rank high or low on all three dimensions of social class. People who rank high on some dimensions and low on others are status inconsistent. The frustration of status inconsistency tends to produce political radicalism.

- Sociologists use two main models to portray the social class structure. Erik Wright developed a four class model based on the ideas of Karl Marx. Dennis Gilbert and Joseph Kahl developed a six class model based on the ideas of Max Weber.

- Social class leaves no aspect of life untouched. Class membership affects life chances, physical and mental health, family life, politics, religion, and education.

- In studying the mobility of individuals within society, sociologists look at intergenerational mobility, the individual changes in social class from one generation to the next; exchange mobility, the movement of large numbers of people from one class to another; and structural mobility, the social and economic changes that affect the social class position of large numbers of people.

- Poverty is unequally distributed in the United States. Latinos, African Americans, Native Americans, children, female-headed households, and the rural poor are more likely to be poor. Sociologists generally focus on structural factors, such as employment opportunities, in explaining poverty. The Horatio Alger myth encourages people to strive to get ahead, and blames failures on individual shortcomings.

LEARNING OBJECTIVES

As you read Chapter 8, use these learning objectives to organize your notes. After completing your reading, briefly state an answer to each of the objectives, and review the text pages in parentheses.

1. Define social class and compare the three components of social class. (178-183)
2. Explain status inconsistency and discuss the consequences in terms of individual behavior. (183-184)
3. Explain Erik Wright's updated model of Marx's class theory. (184)
4. Discuss Gilbert and Kahl's updated model of Weber's perspective. (184-187)
5. Use Gilbert and Kahl's model to explain the reality of social classes in the automobile industry and among our nation's homeless. (187)
6. Examine the consequences of social class in terms of family life, politics, religion, and illness and health care and new technology. (188-191)
7. Distinguish between the different types of social mobility and discuss the patterns of social mobility within the United States. (191-192)
8. Indicate how the poverty line is drawn. State the major characteristics of the poor in the United States. (193-196)
9. Contrast short and long-term poverty. (196-198)

10.   Assess individual versus structural explanations of poverty. (198-201)
11.   Identify the social functions of the Horatio Alger myth. (201)

CHAPTER OUTLINE

I.   **What Is Social Class?**
    A.   Social class can be defined as a large group of people who rank close to each other in wealth, power, and prestige.
    B.   Wealth consists of property (what we own) and income (money we receive). Wealth and income are not always the same--a person may own much property yet have little income, or vice versa. Usually, however, wealth and income go together.
        1.   Ownership of property (real estate, stocks and bonds, etc.) is not distributed evenly: 10 percent of the U.S. population owns 68 percent of the wealth, and the richest 1 percent of U.S. families are worth more than the entire bottom 90 percent of Americans.
        2.   Income is also distributed disproportionately: the top 20 percent of U.S. residents acquire 47 percent of the income; the bottom 20 percent receive less than 5 percent. Each fifth of the U.S. population receives approximately the same proportion of national income today as it did in 1945. The changes that have occurred indicate growing inequality; the richest 20 percent of U.S. families have grown richer while the poorest 20 percent have growth poorer.
        3.   Apart from the very rich, the most affluent group in U.S. society is the executive officers of the largest corporations. Their median compensation is $5.8 million a year. The CEOs' income is 200 times higher than the average pay of U.S. workers.
    C.   Power is the ability to carry out your will in spite of resistance. Power is concentrated in the hands of a few--the "power elite"--who share the same ideologies and values, belong to the same clubs, and reinforce each other's world view. No major decision in U.S. government is made without their approval.
    D.   Prestige is the respect or regard people give to various occupations and accomplishments.
        1.   Occupations are the primary source of prestige. Occupations with the highest prestige pay more, require more education, entail more abstract thought, and offer greater autonomy. Occupational prestige rankings tend to be consistent across countries and over time.
        2.   For prestige to be valuable, people must acknowledge it. The elite traditionally has made rules to emphasize their higher status.
        3.   Status symbols, which vary according to social class, are ways of displaying prestige. In the United States, they include designer label clothing, expensive cars, prestigious addresses, and attending particular schools.
    E.   Status inconsistency is the term used to describe the situation of people who have a mixture of high and low rankings in the three components of social class (wealth, power, and prestige).
        1.   Most people are status consistent--they rank at the same level in all three components. People who are status inconsistent want others to act toward them on the basis of their highest status, but others tend to judge them on the basis of their lowest status.
        2.   Sociologist Gerhard Lenski determined that people suffering the frustrations of

status inconsistency are more likely to be radical and approve political action aimed against higher status groups.

II.   **Sociological Models of Social Class**
    A.   How many classes exist in industrial society is a matter of debate, but there are two main models, one that builds on Marx and the other on Weber.
    B.   Sociologist Erik Wright realized that not everyone falls into Marx's two broad classes (capitalists and workers, which were based upon a person's relationship to the means of productions). For instance, although executives, managers, and supervisors would fall into Marx's category of workers, they act more like capitalists.
        1.   Wright resolved this problem by regarding some people as simultaneously members of more than one class, occupying what he called contradictory class locations.
        2.   Wright identified four classes: capitalists (owners of large enterprises); petty bourgeoisie (owners of small businesses); managers (employees who but have authority over others); and workers (who sell their labor to others).
    C.   Using the framework originally developed by Weber, sociologists Dennis Gilbert and Joseph Kahl created a model to describe class structure in the U.S. and other capitalist countries.
        1.   The capitalist class (1 percent of the population) is composed of investors, heirs, and a few executives; it is divided into "old" money and "new" money. The children of "new" money move into the old money class by attending the right schools and marrying "old" money.
        2.   The upper-middle class (14 percent of the population) is composed of professionals and upper managers, almost all of whom have attended college or university and frequently have postgraduate degrees. Of all classes, this class is the one most shaped by education.
        3.   The lower-middle class (30 percent of the population) is composed of lower managers, craftspeople and foremen. They have at least a high school education.
        4.   The working class (30 percent of the population) is composed of factory workers and low-paid white collar workers. Most have high school educations.
        5.   The working poor (22 percent of the population) is composed of relatively unskilled blue-collar and white-collar workers, and those with temporary and seasonal jobs. If they graduated from high school, they probably did not do well in school.
        6.   The underclass (3 percent of the population) is concentrated in the inner cities and has little connection with the job market. Welfare is their main support.
    D.   The automobile industry provides an example of the social class ladder. At the top is the Ford family, who own and control Ford Motor Co., are at the top of the capitalist class; directly below them are the executives of the company, classified at the lower end of the capitalist class. The owners of a Ford agency would be considered part of the upper middle class, while a salesman would belong to the lower middle class. Mechanics are in the working class; those who "detail" used cars for the agency are working poor. Usually the underclass exists outside the industry.

III.   **Consequences of Social Class**
    A.   Social class plays a role in family life.
        1.   Children of the capitalist class are under great pressure to select the right mate in order to assure the continuity of the family line. Parents in this social class play

a large role in mate selection.

2. Marriages are more likely to fail in the lower social classes; the children of the poor thus are more likely to live in single-parent households.

B. Political views and involvement are influenced by social class.

1. People in lower classes are more likely to vote Democrat, and those in higher classes to vote Republican; parties are seen as promoting different class interests.

2. People in working class are more likely to be liberal on economic issues and more conservative on social issues.

3. Political participation is not equal; people at the bottom of the class structure are less likely to vote and get involved in politics.

C. Religious orientation follow class lines. Classes tend to cluster in different denominations; and patterns of worship also follow class lines.

D. Social class affects our health, with lower classes having more sickness and higher death rates. This pattern is influenced by the unequal access to medical care.

E. Mental health is also affected by social class. Studies show that the mental health of the lower classes is worse than that of the higher classes. These higher rates are due to the stresses of poverty. Social class is also a deciding factor in how the mentally ill are treated, with poorer individuals having less access to mental health facilities.

F. New technologies benefit some classes and hurts others. It opens and closes opportunities for people largely by virtue of where they are located on the social class ladder.

1. For those at the top of the social class ladder, new technology enables them to globalize production, thereby maximizing profits.

2. The educational background of the upper middle class prepares them to take a leading role in managing this new global production system.

3. For those below these two classes, new technology is transforming the workplace, eliminating jobs and causing workers' skills to become outdated. They are hit hardest by technological changes.

IV. **Social Mobility**

A. There are three basic types of social mobility: intergenerational, structural, and exchange.

1. Intergenerational mobility is the change that family members make in their social class from one generation to the next. As a result of individual effort, a person can rise from one level to another; in the event of individual failure, the reverse can be true.

2. Sociologists are more interested in structural mobility--social changes that affect large numbers of people. By way of example, as the economy shifted from factory machines to computers vast numbers of new jobs were created, with shifts from blue-collar jobs to white-collar positions.

3. Exchange mobility is movement of people up and down the social class system, where, on balance, the system remains the same. The term refers to general, overall movement of large numbers of people that leaves the class system basically untouched.

B. Studies of social mobility in the United States have focused on men. Compared with their fathers one-half of all men have moved up in social class; one-third have stayed in the same place; and one-sixth have moved down.

1. In the past it was assumed that women had no class position of their own; they were simply assigned the class of their husbands.

2. Structural changes in the U.S. economy have created opportunities for women to

move up the social class ladder. One study indicated that women that did move up were encouraged by their parents to postpone marriage and get an education.

C.   If the U.S. does not keep pace with global changes, its economic position will decline.

    1.   The U.S. is rushing to integrate advanced technology into all spheres of social life.

    2.   As this happens, the technologically illiterate are being left behind and their future looks grim.

V.   Poverty

A.   The U.S. government classifies the poverty line as being families whose incomes are less than three times a low-cost food budget. Any modification of this measure instantly adds or subtracts millions of people, and thus has significant consequences.

B.   Certain social groups are disproportionately represented among the poor population.

    1.   Poverty is not evenly distributed among the states; the poor are more likely to be clustered in the South and California than in other states. The poverty rate for the rural poor is slightly higher than the national average. While they show the same racial/ethnic characteristics as the nation as a whole, they are less likely to be on welfare or to be single parents, less skilled and less educated, and the jobs available to them pay less.

    2.   Race is a major factor. Although 2 out of 3 poor people are white, racial minorities are much more likely to be poor: 11 percent of whites, 30 percent of Latinos and 29 percent of African-Americans live in poverty.

    3.   Only two percent of people who finish college end up in poverty, compared to one in four of those who drop out of high school.

    4.   The sex of the person who heads a family is the greatest predictor or whether or not a family is poor. Half of all single-parent families headed by women live in poverty. The major causes of this phenomenon, called the feminization of poverty, are divorce, births to unwed mothers, and the lower wages paid to women.

    5.   The percentage of poor people over age 65 is lower than the national average, although elderly Latino and African Americans are almost three times more likely to be poor than elderly white Americans.

C.   Children are more likely to live in poverty than are adults or the elderly. This holds true regardless of race, but poverty is much greater among minority children: two out of every five Latino children and almost one out of every two African-American children are poor.

D.   In the 1960s Michael Harrington and Oscar Lewis suggested that the poor get trapped in a "culture of poverty" as a result of having values and behaviors that make them "fundamentally different" from other U.S. residents.

    1.   Research indicates that most poverty is of short duration, lasting only a year of less, and that most often it is due to a dramatic life change. Only 12 percent of poverty lasts five years or more.

    2.   Since the number of people who live in poverty remains fairly constant, this means that as many people move into poverty as move out of it.

    3.   About one-fourth of the U.S. population is or has ever been poor for at least a year.

E.   In trying to explain poverty, the choice is between focusing on individual explanations or on social structural explanations.

    1.   Sociologists look to such factors as inequalities in education, access to learning job skills, racial, ethnic, age, and gender discrimination, and large-scale economic

change to explain the patterns of poverty in society.

2.   A competing explanation focuses on how characteristics of individuals are assumed to contribute to their poverty. Sociologists reject explanations that focus on qualities of laziness or lack of intelligence as factors to explain poverty.

3.   After decades of debate welfare has been restructured, with limited on how long a person can stay on welfare. Although welfare rolls have dropped, it is too soon to know what the long-term results are.

F.   Sociologists explain such behaviors as a lack of deferred gratification as a consequence of poverty rather than a cause of it. The poor would love opportunities that would allow them the change to practice middle-class virtue of deferred gratification, but the conditions of their lives make such orientation unrealistic.

G.   Despite real-life examples of people from humble origins who climbed far up the social ladder, the widely-held belief of most U.S. residents (including minorities and the working poor) that they have a chance of getting ahead (the Horatio Alger myth) obviously is a statistical impossibility. Functionalists would stress that this belief is functional for society because it encourages people to compete for higher positions, while placing the blame for failure squarely on the individual.

KEY TERMS
After studying the chapter, review each of the following terms.

contradictory class location: Erik Wright's term for a position in the class structure that generates contradictory interests (184)

culture of poverty: the values and behaviors of the poor that are assumed to make them fundamentally different from other people; these factors are assumed to be largely responsible for their poverty, and parents are assumed to perpetuate poverty across generations by passing these characteristics on to their children (196)

deferred gratification: forgoing something in the present in the hope of achieving greater gains in the future (199)

downward social mobility: movement down the social class ladder (191)

exchange mobility: about the same numbers of people moving up and down the social class ladder, such that, on balance, the social class system shows little change (192)

feminization of poverty: a trend in U.S. poverty whereby most poor families are headed by women (196)

Horatio Alger myth: belief that anyone can get ahead if only he or she tries hard enough; encourages people to strive to get ahead and deflects blame for failure from society to the individual (201)

intergenerational mobility: the change that family members make in social class from one generation to the next (191)

poverty line: the official measure of poverty; calculated as three times a low-cost food budget (193)

power: the ability to get your way, even over the resistance of others (181)

power elite: C. Wright Mills's term for the top leaders of corporations, military, and politics who make the nation's major decisions (181)

prestige: respect or regard (182)

social class: a large number of people with similar amounts of income and education who work at jobs that are roughly comparable in prestige (178)

status: the position that someone occupies in society or a social group; one's social ranking (183)

status consistent: people who rank high or low on all three dimensions of social class (183)

status inconsistency: a contradiction or mismatch between statuses; a condition in which a person ranks high on some dimensions of social class and low on others (183)

⊙ **structural mobility:** movement up or down the social class ladder that is attributable to changes in the structure of society, not to individual efforts (191)

underclass: a small group of people for whom poverty persists year after year and across generations (187)

○ **upward social mobility:** movement up the social class ladder (191)

wealth: property and income (178)

KEY PEOPLE

Review the major theoretical contributions or research findings of these people.

William Domhoff: Drawing upon the work of C. Wright Mills, Domhoff analyzed the workings of the ruling class. (181)

Dennis Gilbert and Joseph Kahl: These sociologists developed a more contemporary stratification model based on Max Weber's work. (184)

Ray Gold: In research on status inconsistency, Gold studied tenant reactions to janitors who earned more than they did. He found that the tenants acted "snooty" to the janitors, and the janitors took pleasure in knowing the intimate details of the tenants lives. (183)

Michael Harrington: Harrington analyzed poverty in the 1960s, arguing that the poor get caught in a culture that perpetuates poverty across generations. (196)

Daniel Hellinger and Dennis Judd: In analyzing the exercise of power in the U.S., these two men suggest that there is a "democratic facade" that conceals the real sources of power within this society. (181)

Elizabeth Higginbotham and Lynn Weber: These sociologists studied the mobility patterns for women. They found that those women who experienced upward mobility were most likely to have strong parental support to defer marriage and get an education. (192)

Gerhard Lenski: Lenski noted the everyone wants to maximize their status, but that others often judge them on the basis of their lowest status despite the individual's efforts to be judged on the basis of his highest status.

Oscar Lewis: Back in the 1960s, Lewis suggested that the poor get trapped in a culture of poverty. (196)

Elliot Liebow: Liebow's research on African American street corner men found that their orientation was to the present, since their future did not offer any alternatives to what they currently had. (199)

C. Wright Mills: Mills used the term power elite to describe the top decision-makers in the nation. (181)

Daniel J. Moynihan: Moynihan is a sociologist as well as U.S. senator; he attributes the high rate of child poverty to the breakdown of the U.S. family. (197)

Max Weber: Weber expanded the concept of social class beyond economics--one's relationship to the means of production--to include power and prestige as well. (178)

Erik Wright: Wright proposed an up-dated version of Marx's theory of stratification. (184)

4 classes (capitalist) Dennis Gilbert 8 classes
petty bourgeois

SELF-TEST

After completing this self-test, check your answers against the Answer Key beginning on page 248 of this Study Guide and against the text on page(s) indicated in parentheses.

MULTIPLE CHOICE QUESTIONS

1. According to your text, most sociologists agree that social class: (178)
    a.   has a clear-cut, accepted definition in sociology.
    b.   is best defined by the two classes as set out by Marx.
    c.   is best defined by Weber's dimensions of social class.
    d.   has no clear-cut, accepted definition and, thus, is used differently by all sociologists.

2. It is safe to say that in the United States wealth is: (178)
    a.   fairly evenly distributed among the top one-third of the population.
    b.   concentrated within the largest segment of our population--the middle class.
    c.   concentrated at the top, with about half held by the top 20 percent of U.S. families.
    d.   concentrated, with the top 1 percent of families worth more than the bottom 90 percent.

3. According to Paul Samuelson, if an income pyramid were made out of a child's blocks, most U.S. residents would be: (178)
    a.   near the top of the pyramid.
    b.   near the middle of the pyramid.
    c.   near the bottom of the pyramid.
    d.   None of the above.

4. The term "power elite" was coined by: (181)
    a.   C. Wright Mills.
    b.   G. William Domhoff.
    c.   Gary Marx.
    d.   W. Lloyd Warner.

5. There is a widely-held view among Americans that they indirectly participate in making important governmental decisions because they elect representatives to government. Daniel Hellinger and Dennis Judd call this the _____ that conceals the real source of power in the U.S. (181)
    a.   democratic ideals
    b.   democratic facade
    c.   ideal democracy
    d.   indirect democracy

6. All of the following are true regarding jobs that have the most prestige, <u>except:</u> (182)
    a.   they pay more.
    b.   they require more education.
    c.   they require special talent or skills.
    d.   they offer greater autonomy.

7. Capitalists, petty bourgeoisie, managers, and workers are the four classes in U.S. society, according to: (184)
    a. Erik Wright.
    b. C. Wright Mills.
    c. Dennis Gilbert and Joseph Kahl.
    d. Gary Marx.

8. Capitalist, upper-middle, lower-middle, working class, working poor, and underclass are the six classes in the United States, according to: (184-187)
    a. Erik Wright.
    b. C. Wright Mills.
    c. Dennis Gilbert and Joseph Kahl.
    d. W. Lloyd Warner.

9. According to Gilbert and Kahl, people who have made fortunes in entertainment or sports would be in the _new money_ category. (186)
    a. old money
    b. new money
    c. upper-middle
    d. None of the above.

10. All of the following are characteristics of the working class, except: (186)
    a. most are employed in relatively unskilled blue-collar and white-collar jobs.
    b. most have attended college for one or two years.
    c. most hope to get ahead by achieving seniority on the job.
    d. about thirty percent of the population belong to this class.

11. According to your text, the typical mechanic in a Ford dealership would be in the: (187)
    a. upper-middle class.
    b. lower-middle class.
    c. working class.
    d. underclass.

12. One area of life which is affected by social class is: (188)
    a. choice of mate.
    b. politics.
    c. sickness and health.
    d. all of the above.

13. People in the _working_ class are more likely to be liberal on economic issues and conservative on social issues. (188)
    a. upper
    b. middle
    c. lower
    d. working

14.   Which social class experiences the most stress in daily life? (189)
        a.   upper class
        b.   middle class
        c.   lower class
        d.   All of the above experience about the same amount of stress, although the kind of stress and the source of stress may be different.

15.   A homeless person whose father was a physician has experienced: (191)
        a.   exchange mobility.
        b.   structural mobility.
        c.   upward mobility.
        d.   downward mobility.

16.   As computers were introduced into the workplace many new white-collar jobs opened up overnight. Taking advantage of these new opportunities, many workers switched from blue-collar to white-collar employment. This is an example of: (191)
        a.   exchange mobility.
        b.   structural mobility.
        c.   upward mobility.
        d.   job mobility.

17.   As compared with their fathers, about one-half of men in the U.S. have: (192)
        a.   a status higher than that of their fathers.
        b.   the same status their fathers did.
        c.   a status lower than that of their fathers.
        d.   It is impossible to compare the relative statuses of fathers and sons because of structural mobility.

18.   Research by Higginbotham and Weber on women professionals, managers, and administrators from working class backgrounds indicates that: (192)
        a.   intergenerational mobility was greater for sons than for daughters.
        b.   upwardly mobile women achieved higher positions despite their parents reservations.
        c.   upwardly mobile women achieved higher class positions because of parental encouragement that began when they were just little girls.
        d.   any upward mobility was due entirely to structural changes in the economy rather than individual effort or parental influences.

19.   The official measure of poverty calculated to include those whose incomes equal less than three times a low-cost food budget is the: (193)
        a.   adjusted income level.
        b.   the welfare distribution scale.
        c.   the poverty line.
        d.   the welfare line.

20.   Which of the following is a major cause of the feminization of poverty? (196)
      a.   divorce
      b.   births to unmarried mothers
      c.   lower wages paid to female workers
      d.   all of the above

21.   In the United States, the poor are most likely to be: (196)
      a.   the elderly and women.
      b.   racial minorities, children and women.
      c.   the elderly and children.
      d.   racial minorities and the elderly.

22.   According to Daniel Moynihan, the increase in the rate of child poverty is due to: (197)
      a.   cutbacks in social welfare money.
      b.   the breakdown of the U.S. family.
      c.   the increase in illegal immigration across our borders.
      d.   a liberalization of the definition of poverty.

23.   The assumption that the values and behaviors of the poor make them fundamentally different from
      other people and that these factors are largely responsible for their poverty is referred to as: (196)
      a.   deferred gratification.
      b.   immediate gratification.
      c.   feminization of poverty.
      d.   culture of poverty.

24.   Approximately what portion of the U.S. population is or has ever been poor for at least one year?
      (198)
      a.   one-tenth
      b.   one-quarter
      c.   one-fifth
      d.   one-third

25.   The Horatio Alger myth: (201)
      a.   is beneficial for society, according to the functionalists.
      b.   reduces pressures on the social system.
      c.   motivates people to try harder to succeed because anything is possible.
      d.   all of the above.

TRUE-FALSE QUESTIONS

T F   1.   Most sociologists question Weber's views on social class. (178)
T F   2.   Wealth and income are the same thing. (178)
T F   3.   Sixty-eight percent of the total net worth of all U.S. families is owned by just ten percent
           of those families. (178)
T F   4.   Apart from the very rich, the most affluent group in U.S. society consists of the chief
           executive officers of the nation's largest corporations. (180)
T F   5.   Occupational prestige rankings vary widely across countries and over time. (182)

T F 6. Most U.S. residents are not very conscious of prestige. (183)
T F 7. College professors typically are an example of status inconsistency. (183)
T F 8. According to Gilbert and Kahl, the capitalist class has the ability to shape the consciousness of the nation. (185)
T F 9. The capitalist class is the one most shaped by education. (186)
T F 10. The underclass is concentrated in the inner city and has little or no connection with the job market. (187)
T F 11. In combination, about one-quarter of the U.S. population is part of the working poor or the underclass. (186-187)
T F 12. When it comes to selecting a marriage mate, children of the capitalist class have a wider field of "eligibles" than children of any other social class because of their position at the top of society. (188)
T F 13. Divorce is more common among the middle class than the poor. (188)
T F 14. New technologies open and close opportunities for people largely by virtue of where they are located on the social class ladder. (190)
T F 15. Structural mobility refers to social and economic changes that result in large numbers of people moving up or down the class ladder. (191)
T F 16. Exchange mobility leaves the class system basically untouched. (192)
T F 17. Women were largely excluded from classic studies of occupational mobility. (192)
T F 18. The rural poor do not differ significantly from the urban poor. (194)
T F 19. Most poverty in the U.S. is of short duration, lasting only a year or less. (198)
T F 20. Sociological explanations of poverty tend to focus on structural features of society more than life orientations. (198)

FILL-IN QUESTIONS

1. According to Max Weber, the three dimensions of social class are: (1)_____; (2)_____; and (3)_____. (178)
2. _____, which encompasses buildings, land, cars, stocks, and bank accounts, is a form of wealth. (178)
3. Money received as wages, rents, interest, royalties, or proceeds from a business are _____. (178)
4. According to C. Wright Mills, the _____ makes the big decisions in U.S. society. (181)
5. A person is considered to be _____ if he or she ranks high on some dimensions of social class and low on others. (183)
6. According to Erik Wright, a position in the class structure that generates conflicting interests is _____. (184)
7. According to Gilbert and Kahl, the capitalist class can be divided into two groups: (1) _____ and (2) _____. (185)
8. The _____ consists of a small group of people for whom poverty persists year after year and across generations. (187)
9. _____ is movement up the social class ladder. (191)
10. Movement up or down the social class ladder that is attributed to changes in the structure of society, not to individual efforts, is _____. (191)
11. The official measure of poverty is referred to as _____. (193)
12. _____ is a trend whereby most poor families in the U.S. are headed by women. (196)

13.   That the poor have values and beliefs that set them apart from the rest of society is the main argument of the _____ theory. (196)
14.   Foregoing something in the present in hope of achieving greater gains in the future is _____ . (199)
15.   The _____ is the belief that anyone can get ahead if only he or she tries hard enough. (201)

MATCH THESE SOCIAL SCIENTISTS WITH THEIR CONTRIBUTIONS

___1. Gerhard Lenski
___2. C. Wright Mills
___3. Erik Wright
___4. Dennis Gilbert & Joseph Kahl
___5. William Domhoff
___6. Elliot Liebow
___7. Daniel J. Moynihan
___8. Oscar Lewis

a. *poverty and the breakdown of the U.S. family*
b. *power elite*
c. *status inconsistency*
d. *continued the tradition of C. Wright Mills*
e. *updated Marx's model*
f. *street corner men in Washington, D.C.*
g. *culture of poverty*
h. *updated Weber's model*

ESSAY QUESTIONS
1.   Explain why status inconsistency is often related to political radicalism.
2.   Discuss why you think women have been largely ignored in studies of mobility.
3.   Describe which groups are at greatest risk of poverty and then suggest ways in which poverty can be reduced by targeting these populations.

"DOWN-TO-EARTH SOCIOLOGY"

1.   Study Figure 8.3 on page 180. How could you explain the consistency of income distribution across the years to someone who is unfamiliar with U.S. society?
2.   Do you think it was right to deny Terry Takewell medical treatment because he was too poor to pay his medical bills (p. 187)? Is it right to relegate the poor mentally ill to state hospitals (p. 190)? What do these strategies suggest about our society's values?
3.   After reading about the Asian Indian immigrants (p. 193), what factors can you point to in trying to explain their different experiences in trying to secure a better life for themselves in this country?
4.   Were you surprised at the reality of poverty lying behind the myths (p. 194)? Why do such myths persist?
5.   After reading "Children in Poverty" on page 197, think about the following questions: Is child poverty a concern only for the poor or is it a concern for everyone in society? What steps do you think should be taken to relieve the problem? Where would the money come from to implement your plans?
6.   In your own mind, do you make a distinction between the deserving poor and the undeserving poor (p. 199)? What functions do such distinctions serve?

CHAPTER 9
INEQUALITIES OF RACE AND ETHNICITY

CHAPTER SUMMARY

- Race is a complex and often misunderstood concept. Race is a reality in the sense that inherited physical characteristics distinguish one group from another. However, race is a myth in the sense of one race being superior to another and of there being pure races. The *idea* of race is powerful, shaping basic relationships between people. An ethnic group is a group of people who identify with one another on the basis of common ancestry and cultural heritage. A minority group is defined as one singled out for unequal treatment by members of the dominant group, the group with more power, privilege and social status. Minorities originate with migration and the expansion of political boundaries.

- The extent of ethnic identification depends upon the relative size of the group, its power, broad physical characteristics, and the amount of discrimination. Ethnic work, ranging from efforts to enhance and maintain the group's distinctions to attempts to recover one's heritage, is the process of constructing an ethnic identity.

- Prejudice is an attitude and discrimination is unfair treatment.

- Individual discrimination is the negative treatment of one person by another, while institutional discrimination is discrimination built into society's social institutions.

- Psychological theories explain the origin of prejudice in terms of stress frustration that gets directed towards scapegoats and in terms of the development of authoritarian personalities. Sociologists emphasize how different social environments affect levels of prejudice. They look at the benefits and costs of discrimination, the exploitation of racial-ethnic divisions by those in power, and the self-fulfilling prophecies that are the outcome of labeling.

- Dominant groups typically practice one of five policies toward minority groups: genocide, population transfer, internal colonialism, segregation, assimilation, and multiculturalism.

- From largest to smallest, the major ethnic groups are European Americans, African Americans, Latinos, Asian Americans, and Native Americans.

- While each minority group in the United States has had different experiences, they are all familiar with discrimination. African Americans are increasingly divided into middle and lower classes; Latinos are divided by country of origin; Asian Americans are better off than whites, but their well-being varies by country of origin; Native Americans are concerned with poverty, nationhood, and the settlement of treaty obligations. For all minorities, the overarching issue is overcoming discrimination.

- Today the main issues related to racial/ethnic relations are immigration, affirmative action, and how to develop a true multicultural society.

LEARNING OBJECTIVES
As you read Chapter 9, use these learning objectives to organize your notes. After completing your reading, briefly state an answer to each of the objectives, and review the text pages in parentheses.

1.   Explain how race is defined and how it can be both a reality and a myth. (206-209)
2.   Define ethnicity and explain what an ethnic group is. (209-210)
3.   Define the terms "minority group" and "dominant group" and explain the factors that affect the emergence of minority groups within a society. (209-210)

4.   Outline the factors that heighten or reduce a sense of ethnic identity and explain how the level of ethnic identity contributes to differences in ethnic work. (210-211)
5.   Differentiate between prejudice and discrimination and explain the extent of prejudice among racial and ethnic groups. (210-213)
6.   Compare and contrast individual and institutional discrimination and give examples of each type of discrimination. (213-215)
7.   Compare psychological and sociological perspectives on prejudice. Indicate why sociologists believe psychological explanations are inadequate. (215-217)
8.   List and describe the six patterns of intergroup relations. (217-220)
9.   Discuss the status of White Anglo-Saxon Protestants (WASPs) as a dominant group and, given this, relate the assimilation experiences of white ethnics in the United States. (221-222)
10.   Outline the history of the African American experience in the United States, discussing both the gains and setbacks African Americans have made since the Civil Rights Movement. (222-224)
11.   Summarize the current debate over the importance of race and social class. (225)
12.   Compare and contrast the experiences of different segments of the Latino community, including divisions within each of these broad ethnic groups. (226-227)
13.   Discuss the factors that have contributed to successes within the Asian American community and explain why, despite the successes, Asian Americans should not be viewed as a single group. (227-229)
14.   Describe the treatment of Native Americans and explain why they can be considered an invisible minority. (229-232)
15.   Identify some of the issues related to racial/ethnic relations that are facing the United States today. (232-234)

CHAPTER OUTLINE

I.   **Laying the Sociological Foundation**
      A.   Race is a reality in the sense that humans come in different colors and shapes; however, two myths regarding race are that one race is superior to another, and that a pure race exists. These myths make a difference for social life because people believe they are real and they act on their beliefs.
      B.   Race and ethnicity are often confused due to the cultural differences people see and the way they define race. Ethnicity refers to cultural characteristics that distinguish a people.
      C.   Minority groups are people singled out for unequal treatment and who regard themselves as objects of collective discrimination.
            1.   Shared characteristics of minorities worldwide: the physical or cultural traits that distinguish them are held in low esteem by the dominant group; they are unequally treated by the dominant group; they tend to marry within their own group; and they tend to feel strong group solidarity.
            2.   They are not necessarily in the numerical minority. Sociologists refer to those who do the discriminating as the dominant group--they have greater power, more privileges, and higher social status. The dominant group attributes its privileged position to its superiority, not to discrimination.
            3.   A group becomes a minority through expansion of political boundaries by another group. Another way for group to become a minority is by migration into a territory, either voluntarily or involuntarily.

II.   How People Construct a Racial-Ethnic Identity
   A.   Some people feel an intense sense of ethnic identity while others feel very little.
      1.   An individual's sense of ethnic identity is influenced by the relative size and power of the ethnic group, its appearance, and the level of discrimination aimed at the group.   If a group is relatively small, has little power, has a distinctive appearance, and is an object of discrimination, its members will have a heightened sense of ethnic identity.
      2.   Ethnic work refers to how ethnicity is constructed and includes enhancing and maintaining a group's distinctiveness or attempting to recover ethnic heritage. The idea that the U.S. is a melting pot, with the many different groups quietly blending together into an ethnic stew is undermined by the fact that so many people today are engaged in ethnic work; a better metaphor would be "tossed salad" or "ethnic mosaic."
   B.   Prejudice and discrimination are common throughout the world.
      1.   Discrimination is unfair treatment directed toward someone. When based on race, it is known as racism. It also can be based on features such as age, sex, sexual preference, religion, or politics.
      2.   Prejudice is prejudging of some sort, usually in a negative way.
      3.   Ethnocentrism is so common that each racial/ethnic group views other groups as inferior in at least some way. Studies confirm that there is less prejudice among the more educated and among younger people.
   C.   Sociologists distinguish between individual and institutional discrimination.
      1.   Individual discrimination (negative treatment of one person by another) is too limited a perspective because it focuses only on one individual treating another badly.
      2.   Institutional discrimination (negative treatment of a minority group that is built into a society's institutions) focuses on human behavior at the group level. Examples include certain mortgage lending and health care.

III.   Theories of Prejudice
   A.   Psychological Perspectives
      1.   According to John Dollard, prejudice results from frustration: people unable to strike out at the real source of their frustration find scapegoats to unfairly blame.
      2.   According to Theodor Adorno, highly prejudiced people are characterized by excess conformity, intolerance, insecurity, respect for authority, and submission to superiors; he called this complex of personality traits the authoritarian personality. Subsequent studies have generally concluded that people who are older, less educated, less intelligent and from a lower social class are more likely to be authoritarian.
   B.   Sociological Perspectives
      1.   To functionalists, the social environment can be deliberately arranged to generate either positive or negative feelings about people. Prejudice can be a product of pitting group against group in an "I win/you lose" situation. Prejudice is functional in that it creates in-group solidarity and out-group antagonism. It is dysfunctional in that it destroys social relationships and intensifies conflict.
      2.   To conflict theorists, the ruling class benefits because it systematically pits group against group by: (1) creating a split labor market, dividing workers along racial ethnic lines and weakening solidarity among the workers; and (2) maintaining

higher unemployment rates for minorities, creating a reserve labor force from which owners can draw when they need to expand production temporarily. Workers from different racial and ethnic groups learn to fear and distrust one another, instead of recognizing common class interests and working for their mutual benefit.

3.   To symbolic interactionists, the labels people learn color their perception, leading people to see certain things and be blind to others. Racial and ethnic labels are especially powerful because they are shorthand for emotionally laden stereotypes. These stereotypes that we learn not only justify prejudice and discrimination, but they also lead to a self-fulfilling prophecy, stereotypical behavior in those who are stereotyped.

IV.   Global Patterns of Intergroup Relations

A.   Genocide in the actual or attempted systematic annihilation of a race or ethnic group who has been labeled as less than fully human by the dominant group. Dehumanizing labels are powerful forces that help people to compartmentalize--separate their acts from any feelings that would threaten their self-concept, thereby making it difficult for them to participate in the act. The Holocaust and the treatment of Native Americans are examples.

B.   Population transfer is involuntary movement of a minority group. Indirect transfer involves making life so unbearable that members of a minority then leave; direct transfer involves forced expulsion. A combination of genocide and population transfer occurred in Bosnia, part of the former Yugoslavia, as Serbs engaged in ethnic cleansing, the wholesale slaughter of Muslims and Croats, with survivors forced to flee the area.

C.   Internal colonialism is a society's policy of exploiting a minority by using social institutions to deny it access to full benefits. Slavery is an extreme example.

D.   Segregation, the formal separation of groups, often accompanies internal colonialism. It allows the dominant group to exploit the labor of the minority while maintaining social distance.

E.   Assimilation is the process by which a minority is absorbed into the mainstream. Forced assimilation occurs when the dominant group prohibits the minority from using its own religion, language, customs. Permissive assimilation is when the minority adopts the dominant group's patterns in its own way/at its own speed.

F.   Multiculturalism (pluralism) permits or encourages racial and ethnic variation. Switzerland provides an outstanding example of this.

V.   Race and Ethnic Relations in the United States

A.   The major racial/ethnic groups in the U.S. are European Americans, African Americans, Latinos, Asian Americans, and Native Americans.

B.   In the United States, the dominant group is made up of whites whose ancestors immigrated here from European countries.

1.   White Anglo-Saxon Protestants (WASPs) were highly ethnocentric and viewed white ethnics--the Irish, Germans, Poles, Jews, and Italians--as inferior.

2.   Immigrants were expected to blend into the mainstream, speaking English and adopt the dominant group's way of life. It was the grandchildren of the immigrants, the third generation, who most easily adjusted. As these white ethnics assimilated into Anglo culture, the meaning of WASP was expanded to include them.

3.   Because the English settled in the colonies, they established institutions to which later immigrants had to conform.

C.   African Americans face a legacy of racism.
1.   In 1955, African Americans in Montgomery, Alabama, using nonviolent tactics advocated by Martin Luther King, Jr., protested laws believed to be unjust. This led to the civil rights movement that challenged existing patterns of racial segregation throughout the south.
2.   The 1964 Civil Rights Act (banning discrimination in public facilities) and 1965 Voting Rights Act (banning literacy tests) heightened expectations. Frustration over the slow pace of change led to urban riots and passage of the 1968 Civil Rights Act.
3.   Since then, African Americans have made political and economic progress. For example, African Americans have quadrupled their membership in the U.S. House of Representatives in the past 25 years. As college enrollment continues to increase the middle class has expanded so that now one of every five African American families makes more than $50,000 annually. African Americans such as Jesse Jackson, Douglas Wilder, and Clarence Thomas have gained political prominence.
4.   Despite these gains, however, African Americans continue to lag behind in politics, economics, and education. Only one U.S. senator is African American; African Americans average 60 percent of whites' incomes; only 14 percent of African Americans graduate from college. About one of every five African American families makes less than $10,000 annually
5.   According to William Wilson social class (not race) is the major determinant of quality of life. The African American community today is divided into two groups, the outcome of civil rights legislation that opened new opportunities. Middle-class African Americans seized them and advanced economically, moving out of the inner city; they have moved up the class ladder, live in good housing, have well-paid jobs, and send their children to good schools. However, as opportunities for unskilled labor declined, a large group of poorly educated and unskilled African Americans were left behind; they still live in poverty, face violent crime and dead-end jobs, attend terrible schools, and live in hopelessness and despair.
6.   Charles Willie challenges this, arguing that discrimination on the basis of race persists, despite gains made by some African Americans.
7.   It is likely that both discrimination and social class contribute to the African American experience.
D.   Latinos are the second largest ethnic group in the United States, and include Chicanos, Puerto Ricans, Cuban Americans, and people from Central or South America. Concentrated in four states (California, Texas, New York, and Florida), they are causing major demographic shifts.
1.   The Spanish language distinguishes them from other minorities: perhaps half are unable to speak English without difficulty. This is a major obstacle to getting well-paid jobs.
2.   Divisions based on social class and country of origin prevent political unity.
3.   Compared with non-Hispanic whites and Asian Americans, Latinos are worse off on all indicators of well-being. The country of origin is significant, with Cuban Americans scoring much higher on indicators of well being and Puerto-Rican Americans scoring the lowest.

E.   Asian Americans have long faced discrimination in the United States.

    1.   The history of Asian Americans is one of discrimination and prejudice. Chinese Americans frequently were victims of vigilante groups and anti-Chinese legislation. After the attack on Pearl Harbor in World War II, hostilities towards Japanese Americans increased, with many being imprisoned in "relocation camps."

    2.   When immigrants from Japan began to arrive they experienced "spillover bigotry," a stereotype that lumped all Asians together, depicting them as sneaking, lazy and untrustworthy.

    3.   Today Asian Americans are the fastest growing minority in the U.S. They are a diverse group divided by separate cultures. Although there are variations in income among Asian American groups, on the average Asian Americans have been extremely successful. This success can be traced to four factors: (1) a close family life; (2) a supportive community; (3) educational achievement; and (4) assimilation into the mainstream.

    4.   Recent immigration has been mainly from Vietnam. Despite initial problems of settlement, these immigrants have adjusted well.

F.   Due to the influence of old movie westerns, many Americans tend to hold stereotypes of Native Americans as uncivilized savages, as a single group of people subdivided into separate bands.

    1.   In reality, however, Native Americans represent a diverse group of people with a variety of cultures and languages. Although originally numbering 5 million, their numbers were reduced to a low of 500,000 at the beginning of the 20th century, due to a lack of immunity to European diseases and warfare. Today there are about 2 million Native Americans.

    2.   At first, relations between European settlers and the Native Americans were peaceful. However, as the number of settlers increased, tension increased. Because they stood in the way of expansion, many were slaughtered. Government policy shifted to population transfer, with Native Americans confined to reservations.

    3.   Today, they are an invisible minority. Almost half live in rural areas, with one-third concentrated in Oklahoma, California, and Arizona; most other Americans are hardly aware of them. They have the highest rates of poverty, unemployment, suicide, and alcoholism of any U. S. minority . These negative conditions are the result of Anglo domination.

    4.   In the 1960's Native Americans won a series of legal victories that restored their control over the land and their right to determine economic policy. Many Native Americans have opened businesses on their land, ranging from industrial parks to casinos.

    5.   Many tribes maintain the right to remain separate from the U.S. government and U.S. society; this separatism is a highly controversial issue.

    6.   Today many Native Americans are interested in recovering and honoring their own traditions. Pan-Indianism is an emphasis on common elements that run through Native American cultures in an attempt to develop self-identification that goes beyond any particular tribe.

VI.   Looking toward the Future

A.   As U.S. society moves toward the 21st century, two issues that will have to be resolved are immigration and affirmative action.

B.   Immigration and the fear of its consequences are central to U.S. history.

    1.   The first great wave of immigrants arrived from Europe at the end of the 19th and beginning of the 20th centuries. The second wave, since 1980, has brought immigrants from around the world and is contributing to the changing U.S. racial/ethnic mix.

    2.   In some states, such as California, minorities combined are expected to soon represent the majority of the population.

    3.   Many are concerned that this influx of immigrants will change the character of U.S. society, including the primacy of the English language.

C.   Affirmative action is at the core of the national debate about how to steer a course in race and ethnic relations.

    1.   Some see affirmative action as the most direct way to level the playing field of economic opportunity, while others say that such policies result in reverse discrimination.

    2.   Several controversial rulings suggest that there is still no consensus about the proper role of affirmative action in a multicultural society.

D.   In order to achieve a multicultural society in which different racial/ethnic groups not only co-exist but actually respect one another will require that groups with different histories and cultures learn to accept one another. We must begin to examine our history and question many of the assumptions and symbols.

KEY TERMS

After studying the chapter, review each of the following terms.

assimilation: the process of being absorbed into the mainstream culture (220)

authoritarian personality: Theodor Adorno's term for people who are prejudiced and rank high on scales of conformity, intolerance, insecurity, respect for authority, and submissiveness to superiors (216)

Chicanos: Latinos whose country of origin is Mexico (226)

compartmentalize: to separate acts from feelings or attitudes (219)

discrimination: an act of unfair treatment directed against an individual or a group (211)

dominant group: the group with the most power, greatest privileges, and highest social status (209)

ethnic cleansing: a policy of population elimination, including forcible expulsion and genocide (219)

ethnicity (and ethnic): having distinctive cultural characteristics (209)

ethnic work: activities designed to discover, enhance, or maintain ethnic/racial identification (211)

genocide: the systematic annihilation or attempted annihilation of a race or ethnic group (217)

individual discrimination: the negative treatment of one person by another on the basis of that person's perceived characteristics (213)

institutional discrimination: negative treatment of a minority group that is built into a society's institutions (214)

internal colonialism: the systematic economic exploitation of a minority group (220)

melting pot: the idea that Americans of various backgrounds would melt (or merge), leaving behind their distinctive previous ethnic identities and forming a new ethnic group (211)

minority group: people who are singled out for unequal treatment on the basis of their physical and cultural characteristics, and who regard themselves as objects of collective discrimination (209)

multiculturalism (also called pluralism): a policy that permits or encourages groups to express their individual, unique racial and ethnic identities (220)

pan-Indianism: the emphasis on the common elements in Native American culture in order to develop a mutual self-identity and to work toward the welfare of all Native Americans (231)

population transfer: involuntary movement of a minority group (219)

prejudice: an attitude or prejudging, usually in a negative way (211)

race: inherited physical characteristics that distinguish one group from another (206)

racism: prejudice and discrimination on the basis of race (211)

reserve labor force: the term used by conflict theorists for the unemployed, who can be put to work during times of high production and then discarded when no longer needed (217)

rising expectations: the sense that better conditions are soon to follow, which, if unfulfilled, creates mounting frustration (223)

scapegoat: an individual or group unfairly blamed for someone else's troubles (215)

segregation: the policy of keeping racial or ethnic groups apart (220)

selective perception: seeing certain features of an object or situation but remaining blind to others (217)

split-labor market: a term used by conflict theorists for the practice of weakening the bargaining power of workers by splitting them along racial, ethnic, sex, age, or any other lines (216)

WASP: a white Anglo-Saxon Protestant; narrowly, an American of English descent; broadly, an American of western European ancestry (221)

white ethnics: white immigrants to the United States whose culture differs from that of WASPs (221)

KEY PEOPLE

State the major theoretical contributions or research findings of these people.

Theodor Adorno: Adorno identified the authoritarian personality type. (215)

Lawrence Bobo and James Kluegel: In their research, these sociologists found that prejudice varied by age and educational level. (212)

Emery Cowen, Judah Landes and Donald Schaet: In an experiment, these psychologists found that students directed frustrations onto people who had nothing to do with their problem. (215)

Ashley Doane: Doane identified four factors that affect an individual's sense of ethnic identity. (210)

John Dollard: This psychologist first suggested that prejudice is the result of frustration and scapegoats become the targets for people's frustrations. (215)

Raphael Ezekiel: This sociologist did participant observation of neo-Nazis and the Ku Klux Klan in order to examine racism from inside racist organizations. (218)

Eugene Hartley: This psychologist is known for his work on prejudice. He found that people who are prejudiced against one racial or ethnic group tend to be prejudiced against others and that prejudice is not necessarily based on personal negative experiences. (215)

Marie Krysan and Reynolds Farley: In a random sample of people in Detroit, these researchers found that both whites and African Americans judged Latinos as less intelligent than themselves. (212)

Ashley Montagu: This physical anthropologist pointed out that some scientists have classified humans into two races while others have identifed as many as two thousand. (208)

Donald Muir: Muir measured racial attitudes of white students who belonged to fraternities and sororities and compared them to nonmembers. (213)

Alejandro Portes and Rueben Rumbaut: These sociologists looked at the impact that immigration has had on our country, pointing out that there has always been an anti-immigrant sentiment present. (232)

Muzafer & Carolyn Sherif: The Sherifs researched the functions of prejudice and found that it builds in-group solidarity. (216)

George Simpson and Milton Yinger: These men wrote about the nature of selective perception. (217)

Charles Willie: Willie has criticized William Wilson's work, arguing that race is still an important criterion for discrimination. (225)

William Wilson: Wilson is known for his work on racial discrimination, in which he argues that class is a more important factor than race in explaining patterns of inequality. (225)

Louis Wirth: Wirth offered a sociological definition of minority group. (209)

SELF-TEST

After completing this self-test, check your answers against the Answer Key beginning on page 251 of this Study Guide and against the text on page(s) indicated in parentheses.

MULTIPLE CHOICE QUESTIONS

1. Race: (206)
   a. means having distinctive cultural characteristics.
   b. means having inherited physical characteristics that distinguish one group from another.
   c. means people who are singled out for unequal treatment.
   d. is relatively easy to determine.

2. A minority group: (209)
   a. is discriminated against because of physical or cultural differences.
   b. is discriminated against because of personality factors.
   c. does not always experience discrimination.
   d. All of the above.

3. The dominant group in a society almost always considers its position to be due to: (209)
   a. its own innate superiority.
   b. its ability to oppress minority group members.
   c. its ability to control political power.
   d. All of the above.

4. Which of the following statements about the emergence of minority groups is <u>incorrect</u>? (210)
   a. A minority group is produced when a group expands its political boundaries and incorporates people with different customs, languages, values, and physical characteristics.
   b. A minority group emerges whenever a particular racial or ethnic group constitutes a smaller portion (a minority) of a society's overall population.
   c. A minority group is produced through the voluntary migration of millions of people from one country to another.
   d. A minority group emerges when millions of people are forcibly transported from one society to another.

5. Which of the following is <u>not</u> a factors influencing the sense of ethnic identity? (210)
   a. size of the ethnic group
   b. power of the ethnic group
   c. experiences with discrimination
   d. education

6.   Activities like tracing family lines or preserving food, language and holidays are considered: (211)
        a.   the melting pot.
        b.   ethnic work.
        c.   forced assimilation.
        d.   one's heritage.

7.   Prejudice and discrimination: (211)
        a.   are less prevalent in the United States than in other societies.
        b.   are more prevalent in the United States than in other societies.
        c.   appear to characterize every society.
        d.   appear to characterize only large societies.

8.   Prejudice: (211)
        a.   is an attitude.
        b.   may be positive or negative.
        c.   often is the basis for discrimination.
        d.   All of the above.

9.   The negative treatment of one person by another on the basis of personal characteristics is: (213)
        a.   individual discrimination.
        b.   individual prejudice.
        c.   institutional discrimination.
        d.   institutional prejudice.

10.   As compared with a white baby, an African American baby: (215)
        a.   has a better chance of surviving infancy.
        b.   has the same chance of surviving infancy.
        c.   has a slightly higher chance of dying in infancy.
        d.   has twice the chance of dying in infancy.

11.   The idea that prejudice is the result of frustration was suggested by: (215)
        a.   John Dollard.
        b.   Theodor Adorno.
        c.   Muzafer and Carolyn Sherif.
        d.   George Simpson and Milton Yinger.

12.   An experiment conducted by Muzafer and Carolyn Serif demonstrated that: (216)
        a.   prejudice is learned early in life and cannot be altered.
        b.   prejudice helps to relieve feelings of inferiority and insecurity.
        c.   prejudice is functional and shaped by the social environment.
        d.   prejudice is a deliberate strategy followed by the dominant group against minorities.

13.   According to conflict theorists, prejudice: (216-217)
        a.   benefits capitalists by splitting workers along racial or ethnic lines.
        b.   contributes to the exploitation of workers by producing a split-labor market.
        c.   keeps workers from demanding higher wages and better working conditions.
        d.   All of the above.

14.   _____ refers to the unemployed whose employment depends upon market forces. (217)
   a.   reserve labor force.
   b.   secondary labor force.
   c.   split-labor market.
   d.   the underclass.

15.   Symbolic interactionists stress that prejudiced people: (217)
   a.   are born that way.
   b.   have certain types of personalities.
   c.   learn their prejudices in interaction with others.
   d.   None of the above.

16.   Genocide: (217-219)
   a.   occurred when Hitler attempted to destroy all Jews.
   b.   is the systematic annihilation of a race or ethnic group.
   c.   often requires the cooperation of ordinary citizens.
   d.   All of the above.

17.   When a minority is expelled from a country or one area of a country, the process is called: (219)
   a.   population redistribution.
   b.   direct population transfer.
   c.   indirect population transfer.
   d.   expelled population transfer.

18.   _____ is the use of social institutions to deny minorities access to full social benefits. (220)
   a.   Segregation
   b.   Pluralism
   c.   Internal colonialism
   d.   Genocide

19.   The process of being absorbed into the mainstream culture is: (220)
   a.   pluralism.
   b.   assimilation.
   c.   cultural submersion.
   d.   internal colonialism.

20.   Following the passage of the Civil Rights Act in 1964 and the Voting Rights Act in 1965, many African Americans experienced: (223)
   a.   significantly improved economic opportunities.
   b.   rising expectations about improved social, economic and political conditions.
   c.   sharp gains in political power.
   d.   affirmative action recruitment to colleges and universities.

21. According to _____, social class--not race--is the major determinant of the quality of life for African Americans in the United States today. (225)
    a. Gordon Allport
    b. William Wilson
    c. John Dollard
    d. Robert Merton

22. According to your text, Latinos are distinguished from other ethnic minorities in the United States by: (226)
    a. the Spanish language.
    b. the fact that virtually all Latinos entered the United States illegally.
    c. the length of time Latinos have been in the United States.
    d. All of the above.

23. Today, the fastest-growing minority in the U.S. is: (228)
    a. African Americans.
    b. Asian Americans.
    c. Latinos.
    d. Native Americans.

24. Of all American minorities, the worst off are: (230)
    a. African Americans.
    b. Asian Americans.
    c. Latinos.
    d. Native Americans.

25. The backlash currently directed against immigrants is due to: (232)
    a. concerns that immigrants will undermine social institutions and contribute to social decay.
    b. anxiety that immigrants will take jobs away from native workers.
    c. fears that immigrants will gain political power at the expense of other groups.
    d. All of the above.

TRUE-FALSE QUESTIONS

T F 1. In some societies a "pure" race exists. (207)
T F 2. Sociologists often use the terms race and ethnicity interchangeably. (209)
T F 3. Physical or cultural differences can be a basis of unequal treatment in societies. (209)
T F 4. A group must represent a numerical minority to be considered a minority group. (209)
T F 5. Certain characteristics are shared by minorities worldwide. (209)
T F 6. Minorities often have a shared sense of identity and of common destiny. (209)
T F 7. After the United States defeated Mexico in war and annexed the Southwest, the Mexicans living there were transformed into the dominant group, because they were the majority ethnic group. (209)
T F 8. Sociologists believe that individual discrimination is an adequate explanation for discrimination in the U.S. (213)
T F 9. Research shows that African Americans and Latinos are 60 percent more likely than whites to be rejected for mortgages, all other factors being similar. (214)

T F   10.   People who are prejudiced against one racial or ethnic group are likely to be prejudiced against other groups. (215)

T F   11.   Persons with an authoritarian personality are characterized by prejudice and high rankings on scales of conformity, intolerance, insecurity, and excessive respect for authority. (215-216)

T F   12.   The Sherif study demonstrates that the social environment can be deliberately arranged to generate either positive or negative feelings about people. (216)

T F   13.   Functionalists focus on the role of the capitalist class in exploiting racism and ethnic inequalities. (216)

T F   14.   Symbolic interactionists stress that prejudice is learned through social interaction. (217)

T F   15.   Genocide often relies on labeling and compartmentalization. (219)

T F   16.   Segregation allows the dominant group to exploit the labor of the minority while maintaining social distance. (220)

T F   17.   African Americans today have made such significant gains that they have achieved parity with whites with respect to most aspects of social life. (223-224)

T F   18.   Social class and national origin are major obstacles to Latino political unity. (227)

T F   19.   When the Japanese arrived in the United States they experienced spillover bigotry. (228)

T F   20.   It is accurate to describe the experiences of Native Americans as ranging from genocide to population transfer. (229-232)

FILL-IN QUESTIONS

1.   _____ is inherited physical characteristics that distinguish one group from another. (206)

2.   The systematic annihilation or attempted annihilation of a race or ethnic group is _____ . (207)

3.   Activities designed to discover, enhance, or maintain ethnic and racial identity are called _____ . (211)

4.   _____ is discrimination on the basis of race. (211)

5.   _____ discrimination is the negative treatment of a minority group that is built into a society's institutions. (214)

6.   Theodor Adorno's term for people who are prejudiced and rank high on scales of conformity, intolerance, insecurity, respect for authority, and submissiveness to superiors is _____ . (216)

7.   _____ theorists believe that prejudice can be both functional and dysfunctional. (216)

8.   Split-labor market is used by _____ theorists to explain how the racial and ethnic strife can be used to pit workers against one another. (216)

9.   The term used to describe the unemployed who can be put to work during times of high production and then discarded when no longer needed is _____ . (217)

10.   _____ is the ability to see certain points but remain blind to others. (217)

11.   The types of population transfer are: (1) _____ and (2) _____ . (219)

12.   The policy of forced expulsion and genocide is referred to as _____ . (219)

13.   _____ is the process of being absorbed into the mainstream culture. (220)

14.   In the period immediately following passage of the Civil Rights Act, many African Americans experienced _____ , a belief that better conditions were in sight. (223)

15.   Emphasizing the common elements that run through Native American cultures in the attempt to develop a self-identity that goes beyond the tribe is the goal of _____ . (231)

MATCH THESE SOCIAL SCIENTISTS WITH THEIR CONTRIBUTIONS

___1. Theodor Adorno   a. *measured racial attitudes of white students*
___2. Ashley Doane   b. *argues that class is more important than race in explaining inequality*
___3. John Dollard   c. *prejudice varies by age and educational level*
___4. Raphael Ezekiel   d. *identified the authoritarian personality type*
___5. Louis Wirth   e. *argues that race is still an important criterion for discrimination*
___6. Eugene Hartley   f. *identified four factors that affect an individual's sense of ethnic identity*
___7. Donald Muir   g. *suggested that prejudice is the result of frustration*
___8. William Wilson   h. *prejudice against one group leads to prejudice against other groups*
___9. Charles Willie   I. *offered a sociological definition of minority groups*
___10. Bobo & Kluegel   j. *studied racism in neo-Nazis and KKK organizations*

ESSAY QUESTIONS

1. Explain what the author means when he says that race is both a myth and a reality.
2. Explain how both psychological and sociological theories can be used together to gain a deeper understanding of prejudice and discrimination.
3. Using the experiences of different racial and ethnic groups in the U.S., identify and discuss the six patterns of intergroup relations.

"DOWN-TO-EARTH SOCIOLOGY"

1. Do you think that the census should include questions about race (p.208)? Is it important for the government to have such information?
2. What was the message that Henslin was trying to send in recounting his experiences in Barcelona (p. 210)? What could he have done differently? What does this story suggest to you about ethnic identity and inter-ethnic relations?
3. Read "Self-Segregation: Help or Hindrance for Race Relations on Campus" (p. 213). What are the arguments in favor of self-segregation? What are the arguments in opposition? Which argument do you find more compelling? Why?
4. After reading about "The Racist Mind" on page 218, why do you think the number of hate groups has been increasing? What changes in our society contribute to their emergence? How does Ezekiel's research findings fit with Adorno's concept of the authoritarian personality?
5. After reading about the Haitian experience with assimilation (p.221), why do you think it is more difficult for black immigrants than non-black immigrants to assimilate? Why or why not? Would the social class background of the immigrant make a difference?
6. Think back over history textbooks you read in school. Were they balanced in presenting the accomplishments of diverse groups? Why or why not? What new information about the history of U.S. race/ethnic relations did you learn from reading this chapter?

CHAPTER 10
INEQUALITIES OF GENDER AND AGE

CHAPTER SUMMARY

- Each society establishes a structure that, on the basis of sex and gender, permits or limits access to power, property, and prestige; this structure is referred to as gender stratification. Sex refers to biological distinctions between males and females; gender refers to what a society considers to be proper behaviors and attitudes for its males and females. In the "nature versus nurture" debate, almost all sociologists take the side of nurture.

- Male dominance, or patriarchy, appears to be universal. The primary theory about how women became a minority group in their own society focuses on the physical limitations imposed by childbirth.

- Although feminist movements in the United States have battled to eliminate some of the most blatant forms of gender discrimination, there are still many areas of inequality. More females than males now attend college, but both generally end up in gender-biased academic fields. There are signs of change, as indicated by the growing number of women in such fields as law and medicine.

- Over the course of this century women have made up an increasing proportion of the workforce. Women continue to face sexual harassment in the workplace and discrimination in pay.

- Women are generally the victims of battering, rape, incest, and murder; female circumcision is a special case of violence against women. According to conflict theory, men use violence against women to maintain their position of power.

- The traditional expectations associated with women's roles have kept them out of politics. Although still underrepresented, there is a trend toward greater political equality.

- As women's decision-making roles continue to expand, a reasonable goal is greater appreciation of differences combined with greater equality of opportunity.

- Attitudes, beliefs, and policies regarding the aged vary from one society to another; they range from exclusion and killing to integration and honor. The global trend is for people to live longer.

- The symbolic interaction perspective stresses the social construction of aging, emphasizing that age has no meaning in and of itself, but is given a meaning by society. Ageism is based on stereotypes which are influenced by the mass media.

- The functional perspective analyzes the withdrawal of the elderly from positions of responsibility. Disengagement and activity theories are two functional theories arising from research in this area.

- Conflict theorists study the competition for scarce resources by rival interest groups (e.g., how different age cohorts may be on a collision course regarding Social Security, Medicare, and Medicaid).

LEARNING OBJECTIVES

As you read Chapter 10, use these learning objectives to organize your notes. After completing your reading, briefly state an answer to each of the objectives, and review the text pages in parentheses.

1. Define gender stratification and differentiate between sex and gender. (240)
2. Discuss the continuing controversy regarding biological and cultural factors which come into play in creating gender differences in societies. (240-242)
3. Explain why women are considered to be a minority group and summarize the theory of how male dominance occurred. (242-244)

4. Describe the major factors which led to the rise of feminism in the United States and note how successful this movement has been up to this point in time. (244-245)
5. Discuss ways in which educational systems may perpetuate gender inequality. (245-246)
6. Identify some of the ways in which the field of health care reflects gender inequality. (246-247)
7. Explain gender relations in the workplace, including changes in the labor force participation rate that produced the quiet revolution, the pay gap, the "glass ceiling," the "glass escalator," and sexual harassment. (247-252)
8. Discuss the patterns of violence against women, explain why female circumcision is a special case of violence leveled against women, and summarize the feminist explanation. (252-255)
9. Explain why women historically have not taken over politics and transformed American life. (255-256)
10. Describe what the future looks like in terms of gender relations in the United States. (256)
11. Analyze the social factors in aging, using the Abkhasians' culture as an example. (257-258)
12. Discuss what effects industrialization has had on the aging process and identify factors involved in the "graying" of industrialized nations. (258-260)
13. Discuss the major conclusions drawn by symbolic interactionists regarding aging. (261-262)
14. Summarize the functional perspective on aging and explain disengagement theory and activity theory. (262-263)
15. Explain why conflict theorists see social life as a struggle between groups for scarce resources and note how this impacts different age cohorts. (263-266)

CHAPTER OUTLINE

INEQUALITIES OF GENDER
I. **Issues of Sex and Gender**
    A. Gender stratification refers to men's and women's unequal access to power, prestige, and property.
    B. Sex and gender reflect different bases.
        1. Sex is biological characteristics distinguishing males and females--primary sex organs (organs related to reproduction) and secondary sex organs (physical distinctions not related to reproduction).
        2. Gender is a social characteristic which varies from one society to another and refers to what the group considers proper for its males and females.
        3. The sociological significance of gender is that it serves as a primary sorting device by which society controls its members and thus is a structural feature of society.
    C. There is disagreement as to what produces gender differences in behavior.
        1. Some researchers argue that biological factors (two X chromosomes in females, one X and one Y in males) result in differences in the behavior of males (more aggressive and domineering) and females (more comforting and nurturing).
        2. The dominant sociological position is that gender differences result from sex being used to mark people for special treatment. Society interprets the physical differences; males and females then take the relative positions that society assigns to them.
    D. Alice Rossi suggested that women are better prepared biologically for "mothering" than are men; nature provides biological predispositions which are overlaid with culture. Medical accidents and studies such as the one involving Vietnam veterans suggest that the relationship between biology and social learning is a complex one.

II. **How Females became a Minority Group**
    A.   Around the world, gender is *the* primary division between people. Because society sets up barriers to deny women equal access, they are referred to as a minority even though they outnumber men.
    B.   Although the origin of patriarchy (male dominance) is unknown, one theory points to the social consequences of human reproduction.
        1.   As a result of pregnancy and breast-feeding, women were limited for much of their lives; they assumed tasks associated with the home and child care.
        2.   Men took over tasks requiring greater speed and longer absences, such as hunting animals. This enabled men to make contact with other tribes and to wage war; male prestige was the result of their accumulation of possessions through trade and war with other groups. Little prestige was given to women's routine tasks; they were not perceived as risking their lives for the group.
        3.   Eventually men took over society, using their weapons, their possessions, and their knowledge to guarantee that they held more social power than women.
    C.   There is no way to test this theory because answers lie buried in history. There may be many different causes, other than the biology of human reproduction.
        1.   Marvin Harris argued that in prehistoric times, each group was threatened with annihilation by other groups, and each had to recruit members to fight enemies in dangerous, hand-to-hand combat. Men (bigger and stronger) were coaxed into this bravery by promises of rewards--sexual access to females.
        2.   Frederick Engels suggested that male dominance developed in society with the emergence of private property.
        3.   Today, male dominance is a continuation of millennia-old patterns.

III. **Gender Inequality in the United States**
    A.   Women's rights resulted from a prolonged and bitter struggle.
        1.   U.S. women could not vote, hold property, or serve on a jury until this century. Males did not willingly surrender their privileges; but used social institutions to maintain their position.
        2.   Feminism, the view that biology is not destiny and that gender stratification is wrong and should be resisted, met with strong opposition.
        3.   The first wave of the women's movement had a radical branch, that wanted to reform all social institutions, and a conservative branch, that concentrated on winning the vote for women; the conservative branch dominated and the movement more or less disappeared after achieving suffrage.
        4.   The second wave began in the 1960s; its goals range from changing women's work roles to changing policies on violence against women.
        5.   While women enjoy more rights today, gender inequality still exists.
    B.   Despite evidence of educational gains made by women--more females than males are enrolled in U.S. colleges and universities and females earn 55 percent of all bachelor's degrees--some traditional male-female distinctions persist.
        1.   At college males and females are channeled into different fields; 90 percent of nursing degrees are awarded to females; 85 percent of engineering degrees are awarded to males.
        2.   The proportion of females decreases in post-graduate work.
        3.   There is gender stratification in both the rank and pay within higher educational institutions. Women are less likely to be in the higher ranks of academia, and at

all levels are paid less than their male counterparts.

4. Changes are taking place; the proportion of professional degrees earned by women has increased in recent years.

C. Researchers have found sex discrimination in the area of medicine and health care.

1. Physicians sometimes dismiss the complaints of female patients as not serious. This neglect could be a matter of life and death; one example is in the area of heart disease.

2. Physicians regard women's reproductive organs as "potentially disease producing" and largely unnecessary after childbearing years. They recommend removal.

3. Surgeons make money from the unnecessary removal of these organs.

D. There have been significant changes in the workforce, as the number of working women has increased. However, discrimination against women is still very visible.

1. In 1900, one in five workers was female; today it is almost one in two.

2. Sociologists refer to the continuing increase in the proportion of women in the workforce as a "quiet revolution." It has had profound effects on consumer patters, relations at work, self-concepts, and relationships with significant others.

3. Women who work full-time average only 66 percent of men are paid. Despite the level of educational achievement women earn less than men; this is true even when they have more qualifications that male counterparts. Half of this pay gap results from women entering lower-paying jobs.

4. One study found that, in their first jobs, women business majors at one university averaged 11 percent less annual starting salary than their male counterparts, even though they had higher grades and more internship experiences. Five years after graduation from college, the pay gap was even wider than it was upon entering the job market.

5. "Glass ceiling" describes an invisible barrier that women face in the work force. Men, who dominate the executive suites, stereotype potential leaders as people who look like themselves. Women lack mentors; male executives are reluctant to get close to female subordinates because they fear gossip and sexual harassment charges, or they believe that women are weak.

6. For men, employment in a non-traditional occupation (nursing, elementary school teaching, social work) meant increased job opportunities, more desirable work assignments, higher-level positions, and larger salaries. Christine Williams refers to this as the "glass escalator."

E. Until the 1970s, women did not draw a connection between unwanted sexual advances on the job and their subordinate positions at work.

1. As women began to discuss the problem, they named it and came to see unwanted sexual advances by men in powerful positions as a structural problem. The change resulted from reinterpreting women's experiences--giving them a name.

2. As more women move into positions of authority over men, the problem of sexual harassment is no longer exclusively a female problem.

F. Women are more likely to be victims of violence than men.

1. Every year in the U.S. 1 out of every 1,000 females aged 12 and older is raped; the typical rapist is under the age of 30.

2. Of increased concern today is the widespread incidence of date rape. Studies show that this occurs most commonly between couples who have known each other about one year; most go unreported.

3.   Males are more likely to commit murder than females; males commit 91 percent of the murders involving women victims.

4.   Women are also disproportionate victims of family violence--spouse battering, marital rape, and incest--and of genital circumcision.

5.   Feminists use symbolic interactionism to understand violence against women. They stress that U.S. culture promotes violence by males. It teaches men to associate power, dominance, strength, virility and superiority with masculinity. Men use violence to try and maintain a higher status.

6.   To solve violence we must first break the link between violence and masculinity, possibly through educational programs involving schools, churches, homes and the media.

IV.   The Changing Face of Politics

A.   Despite the gains U.S. women have made in recent elections, they continue to be underrepresented in political office, especially in higher office. There are different factors that contribute to this pattern.

1.   Women are still underrepresented in law and business, the careers from which most politicians are drawn.

2.   Women do not see themselves as a voting bloc who need political action to overcome discrimination.

3.   Women still find the roles of mother and politician incompatible.

4.   Males seldom incorporate women into the centers of decision making or present them as viable candidates.

B.   Trends in the 1990s indicate that women will participate in political life in far greater numbers than in the past.

C.   As women play a fuller role in society, further structural obstacles to women's participation in society will give way. Relationships between men and women will change and certain distinctions between the sexes will disappear. The goal will be a greater appreciation of sexual differences coupled with increased equality of opportunity.

INEQUALITIES OF AGING

V.   Aging in a Global Perspective

A.   Every society must deal with the process of people aging.

1.   In Abkhasia (a remote agricultural region in the former Soviet Union) the people commonly live to be 100, or even older. Possible reasons for their longevity include diet and eating customs (overeating is considered dangerous); lifelong physical activity (they don't begin to slow down until age 80); and social integration (active, valued, contributing members of the society, never isolated from family and community).

2.   This reveals an important sociological principle, that aging is socially constructed. Attitudes towards aging are rooted in society and therefore differ from one social group to the next.

B.   In industrialized nations, life expectancy increases because of a more plentiful food supply, safer water supply and the control of certain diseases.

1.   As the elderly population increases, so does the bill for meeting their particular needs; this has become a major social issues in the Most Industrialized Nations as the young face a growing tax burden to pay for benefits to the elderly.

2.   In the Least Industrialized Nations, there are no social security taxes and families are expected to take care of their own elderly.

C.   The graying of America refers to the proportion of older persons in the U.S. population. Almost 13 percent of the population has achieved age 65.

    1.   There are now 8 million more elderly Americans than teenagers.

    2.   The maximum length of life, the life span, has not increased.

VI.   The Symbolic Interactionist Perspective

A.   Robert Butler coined the term ageism to refer to prejudice, discrimination, and hostility directed at people because of their age.

B.   While in U.S. society today the general image of old age is negative, researchers have found that at one time, old age had more positive meanings.

    1.   Few made it to old age, so those who did were respected.

    2.   In the days before Social Security provided for retirement, the elderly worked and were seen as wise and knowledgeable about work skills.

    3.   Industrialization eroded traditional bases of respect. With improved sanitation and health care, living to an old age was no longer unique. The mystique that the elderly possessed superior knowledge was stripped away by mass education.

    4.   The aging baby boom generation, because of their size and their better financial standing, will very likely contribute to more positive symbols of aging.

VII.   The Functionalist Perspective

A.   Functionalists examine age from the standpoint of how those persons who are retiring and those who will replace them in the work force make mutual adjustments.

B.   Elaine Cumming and William Henry developed disengagement theory to explain how society prevents disruption to society when the elderly retire. The elderly are rewarded in some way (pensions) for giving up positions rather than wait until they become incompetent or die; this allows for a smooth transition of positions. It is criticized because it assumes that the elderly disengage and then sink into oblivion.

C.   Activity theory examines people's reactions to exchanging one set of roles for another. Older people who maintain a high level of activity tend to be more satisfied with life than those who do not. Level of activity is connected to key factors such as social class, health, and individual orientation.

VIII.   The Conflict Perspective

A.   Conflict theorists examine social life as a struggle between groups for scarce resources. Social Security legislation is an example of that struggle.

    1.   In the 1920s-30s, two-thirds of all citizens over 65 had no savings and could not support themselves. Francis Townsend enrolled one-third of all Americans over 65 in clubs that sought a national sales tax to finance a monthly pension for all Americans over age 65. To avoid the plan without appearing to be opposed to old-age pensions, Social Security was enacted by Congress.

    2.   Conflict theorists state that Social Security was not a result of generosity, but rather of competition among interest groups.

B.   Since equilibrium is only a temporary balancing of social forces, some form of continuing conflict between the younger and the older appears inevitable.

    1.   The huge costs of Social Security have become a national concern. The dependency ratio (number of workers compared with number of recipients) is currently five working-age Americans paying to support each person over 65. Meanwhile, other groups are organizing to fight the elderly for these resources.

    2.   Some argue that the elderly and children are on a collision course. Data indicate that as the number of elderly poor decreased, children in poverty increased. It has

been argued that the comparison is misleading because the money that went to the elderly did not come from money intended for the children. Framing the issue in this way is an attempt to divide the working class, and to force a choice between suffering children and suffering elderly.

KEY TERMS

After studying the chapter, review each of the following terms.

activity theory: the view that satisfaction during old age is related to a person's level and quality of activity (263)

age cohort: people born at roughly the same time who pass through the life course together (262)

ageism: prejudice, discrimination, and hostility directed against people because of their age; can be directed against any age group, including youth (261)

dependency ratio: the number of workers required to support one person on Social Security (265)

disengagement theory: the view that society prevents disruption by having the elderly vacate their positions of responsibility so that the younger generation can step into their shoes (262)

feminism: the philosophy that men and women should be politically, economically, and socially equal; organized activity on behalf of this principle (244)

gender: the social characteristics that a society considers proper for its males and females; masculinity and femininity (240)

gender stratification: males' and females' unequal access to power, prestige, and property on the basis of sex (240)

graying of America: older people making up an increasing proportion of the U.S. population (259)

life expectancy: the age to which people can expect to live (258)

life span: the maximum length of life (260)

patriarchy: a society in which authority is vested in males; control by men of a society or group (243)

quiet revolution: the fundamental changes in society that follow when vast numbers of women enter to work force (247)

sex: biological characteristics that distinguish females and males, consisting of primary and secondary sex characteristics (240)

sexual harassment: unwanted sexual advances, usually within an occupational or educational setting (252)

KEY PEOPLE

State the major theoretical contributions or research findings of these people.

Robert Butler: Butler coined the term "ageism" to refer to prejudice, discrimination and hostility directed against people because of their age. (261)

Elaine Cumming and William Henry: These two developed disengagement theory to explain how society prevents disruption when the elderly vacate their positions of responsibility. (262)

Janet Chafetz: Chafetz studied the second wave of feminism in the 1960s, noting that as large numbers of women began to work in the economy, they began to compare their working conditions with those of men. (244)

Frederick Engels: Engels was a colleague of Karl Marx and wrote a book about the origins of the family in which he argued that male dominance developed with the origin of private property. (243)

Sue Fisher: Fisher's participant observation in a hospital uncovered evidence of doctors' recommending unnecessary surgery for female patients. (246)

Rex Fuller and Richard Schoenberger: These economists examined the starting salaries of business majors and found that women averaged 11 percent lower pay than men right out of college, and that the gap grew to 14 percent after five years in the workforce. (251)

Marvin Harris: This anthropologist suggested that male dominance grew out of the greater strength that men had which made them better suited for the hand-to-hand combat of tribal societies; women became the reward to entice men into battle. (243)

Charles Hart: An anthropologist who did his field work during the 1920s among the Tiwi. (256)

Dorothy Jerrome: This anthropologist is critical of disengagement theory, pointing out that it contains implicit bias against old people. (263)

Gerda Lerner: While acknowledging that in all societies women--as a group--have never had decision-making power over men, Lerner suggested that patriarchy may have had different origins in different places around the globe. (243)

Meredith Minkler and Ann Robertson: These conflict sociologists investigated whether or not the government expenditures allocated for the elderly were at the expense of children and found there was no evidence of that. (265)

Alice Rossi: This feminist sociologist has suggested that women are better prepared biologically for "mothering" than are men. (241)

Felice Schwartz: Schwartz is the founder of Catalyst, an organization that focuses on women's issues in the workplace. (251)

Diana Scully: Scully did research on physicians' attitudes towards female patients. (247)

Christine Williams: Williams found that men in non-traditional careers and occupations often experience a glass escalator -- moving more quickly than women into desirable work assignments, higher-level positions, and larger salaries. (252)

SELF-TEST

After completing this self-test, check your answers against the Answer Key beginning on page 255 of this Study Guide and against the text on page(s) indicated in parentheses.

MULTIPLE CHOICE QUESTIONS

1. Gender stratification: (240)
    a.   cuts across all aspects of social life.
    b.   represents a primary division between people.
    c.   refers to men's and women's unequal access to power, prestige, and property on the basis of their sex.
    d.   All of the above.

2. The term "sex" refers to: (240)
    a.   the social characteristics that a society considers proper for its males and females.
    b.   the biological characteristics that distinguish females and males.
    c.   masculinity and femininity.
    d.   All of the above.

3. According to sociologists, if biology were the principal factor in human behavior, around the world we would find: (241)
    a.   things to be just like they are.
    b.   men and women to be much more like each other than they currently are.
    c.   women to be one sort of person and men another.
    d.   None of the above.

4.   In early hunting and gathering societies little prestige was accorded to the ordinary, routine, taken-for-granted activities of women. The author of the text suggests this is because: (243)
      a.   what women did was less important.
      b.   women didn't want to take away from the achievements of men.
      c.   women's contributions were not seen as crucial for social survival.
      d.   women were not seen as risking their lives for the group.

5.   Patriarchy: (243)
      a.   is a society in which men dominate women.
      b.   has existed throughout most of history.
      c.   is universal.
      d.   All of the above.

6.   Feminism is the view that: (244)
      a.   female traits are superior to male traits.
      b.   gender stratification is wrong and should by resisted.
      c.   females should have dominance over males.
      d.   All of the above

7.   Gender inequality in education: (245)
      a.   has virtually disappeared today.
      b.   is allowed by law.
      c.   is perpetuated by tracking students into different academic disciplines based on their sex.
      d.   None of the above.

8.   The increased number of women in the workforce is called the "quiet revolution" because: (247)
      a.   women are generally quieter than men.
      b.   the changes have been gradual, while the implications are profound.
      c.   most people aren't even aware of it, because their lives are not affected by it.
      d.   women have been employed in "quiet" occupations like clerical or nursing.

9.   The pay gap between men and women: (249)
      a.   is found primarily in jobs that require little education.
      b.   is found primary in the professional jobs requiring college or more.
      c.   is found in jobs that require little education as well as those that require a lot.
      d.   largely has disappeared in both low-skilled jobs and in the professions.

10.   According to researchers, what keeps women from breaking through the glass ceiling? (251)
      a.   a lack of self-confidence on the part of the women themselves
      b.   being "detoured" away from core positions from which executives are recruited
      c.   a lack of educational credentials
      d.   the burden of childcare responsibilities

11. The use of one's position to force unwanted sexual demands on someone is referred to as: (252)
    a. sexual harassment.
    b. sexual provocation.
    c. sexual maladjustment.
    d. sexual conquest.

12. Sexual harassment: (252)
    a. is still exclusively a female problem.
    b. has a clear legal definition based on Supreme Court rulings.
    c. involves a person in authority using the position to force unwanted sex on subordinates.
    d. All of the above.

13. The pattern of date rape shows: (253-254)
    a. that it is not an isolated event.
    b. that it is more likely to happen with couples who have dated for a period of time.
    c. that most date rapes go unreported.
    d. All of the above.

14. Women continue to be underrepresented in politics because: (256)
    a. they are not really interested in pursuing political careers.
    b. they are not viewed as serious candidates by the voters.
    c. their roles as mothers and wives are incompatible with political roles.
    d. they lack the proper educational backgrounds.

15. According to the author, which of the following is most likely to result in breaking the stereotypes that lock both males and females into traditional gender activities? (256)
    a. stricter laws
    b. equal pay
    c. increased female participation in the decision-making processes of social institutions
    d. increased male participation in nurturing activities

16. The Abkhasians are an interesting example regarding age because they: (258)
    a. live such short lives.
    b. live such long lives.
    c. have so many words in their language for "old people."
    d. quit working when they were quite young.

17. The principle that attitudes towards the aged are rooted in society and therefore differ from one social group to another is referred to as: (258)
    a. variability of aging.
    b. ageism.
    c. the social construction of aging.
    d. the aging principle.

18.   The increase in life expectancy in industrialized nations is due to: (258)
        a.   improvements in sanitation.
        b.   developments in medicine.
        c.   the control of deadly childhood diseases.
        d.   All of the above.

19.   The trend for older persons to make up a growing percentage of the U.S. population is the: (259)
        a.   the aging process.
        b.   the graying of America.
        c.   the gentrification process.
        d.   None of the above.

20.   Prior to industrialization, old people in U.S. society: (261)
        a.   were considered a burden.
        b.   were generally neglected by their families.
        c.   were viewed in a positive light, seen as wise and virtuous.
        d.   were not as productive as they are today.

21.   Researchers believe that the process of disengagement actually begins: (262)
        a.   when a person first starts a job.
        b.   during middle age.
        c.   at retirement.
        d.   about one year after retirement.

22.   _____ suggests that satisfaction in old age depends on one's level/quality of activity. (263)
        a.   activity theory.
        b.   recreational theory.
        c.   satisfaction theory.
        d.   None of the above.

23.   Conflict theorists believe that retirement benefits are the result of: (264)
        a.   generous hearts in Congress.
        b.   a struggle between competing interest groups.
        c.   many years of hard work by elderly Americans.
        d.   None of the above.

24.   The dependency ratio refers to: (265)
        a.   the number of dependents in a household relative to the number of working people.
        b.   the number of workers it takes to pay one person's Social Security.
        c.   the number of welfare recipients relative to employed workers.
        d.   the number of working women relative to non-working women.

25.   Trends over the past 30 years indicate that: (265)
        a.   the percentage of elderly who are poor has increased.
        b.   the percentage of elderly who are poor has decreased.
        c.   both childhood and elderly poverty has decreased.
        d.   elderly poverty has increased and childhood poverty has decreased.

TRUE-FALSE QUESTIONS

T F   1.   The terms sex and gender basically mean the same thing to sociologists. (240)

T F   2.   Sociologist Alice Rossi has argued that nature provides biological predispositions which are overlaid with culture. (241)

T F   3.   Women are considered to be a minority group because there are fewer women than men in the United States. (242)

T F   4.   Patriarchy is a society in which men dominate women. (243)

T F   5.   According to anthropologist Marvin Harris, females became the reward to encourage males to become a society's defenders and attackers. (243)

T F   6.   In the U.S. women's rights were gained by a prolonged and bitter struggle. (244)

T F   7.   While women outnumber men on college campuses today, they earn less than one-half of all bachelor's degrees. (245)

T F   8.   Researchers have found that physicians do not treat men and women equally when it comes to the diagnosis and treatment of heart disease. (246)

T F   9.   Today nearly one out of every two workers in the U.S. is a woman. (247)

T F   10.   The pay gap in men's and women's earnings is due almost entirely to women's lower educational levels. (250)

T F   11.   Women today who are employed in non-traditional occupations are finding new opportunities for advancement and higher pay, which sociologists refer to as the glass escalator. (252)

T F   12.   Once sexual harassment was defined as a problem, women saw some of their experiences in a different light. (252)

T F   13.   Both males and females are equally likely to be victims of violence. (252)

T F   14.   Feminists argue that female circumcision reflects the powerlessness of women in societies that are extremely male dominated. (255)

T F   15.   Women in the United States are still vastly underrepresented in political decision making. (256)

T F   16.   One reason why the Abkhasians live so long is because they retire while they are still young enough to enjoy life. (258)

T F   17.   Not all industrialized nations have the increase in life expectancy experienced in the United States. (258)

T F   18.   In the Least Industrialized Nations there are no social security taxes and families are expected to take care of their elderly. (258)

T F   19.   The dependency ratio is the number of workers required to support one person on Social Security. (265)

T F   20.   According to conflict theorists Meredith Minkler and Ann Robertson, the increase in child poverty has paralleled the decrease in elderly poverty is the result of shifting funds away from children and towards old people. (265)

FILL-IN QUESTIONS

1.   _____ refers to biological characteristics that distinguish females and males, consisting of primary and secondary sex characteristics. (240)

2.   Around the world, _____ is the primary division between people. (240)

3.   Frederick Engels proposed that _____ developed with the origin of private property. (243)

4. Patriarchy was attributed to warfare and physical strength by anthropologist _____. (243)
5. _____ is the philosophy that gender stratification is wrong and should be resisted. (244)
6. The _____ prevents women from advancing to top executive positions. (251)
7. Men in non-traditional jobs often ride the _____ to more desirable work assignments, higher-level positions, and larger salaries. (252)
8. _____ is a particular form of violence directed exclusively against women. (254)
9. The process by which older persons make up an increasing proportion of the United States population is called _____. (259)
10. The maximum length of life is referred to as the _____. (260)
11. _____ is the discrimination against people because of their age. (261)
12. People who are born at roughly the same time and who pass through the life course together are considered a(n) _____. (262)
13. The belief that society prevents disruption by having the elderly vacate their positions of responsibility is _____. (262)
14. _____ theory asserts that satisfaction during old age is related to a person's level and quality of activity. (263)
15. The number of workers it takes to pay one person's Social Security is a _____. (265)

MATCH THESE SOCIAL SCIENTISTS WITH THEIR CONTRIBUTIONS

___1. Janet Chafetz
___2. Alice Rossi
___3. Christine Williams
___4. Sue Fisher
___5. Felice Schwartz
___6. Robert Butler
___7. Dorothy Jerrome
___8. Cumming & Henry
___9. Robertson & Minkler
__10. Charles Hart

a. *men in non-traditional occupations often experience a glass escalator*
b. *founder of Catalyst*
c. *found no evidence that the elderly gained at children's expense*
d. *developed disengagement theory*
e. *documented physicians' practice of recommending unnecessary surgery*
f. *coined "ageism" to refer to prejudice or discrimination based on age*
g. *women are better prepared biologically for "mothering" than are men*
h. *studied the second wave of feminism in the 1960s*
I. *criticized disengagement theory for its implicit bias against the old*
j. *anthropological study of the Tiwi tribe*

ESSAY QUESTIONS

1. Summarize the sociobiology argument concerning behavioral differences between men and women. Explain which position most closely reflects your own -- biological, sociological, or sociobiological.

2. Compare and contrast the two waves of the feminist movement in this country by identifying the forces that contributed to both waves.

3. Choose one of the three different perspectives and discuss how that perspective approaches the subject of aging. Consider both the strengths and the weaknesses of the perspective you choose.

"DOWN-TO-EARTH SOCIOLOGY"

1.   What factors do you think were responsible for the break-up of Altagracia Ortiz's marriage (p. 249)? Could the couple have done anything differently in order to hold their marriage together? Where does the blame for the failure lie?

2.   On which side of the debate over women in the military would you place yourself (p. 253)? Can you think of any social structural factors that help to explain the pattern of sexual harassment? What changes, if any, would you recommend to address this issue?

3.   What was your reaction to the piece on female circumcision (pp. 254-255)? How is the purpose of this procedure fundamentally different from male circumcision? Do you think that international pressure should be applied to end this procedure? Why or why not?

4.   After reading about how some other cultures view their elderly, think again about our own society. What are some of the social factors that influence how different societies treat their elderly? Where would you like to live when you're old?

5.   What do you think should be the basis for making decisions about who receives the benefits of new medical technologies (p. 266)? Should it be based on the person's ability to pay? Or the contribution that person could make to society? Should it go to the young? or to the old?

CHAPTER 11
POLITICS AND THE ECONOMY:
LEADERSHIP AND WORK IN THE GLOBAL VILLAGE

CHAPTER SUMMARY

- Authority refers to the legitimate use of power, while coercion is viewed as unjust. The state is a political entity that claims a monopoly on violence over a particular territory. Max Weber identified three types of authority--traditional, rational-legal, and charismatic. The orderly transfer of authority at the death, resignation, or incapacitation of a leader is critical for social stability.

- Three forms of government are monarchies (power is based on hereditary rule), democracies (power is given by the citizens), and dictatorships (power is seized by an individual or a small group).

- In the United States, with its winner-takes-all electoral system, the two main political parties must appeal to the center, and minority parties make little headway. The more people feel they have a stake in the political system, the more likely they are to vote. Special interest groups, with their lobbyists and PACs, play a significant role in U.S. politics.

- Functionalists and conflict theorists have very different views on who rules the United States. According to the functionalists, no one group holds power; the outcome is that the competing interest groups balance one another (pluralism). According to conflict theorists, the United States is governed by a ruling class made up of members drawn from the elite (power elite).

- The earliest hunting and gathering societies were characterized by subsistence economies; economic systems became more complex as people discovered how to cultivate (horticultural and pastoral societies), farm (agricultural societies) and manufacture (industrial societies). Trade followed the emergence of a surplus; one outcome of trade was the creation of social inequality, as some people began to accumulate more than others.

- The two major economic systems are capitalism, in which the means of production are privately owned, and socialism, in which the means of production are state owned. In recent years, each of these systems has adopted features of the other.

- The term corporate capitalism is used to describe the economic dominance by giant corporations today. Those in the inner circle are intent on making sure that corporate capitalism is protected; the interests of this inner circle lies beyond national boundaries.

- There are indications that a new world order is developing, as communications, transportation, and trade expand globally. The consequences of this transformation for human welfare are still unclear; predictions range from excellent to calamitous.

LEARNING OBJECTIVES

As you read Chapter 11, use these learning objectives to organize your notes. After completing your reading, briefly state an answer to each of the objectives, and review the text pages in parentheses.

1. Distinguish between power, authority, and coercion and discuss the role of the state in the exercise of legitimate violence. (272-273)
2. Describe the sources of authority identified by Weber, and explain how the orderly transfer of authority is achieved under each type of authority. (273-275)
3. Differentiate between monarchies, democracies, and dictatorships and oligarchies. (275-277)
4. Explain the nature of the two-party system in the United States and consider why third parties do poorly within this system. (277-278)

5. Describe American voting patterns, identify those most and least likely to vote in elections, and explain the social factors behind these patterns. (278-279)
6. Analyze the ways in which special-interest groups influence the political process. (279-281)
7. Distinguish between the functionalist and conflict perspectives on how the U.S. political process operates, and compare the power elite perspective of C. Wright Mills with William Domhoff's ruling class theory. (281-282)
8. Trace the transformation of the economic systems through each of the historical stages and state the degree to which social inequality existed in each of the economies. (282-285)
9. Discuss some of the ominous contemporary trends within the U.S. economy, including downsizing, the "Great U-Turn," the growing inequality in the U.S., and the U.S.'s status as the world's largest debtor. (285-287)
10. State the essential features of capitalism and socialism and explain why neither exists in its "pure" form. (287-289)
11. Identify the ideologies of capitalism and socialism. (289-290)
12. State criticisms of capitalism and socialism, describe the recent changes in socialist economies, and explain why some theorists believe the two systems are converging. (290)
13. Define corporations, interlocking directorates, and multinational corporations and discuss the role each plays in the global economy. (290-292)
14. Explain why some theorists believe that there is a possibility that global political and economic unity could come about. (292-293)

CHAPTER OUTLINE

POLITICS: ESTABLISHING LEADERSHIP
I. **Power and Authority and Violence**
   A. Max Weber noted that power--the ability to get your way, even over the resistance of others--can be either legitimate or illegitimate. Authority is legitimate power that people accept as right, while coercion is power that people do not accept as just.
   B. The state is the source of legitimate force or violence in society; violence is the ultimate foundation of political order. The ultimate proof of the state's authority is that the state can kill someone because he or she has done something which is considered absolutely horrible; an individual can't, without facing consequences.
   C. Weber identified three sources of authority.
      1. Traditional authority (based on custom) is prevalent in preliterate groups, where custom sets relationships. When society changes, traditional authority is undermined, but does not die, even in postindustrial societies. For example, parental authority is a traditional authority.
      2. Rational-legal authority (based on written rules, also called bureaucratic authority) derives from the position an individual holds, not from the person. Everyone (no matter how high the office) is subject to the rules.
      3. Charismatic authority (based on an individual's personal following) may pose a threat. Because charismatic leaders work outside the established political system and may threaten it, the authorities are often quick to oppose this type of leader.
   D. Orderly transfer of authority upon death, resignation, or incapacity of a leader is critical for stability. Succession is more of a problem with charismatic authority than with traditional or rational-legal authority. Routinization of charisma refers to the transfer of authority from a charismatic leader to either traditional or rational-legal authority.

II.   Types of Government

A.   As cities developed, each city-state (an independent city whose power radiated outward, bringing adjacent areas under its rule) had its own monarchy, a type of government headed by a king or queen.

    1.   As city-states warred with one another, the victors would extend their rule, eventually over an entire region.

    2.   As the size of these regions grew, people developed an identification with the region; over time this gave rise to the state.

B.   A democracy is a government whose authority derives from the people.

    1.   Direct democracy (voters meet together to discuss issues and make decisions) existed about 2,000 years ago in Athens. This type of democracy was appropriate in small communities.

    2.   Representative democracy (voters elect representatives to govern and make decisions on their behalf) emerged as the United States became more populous, making direct democracy impossible. This concept was revolutionary; its implementation meant the reversal of traditional ideas, for the government was to be responsive to the people's wishes, not the people to the wishes of the government.

    3.   Today, citizenship (citizens have basic rights) is taken for granted in the U.S. Universal citizenship (everyone having the same basic rights) came into practice very slowly and only through fierce struggle.

C.   Dictatorship is government where power is seized and held by an individual; oligarchy results when a small group of individual seizes power. Dictators and oligarchies can be totalitarian; this is when the government exercises almost total control of a people.

III.   The U.S. Political System

A.   The Democratic and Republican parties emerged by the time of the Civil War.

    1.   The Democrats are often associated with the poor and the working class and the Republicans with people who are financially better off.

    2.   Since each appeals to a broad membership, it is difficult to distinguish conservative Democrats from liberal Republicans; however, it is easy to discern the extremes. Those elected to Congress may cross party lines, because although office holders support their party's philosophy, they do not necessarily support all of its specific proposals.

    3.   Despite their differences, however, both parties support fundamentals of U.S. society such as freedom of religion, free public education, and capitalism.

    4.   Third parties do play a role in U.S. politics, although generally they receive little public support. Ross Perot's "United We Stand" party is one exception.

B.   Voting Patterns

    1.   U.S. voting patterns are consistent: the percentage of people who vote increases with age; whites are more likely to vote than African Americans or Asian Americans, while Latinos are considerably less likely to vote than either; those with higher levels of education are more likely to vote, as are people with higher levels of income; females are slightly more likely to vote in presidential elections than males.

    2.   The more that people feel they have a stake in the system, the more likely they are to vote. Those who have been rewarded by the system feel more socially integrated and perceive that elections directly affect their lives and the society in

which they live.
3.   People who gain less from the system in terms of education, income, and jobs are more likely to be alienated.
4.   Voter apathy is indifference/inaction to the political process. As a result of apathy, two out of five eligible American voters do not vote for president; less than half of the nation's eligible voters vote for members of Congress.
C.   Special-interest groups are people who think alike on a particular issue and can be mobilized for political action.
1.   Lobbyists are people who try to influence legislation on behalf of their clients; they have become a major force in politics. In an effort to curb the influence of lobbyists, Congress passed legislation in the 1970s that set limits on the amount of money that special-interest groups can donate to political candidates.
2.   Political action committees (PACs) solicit and spend funds to influence legislation and bypass laws intended to limit the amount any individual, corporation, or group can give a candidate. PACs have become a powerful influence, bankrolling lobbyists and legislators, and PACs with the most clout gain the ear of Congress.
D.   The major criticism against lobbyists and PACs is that their money buys votes. Rather than representing the people who elected them, legislators support the special interests of groups able to help them stay in power.

IV.   **Who Rules the United States?**
A.   The functionalists say that pluralism, the diffusion of power among interest groups, prevents any one from gaining control of the government. Functionalists believe it helps keep the government from turning against its citizens.
1.   To balance the interests of competing groups, the founders of the U.S. system of government created a system of checks and balances in which separation of powers among the three branches of government ensures that each is able to nullify the actions of the other two, thus preventing the domination of any single branch.
2.   According to this perspective, each group within society pursues its own interests and is balanced by other groups pursuing theirs. As groups negotiate with one another and reach compromises, conflict is minimized.
B.   According to the conflict perspective, lobbyists and even Congress are not at the center of decision making; rather, the power elite makes the decisions that direct the country and shake the world.
1.   As stated by C. Wright Mills, the power elite (heads of leading corporations, powerful generals and admirals in the armed forces, and certain elite politicians) rule the United States. The power elite views capitalism as essential to the welfare of the country; thus, business interests come first.
2.   According to William Domhoff, the ruling class (the wealthiest and most powerful individuals in the country) run the United States. Its members control the U.S.'s top corporations and foundations; presidential cabinet members and top ambassadors to the most powerful countries are chosen from this group, which promotes the view that positions come through merit and that everyone has a chance of becoming rich.
3.   The ruling class does not act in complete unity; the interests of one segment may conflict with those of another. At the same time the members generally see eye to eye; they have a mutual interest in solving the problems of business.

C.   While the functionalist and conflict views of power in U.S. society cannot be reconciled. it is possible to employ both. The middle level of C. Wright Mills's model best reflects the functionalist view of competing interests holding each other at bay. At the top is an elite that follows its special interests, as conflict theorists suggest.

THE ECONOMY: WORK IN THE GLOBAL VILLAGE

V.   **The Transformation of Economic Systems**

A.   The economy is a system of producing and distributing goods and services. It has evolved over time from preindustrial, to industrial, to postindustrial.

B.   The transformation of preindustrial societies, from hunting-and-gathering to agricultural, was accompanied by growing inequality.

1.   Earliest hunting and gathering societies had subsistence economies, characterized by little trade with other groups, and a high degree of social equality.

2.   In pastoral and horticultural economies, people created more dependable food supplies. The creation of a surplus allowed groups to grow in size, to settle in a single place, to develop a specialized division of labor, and to trade with other groups, all of which fostered social inequality.

3.   Agricultural economies brought even greater surpluses, magnifying prior trends in social, political and economic inequality. More people were freed from food production, a more specialized division of labor developed, and trade expanded.

C.   The surplus (and greater inequality) grew in industrial societies. As the surplus increased emphasis changed from production of goods to consumption (Thorstein Veblen coined the term conspicuous consumption).

D.   Postindustrial societies are characterized by three types of work: primary (extraction of natural resources from the environment), secondary (processing of raw materials into finished products), and tertiary (provision of services).

1.   According to Daniel Bell, postindustrial economies have six traits: (1) a service sector so large that it employs the majority of workers; (2) a large surplus of goods; (3) even more extensive trade among nations; (4) a wide variety and amount of goods available to the average person; (5) an information explosion; and (6) a "global village" with instantaneous, worldwide communications.

2.   The key to the postindustrial society is the "information explosion" with large numbers of people managing information and designing and servicing products.

3.   The consequence of this explosion is that the transformation of the world is uneven; some will live comfortably while others will continue the struggle just to survive.

E.   In recent years some ominous economic trends have emerged within the United States.

1.   To reduce costs, U.S. firms are downsizing. "Expensive" full-time workers are fired and temporary workers are hired in their place. In this way, firms do not have to spend money on expensive frills like vacation pay and retirement benefits.

2.   Many Americans find their standard of living stagnating or even declining. There has been a net decline in wages and the standard of living (the great American U-Turn) since the early 1970s.

3.   Income inequalities continue to plague our society. The distribution of income reassembles an inverted pyramid.

4.   The United States has gone from being the world's largest creditor to the world's largest debtor in the space of a few short years. The national debt is so large that the interest alone is greater that the combined expenditures for health, science,

space, agriculture, housing, protecting the environment, and the entire justice system.

5.   If these trends continue, the United States will become a "two-thirds society." At the top would be the one-third of the population that is well-educated and securely employed. In the middle third would be the working class, insecure in their jobs, earning a more-or-less adequate income. At the bottom would be the unemployed and the underemployed.

VI.   **World Economic Systems**

A.   Capitalism has three essential features: (1) the private ownership of the means of production; (2) the pursuit of profit; and (3) market competition.

    1.   Pure (laissez faire) capitalism exists only when market forces are able to operate without interference from the government.

    2.   The United States today has welfare (or state) capitalism. Private citizens own the means of production and pursue profits, but do so within a vast system of laws designed to protect the public welfare (market restraints).

B.   Socialism also has three essential features: (1) the public ownership of the means of production; (2) central planning; and (3) the distribution of goods without a profit motive.

    1.   Under socialism, the government owns the means of production, and a central committee determines what the country needs instead of allowing supply and demand to control production and prices.

    2.   Socialism is designed to eliminate competition, to produce goods for the general welfare, and to distribute them according to people's needs, not their ability to pay.

    3.   Socialism does not exist in pure form. Although the ideology of socialism calls for resources to be distributed according to need rather than position, socialist nations found it necessary to offer higher salaries for some jobs in order to entice people to take greater responsibilities.

    4.   Some nations (e.g., Sweden and Denmark) have adopted democratic or welfare socialism: both the state and individuals engage in production and distribution, although the state owns certain industries (steel, mining, forestry, telephones, television stations, and airlines) while retail stores, farms, and most service industries remain in private hands.

C.   Capitalism and socialism represent distinct ideologies.

    1.   Capitalists believe that market forces should determine both products and prices, and that it is good for people to strive for profits. Capitalists see that socialists violate basic human rights of freedom of decision and opportunity.

    2.   Socialists believe that profit is immoral and represents excess value extracted from workers. Socialists see that capitalists violate basic human rights of freedom from poverty.

    3.   Each ideology sees the other as a system of exploitation.

D.   The primary criticism of capitalism is that it leads to social inequality (a top layer of wealthy, powerful people, and a bottom layer of people who are unemployed or underemployed). Socialism has been criticized for not respecting individual rights, and for not being capable of producing much wealth (thus the greater equality of socialism actually amounts to almost everyone having an equal chance of being poor).

E.   As societies industrialize they display comparable divisions of labor, a similar emphasis on higher education, and a trend towards extensive urbanization. According to convergence theory, as both capitalist and socialist systems adopt features of the other, the result may be the emergence of a hybrid or mixed economy in the future.

VII.   **Capitalism in a Global Economy**
   A.   The corporation (joint ownership of a business enterprise, whose liabilities are separate from those of its owners) has changed the face of capitalism.
      1.   Corporate capitalism refers to the domination of the economic system by giant corporations. One of the most significant aspects of large corporations is the separation of ownership and management, producing ownership of wealth without appreciable control, and control of wealth without appreciable ownership.
      2.   Because of the dispersion of ownership, a power vacuum is created. Often, stockholders will simply rubber-stamp management's recommendations at annual stockholders' meetings. However, a stockholders' revolt (stockholders of a corporation refuse to rubber stamp decisions made by the management) is likely to occur if the profits do not meet expectations.
   B.   Interlocking directorates occur when individuals serve as directors of several companies, concentrating power and minimizing competition.
   C.   As corporations have outgrown national boundaries, the result is the creation of multinational corporations.
      1.   As multinationals move investments and production from one part of the globe to another in search of profits, the result is a flood of low-priced consumer goods.
      2.   This comes at a cost. Millions of U.S. jobs have been lost, while workers in the Least Industrialized Nations are exploited and the environments in these nations are often polluted.

VIII.   **A New World Order?**
   A.   New technologies underlay the globalization of capitalism, allowing a worldwide flow of information, capital and goods. New alliances among nations have emerged, creating new possibilities for world peace.
   B.   At the same time, multinationals owe their allegiance to profits; national boundaries become meaningless. These businesses have become detached from the interests and values of their country of origin.
   C.   As the power of multinationals continues to grow, their elites are likely to become more interconnected, forging partnerships with national elites. The end result may be that the multinationals and their new trade agreements will become a force for peace, but the price may be high if it means that the new world order is dominated by a handful of the world's top corporate leaders.

KEY TERMS
After studying the chapter, review each of the following terms.

anarchy: a condition of lawlessness or political disorder caused by the absence or collapse of governmental authority (281)

authority: power that people accept as rightly exercised over them (272)

capitalism: an economic system characterized by the private ownership of the means of production, the pursuit of profit, and market competition (282)

charismatic authority: authority based on an individual's outstanding traits, which attract followers (274)

checks and balances: the separation of powers among the three branches of U.S. government--legislative, executive and judicial--so that each is able to nullify the actions of the other two, thus preventing the domination any single branch (281)

citizenship: the concept that birth (and residence) in a country impart basic rights (276)

city-state: an independent city whose power radiates outward, bringing the adjacent areas under its rule (275)

coercion: illegitimate power that people do not accept as just (272)

conspicuous consumption: Thorstein Veblen's term for a change from the Protestant ethic to an eagerness to show off wealth by the elaborate consumption of goods (283)

convergence theory: the view that as capitalist and socialist economic systems each adopt features of the other, a hybrid (or mixed) economic system may emerge (290)

corporate capitalism: the domination of the economic system by giant corporations (290)

corporation: the joint ownership of a business enterprise, whose liabilities and obligations are separate from those of the owners (290)

democracy: a system of government in which authority derives from the people (275)

democratic socialism: a hybrid economic system in which capitalism is mixed with state ownership (288)

dictatorship: a form of government in which power is seized by an individual (276)

direct democracy: a form of democracy in which voters meet together to discuss issues and make their decisions (276)

economy: a system of distribution of goods and services (283)

interlocking directorates: individuals serving on the board of directors in several companies (291)

laissez-faire capitalism: unrestrained manufacture and trade (literally, "hands off" capitalism) (288)

lobbyists: people who try to influence legislation on behalf of their clients or interest groups (280)

market forces: the law of supply and demand (288)

market restraints: laws and regulations govern the manufacture and sell of products (288)

monarchy: a form of government headed by a king or queen (275)

multinational corporation: companies that operate across national boundaries (291)

nationalism: identify with and loyalty towards a nation (293)

oligarchy: a form of government in which power is held by a small group of individuals; the rule of the many by the few (276)

pluralism: the diffusion of power among many interest groups, preventing any single group from gaining control of the government (281)

political action committee (PAC): an organization formed by one or more special-interest groups to solicit and spend funds for the purpose of influencing legislation (280)

power: the ability to get your way, even over the resistance of others (272)

power elite: C. Wright Mills's term for the top leaders of U.S. corporations, military, and politics who make the nation's major decisions (281)

rational-legal authority: authority based on law or written rules and regulations; also called *bureaucratic authority* (273)

representative democracy: a form of democracy in which voters elect representatives to govern and make decisions on their behalf (276)

routinization of charisma: the transfer of authority from a charismatic figure to either a traditional or a rational-legal form of authority (275)

socialism: an economic system characterized by the public ownership of the means of production, central planning, and the distribution of goods without a profit motive (288)

special-interest group: people who share views on a particular issue and can be mobilized for political action (280)

state: the political entity that claims a monopoly on the use of violence within a territory (273, 275)

stockholders' revolt: the refusal of a corporation's stockholders to rubber-stamp decisions made by its managers (291)

subsistence economy: the type of economy in which human groups live off the land with little or no surplus (283)

totalitarianism: a form of government that exerts almost total control over the people (276)

traditional authority: authority based on custom (273)

universal citizenship: the idea that everyone has the same basic rights by virtue of being born in a country (or by immigrating and becoming a naturalized citizen) (276)

voter apathy: indifference and inaction on the part of individuals or groups with respect to the political process (278)

welfare (or state) capitalism: an economic system in which individuals own the means of production but the state regulates many economic activities for the welfare of the population (288)

KEY PEOPLE

Review the major theoretical contributions or research findings of these people.

Daniel Bell: Bell identified six characteristics of the postindustrial society. (284)

Peter Berger: Berger argued that violence is the ultimate foundation of any political order. (272)

William Domhoff: Like Mills, Domhoff saw that power resides in the hands of an elite, which he referred to as the ruling class. He focused on the top one percent of Americans who belong to the super rich. (281)

William Form: A supporter of convergence theory, Form has studied aspects of capitalist and socialist systems that have been borrowed from each other. (290)

Bennett Harrison and Barry Bluestone: These social analysts have used the expression "the great American U-turn" to describe the stagnating/declining standard of living of many Americans today. (286)

C. Wright Mills: Mills suggested that power resides in the hands of an elite made up of the top leaders of the largest corporations, the most powerful generals of the armed forces, and certain elite politicians. (281)

Michael Useem: Using a conflict perspective, Useem studied the activities of the "inner circle" of corporate executives. (290)

Thorstein Veblen: Veblen created the term "conspicuous consumption" to refer to the eagerness to show off one's wealth through the elaborate consumption of material goods. (283)

Max Weber: Weber identified three different types of authority: traditional, rational-legal, and charismatic. (272)

SELF-TEST

After completing this self-test, check your answers against the Answer Key beginning on page 259 of this Study Guide and against the text on page(s) indicated in parentheses.

MULTIPLE CHOICE QUESTIONS

1. Power: (272)
    a. was defined by Max Weber.
    b. is the ability to carry out one's will in spite of resistance from others.
    c. is an inevitable part of everyday life.
    d. All of the above.

2.   According to Weber, the _____ claims a monopoly on legitimate force or violence. (273)
        a.   clergy
        b.   family
        c.   state
        d.   individual citizen

3.   Traditional authority: (273)
        a.   is the hallmark of preliterate groups.
        b.   is based on custom.
        c.   was identified by Max Weber.
        d.   All of the above.

4.   The least stable type of authority is the: (275)
        a.   traditional.
        b.   rational-legal.
        c.   charismatic.
        d.   monarchy.

5.   Democracy: (275)
        a.   first occurred in the United States.
        b.   is a system of government in which authority derives from elected officials.
        c.   is basically a modern idea.
        d.   None of the above.

6.   An individual who seizes power and imposes his will onto the people is known as a: (276)
        a.   charismatic leader.
        b.   dictator.
        c.   totalitarian leader.
        d.   monarch.

7.   A form of government that exerts almost total control over the people is a(n): (276)
        a.   monarchy.
        b.   dictatorship.
        c.   totalitarian regime.
        d.   oligarchy.

8.   Studies of voting patterns in the United States: (278)
        a.   are inconsistent.
        b.   show that voting varies by age, race/ethnicity, education, employment, and income.
        c.   show that younger people are more likely to vote than older individuals.
        d.   All of the above.

9.   Today in the U.S., how many eligible voters do not vote for the President? (279)
        a.   one in five
        b.   two in five
        c.   three in ten
        d.   four in eight

10.	Lobbyists: (280)
	a.	are people paid to influence legislation on behalf of their clients.
	b.	are employed by special-interest groups.
	c.	are a major force in American politics.
	d.	All of the above.

11.	Functionalists believe that any one group is prevented from gaining control of the government because of: (281)
	a.	the existence of pluralism.
	b.	the use of checks and balances.
	c.	the presence of many interest groups to which politicians must pay attention.
	d.	All of the above.

12.	According to conflict theorists, the ruling class is: (282)
	a.	a group that meets together and agrees on specific matters.
	b.	a group which tends to have complete unity on issues.
	c.	made up of people whose backgrounds and orientations to life are so similar that they automatically share the same goals.
	d.	a myth.

13.	Hunting and gathering societies are characterized by a: (283)
	a.	market economy.
	b.	surplus economy.
	c.	subsistence economy.
	d.	maintenance economy.

14.	Industrial economies: (283)
	a.	are based on machines powered by fuels.
	b.	created a surplus unlike anything the world had seen.
	c.	emerged following the invention of the steam engine.
	d.	All of the above.

15.	Workers who package fish, process copper into wire, and turn trees into lumber are in the: (284)
	a.	primary sector.
	b.	secondary sector.
	c.	tertiary sector.
	d.	None of the above.

16.	Postindustrial economies are characterized by: (285)
	a.	a large surplus of goods.
	b.	extensive trade among nations.
	c.	a "global village."
	d.	All of the above.

17. Studies show that since 1970, the buying power of the American workers' paychecks has: (286)
    a. improved.
    b. worsened.
    c. remained the same.
    d. been impossible to calculate.

18. Private ownership of the means of production is an essential feature of: (287)
    a. communism.
    b. socialism.
    c. democracy.
    d. capitalism.

19. The term "welfare capitalism" refers to a system in which: (288)
    a. the government gives financial breaks to businessmen.
    b. former socialist economies are replaced by a "kinder and gentler" form of capitalism.
    c. a kind of underground economy in which the entrepreneurs are not only receiving welfare but are also engaged in economic activities that generate a profit.
    d. private individuals own the businesses and pursue profits, but they do so within a system of laws designed to protect the welfare of the population.

20. An economic system characterized by the public ownership of the means of production, central planning, and the distribution of goods without a profit motive is: (288)
    a. democratic socialism.
    b. socialism.
    c. capitalism.
    d. communism.

21. Which of the following views profits as immoral? (289)
    a. capitalism
    b. welfare capitalism
    c. the new world order
    d. socialism

22. Unemployment compensation, housing subsidies, minimum wage, and Social Security are examples of: (290)
    a. government handouts.
    b. outdated Democratic party programs.
    c. socialist practices.
    d. inflated government budget expenditures.

23. The joint ownership of a business enterprise, whose liabilities and obligations are separate from those of its owners is a(n): (290)
    a. oligopoly.
    b. monopoly.
    c. corporation.
    d. interlocking directorate.

24.   The elite who sit on the boards of directors of not just one but several companies are referred to as: (291)
    a.   vertical integrators.
    b.   interlocking trustees.
    c.   interlocking directorates.
    d.   oligopolies.

25.   The sociological significance of multinational corporations is that: (292)
    a.   it is easier for government to regulate their business affairs.
    b.   increasingly they have become detached from the interests and values of their country of origin.
    c.   they help to control the problem of interlocking directorates because they recruit an international elite to serve on their boards.
    d.   the are less likely to exploit labor and natural resources because they operate in a world economy rather than a national economy.

TRUE-FALSE QUESTIONS

T F   1.   In every group, large or small, some individuals have power over others. (272)
T F   2.   Coercion refers to legitimate power. (272)
T F   3.   Even with industrialization some forms of traditional authority go unchallenged. (273)
T F   4.   Rational-legal authority is based on written rules. (273)
T F   5.   Routinization of charisma involves the transfer of authority from a charismatic leader to either traditional or rational-legal authority. (275)
T F   6.   Direct democracy was impossible in the U.S. as population grew and spread out. (276)
T F   7.   The concept of representative democracy based on citizenship may be the greatest gift the United States has given to the world. (276)
T F   8.   The idea of universal citizenship caught on quickly in the United States. (276)
T F   9.   Employment and income do not affect the probability that people will vote. (278)
T F   10.   Most political action committees represent broad social interests such as environmental protection. (280)
T F   11.   Functionalists believe that pluralism prevents any one group from gaining control of the government and using it to oppress the people. (281)
T F   12.   Conflict theorists believe that the ruling class is a group that meets together and agrees on specific matters. (282)
T F   13.   Hunting and gathering societies were the first economies to have a surplus. (283)
T F   14.   In pastoral and horticultural economies, some individuals were able for the first time in human history to develop their energies to tasks other than food production. (283)
T F   15.   Industrial economies are based on information processing and providing services. (284)
T F   16.   The richest fifth of Americans earn about 47 percent of all the income in the United States. (286)
T F   17.   In welfare capitalism, private citizens own the means of production and pursue profits, but do so within a vast system of laws. (288)
T F   18.   Under democratic socialism, both the state and individuals engage in production and distribution of economic goods. (289)
T F   19.   According to convergence theory, as nations industrialize they are likely to adopt more and more of the characteristics of capitalism rather than socialism. (290)

T F   20.   The term "corporate capitalism" is used to describe the dominance of the economic system by giant corporations. (290)

FILL-IN QUESTIONS

1.   _____, synonymous with government, is the source of legitimate violence in society. (273)
2.   _____ is authority based on custom. (273)
3.   Bureaucratic authority is also called _____. (273)
4.   An independent city whose power radiates outward, bringing the adjacent area under its rule is a _____. (275)
5.   _____ is a form of democracy in which the eligible voters meet together to discuss issues and make their decisions. (276)
6.   The concept that birth and residence in a country impart basic rights is known as _____. (276)
7.   A form of government that exerts almost total control over the people is _____. (276)
8.   _____ refers to indifference and inaction on the part of individuals or groups with respect to the political process. (278)
9.   _____ refers to the top people in leading corporations, the most powerful generals and admirals of the armed forces, and certain elite politicians. (281)
10.   _____ is the term for a system of distribution of goods and services. (283)
11.   Barry Bluestone and Bennett Harrison use the expression " _____ " to refer to the net decline in the wages and standard of living of U.S. workers. (286)
12.   A type of economic system in which market forces operate without interference from the government would be _____. (288)
13.   The view that as capitalist and socialist economic systems each adopt features of the other, a hybrid (or mixed) economic system may emerge is _____. (290)
14.   The refusal of a corporation's stockholders to rubber-stamp decisions made by its managers is referred to as _____. (291)
15.   When individuals serve on the board of directors of several companies simultaneously, the result is the emergence of _____. (291)

MATCH THESE SOCIAL SCIENTISTS WITH THEIR CONTRIBUTIONS

___1. Daniel Bell   a. *supported convergence theory*
___2. Peter Berger   b. *created the term "conspicuous consumption"*
___3. Michael Useem   c. *ruling class*
___4. William Domhoff   d. *three types of authority*
___5. Thorstein Veblen   e. *studied the activities of the "inner circle"*
___6. C. Wright Mills   f. *identified the characteristics of postindustrial societies*
___7. Max Weber   g. *power elite*
___8. William Form   h. *violence is the foundation of the political order*

ESSAY QUESTIONS

1.   Discuss the three sources of authority and the issues related to the transfer of authority.

2.   Discuss the system of democracy found in the U.S. and consider how some of the problems

associated with our system -- voter apathy and the power of political action committees -- are related to our system of government.

3. Discuss the advantages and disadvantages of both capitalism and socialism as ideologies and as economic systems.

"DOWN-TO-EARTH SOCIOLOGY"

1. Were you surprised at the profile of the American voter that is contained in Table 11.2 on page 278? How would you characterize you own attachment to the political process? Do you vote? Do your friends vote? Why or why not?

2. After reading "Ethnicity and Class in the Path of Political Participation," (p. 279), do you think that recent immigrants will follow the same political route to overcoming discrimination that earlier immigrants took? In what ways might this be more difficult today than in the past? In what ways might it be easier?

3. From the discussion of technology and the restructuring of work (p. 286), what kind of future do you see? Will the economy be able to absorb those workers who are displaced by the new technology? If not, what do you think will happen to them?

4. In what ways does the rise of nationalism undermine the continuing globalization of capitalism and efforts at building a new world order (pp. 292-293)? Do you consider nationalism a positive or negative development? Why?

CHAPTER 12
MARRIAGE AND FAMILY

CHAPTER SUMMARY

- Because there are so many cultural variations on family structure, it is hard to define. Nevertheless, family is defined broadly as two or more people who consider themselves related by blood, marriage or adoption. Marriage and family patterns vary remarkably across cultures, but four universal themes in marriage are mate selection, descent, inheritance, and authority.

- According to the functionalist perspective, the family carries out important social functions. Conversely, conflict theorists focus on how families help perpetuate inequality, especially gender relations. Symbolic interactionists focus on the meanings that people give their marital relationships, particularly in regard to the household division of labor.

- The family life cycle is analyzed in terms of love and courtship, marriage, childbirth, child rearing, and the family in later life. Within the United States, patterns of marriage vary by social class, age, religion, and race; patterns of childbearing and childrearing vary by social class.

- Family diversity in U.S. culture is related to social class rather than race or ethnicity. One-parent families, childless families, blended families, and gay families represent some of the different types of families today. Poverty is especially significant for one-parent families, most of whom are headed by women.

- Major trends in U.S. families today include postponement of first marriage, cohabitation, and the emergence of the "sandwich generation," middle-aged couples who are caught between caring for their own children and caring for their elderly parents.

- Studies on divorce have focused on problems in measuring divorce, the impact of divorce on children and ex-spouses, and remarriage. While time seems to heal most children's wounds over the divorce of their parents, research suggests that a minority carry the scars of divorce into adulthood. Men and women experience divorce differently; for men, this event often results in a weakening of their relationships with children, for women it means a decline in their standard of living. Although most divorced people remarry, their rate of remarriage has slowed considerably.

- Violence and abuse--including battering, child abuse, and incest--are the "dark side" of family life. Researchers have identified variables that help marriages last and be happy.

- The trends for the future include a continued increased in cohabitation, births to unmarried mothers, and postponement of marriage. The continuing growth in the numbers of working wives will impact on marital balance of power.

LEARNING OBJECTIVES

As you read Chapter 12, use these learning objectives to organize your notes. After completing your reading, briefly state an answer to each of the objectives, and review the text pages in parentheses.

1. Explain why it is difficult to define the term "family." (298-299)
2. Identify the common cultural themes that run through marriage and the family. (299-300)
3. Discuss the functionalists, conflict, and symbolic interaction perspectives regarding marriage and family. (300-304)
4. Outline the major developments in each stage of the family life cycle. (304-309)
5. State the unique problems experienced by African-American, Latino, Asian-American, and Native-American families. (309-312)

6. Identify the major concerns of one-parent families, families without children, blended families, and gay and lesbian families. (312-313)
7. Describe the current trends affecting marriage and family life in the United States. (313-316)
8. State why it is difficult to measure divorce accurately. (316-317)
9. Note some of the adjustment problems of children and ex-spouses following divorce. (318-320)
10. Explain the "dark side" of family life. (320-322)
11. List some of the characteristics which tend to be present in marriages that work. Explain how happy couples approach problems. (322)
12. Summarize conclusions regarding the future of marriage and family in the United States. (322)

CHAPTER OUTLINE

I. **Marriage and Family in Global Perspective**
    A. The term family is difficult to define as there are many types.
        1. In some societies men have more than one wife (polygyny) or women have more than one husband (polyandry).
        2. A broad definition of family is a group of two or more people who consider themselves related by blood, marriage, or adoption, and lives together (or has lived together). A household, in contrast to a family, consists of all people who occupy the same housing unit.
        3. A family is classified as a nuclear family (husband, wife, and children) or an extended family (a nuclear family plus other relatives who live together).
        4. The family of orientation is the family in which a person grows up, while the family of procreation is the family formed when a couple's first child is born. A person who is married but has not had a child is part of a couple, not a family.
        5. Marriage is a group's approved mating arrangements, usually marked by a ritual.
    B. Despite diversity, several common themes run through marriage and family.
        1. Each group establishes norms to govern who can and cannot marry. Endogamy is the practice of marrying within one's own group, while exogamy is the practice of marrying outside of one's own group. Some norms of mate selection are written into law, others are informal.
        2. Three major patterns of descent (tracing kinship over generations) are: (a) bilateral (descent traced on both the mother's and the father's side); (b) patrilineal (descent traced only on the father's side); and © matrilineal (descent traced only on the mother's side).
        3. Mate selection and descent are regulated in all societies in order to provide an orderly way of passing property, etc., to the next generation. In a bilateral system, property passes to males and females; in a patrilineal system, property passes only to males; in a matrilineal system, property passes only to females.
        4. Patriarchy, found in all societies, is a social system in which men dominate women. No historical records exist of a true matriarchy (a system in which women as a group dominate men). In an egalitarian social system authority is more or less equally divided between men and women.
II. **Marriage and Family in Theoretical Perspective**
    A. Functionalists stress that to survive, a society must meet certain basic needs; they examine how the family contributes to the well-being of society.
        1. The family is universal because it serves functions essential to the well-being of

society: economic production, socialization of children, care of the sick and aged, recreation, sexual control, and reproduction.

    2.   The incest taboo (rules specifying which people are too closely related to have sex or marry) helps the family avoid role confusion and forces people to look outside the family for marriage partners, creating a network of support.

    3.   The nuclear family has few people it can depend on for material and emotional support; thus, the members of a nuclear family are vulnerable to "emotional overload." The relative isolation of the nuclear family makes it easier for the "dark side" of families (incest and other types of abuse) to emerge.

    B.   To conflict theorists, the issue is the struggle over scarce resources; they argue that within the family, the conflict over housework is really about control over scarce resources--time, energy, and the leisure to pursue interesting activities.

    1.   Most men resist doing housework and working wives end up doing almost all of it, even though men think that they are splitting the work fifty-fifty.

    2.   Arlie Hochschild found that after an 8-hour day at work, women typically work a "second shift" at home; this means that wives work an extra month of 24-hour days each year. The result is that working wives feel deep discontent.

    C.   Symbolic interactionists look at the meanings that people give to their experiences; they are interested in how husbands view housework.

    1.   Research indicates that the closer a husband's and wife's earnings are, the more likely they are to share housework. When husbands are laid off from work, their contribution decreases. And husbands who earn less than their wives do the least housework.

    2.   The key to understanding this pattern is gender role. When a wife earns more than her husband, his masculinity is threatened; to do housework is even more threatening. By not doing it, he is able to "reclaim" his masculinity.

III.   The Family Life Cycle

    A.   Romantic love provides the ideological context in which people in the U.S. seek mates and form families. Romantic love has two components: (1) emotional, a feeling of sexual attraction; and (2) cognitive, the feeling we describe as being "in love."

    B.   The social channels of love and marriage in the United States include age, education, social class, race, and religion.

    1.   Homogamy is the tendency of people with similar characteristics to marry one another, usually resulting from propinquity (spatial nearness). People living near one another tend to marry.

    2.   Interracial marriage is an exception to these social patterns. In the U.S., about 6 percent of the population marries someone from a different race. At the same time, interracial marriages are becoming more acceptable.

    C.   Marital satisfaction usually decreases with the birth of a child, according to Martin Whyte. Lillian Rubin found that social class influences how couples adjust to children. Working-class couples are more likely to have a baby nine months after marriage and have major interpersonal and financial problems; middle-class parents are more prepared because of more resources, postponement of the birth of the first child, and more time to adjust to one another.

    D.   Traditionally childrearing automatically fell on the mother. As more mothers become employed outside the home, this has changed.

    1.   The overall child care arrangements appear to be quite similar for married couples

and single mothers. The main difference is the role played by the child's father while the mother is at work. For married couples, almost one of four children is cared for by the father, while for single mothers this arrangement occurs for about only one of fourteen children. Grandparents often help to fill the child care gap left by absent fathers in single mother homes.

2. Social class is also important in child rearing. According to Melvin Kohn, parents socialize children into the norms of their respective work worlds. Working-class parents want their children to behave in conformity with social expectations. Middle-class parents are more concerned that their children develop curiosity, self-expression, and self-control.

3. Birth order is significant in child rearing: first-borns tend to be disciplined more than children who follow but also receive more attention; when the next child arrives, the first born competes to maintain attention.

E. Later stages of the family life cycle bring their own pleasures and problems.

1. The empty-nest is thought to signal a difficult adjustment for women; however Lillian Rubin argues that this syndrome is largely a myth because women's satisfaction generally increases when the last child leaves home. Most women feel relieved at being able to spend more time on themselves. Many couples report a renewed sense of companionship at this time.

2. With prolonged education and a growing cost of establishing households, U.S. children are leaving home later, or after initially leaving home they are returning.

3. Women are more likely than men to face the problem of adjusting to widowhood; not only does the average woman live longer than a man but she has also married a man older than herself.

IV. **Diversity in U.S. Families**

A. As with other groups, the family life of African Americans differs with social class.

1. The upper class is concerned with maintaining family lineage and preserving their privilege and wealth; the middle-class focuses on achievement and respectability; poor African-American families face the problems that poverty brings.

2. Marriage squeeze (fewer unmarried males than unmarried females) exists among African Americans; women thus are more likely to marry men with less education, or who are unemployed or divorced, or to remain single.

B. The effects of social class on families also apply to Latinos. In addition, families differ by country of origin.

1. Latino families are distinguishable by the Spanish language, Roman Catholic religion, and strong family ties with a disapproval of divorce.

2. Machismo, the emphasis on male strength and dominance, also seems to be a characteristic of Latino families. As a result, the husband-father plays a stronger role than in white or African-American families, and the wife-mother deals with family and child-related decisions.

C. Bob Suzuki points out that while Chinese-American and Japanese-American families have adopted the nuclear family pattern of the United States, they have retained Confucian values that provide a distinct framework to family life: humanism, collectivity, self-discipline, hierarchy, respect for the elderly, moderation, and obligation.

D. Perhaps the most significant issue facing Native-American families is whether to follow traditional values or to assimilate; traditionals speak native languages and emphasize distinctive values and beliefs, while those who have assimilated to not.

E. There has been an increase in one-parent families.
1. This increase is due to the high divorce rate and the sharp increase in unwed motherhood.
2. Most of these families are poor; the reason for the poverty is that most are headed by women who earn less than men.
3. Children from one-parent families are more likely to drop out of school, become delinquent, be poor as adults, divorce, and have children outside of marriage.

F. There are a growing number of families who are voluntarily childless. The percentage varies with the education of the woman; the more education she has, the more likely she is to expect to bear no children. Latinas are much less likely to expect to remain childless than whites and African Americans.
1. There are different reasons why a couple chooses not to have a child: a weak relationship, financial constraints, or a demanding career are among the reasons researchers have identified.
2. More education, careers for women, effective contraception, abortion, the costs of rearing children, as well as changing attitudes toward children and goals in life, all contribute the increase in childless and childfree marriages.

G. A blended family is one whose members were once part of other families (two divorced persons marry, bringing children into a new family unit). Blended families are increasing in number and often experience complicated family relationships.

H. Although marriage between homosexuals is illegal in the United States, many homosexual couples live in monogamous relationships that they refer to as marriage. They have the usual problems of heterosexual marriages: housework, money, careers, problems with relatives, and sexual adjustment.

V. **Trends in U.S. Families**
A. The average age of U.S. brides is the oldest it has been since records first were kept. Many young people postpone marriage, but not cohabitation; if cohabitation were counted as marriage, rates of family formation and age at first marriage would show little change.
B. Cohabitation, living together as an unmarried couple, is eight times more common today than 25 years ago. About half the couples who marry have cohabited; this rate is lower in the United States than in Canada and most European countries. Commitment is the essential difference between cohabitation and marriage: marriage assumes permanence; cohabiting assumes remaining together "as long as it works out."
C. As previously discussed, there has been an increase in the number of births to unmarried mothers.
1. In the ten industrialized nations for which data are available, all except Japan have experienced sharp increases in births to unmarried mothers--the U.S. rate falls in the middle third of these nations.
2. Industrialization alone is too simple an explanation for this increase. To more fully understand this trend, future research must focus on customs and values embedded within particular cultures.
D. The "sandwich generation" refers to people who find themselves sandwiched between two generations, responsible for the care of their children and for their own aging parents.
1. These people are typically between the ages of 40 and 55.
2. More businesses offer elder care assistance to their employees. With people living longer, this issue is likely to become even more urgent in the future.

VI. Divorce and Remarriage

    A. The United States has the highest divorce rate in the industrialized world; estimates suggest that half or more of all couples getting married today may eventually divorce.

        1. Although the divorce rate is reported at 50 percent, this statistic is misleading because with rare exceptions those who divorce do not come from the group who married that year.

        2. An alternative is to compare the number of divorces in a given year to the entire group of married couples; this amount to 2.1 percent of all married couples getting a divorce.

        3. A third way is to calculate the number of divorce persons for every thousand married people; this measure shows that divorce has tripled in the last two decades, although it leveled off in about 1981.

    B. Each year over one million children are in families affected by divorce. Divorce threatens a child's world.

        1. Research has found that the grown children of divorce feel more distant from parents than children from intact families.

        2. A study of students at McGill University showed that children's adjustment was affected by the relationship(s) their mothers formed after divorce. Those whose mothers entered into a single, stable relationship after divorce had the best adjustment.

        3. Several factors help children adjust to divorce: both parents show understanding and affection; the parent with whom the child lives is making a good adjustment; family routines are consistent; the family has adequate money for its needs; and, according to preliminary studies, the child lives with the parent of the same sex.

        4. Children adjust better when a second adult can be counted on for support.

    C. A new fathering pattern known as serial fatherhood is beginning to emerge.

        1. Divorced fathers tend to live with, support, and play an active fathering role with children of the woman to whom they are currently married or with whom they are currently living.

        2. Over time, contact with their children from a previous marriage diminishes; one study found that only about one-sixth of children who live apart from their fathers see than as often as every week.

    D. Women are more likely than men to feel divorce gives them a new chance at life. Divorce likely spells economic hardship for women, especially mothers of small children; in the first post-divorce year, the standard of living for women with dependent children declines significantly. The ex-husband's standard of living is likely to increase.

    E. Most divorced persons eventually remarry, with an average lapse between divorce and remarriage of about five years for women.

        1. Most divorced people remarry other divorced people.

        2. Women with small children, and women with less than a high school education, are most likely to remarry.

        3. Men are more likely than women to remarry, perhaps because they have a larger pool of potential mates from which to select.

        4. The divorce rate for remarried people without children is the same as that of first marriages. Those who bring children into their new marriage, however, are more likely to divorce again; this suggests that remarriages with children are more difficult because there are not yet norms governing these relationships.

VII.   Two Sides of Family Life

    A.   The dark side of family life deals with events that people would rather keep in the dark--battering, child abuse, and incest

        1.   Although wives are about as likely to attack their husbands as husbands are to attack their wives, it is generally the husband who lands the last and most damaging blow. Living in a sexist society, men who batter think they are superior and that they have a right to force their will on their wives.

        2.   Child abuse is extensive. Each year, three million U.S. children are reported to the authorities as victims of abuse or neglect.

        3.   Incest is sexual relations between relatives, such as brothers and sisters or parents and children. It is most likely to occur in families that are socially isolated, and is more common than it previously was thought to be. The most common offenders are first cousins, followed by fathers/stepfathers, brothers, and finally other male relatives.

    B.   There are a number of factors that make marriages work. Variables that produce happy marriages include: spending time together, appreciating one another, having a commitment to the marriage, using good communications, confronting and working through problems together, and putting more into the marriage than you take out.

VIII.   The Future of Marriage and Family

    A.   Despite its problems, marriage is not likely to disappear as a social institution because it is functional; we see it as vital to our welfare.

    B.   It is likely that cohabitation will increase, as will the age at first marriage, and the number of women joining the work force, with a resulting shift in marital power toward a more egalitarian norm.

    C.   Sociology can play a role in correcting some of the distortions associated with marriage and family life as well as help to formulate social policy that will enhance family life.

KEY TERMS

After studying the chapter, review each of the following terms.

bilateral system: a system of reckoning descent that counts both the mother's and the father's side (300)

blended family: a family whose members were once part of other families (313)

cohabitation: unmarried people living together in a sexual relationship (314)

empty nest: a married couple's domestic situation after the last child has left home (309)

endogamy: the practice of marrying within one's group (299)

exogamy: the practice of marrying outside one's group (299)

extended family: a nuclear family plus other relatives, such as grandparents, uncles and aunts, who live together (299)

family: two or more people who consider themselves related by blood, marriage, or adoption (299)

family of orientation: the family in which a person grows up (299)

family of procreation: the family formed when a couple's first child is born (299)

homogamy: the tendency of people with similar characteristics to marry one another (306)

household: all persons who occupy the same housing unit (299)

incest taboo: rules specifying the degrees of kinship that prohibit sex or marriage (299)

machismo: an emphasis on male strength and dominance (310)

marriage: a group's approved mating arrangements, usually marked by a ritual of some sort (299)

matriarchy: a society or group in which authority vested in females (300)

matrilineal system: a system of reckoning descent that counts only the mother's side (300)

nuclear family: a family consisting of a husband, wife, and child(ren) (299)

patriarchy: a society or group in which authority is vested in men (300)

patrilineal system: a system of reckoning descent that counts only the father's side (300)

polyandry: a marriage in which a woman has more than one husband (298)

polygyny: a marriage in which a man has more than one wife (298)

romantic love: feelings of erotic attraction accompanied by an idealization of the other (304)

serial fatherhood: a pattern of parenting in which a father, after divorce, reduces contact with his own children, serves as a father to the children of the woman he marries or lives with, then ignores them after moving in with or marrying another woman; this pattern repeats (319)

system of descent: how kinship is traced over the generations (299)

KEY PEOPLE
Review the major theoretical contributions or research findings of these people.

Philip Blumstein and Pepper Schwartz: These two sociologists interviewed same-sex couples and found their main struggles were the same ones facing heterosexual couples. (313)

Urie Bronfenbrenner: This sociologist studied the impact of divorce on children and found that children adjust better if there is a second adult who can be counted on for support. (319)

Andrew Cherlin: Cherlin notes that our society has not yet developed adequate norms for remarriage. (320)

Donald Dutton and Arthur Aron: These researchers compared the sexual arousal levels of men who are in dangerous situations with men in safe situations and found that the former were more sexually aroused than the latter. (305)

Kathleen Gerson: Gerson found that there are different reasons why some couples choose not to have children--weak marriages, expenses associated with raising children, diminished career opportunities. (312)

Alex Heckert, Thomas Nowak and Kay Snyder: These researchers did secondary analysis of data gathered on a nationally representative sample and found that divorce increases when women earn more than their husbands, the wife's health is poorer than her husband's, or the wife does less housework. (317)

Arlie Hochschild: Hochschild conducted research on families in which both parents are employed full-time in order to find out how household tasks are divided up. She found that women did more of the housework than their husbands, resulting in women putting in a *second shift* at home after their workday has ended. (302)

William Jankowiak and Edward Fischer: These anthropologists surveyed data on 166 societies and found that the majority of them contained the ideal of romantic love. (304)

Melvin Kohn: Kohn studied social class differences in child-rearing. (307)

Jeanette & Robert Lauer: These sociologists interviewed 351 couples who had been married fifteen years or longer in order to find out what makes a marriage successful. (322)

Lillian Rubin: Rubin compared working and middle class couples and found the key to how well the couple adjusts to the arrival of children is social class. Rubin also interviewed both career women and homemakers found that the notion of the "empty-nest" as a difficult time for women is largely a myth and that most women's satisfaction increased when the last child left home. (307, 309)

Diana Russell: Russell found that incest victims who experience the most difficulty are those who have been victimized the most often, over longer periods of time, and whose incest was "more intrusive." (321)

Nicholas Stinnett: Stinnett studied 660 families from all regions of the U.S. and parts of South America in order to find out what the characteristics of happy families are. (322)

Murray Straus: This sociologist has studied domestic violence and found that, while husbands and wives are equally likely to attack one another, men inflict more damage on women than the reverse. (313)

Bob Suzuki: This sociologist studied Chinese-American and Japanese-American families and identified several distinctive characteristics of this type of family. (311)

Martin Whyte: Whyte interviewed married women in the greater Detroit area and found that marital satisfaction tended to decrease with the birth of a child. (306)

SELF-TEST

After completing this self-test, check your answers against the Answer Key beginning on page 263 of this Study Guide and against the text on page(s) indicated in parentheses.

MULTIPLE CHOICE QUESTIONS

1.   Polyandry is: (298)
     a.   a marriage in which a woman has more than one husband.
     b.   a marriage in which a man has more than one wife.
     c.   male control of a society or group.
     d.   female control of a society or group.

2.   The family of orientation: (299)
     a.   is the family formed when a couple's first child is born.
     b.   is the same thing as an extended family.
     c.   is the same as the family of procreation.
     d.   None of the above.

3.   Endogamy: (299)
     a.   is the practice or marrying outside one's group.
     b.   is the practice of marrying within one's own group.
     c.   is the practice of marrying someone within one's own family.
     d.   None of the above.

4.   In a matrilineal system: (300)
     a.   descent is figured only on the mother's side.
     b.   children are not considered related to their mother's relatives.
     c.   descent is traced on both the mother's and the father's side.
     d.   descent is figured only on the father's side.

5.   According to functionalists, the family: (300)
     a.   serves very different functions from society to society.
     b.   serves certain essential functions in all societies.
     c.   has very few functions left.
     d.   is no longer universal.

6.   The incest taboo: (300-301)
        a.   is rules specifying the degrees of kinship that prohibit sex or marriage.
        b.   helps families avoid role confusion.
        c.   facilitates the socialization of children.
        d.   All of the above.

7.   According Hochschild, which is <u>not</u> a resistance strategy used by men to avoid housework? (303-304)
        a.   waiting it out
        b.   purchasing services
        c.   needs reduction
        d.   playing dumb

8.   What factor is associated with a husband's likelihood of doing his share of the housework? (302)
        a.   his level of education
        b.   the social class of the couple
        c.   his earnings relative to his wife's
        d.   his ethnicity

9.   Among most people in the U.S., romantic love: (304)
        a.   is considered to be a relic of the past.
        b.   is considered to be the single most important factor in marriage.
        c.   is considered to be somewhat less important than the financial potential of the spouse.
        d.   None of the above.

10.   The tendency of people with similar characteristics to marry one another is: (306)
        a.   propinquity.
        b.   erotic selection.
        c.   homogamy.
        d.   heterogamy.

11.   What was the key Lillian Rubin identified to explain how couples adjust to the arrival of children? (307)
        a.   race of parents
        b.   age of mother at time of first birth
        c.   educational level of parents
        d.   social class of parents

12.   A national survey found that among married couples, fathers are the caregivers for almost _____ percent of children. (307)
        a.   25
        b.   30
        c.   35
        d.   40

13. The empty nest syndrome: (309)
    a. is not a reality for most parents.
    b. causes couples to feel a lack of companionship.
    c. is easier for women who have not worked outside the home.
    d. None of the above.

14. Who is likely to face problems adjusting to widowhood, men or women? (309)
    a. men
    b. women
    c. both; it is equally difficult for men and women to adjust to the loss of a spouse
    d. neither; research shows that both adjust relatively easily.

15. According to your text, a major concern of upper class African-American families is: (309)
    a. achievement and respectability.
    b. problems of poverty.
    c. maintaining family lineage.
    d. All of the above.

16. Machismo: (310)
    a. distinguishes Latino families from other groups.
    b. is an emphasis on male strength and dominance.
    c. exists where the Chicano husband-father plays a strong role in his family.
    d. All of the above.

17. The most significant issue facing Native-American families today is: (311)
    a. whether to move off the reservations or not.
    b. whether to follow traditional values or assimilate.
    c. whether to send their children to Anglo colleges and universities.
    d. whether to be permissive or authoritative with their children.

18. The primary source of strain for one-parent families is: (312)
    a. divorce.
    b. poverty.
    c. delinquency.
    d. All of the above.

19. Children from single-parent families are more likely to: (312)
    a. drop out of school.
    b. become delinquent.
    c. be poor as adults.
    d. All of the above.

20. A family whose members were once part of other families is known as a: (313)
    a. reconstituted family.
    b. mixed family.
    c. blended family.
    d. multiple nuclei family.

21.   Cohabitation: (314)
        a.   is the condition of living together as an unmarried couple.
        b.   has increased about eight times in just 25 years.
        c.   has occurred before about half of all couples marry.
        d.   All of the above.

22.   The "sandwich generation" refers to: (315)
        a.   grandparents who are primary caregivers for latchkey grandchildren.
        b.   children who survive on peanut butter sandwiches.
        c.   people who find themselves responsible for the care of children and aging parents.
        d.   people caught between families due to divorce.

23.   The pattern of parenting in which contact with one's children from a previous relationship is reduced as new relationships with another woman and her children are formed is: (319)
        a.   sequential fatherhood.
        b.   serial fatherhood.
        c.   temporary fatherhood.
        d.   modern fatherhood.

24.   Today, the average divorced woman will wait about _____ years to remarry. (320)
        a.   two
        b.   three
        c.   four
        d.   five

25.   According to Murray Straus, _gender_ _____ underlies much marital violence. (321) _inequality_
        a.   economic woes
        b.   gender inequality
        c.   alcohol
        d.   ignorance

TRUE-FALSE QUESTIONS

T F   1.   Families are people who live together in the same housing unit. (299)
T F   2.   The best example of endogamy is the incest taboo, which prohibits sex and marriage among certain relatives. (299)
T F   3.   Functionalists believe that the incest taboo helps the family to avoid role confusion. (300)
T F   4.   The phrase "second shift" refers to the time a person spends on household chores following a full day's work. (303)
T F   5.   According to Arlie Hochschild, it is very important for a husband to express appreciation to his wife for her being so organized that she can handle both work for wages and the second shift at home. (304)
T F   6.   Of all categories of husbands, those who earn less than their wives do the most housework. (303)
T F   7.   Love and marriage channels include age, education, social class, race, and religion. (306)
T F   8.   The birth of a child usually increases the level of marital satisfaction. (306)
T F   9.   For working single mothers, grandparents are twice as likely as fathers to step in and

provide child care while the woman is working. (307)

T F   10.   Firstborns tend to be disciplined more than children who follow. (308)

T F   11.   Regardless of the type of household, less than one in five preschoolers of working parents is cared for in organized child care facilities. (308)

T F   12.   Researchers have found that most husbands and wives experience the empty nest when their last child leaves home. (309)

T F   13.   Because of the marriage squeeze, African-American women are more likely than other racial groups to marry men who are less educated than themselves, who are unemployed, or who are divorced. (310)

T F   14.   Marriage between homosexuals is legal in several states, including California. (313)

T F   15.   Americans have become more tolerant of cohabitation. (314)

T F   16.   Among industrialized nations, the United States ranks at the top in terms of the rate of births to unmarried women. (315)

T F   17.   Children of divorce feel more distant from their parents than do children from intact families. (318)

T F   18.   The usually pattern of father-child contact following a divorce is for the contact to be fairly high for several years while the child is young, but then to drop off significantly as the child moves through adolescence. (319)

T F   19.   On the average, a divorced woman waits five years before remarrying. (320)

T F   20.   In the future, the estimates are that the majority of Americans will continue to marry because they see it a vital to their welfare. (322)

FILL-IN QUESTIONS

1.   A marriage in which a man has more than one wife is _polygamy_. (298)

2.   A _household_ consists of all people who occupy the same housing unit. (299)

3.   A(n) _nuclear family_ is a family consisting of a husband, wife, and child(ren). (299)

4.   The family you grow up in is called your _____. (299)

5.   A social group's approval arrangement for mating, usually marked by a ritual ceremony of some sort, is _marriage_. (299)

6.   _Exogamy_ is the practice of marrying outside one's group. (299)

7.   Those societies in which descent is only counted on the father's side are _patrilineal_. (300)

8.   Female control of a society or group is a(n) _matriarchy_. (300)

9.   Feelings of erotic attraction, accompanied by an idealization of the other, is the definition of _romantic love_. (304)

10.   _Homogamy_ is the tendency of people with similar characteristics to get married. (306)

11.   A married couple's domestic situation after the last child has left home is sometimes referred to as the _empty nest_. (309)

12.   An emphasis on male strength and dominance is _Patriarchy_. (310)

13.   A _blended family_ is one whose members were once part of other families. (313)

14.   The term sociologists use to describe adults who are living together in a sexual relationship without being married is _cohabitation_. (314)

15.   The pattern of divorced fathers living with, supporting, and playing an active fathering role with the children of the woman with whom they are currently involved is known as _Serial fatherhood_ (319)

MATCH THESE SOCIAL SCIENTISTS WITH THEIR CONTRIBUTIONS

___ 1. Blumstein & Schwartz   a. *factors associated with successful marriages*
___ 2. Dutton & Aron   b. *studied household issues of same-sex couples*
___ 3. Andrew Cherlin   c. *found that women's satisfaction increased after last child moved out*
___ 4. Lauer & Lauer   d. *studied incest victims*
___ 5. Kathleen Gerson   e. *identified reasons why couples choose to be child-free*
___ 6. Arlie Hochschild   f. *studied the relationship between danger and sexual arousal*
___ 7. Melvin Kohn   g. *identified distinctive characteristics of Asian American families*
___ 8. Lillian Rubin   h. *noted lack of norms regarding remarriage*
___ 9. Diana Russell   i. *studied social class differences in child-rearing*
___ 10. Bob Suzuki   j. *identified the second shift*

ESSAY QUESTIONS

1.   Explore why it is so difficult to answer the question "What is a family, anyway?"

2.   Identify the stages in the family life cycle, discussing what tasks are accomplished in each stage and what event marks that transition from one stage to the next.

3.   Discuss the impact that divorce has on family members -- men, women and children.

"DOWN-TO-EARTH SOCIOLOGY"

1.   What was your reaction to the description family life in Sweden (p. 301)? Should similar benefits be available to new families in the U.S.? What consequences would this have for family life? What are some of the obstacles to having such a program in this country?

2.   Do you think the second shift (pp. 303-304), is a temporary problem or a long-range problem in many families? How will you resolve problems such as this in your family?

3.   Would you like to have your marriage arranged for you by your parents? Consider this as you read "East is East and West is West" (p. 305). What would you gain and lose by this?

4.   After reading about marriage and family life in this chapter consider the three research findings reported on page 317. Try and develop some explanations for each, based on your new sociological knowledge, then turn to page 318 and see whether or not the experts' explanations are similar to your own. In what ways did yours differ?

5.   What are your own views on "covenant marriage?" As you read more about it on page 319, did you feel that this was a solution to the problem of high divorce rates? Why or why not?

CHAPTER 13
EDUCATION AND RELIGION

CHAPTER SUMMARY

- Industrialized societies are credential societies; employers use diplomas and degrees to determine who is eligible for jobs. Educational certification provides evidence of a person's ability in societies that are large and anonymous and people lack personal knowledge of one another.

- In general, formal education is more extensive in the Most Industrialized Nations, undergoing extensive change in the Industrializing Nations, and very spotty in the Least Industrialized Nations.

- Functionalists emphasize the functions of education, including teaching knowledge and skills, transmitting cultural values, social integration, gatekeeping, and mainstreaming.

- Conflict theorists view education as a mechanism for maintaining social inequality and reproducing the social class system. Accordingly, they stress how mechanisms such as unequal funding of schools, culturally biased IQ tests, tracking, and the hidden curriculum reinforce basic social inequality.

- Symbolic interactionists examine classroom interaction. They study how teacher expectations cause a self-fulfilling prophecy, producing the very behavior the teacher is expecting.

- In addition to violence, the problems facing the current U.S. educational system include falling SAT scores, grade inflation, social promotion, and functional illiteracy. Suggestions for reform include increasing academic standards and expectations for both students and teachers.

- Durkheim identified the essential elements of religion: beliefs that separate the profane from the sacred, rituals, and a moral community.

- According to the functionalist perspective, religion meets basic human needs such as answering questions about ultimate meaning, providing social solidarity, guidelines for everyday life, adaptation, support for the government, and social change. Functionalists also believe religion has two main dysfunctions: war and religious persecution.

- Symbolic interactionists focus on how religious symbols communicate meaning and how rituals, beliefs, and experiences unite people into a community.

- Conflict theorists see religion as a conservative force that serves the needs of the ruling class by reflecting and reinforcing social inequality.

- Unlike Marx, Weber saw religion as a powerful force for social change. He analyzed how Protestantism gave rise to an ethic that stimulated "the spirit of capitalism." The result was capitalism, which transformed society.

- Sociologists have identified cults, sects, churches, and ecclesia as distinct types of religious organizations. All religions began as cults; although most ultimately fail, those that survive become sects. As a sect grows it may change into a church. Ecclesiae, or state religions, are rare.

- Religion in the United States is characterized by diversity, pluralism and freedom, competition, a fundamentalist revival, and the electronic church. Secularization, a shift from spiritual concerns to those of "this world," is the force behind the dynamics of religious organization. As a cult or sect evolves into a church, its teachings are adapted to reflect changes in the social status of its members. Dissatisfied members break away to form new cults or sects.

- Even in countries where a concerted effort was made to eliminate it, religion has continued to thrive. Religion apparently will continue to exist as long as humanity does.

LEARNING OBJECTIVES

As you read Chapter 13, use these learning objectives to organize your notes. After completing your reading, briefly state an answer to each of the objectives, and review the text pages in parentheses.

1.   Explain why the United States has become a credential society. (328-329)
2.   Outline the major differences in the educational systems of Japan, the former Soviet Union, and Egypt. (329-330)
3.   List and briefly explain the functions of education. (330-332)
4.   Explain how education maintains social inequality, according to conflict theorists. (332-335)
5.   Summarize symbolic interaction research regarding teacher expectations and the self-fulfilling prophecy. (335)
6.   Identify the major problems with the U.S. educational system and discuss solutions. (336-339)
7.   Define religion and explain Durkheim's essential elements of religion. (339-340)
8.   Describe the functions and the dysfunctions of religion. (340-342)
9.   Explain what aspects of religion are focused on by symbolic interactionists. (342-343)
10.   Identify the conflict perspective on religion and note Marx's influence. (343-344)
11.   Describe the relationship between religion and capitalism, as seen by Weber. (344-345)
12.   Define cult, sect, church, and ecclesia, and describe the process by which some groups have moved from one category to another. (345-347)
13.   State the major characteristics of religion in the U.S. (348-350)
14.   Explain what is meant by secularization of religion. (351-352)
15.   Analyze the future of religion. State whether or not you agree with the author's assertion that "religion will last as long as humanity lasts," and defend your answer. (352)

CHAPTER OUTLINE

EDUCATION: TRANSFERRING KNOWLEDGE AND SKILLS

I.   **Education in Global Perspective**
  A.   A credential society is one in which employers use diplomas and degrees to determine job eligibility.
   1.   The sheer size, urbanization and consequent anonymity of U.S. society is a major reason why credentials are required. Diplomas/degrees often serve as sorting devices for employers; because they don't know the individual personally, they depend on schools to weed out the capable from the incapable.
   2.   As technology and knowledge change, simple on-the-job training will not do; specific job skills must be mastered before an individual is allowed to do certain kinds of work.
   3.   Without the right credentials, a person will not get hired despite the person's ability to do the job better than someone else.
  B.   Education in the Most Industrialized Nations: Japan
   1.   Japanese education reflects a group-centered ethic. Children in grade school work as a group, mastering the same skills/materials; cooperation and respect for elders (and positions of authority) is stressed.
   2.   College admission procedures are based on test scores; only the top scorers are admitted, regardless of social class.
  C.   Education in the Industrializing Nations: Post-Soviet Russia
   1.   After the Revolution of 1917, the government insisted that socialist values dominate education, seeing education as a means to undergird the new political

system; children were taught that capitalism was evil and communism was the salvation of the world. Education was centralized, with all schools following the same curriculum.

2.   Today, Russians are in the midst of "reinventing" education. Private, religious, and even foreign-run schools are operating, and students are encouraged to think for themselves.

3.   The primary difficulty facing the post-Soviet educational system is the rapidly changing values and world views currently underway in Russia.

D.   Education in the Least Industrialized Nations: Egypt

1.   Several centuries before the birth of Christ, Egypt was a world-renowned center of learning. Primary areas of study during this period were physics, astronomy, geometry, geography, mathematics, philosophy, and medicine. After defeat in war, education declined, never to rise to its former prominence.

2.   Today, education is free at all levels, including college; however, qualified teachers are few, classrooms are crowded, and education is highly limited. Although it is free at all levels, children of the wealthy are still several times as likely to get a college education.

II.   The Functionalist Perspective: Education's Social Benefits

A.   A central position of functionalism is that when the parts of society are working properly, each contributes to the stability of society. For education, both manifest and latent functions can be identified.

B.   The functions of education include: (1) teaching knowledge and skills; (2) cultural transmission of values (individualism, competition, and patriotism); (3) social integration (molding students into a more or less cohesive unit); and (4) gatekeeping (determining who will enter what occupations, through tracking and social placement).

C.   Schools have assume many functions previously fulfilled by the family (e.g., child care and sex education).

III.   The Conflict Perspective: How Education Reproduces the Social Class Structure

A.   The educational system is a tool used by those in the controlling sector of society to maintain their dominance. Education reproduces the social class structure.

B.   Regardless of ability, children of the wealthy are usually placed in college-bound tracks and children of the poor in vocational tracks. Whites are more likely to complete high school, go to college, and get a degree than African Americans and Latinos. The education system helps pass privilege (or lack thereof) across generations.

C.   The hidden curriculum is unwritten rules of behavior and attitude (e.g., obedience to authority, conformity to cultural norms) taught in school in addition to the formal curriculum.

D.   Conflict theorists criticize IQ (intelligence quotient) testing because they not only measure intelligence but also culturally acquired knowledge. By focusing on these factors, IQ tests reflect a cultural bias that favors the middle class and discriminates against minority and lower class students.

E.   Because public schools are largely financed by local property taxes, there are rich and poor school districts. Unequal funding stacks the deck against minorities and the poor.

IV.   The Symbolic Interaction Perspective

A.   Symbolic interactionists study face-to-face interaction inside the classroom. They have found that expectations of teachers are especially significant in determining what students learn.

B.   The Rist research (participant observation in an African-American grade school with an African-American faculty) found tracking begins with teachers' perceptions.

    1.   After eight days--and without testing for ability--teachers divided the class into fast, average, and slow learners; social class was the basis for the assignments.

    2.   Students from whom more was expected did the best; students in the slow group were ridiculed and disengaged themselves from classroom activities.

    3.   The labels applied in kindergarten tended to follow the child through school.

C.   George Farkas found students scoring the same on course matter may receive different grades: females get higher grades, as do Asian Americans. Some students signal that they are interested in what the teacher is teaching; teachers pick up these signals.

V.   Problems in U.S. Education--and Their Solutions

A.   A variety of factors have been identified as the major problems facing the U.S. educational system today. These problems include: the rising tide of mediocrity, grade inflation, and how it relates to social promotion and functional illiteracy; and violence in schools.

B.   A number of solutions have been offered to address these problems, including creating a secure learning environment and establishing higher academic standards and expectations.

RELIGION: ESTABLISHING MEANING

VI.   What Is Religion?

A.   According to Durkheim, religion is the beliefs/practices separating the profane from the sacred, uniting adherents into a moral community.

    1.   Sacred refers to aspects of life having to do with the supernatural that inspire awe, reverence, deep respect, or deep fear.

    2.   Profane refers to the ordinary aspects of everyday life.

B.   He found religion to be defined by three elements: (1) beliefs that some things are sacred (forbidden, set off from the profane); (2) practices (rituals) concerning things considered sacred; and (3) a moral community (a church) resulting from a group's beliefs and practices.

VII.   The Functionalist Perspective

A.   Religion performs functions such as: (1) answering questions about ultimate meaning (the purpose of life, why people suffer); (2) uniting believers into a community that shares values and perspectives; (3) providing guidelines for life; (4) controlling behavior; (5) providing support for the government; and (6) spearheading social change (on occasion, as in the case of the civil rights movement in the 1960s).

B.   War and religious persecution are dysfunctions of religion.

VIII.   The Symbolic Interactionist Perspective

A.   Religions use symbols to provide identity and social solidarity for members. For members, these are not ordinary symbols, but sacred symbols evoking awe and reverence, which become a condensed way of communicating with others.

B.   Rituals are ceremonies or repetitive practices that unite people into a moral community. Some are designed to create a feeling of closeness with God and unity with one another.

    1.   Symbols, including rituals, develop from beliefs. A belief may be vague ("God is") or specific ("God wants us to prostrate ourselves and face Mecca five times each day").

    2.   Religious beliefs include values and a cosmology (unified picture of the world).

C.   Religious experience is a sudden awareness of the supernatural or a feeling of coming in contact with God. Some Protestants use the term "born again" to describe people who have undergone a religious experience.

IX.   The Conflict Perspective

A.   Conflict theorists are highly critical of religion. Karl Marx called religion the "opium of the people" because he believed that the workers escape into religion. He argued that religion diverts the energies of the oppressed from changing their circumstances because believers focus on the happiness they will have in the coming world rather than on their suffering in this world.

B.   Religious teachings and practices reflect a society's inequalities. Religion legitimates social inequality; it reflects the interests of those in power by teaching that the existing social arrangements of a society represent what God desires.

X.   Religion and the Spirit of Capitalism

A.   Observing that European countries industrializing under capitalism, Weber questioned why some societies embraced capitalism while others clung to traditional ways. He concluded that religion held the key to modernization (transformation of traditional societies into industrial societies).

B.   Weber concluded that:

1.   Religion (including a Calvinistic belief in predestination and the need for reassurance as to one's fate) is the key to why the spirit of capitalism developed in Europe.

2.   A change in religion (from Catholicism to Protestantism) led to a change in thought and behavior. The result was the Protestant Ethic, a commitment to live a moral life and to work and be frugal.

3.   The spirit of capitalism (desire to accumulate capital as a duty, as an end in itself), which resulted from this new ethic, was a radical departure from the past.

C.   Today the spirit of capitalism and the Protestant ethic are by no means limited to Protestants; they have become cultural traits that have spread throughout the world.

XI.   Types of Religious Groups

A.   A cult is a new religion with few followers, whose teachings and practices put it at odds with the dominant culture and religion.

1.   All religions began as cults. Cults often emerge with the appearance of a charismatic leader (exerting extraordinary appeal to a group of followers).

2.   Each cult meets with rejection from society. The message given by the cult is seen as a threat to the dominant culture.

B.   A sect is larger than a cult, but still feels substantial hostility from and toward society. If a sect grows, its members tend to become respectable in society, and the sect is changed into a church.

C.   A church is a large, highly organized religious group with formal, sedate services and less emphasis on personal conversion. The religious group is highly bureaucratized (including national and international offices that give directions to local congregations). Most new members come from within the church, from children born to existing members, rather than from outside recruitment.

D.   An ecclesia is a religious group so integrated into the dominant culture that it is difficult to tell where one begins and the other leaves off. The government and religion work together to shape the society. There is no recruitment of members, for citizenship makes everyone a member. The majority of the society belong to the religion in name only.

E.   Although religions began as cults, not all varieties of a religion have done so. A denomination, a "brand name" within a religion (e. g., Methodist), begins as a splinter group. On occasion a large group within a church may disagree on some of the church's teachings (but not its major message) and break away to form its own organization.

XII. **Religion in the United States**

    A.   Characteristics of membership in U.S. churches:

        1.   Membership is highest in the South, followed by the Midwest and the East.

        2.   Each religious group draws members from all social classes, although some are more likely to draw members from the top of the social class system and others from the bottom. The most top-heavy are Episcopalians and Jews, the most bottom-heavy the Baptist and Evangelicals.

        3.   All major religious groups in the United States draw from various racial and ethnic groups; however, persons of Hispanic or Irish descent are likely to be Roman Catholics, those of Greek origin to belong to the Greek Orthodox church, while African Americans are likely to be Protestants.

        4.   Membership rate increases steadily with age.

    B.   Characteristics of Religious Groups

        1.   There is a diversity of religious groups--no state church, no ecclesia, and no single denomination dominates.

        2.   The many religions compete with one another for members.

        3.   Today there is a fundamentalist revival because mainstream churches fail to meet basic religious needs of large numbers of people.

        4.   The electronic church, in which tele-evangelists reach millions of viewers and raise millions of dollars, has grown. Recently, the electronic church has moved to the Internet. Some feel that the Internet may fundamentally change our ideas about God.

    C.   The history of U.S. churches is marked by secularization and the splintering of religious groups.

        1.   Initially, the founders of religious sects felt alienated from the general culture, their values and lower social class position setting them apart.

        2.   As time passes, the members of the group become successful, acquiring more education, becoming middle class, and growing more respectable. They no longer feel alienated from the dominant culture. There is an attempt to harmonize religious beliefs with the new cultural orientation.

        3.   This process is the secularization of religion, of shifting the focus from religious matters to affairs of this world.

        4.   Those who have not achieved worldly success feel betrayed and break away to form a new sect.

XIII. **The Future of Religion**

    A.   Science cannot answer questions about four concerns many people have: the existence of God; the purpose of life; morality; and the existence of an afterlife.

    B.   Neither science nor political systems can replace religion, and religion will last as long as humanity lasts.

KEY TERMS

After studying the chapter, review each of the following terms.

born again: a term describing Christians who have undergone a life-transforming religious experience so radical that they feel they have become a "new person" (343)

charisma: literally, an extraordinary gift from God; more commonly, an outstanding, "magnetic" personality (346)

charismatic leader: literally, someone to whom God has given an extraordinary gift; more commonly, someone who exerts extraordinary appeal to a group of followers (346)

church: According to Durkheim, one of the three essential elements of religion--a moral community of believers (340); used by other sociologists to refer to a highly organized religious organization (347)

cosmology: teachings or ideas that provide a unified picture of the world (343)

credential society: a group that uses of diplomas and degrees to determine who is eligible for jobs, even though the diploma or degree may be irrelevant to the actual work (328)

cult: a new religion with few followers, whose teachings and practices put it at odds with the dominant culture and religion (345)

cultural transmission: in reference to education, the ways in which schools transmit a society's culture, especially its core values (331)

ecclesia: a religious group so integrated into the dominant culture that it is difficult to tell where the one begins and the other leaves off (347)

functional illiterate: a high school graduate who has difficulty with basic reading and math (337)

gatekeeping: the process by which education opens and closes doors of opportunity; another term for the social placement function of education (332)

grade inflation: giving higher grades given for the same work; a general rise in student grades without a corresponding increase in learning or test scores (336)

hidden curriculum: the unwritten goals of schools, such as teaching obedience to authority and conformity to cultural norms (333)

latent functions: unintended consequences of people's actions that helps to keep a social system in equilibrium (330)

mainstreaming (or inclusion): helping people to become part of the mainstream of society (331)

manifest functions: intended consequences of people's actions designed to help some part of a social system (330)

modernization: the transformation of traditional societies into industrial societies (344)

profane: Durkheim's term for common elements of everyday life (340)

Protestant Ethic: Max Weber's term to describe the ideal of a self-denying, highly moral life, accompanied by hard work and frugality (345)

religion: according to Emile Durkheim, beliefs and practices that separate the profane from the sacred and unite its adherents into a moral community (339)

religious experience: an awareness of the supernatural or a feeling of coming into contact with God (343)

rituals: ceremonies or repetitive practices; in this context, religious observances or rites, often intended to evoke a sense of awe of the sacred (343)

sacred: Durkheim's term for things set apart or forbidden, which inspire fear, awe, reverence, or deep respect (340)

sect: a group larger than a cult that still feels substantial hostility from and toward society (347)

secularization of religion: the replacement of a religion's "otherworldly" concerns with concerns about "this world" (352)

social placement: a function of education; funneling people into a society's various positions (332)

social promotion: passing students to the next grade even though they have not mastered basic materials (336)

spirit of capitalism: Weber's term for the desire to accumulate capital as a duty--not to spend it, but as an end in itself--and to constantly reinvest it (344)

tracking: the sorting of students into different educational programs on the basis of real or perceived abilities (332)

KEY PEOPLE

Review the major theoretical contributions or research findings of these people.

James Coleman and Thomas Hoffer: A study of students in Catholic and public high schools by these two sociologists demonstrated that performance was based on setting higher standards for students rather than on individual ability. (337)

Randall Collins: Collins studied the credential society. (328)

Kingsley Davis and Wilbert Moore: Davis and Moore argue that a major task of society is to fill social positions with capable people and that one of the functions of schools is gatekeeping -- the funneling of people into these positions based on merit.(332)

Emile Durkheim: Durkheim investigated world religions and identified elements that are common to all religions--separation of sacred from profane, beliefs about what is sacred, practices surrounded the sacred, and a moral community. (339)

George Farkas: Farkas and a team of researchers investigated how teacher expectations affect student grades. They found that students signal teachers that they are good students by being eager, cooperative and working hard. (335)

Benton Johnson: Johnson analyzed types of religious groups--cults, sects, churches, and ecclesia. (345)

Karl Marx: Marx was critical of religion, calling it the opium of the masses. (343)

Richard Niebuhr: This theologian suggested that the splintering of Christianity into numerous branches has more to do with social change than with religious conflict. (351)

Talcott Parsons: Another functionalist who suggested that a function of schools is to funnel people into social positions. (332)

Liston Pope: Another sociologist who studied types of religious groups. (345)

Ray Rist: This sociologist's classic study of an African-American grade school uncovered some of the dynamics of educational tracking. (335)

Thomas Sowell: Sowell has studied international differences in student performance. (336)

Ernst Troeltsch: Yet another sociologist who is associated with types of religious groups from cults to eccelsia. (345)

Max Weber: Weber studied the link between Protestantism and the rise of capitalism and found that the ethic associated with Protestant denominations was compatible with the early needs of capitalism. (344)

SELF-TEST

After completing this self-test, check your answers against the Answer Key beginning on page 266 of this Study Guide and against the text on page(s) indicated in parentheses.

MULTIPLE CHOICE QUESTIONS

1. Using diplomas to hire employees, even when diplomas are irrelevant to the work, is: (328)
    a. a credential society.
    b. a certification mill.
    c. employer discretion in hiring.
    d. None of the above.

2.   In Japan, college admission is based on: (329)
    a.   the ability of parents to pay the tuition.
    b.   making a high score on a national test.
    c.   being known by teachers as a "hard worker."
    d.   the same procedures that prevail in the United States.

3.   The function of education that sorts people into a society's various positions is: (332)
    a.   functional placement.
    b.   social placement.
    c.   railroading.
    d.   social promotion.

4.   From a conflict perspective, the real purpose of education is to: (332)
    a.   perpetuate existing social inequalities.
    b.   provide educational opportunities for students from all types of backgrounds.
    c.   teach patriotism, teamwork, and cooperation.
    d.   replace family functions which most families no longer fulfill.

5.   The hidden curriculum is based on: (333)
    a.   functionalism.
    b.   symbolic interactionism.
    c.   the conflict perspective.
    d.   ethnomethodology.

6.   Public schools are largely supported by: (334)
    a.   state funding.
    b.   federal funding.
    c.   local property taxes.
    d.   None of the above.

7.   Teacher expectations and face-to-face interactions are of interest to _____ theorists. (335)
    a.   functionalist
    b.   conflict
    c.   symbolic interaction
    d.   educational

8.   Research by George Farkas focused on: (335)
    a.   education of elite children.
    b.   how teacher expectations affect a kindergarten class.
    c.   how teacher expectations are influenced by students' alleged IQ scores.
    d.   how teacher expectations affect students' grades.

9.   During the past twenty to thirty years, combined scores on tests such as the SAT: (336)
    a.   have continued to improve.
    b.   have continued to decline.
    c.   have remained about the same.
    d.   None of the above.

10. High school graduates who have difficulty with basic reading and math are known as: (337)
    a. "boneheads."
    b. functional literates.
    c. functional illiterates.
    d. underachievers.

11. Which of the following is not a solution to the problems of the U.S. education: (337)
    a. providing a safe learning environment
    b. setting higher expectations
    c. increasing parental involvement
    d. eliminating the hidden curriculum

12. According to Durkheim, a church: (340)
    a. is a large, highly organized religious group.
    b. has little emphasis on personal conversion.
    c. is any group of believers sharing a set of beliefs and practices regarding the sacred.
    d. All of the above.

13. All of the following are functions of religion, except: (340-341)
    a. encouraging wars for holy causes.
    b. instilling the values of patriotism.
    c. spearheading social change.
    d. providing guidelines for daily life.

14. War and religious persecution are: (341)
    a. manifest functions of religion.
    b. latent functions of religion.
    c. dysfunctions of religion.
    d. functional equivalents of religion.

15. Religion is the opium of the people according to some: (343)
    a. conservatives.
    b. functionalists.
    c. conflict theorists.
    d. symbolic interactionists.

16. An example of the use of religion to legitimize social inequalities is: (344)
    a. the divine right of kings.
    b. a declaration that the Pharaoh or Emperor is god or divine.
    c. the defense of slavery as being God's will.
    d. All of the above.

17. Weber believed that religion held the key to: (344)
    a. modernization.
    b. bureaucratization.
    c. institutionalization.
    d. socialization.

18.   The spirit of capitalism is: (344)
    a.   the desire to accumulate capital so one can spend it to show how one "has it made."
    b.   Marx's term for the driving force in the exploitation of workers.
    c.   the ideal of a highly moral life, hard work, industriousness, and frugality.
    d.   None of the above.

19.   A cult: (345-347)
    a.   is a new religion with few followers.
    b.   has teachings and practices which put it at odds with the dominant culture.
    c.   often is at odds with other religions.
    d.   All of the above.

20.   Although larger than a cult, a _____ may still feel substantial hostility from society. (347)
    a.   commune.
    b.   ecclesia.
    c.   sect.
    d.   church.

21.   Churches: (347)
    a.   are highly bureaucratized.
    b.   have more sedate worship services.
    c.   gain new members from within, from children born to existing members.
    d.   All of the above.

22.   A "brand name" within a major religion is a(n): (347)
    a.   denomination.
    b.   faction.
    c.   cult.
    d.   sect.

23.   Church membership is highest in: (348)
    a.   the South and Midwest.
    b.   the Midwest and the West.
    c.   the Northeast.
    d.   the Northwest.

24.   _____ churches teach that the Bible is literally true and that salvation comes only through a personal relationship with Jesus Christ. (350)
    a.   Denominational
    b.   Roman Catholic
    c.   Fundamentalist
    d.   Orthodox

25.   Questions that science cannot answer include: (352)
    a.   is there a God?
    b.   what is the purpose of life?
    c.   what happens when a person dies?
    d.   All of the above.

TRUE-FALSE QUESTIONS

T F   1.   In the United States, employers use diplomas and degrees to determine who is eligible for a job. (328)

T F   2.   Japanese schools teach the value of competition to their students. (329)

T F   3.   In Post-Soviet Russia, private, religious, and foreign-run schools are not allowed to operate. (330)

T F   4.   Because Egyptian education is free at all levels, including college, children of the wealthy are no more likely than children of the poor to get a college education. (330)

T F   5.   Education's most obvious manifest function is to teach knowledge and skills. (330)

T F   6.   American schools discourage individualism and encourage teamwork. (331)

T F   7.   Students everywhere are taught that their country is the best country in the world. (331)

T F   8.   Functional theorists believe that social placement is harmful to society. (332)

T F   9.   Functionalists emphasize the hidden curriculum in their analysis of U.S. education. (333)

T F   10.   According to conflict theorists, unequal funding for education automatically stacks the deck against children from lower income families. (334)

T F   11.   Research by Ray Rist concluded that the child's journey through school was preordained by the end of the first year of kindergarten. (335)

T F   12.   George Farkas's research demonstrated that teachers discriminate against women and some minorities because they do not fit their expectations of what a good student should be. (335)

T F   13.   Research by Coleman and Hoffer demonstrated that the superior test performance of Catholic school students was due to the higher standards that teachers maintained. (337)

T F   14.   The goal of the sociological study of religion is to determine which religions are most effective in people's' lives. (339)

T F   15.   According to Durkheim, all religions separate the sacred from the profane. (340)

T F   16.   That the U.S. flag is prominently displayed in many churches is an example of how religion instills the value of patriotism in its believers. (341)

T F   17.   The term "born again" is a term used to describe the Hindu belief in reincarnation. (343)

T F   18.   Conflict theorists believe that religion mirrors and legitimates social inequalities of the larger society. (344)

T F   19.   Emile Durkheim wrote <u>The Protestant Ethic and the Spirit of Capitalism</u>. (344)

T F   20.   Cults often begin with the appearance of a charismatic leader. (346)

T F   21.   The terms church and state religion mean the same thing. (347)

T F   22.   Denominations may begin as splinter groups of a church. (347)

T F   23.   Sunday morning between 10 and 11 a.m. has been called "the most segregated hour in the United States." (347)

T F   24.   The racial segregation observed in church membership is based on religious teachings, not social custom. (349)

T F   25.   Fundamentalism is the belief that modernism threatens religion and that the faith as it was originally practiced should be restored. (350)

FILL-IN QUESTIONS

1. Using diplomas and degrees to determine who is eligible for jobs, even though the diploma or degree may be irrelevant to the actual work, is a characteristic of _____. (328)
2. _____ are the intended consequences of people's actions designed to help some part of the social system. (330)
3. The function of _____ is intended to help people become part of the mainstream of society. (331)
4. The process by which education opens and closes doors of opportunity for individuals in a society is the _____ function of education. (332)
5. Many U.S. schools practice _____, the sorting of students into different educational programs based on their real or perceived abilities. (332)
6. The unwritten goals of schools, such as teaching obedience to authority and conformity to cultural norms, is referred to as _____. (333)
7. A high school graduate who has difficulty with basic reading and math is _____. (337)
8. Durkheim's term for common elements of everyday life was _____. (340)
9. Answering questions about ultimate meaning, providing emotional comfort, and social solidarity are _____ of religion. (340)
10. For Muslims, the crescent moon and star, for Jews the Star of David, and for Christians the cross, all are examples of _____. (342)
11. _____ is teachings or ideas that provide a unified picture of the world. (343)
12. According to conflict theorists, religion is the _____. (343)
13. _____ is Weber's term to describe the ideal of a highly moral life, hard work, industriousness, and frugality. (345)
14. A(n) _____ is someone who exerts extraordinary appeal to a group of followers. (346)
15. _____ is the replacement of a religion's "otherworldly" concerns with concerns about "this world." (352)

MATCH THESE SOCIAL SCIENTISTS WITH THEIR CONTRIBUTIONS

___1. Randall Collins
___2. Ray Rist
___3. George Farkas
___4. Talcott Parsons
___5. Emile Durkheim
___6. Max Weber
___7. Karl Marx
___8. Ernst Troeltsch

a. *cult-sect-church-ecclesia typology*
b. *the gatekeeping function of education*
c. *credential society*
d. *The Elementary Forms of Religious Life*
e. *"religion is the opium of the people"*
f. *expectations of kindergarten teachers*
g. *teacher expectations in grading students*
h. *The Protestant Ethic and the Spirit of Capitalism*

ESSAY QUESTIONS

1. Select one of the three perspectives and design a research project to test the claims of that perspective about the nature of education.
2. In discussing solutions to educational problems, the author suggests that one direction in which schools should go is towards setting higher educational standards. Both the research by James Coleman and Thomas Hoffer, and the success of Jaime Escalante, support this. Discuss social factors that might explain why such a proposal has not been widely adopted by public schools across the country.

3.   Assume that you have been asked to make a presentation about religion to a group of people who have absolutely no idea what religion is. Prepare a speech in which you define religion and explain why it exists.

"DOWN-TO-EARTH SOCIOLOGY"

1.   In his classroom Jaime Escalante has challenged many of the assumptions about educating low income students (p. 338). Is his success due to his extraordinary teaching skills or is it possible to extend his successes into classrooms across the country? If so, what changes would have to be made in education?
2.   Why do you think we are so fascinated with cults such as the Heaven's Gate cult (p. 346)? What is it about the nature of social life today that produces so many cults? What does this tell you about the functions of religion is social life?
3.   After reading about "Bikers and Bibles" (p. 351), why do you think Herbie Shreve does what he does? Using concepts presented in this chapter, try and explain why Herbie and his father were often snubbed by fellow Christians for their work among the bikers.

CHAPTER 14
POPULATION AND URBANIZATION

CHAPTER SUMMARY

- Demography is the study of the size, composition, growth, and distribution of human populations. Over 200 years ago Thomas Malthus observed that populations grow geometrically while food supplies increase arithmetically; he argued that the population of the world would eventually outstrip its food supply. The debate between those who agree with his predictions (the New Malthusians) and those who disagree (the Anti-Malthusians) continues. Today, the basic cause of starvation is the global maldistribution of food rather than world overpopulation.

- People in the Least Industrialized Nations have large families because children play a very different role in the cultures of the Least Industrialized Nations. To project population trends, demographers use three demographic variables: fertility, mortality, and migration. A nation's growth rate is affected by unanticipated variable, such as wars, plagues, and famines, as well as government policies and industrialization.

- Urbanization, the process by which an increasing proportion of a population lives in cities, represents the greatest mass migration in human history. Cities can only develop if there is an agricultural surplus. Until the Industrial Revolution cities were small; as transportation and communication systems grew out of the Industrial Revolution, the infrastructure of modern cities developed and cities grew larger.

- Urbanization today is so extensive that some cities have become metropolises; in some cases metropolises have merged to form a megalopolis. Within the U.S., the trends are gentrification and regional migration.

- Three major models have been proposed to explain how cities expand: the concentric-zone, sector, and multiple-nuclei models. No one model is adequate in explaining completely the complexities of urban growth.

- Some people find a sense of community in cities; others find alienation. What people find depends largely on their background and urban networks. Herbert Gans identified five types of city dwellers: cosmopolites, singles, ethnic villages, the deprived, and the trapped. To develop community in the city, people personalize their shopping, identify with sports teams, and even become sentimental about objects in the city. Noninvolvement is generally functional for urbanites, but it impedes giving help in emergencies.

- Cities in the U.S. are subject to constant change, including disinvestment, suburbanization, and deindustrialization. Guiding principles for developing social policy are scale, livability, and social justice.

LEARNING OBJECTIVES

As you read Chapter 14, use these learning objectives to organize your notes. After completing your reading, briefly state an answer to each of the objectives, and review the text pages in parentheses.

1. Discuss the Malthus theorem and identify key issues in the debate between New Malthusians and Anti-Malthusians regarding the specter of overpopulation. (358-362)
2. Explain why there is starvation. (362-364)
3. Explain why people in the Least Industrialized Nations have so many children and note the implications of different rates of population growth. (364-365)

4.   State the three demographic variables used in estimating population growth and explain why it is difficult to forecast population growth. (365-369)
5.   Describe urbanization and outline the history of how cities came into existence. (370)
6.   Identify the trends that have contributed to the growth of metropolises and megalopolises. (370-371)
7.   Discuss urbanization in the U.S. (371-373).
8.   Discuss the three models of urban growth and critique the models. (373-375)
9.   Explain why many people feel a sense of alienation by living in large urban areas. (376)
10.   Define the urban village and briefly describe the five different types of people who live in the city, as identified by sociologist Herbert Gans. (376-377)
11.   Describe ways in which city people create a sense of intimacy for themselves in large urban areas. (378)
12.   Explain why the norm of noninvolvement and the diffusion of responsibility, which help urban dwellers get through everyday city life may be dysfunctional in some situations. (378)
13.   Outline the major changes facing U.S. cities regarding suburbanization, disinvestment, and deindustrialization. (380-381)
14.   Identify the guiding principles for developing solutions to urban problems. (381-382)

CHAPTER OUTLINE

POPULATION IN GLOBAL PERSPECTIVE
I.   **A Planet with No Space to Enjoy the Good Life?**
A.   Demography is the study of size, composition, growth, and distribution of populations.
B.   Thomas Malthus wrote *An Essay on the Principle of Population* (1798) stating the Malthus theorem--population grows geometrically while food supply increases arithmetically; thus, if births go unchecked, population will eventually outstrip food supply.
C.   New Malthusians believe Malthus was correct. The world's population is following an exponential growth curve (where numbers increase in extraordinary proportions): 1800, one billion; 1930, two billion; 1960, three billion; 1975, four billion; and 1987, five billion. Right now, the world population is almost six billion.
D.   Anti-Malthusians believe that people do not blindly reproduce until there is no room left.
        1.   They cite three stages of the demographic transition in Europe as an example: Stage 1, a fairly stable population (high birth rates offset by high death rates); Stage 2, "population explosion" (high birth rates and low death rates); and Stage 3, population stability (low birth rates and low death rates).
        2.   They assert this transition will happen in the Least Industrialized Nations, which currently are in the second stage.
        3.   Population shrinkage (a country's population is smaller because birth rate and immigration cannot replace those who die and emigrate) has occurred in Europe.
E.   Who is correct?
        1.   There is no question that the Least Industrialized Nations are in Stage 2, but there is a question about when they will reach Stage 3. Death rates have dropped but birth rates remain high.

2.   Leaders of the Most Industrialized Nations, fearing that these growing nations would upset the international balance of power, used the United Nations to spearhead global efforts to reduce world population growth.

3.   The population of the Least Industrialized Nations is still increasing, only at a slower rater. To the New Malthusians, the catastrophe is still coming; to Anti-Malthusians, this is a sign that the Least Industrialized Nations are approaching Stage 3.

4.   Only the future will prove the accuracy of either side's projections.

F.   Why are people starving? Does the world produce enough food to feed everyone?

      1.   Anti-Malthusians note that the amount of food produced for each person in the world has increased: famines are not the result of too little food production, but result from the global maldistribution of existing food.

      2.   The New Malthusians counter that the world's population continues to grow and the earth may not be able to continue to produce sufficient food.

      3.   New Malthusians promote policies that attempt to reduce the size of populations, while Anti-Malthusians concentrate on policies that focus on a more equitable distribution of food.

      4.   Recently, famines have been concentrated in Africa. However, these famines are not due to too many people living on too little land. Rather, these famines are due to outmoded farming techniques and ongoing political instability that disrupt harvests and food distribution.

II.   Sociological Perspectives on Population Growth

A.   There are different reasons why people in the Least Industrialized Nations have so many children.

      1.   Parenthood is a significant status. For women, motherhood is the most exalted status a woman can achieve--the more children, the higher the status. For men, their manhood is proven if they father many children, especially male children.

      2.   The community supports this view, awarding or withholding status.

      3.   Children are a sign of God's blessing; couples are expected to have many children.

      4.   Children are considered to be economic assets (the parents rely on the children to take care of them in their old age).

      5.   The conflict perspective stresses the domination of females by males in all spheres of life, including reproduction. Male dominance includes fathering many children as a means of achieving status in the community.

B.   Demographers use population pyramids (graphic representations of a population, divided into age and sex) to illustrate a country's population dynamics (e.g., Mexico's doubling rate is only 30 years).

      1.   Different population growth rates have different implications. Countries with slow growth rates have fewer people on which to spend their resources, while countries with rapid growth rates have to cope with increased numbers of people among whom to share resources.

      2.   A declining standard of living may result in political instability followed by severe repression by the government.

C.   Estimated population growth is based on three demographic variables.

      1.   Fertility, measured by the fertility rate (number of children an average woman bears), is sometimes confused with fecundity (number of children a woman

theoretically can bear). To compute a country's fertility rate, demographers use crude birth rate (annual number of births per 1,000 people).

2. Mortality is measured by the crude death rate (number of deaths per 1,000 people).

3. Migration is measured by the net migration rate (difference between the number of immigrants moving in and emigrants moving out per 1,000 population); it may be voluntary or forced. Push factors make people want to leave where they are living (e.g., poverty, persecution, lack of economic opportunity); pull factors attract people (e.g., opportunities for higher wages or better jobs in the new locale). The flow of migration is from the Least Industrialized Nations to the industrialized countries, with the U.S. being the world's number one choice of immigrants.

D. The growth rate equals births minus deaths, plus net migration.

1. Economic changes, government policies, and behavioral changes make it difficult to forecast population growth. The primary factor that influences a country's growth rate is its rate of industrialization--in every country that industrializes, the growth rate declines.

2. Because of the difficulties in forecasting population growth, demographers formulate several predictions simultaneously, each depending on different assumptions.

URBANIZATION
III. The Development of Cities

A. A city is a place in which a large number of people are permanently based and do not produce their own food.

1. Small cities with massive defensive walls existed as far back as 10,000 years ago; cities on a larger scale originated about 3500 B. C. as a result of the development of more efficient agriculture and of a surplus.

2. The Industrial Revolution drew people to cities to work.

3. Today urbanization not only means that more people live in cities, but also that today's cities are larger; about 300 of the world's cities contain at least one million people.

B. Urbanization is the process by which an increasing proportion of a population lives in cities. There are specific characteristics of cities, such as size and anonymity, that give them their unique urban flavor.

1. Metropolis refers to cities that grow so large that they exert influence over a region; the central city and surrounding smaller cities and suburbs are connected economically, politically, and socially.

2. Megalopolis refer to an overlapping area consisting of at least two metropolises and their suburbs, connected economically, socially, and sometimes politically.

C. In 1790, only about 5 percent of Americans lived in cities; by 1920, 50 percent of the U.S. population lived in urban areas; today, between 75 and 80 percent of Americans live in urban areas.

1. The U.S. Census Bureau divided the country into 269 metropolitan statistical areas (MSAs)--a central city and the urbanized counties that are linked to it.

2. Over half of the entire U.S. population lives in just 45 MSAs.

3. As Americans migrate in search of work and better life styles, distinct patterns appear. The general movement is from the North and East to the West and the

South--from the "snow belt" to the "sun belt."

4.   As Americans migrate and businesses move to serve them, edge cities have developed (a clustering of service facilities and residential areas near highway intersections).

5.   Gentrification, the movement of middle-class people into rundown areas of a city, is another major U.S. urban pattern.

E.   Robert Park coined the term human ecology to describe how people adapt to their environment (known as "urban ecology"); human ecologists have constructed three models which attempt to explain urban growth patterns.

     1.   Ernest W. Burgess proposed the concentric-zone model, which views the city as a series of zones emanating from its center, with each characterized by a different group of people and activity: Zone 1, central business district; Zone 2, in transition with deteriorating housing and rooming houses; Zone 3, area to which thrifty workers have moved to escape the zone in transition, yet maintain access to work; Zone 4, more expensive apartments, single-family dwellings, and exclusive areas where the wealthy live; and Zone 5, commuter zone consisting of suburban areas or cities that have developed around rapid transit routes.

     2.   The sector model sees urban zones as wedge-shaped sectors radiating out from the center. A zone might contain a sector of working-class housing, another sector of expensive housing, a third of businesses, and so on, all competing with one another for the same land. In an invasion-succession cycle, when poor immigrants move into a city, they settle in the lowest-rent area available and, as their numbers grow, begin to encroach on adjacent areas. As the poor move closer to the middle class, the middle class leave, expanding the sector of lower-cost housing.

     3.   The multiple-nuclei model views the city as comprised of multiple centers or nuclei, each of which focuses on a specialized activity (e.g., retail districts, automobile dealers, etc.).

     4.   Cities are complex, and no single model yet developed does justice to this complexity; the models do not make allowances for the extent to which elites influence the development of cities.

IV.   **City Life: Alienation and Community**

A.   For some, cities provide a sense of community--a feeling that people care about what happens to each other, and they depend upon one another. For others, the city is alienating.

B.   Louis Wirth argued that the city undermines kinship and neighborhood, which are the traditional bases of social control and social solidarity.

     1.   Urban dwellers live in anonymity, their lives marked by segmented and superficial encounters which make them grow aloof from one another and indifferent to other people's problems.

     2.   This is similar to the idea that *Gemeinschaft* (a sense of community that comes from everyone knowing everyone else) disappears as a country industrializes, and *Gesellschaft* (a society characterized by secondary, impersonal relationships which result in alienation) replaces it.

C.   Herbert Gans uses the term urban village to refer to an area of the city that people know well and in which they live, work, shop, and play.

D.   Gans identified five types of people who live in the city.

     1.   Cosmopolites--intellectuals and professionals, students, writers, and artists who

                  live in the inner city to be near its conveniences and cultural benefits.

        2.   Singles--young, unmarried people who come seeking jobs and entertainment.

        3.   Ethnic villagers--live in tightly knit neighborhoods that resemble villages and small towns, united by race and social class.

        4.   The deprived--the very poor, the emotionally disturbed, and the handicapped who live in neighborhoods more like urban jungles than urban villages.

        5.   The trapped--who consist of four subtypes: those who can not afford to move when their neighborhood is invaded by another ethnic group; downwardly mobile persons who have fallen from a higher social class; elderly people who have drifted into the slums because they are not wanted elsewhere and are powerless to prevent their downward slide; and alcoholics and drug addicts.

    E.   Sociologists have analyzed how urban dwellers build community in the city.

        1.   City people create a sense of intimacy for themselves by personalizing their shopping (by frequenting the same stores and restaurants, people become recognized as "regulars").

        2.   Spectator sports also engender community identification.

    F.   Urban dwellers are careful to protect themselves from the unwanted intrusions of strangers.

        1.   They follow a norm of noninvolvement--such as using a newspaper or a Walkman to indicate inaccessibility for interaction--to avoid encounters with people they do not know.

        2.   The more bystanders there are to an incident, the less likely people are to help because people's sense of responsibility becomes diffused. The norm of noninvolvement and the diffusion of responsibility may help urban dwellers get through everyday city life, but they are dysfunctional because people do not provide assistance to others.

V.   **Urban Problems and Social Policy**

    A.   Suburbanization--the movement from the city to the suburbs--has had a profound effect on U.S. cities.

        1.   People have moved for over 100 years to towns next to the cities in which they worked; today the speed and extent to which people have left the city is new.

        2.   Central cities have lost residents, businesses, and jobs, causing the cities' tax base (which supports essential city services and schools) to shrink; people left behind are those with limited financial means.

        3.   According to William Wilson, the term ghetto reflects a social transformation; groups represented in these areas today are more socially isolated than those who lived in these communities in the past.

        4.   Suburbanites prefer the city to keep its problems to itself and fight movements to share suburbia's revenues with the city. However, the time may come when suburbanites may have to pay for their attitudes toward the city.

    B.   By the 1940's, the movement to suburbs began to undermine the cities' tax base, a problem accelerated as huge numbers of poor rural migrants moved into northern cities.

        1.   As the tax base eroded, services declined, buildings deteriorated, and banks began red lining (drawing a line on a map around problem areas and refusing to make loans to living and working in these areas). This disinvestment pushed these areas into further decline.

        2.   The development of a global market has led to deindustrialization. Manufacturing

            firms have relocated from the inner city to areas where production costs are lower. The inner-city economies have not been able to provide alternative employment for poor residents, thereby locking them out of the economy.

    C.   Social policy usually takes one of two forms.

        1.   Urban renewal involves tearing down and rebuilding the buildings in an area. As a result of urban renewal, the areas residents can no longer afford to live in the area and are displaced to adjacent areas.

        2.   Enterprise zones are economic incentives to encourage businesses to move into the area. Most business, however, refuse to move into high- crime areas.

        3.   If U.S. cities are to change, they must become top agenda items of the U.S. government, with adequate resources in terms of money and human talents focused on overcoming urban woes.

    D.   William Flanagan suggests three guiding principles for working out specific solutions to urban problems: (1) regional and national planning is necessary; (2) growth needs to be channeled in such a way that makes city living attractive; and (3) social policy must be evaluated by its effects on people. Finally, unless the root causes of urban problems-- housing, education, and jobs--are addressed, solutions will only serve as band-aids that cover the real problems.

KEY TERMS

After studying the chapter, review each of the following terms.

alienation: a sense of not belonging, and a feeling that no one cares what happens to you (376)

basic demographic equation: growth rate = births - deaths + net migration (368)

city: a place in which a large number of people are permanently based and do not produce their own food (366)

community: a place people identify with, where they sense that they belong and that others care what happens to them (376)

crude birth rate: the annual number of births per 1,000 population (366)

crude death rate: the annual number of deaths per 1,000 population (366)

demographic transition: a three-stage historical process of population growth; first, high birth rates and high death rates; second, high birth rates and low death rates; and third, low birth rates and low death rates (360)

demographic variables: the three factors that influence population growth: fertility, mortality, and net migration (366)

demography: the study of the size, composition, growth, and distribution of human populations (358)

disinvestment: the withdrawal of investments by financial institutions, which seals the fate of an urban area (380)

edge city: a large clustering of service facilities and residences near a highway intersection that provides a sense of place to people who live, shop, and work there (373)

enterprise zone: the use of economic incentives in a designated area with the intention of encouraging investment there (382)

exponential growth curve: a pattern of growth in which numbers double during approximately equal intervals, accelerating in the latter stages (359)

fertility rate: the number of children that the average woman bears (366)

gentrification: the displacement of the poor in a section of a city by the relatively affluent, who renovate the former's homes (373)

growth rate: the net change in a population after adding births, subtracting deaths, and either adding or subtracting net migration (368)

human ecology: Robert Park's term for the relationship between people and their environment (natural resources such as land) (373)

invasion-succession cycle: the process of one group of people displacing a group whose racial-ethnic or social class characteristics differ from their own (374)

Malthus theorem: an observation by Thomas Malthus that although the food supply increases only arithmetically (from 1 to 2 to 3 to 4 and so on), population grows geometrically (from 2 to 4 to 8 to 16 and so forth) (358)

megalopolis: an urban area consisting of at least two metropolises and their many suburbs (371)

metropolis: a central city surrounded by smaller cities and their suburbs (371)

net migration rate: the difference between the number of immigrants and emigrants per 1,000 population (366)

population pyramid: a graphic representation of a population, divided into age and sex (365)

population shrinkage: the process by which a country's population becomes smaller because its birth rate and immigration are too low to replace those who die and emigrate (361)

redlining: the officers of a financial institution deciding not to make loans in a particular area (380)

suburbanization: the movement from the city to the suburbs (380)

suburbs: the communities adjacent to the political boundaries of a city (380)

urbanization: an increasing proportion of a population living in cities and those cities having an increasing influence in their society (370)

urban renewal: the rehabilitation of a rundown area, which usually results in the displacement of the poor who are living in that area (382)

zero population growth: a demographic condition in which women bear only enough children to reproduce the population (369)

KEY PEOPLE

State the major theoretical contributions or research findings of these people.

Ernest Burgess: Burgess developed the concentric zone model of urban development. (373)

Paul and Ann Ehrlich: These demographers predict that there will be a worldwide catastrophe if something is not done quickly to halt the population explosion. (361)

William Flanagan: Flanagan has suggested three guiding principles for finding solutions to pressing urban problems--use of regional planning, awareness of human needs, and equalizing the benefits as well as the impact of urban change. (382)

Herbert Gans: Gans studied urban neighborhoods, with the result that he documented the existence of community within cities and identified the several different types of urban dwellers that live there. (376)

Chauncey Harris and Edward Ullman: These two geographers developed the multiple-nuclei model of urban growth. (374)

Homer Hoyt: Hoyt modified Burgess's model of urban growth with the development of the sector model. (374)

David Karp and William Yoels: These sociologists note that identification with a city's sports teams can be so intense that even after an individual moves away from the city, he continues to root for the team.(378)

Thomas Malthus: Malthus was an economist who made dire predictions about the future of population growth. (358)

Robert Park: Park coined the term "human ecology" to describe how people adapt to their environment. (373)

Julian Simon: Simon is an anti-Malthusian who believes people do not just reproduce blindly but act intelligently and plan rationally. Simon has also argued that immigrants are a net contributor on the U.S. economy. (360)

Louis Wirth: Wirth wrote a classic essay, "Urbanism as a Way of Life," in which he argued that city life undermines kinship and neighborhood. (376)

SELF-TEST

After completing this self-test, check your answers against the Answer Key beginning on page 270 of this Study Guide and against the text on page(s) indicated in parentheses.

<u>MULTIPLE CHOICE QUESTIONS</u>

1. The proposition that the population grows geometrically while food supply increases arithmetically is known as the: (358)
    a. food surplus equation.
    b. Malthus theorem.
    c. exponential growth curve.
    d. demographic transition.

2. The New Malthusians point out that the world's population is: (359)
    a. in the midst of the demographic transition.
    b. becoming increasingly more urban.
    c. experiencing zero population growth.
    d. following an exponential growth curve.

3. Anti-Malthusians believe that: (360-361)
    a. people will blindly reproduce until there is no room left on earth.
    b. it is possible to project the world's current population growth into the indefinite future.
    c. most people do not use intelligence and rational planning when it comes to having children.
    d. None of the above.

4. The three-stage historical process of population growth is known as the: (360)
    a. demographic equation.
    b. demographic transition.
    c. exponential growth curve.
    d. implosion growth curve.

5. The process by which a country's population becomes smaller because its birth rate and immigration are too low to replace those who die and emigrate is: (361)
    a. population transfer.
    b. population annihilation.
    c. population shrinkage.
    d. population depletion.

6. According to Anti-Malthusians, people are starving because: (362)
    a.   there are too many people.
    b.   there is too little food.
    c.   there is a mismatch between where the greatest supply of food is and where the greatest demand for it is.
    d.   people are greedy.

7. People in the Least Industrialized Nations have so many children because: (364)
    a.   parenthood provides status.
    b.   children are considered to be an economic asset.
    c.   the community encourages people to have children.
    d.   All of the above.

8. Demographers use _____ to describe the age and sex distribution of a nation. (365)
    a.   computer simulations
    b.   population equations
    c.   population pyramids
    d.   graphic pyramids

9. Factors that influence population growth: fertility, mortality, and net migration are: (366)
    a.   demographic variables.
    b.   demographic transitions.
    c.   demographic equations.
    d.   demographic constants.

10. The annual number of deaths per 1,000 population is the: (366)
    a.   crude death rate.
    b.   crude mortality rate.
    c.   crude life expectancy rate.
    d.   net death rate.

11. Factors pushing someone to migrate include: (367)
    a.   poverty.
    b.   lack of religious and political freedom.
    c.   political persecution.
    d.   All of the above.

12. According to your text, it is difficult to forecast population growth because of: (368)
    a.   government programs.
    b.   dishonesty in reporting data.
    c.   lack of computer programs to deal with data adequately.
    d.   All of the above.

13. The key to the origin of cities is: (370)
    a. increased literacy of the world's population.
    b. more efficient agriculture.
    c. warfare and the need to build fortified settlements.
    d. large-scale trade and commerce.

14. The process by which an increasing proportion of a population lives in cities is: (370)
    a. suburbanization.
    b. gentrification.
    c. megalopolitanism.
    d. urbanization.

15. The area in Florida between Miami, Orlando, and Tampa is considered: (371)
    a. prime vacation property.
    b. a megalopolis.
    c. a metropolis.
    d. urban sprawl.

16. Edge cities: (373)
    a. consist of malls, office parks, and residential areas near major highway intersections.
    b. overlap political boundaries and include parts of several cities or towns.
    c. provide a sense of place to whose who live there.
    d. All of the above.

17. The movement of middle-class people into rundown areas of a city is called: (373)
    a. urban renewal.
    b. urban homesteading.
    c. gentrification.
    d. reverse migration.

18. The _____ model suggests that land use in cities is based on several centers. (374)
    a. sector model.
    b. concentric-zone model.
    c. multiple-nuclei model.
    d. commerce model.

19. As the number of low-income neighborhood residents increases, they begin to spill over into adjacent middle-class neighborhoods. The consequences is that the middle class begins to move out, thereby expanding the sector of low-income housing. Sociologists refer to this as: (374)
    a. reverse gentrification.
    b. disinvestment.
    c. concentric zone development.
    d. invasion-succession cycle.

20. The different models of urban growth have been criticized because: (374)
    a. they do not adequately explain urban growth in the Least Industrialized Nations.
    b. they do not take into consideration deliberate policies like redlining.
    c. they do not allow for the development of edge cities.
    d. the underestimate the amount of urban renewal that actually takes place.

21. Alienation can result in societies characterized by: (376)
    a. *Gemeinschaft.*
    b. *Gesellschaft.*
    c. norms of non-involvement.
    d. diffusion of responsibility.

22. According to Gans's typology, the trapped includes: (377-378)
    a. downwardly mobile persons.
    b. elderly persons.
    c. alcoholics and drug addicts.
    d. All of the above.

23. The Kitty Genovese case in an example of: (378)
    a. ethnic villagers.
    b. cosmopolites.
    c. alienation.
    d. community.

24. Suburbanization is the: (380)
    a. movement from the suburbs to edge cities.
    b. movement from the city to the suburbs.
    c. movement from rural areas to suburbs.
    d. displacement of the poor by the relatively affluent, who renovate the former's homes.

25. In many urban neighborhoods, as the tax base began to erode and services decline, banks adopted policies of refusing to make loans for housing or business. This practices is called: (380)
    a. redlining.
    b. fecundiary withdrawal.
    c. invasion-succession cycle.
    d. destablization.

TRUE-FALSE QUESTIONS

T F 1. Thomas Malthus was a sociologist at the University of Chicago in the 1920s. (358)
T F 2. The exponential growth curve is based on the idea that if growth doubles during approximately equal intervals of time, it accelerates in the latter stages. (359)
T F 3. There are four stages in the process of demographic transition. (360)
T F 4. The major reason why people in the Least Industrialized Nations have so many children is because they do not know how to prevent conception. (364)
T F 5. Population pyramids represent a population, divided into race, age, and sex. (365)

T F   6.   Demographers analyze fertility, mortality, and migration to project a country's population trends. (366)

T F   7.   The fertility rate and fecundity are different terms to express the same idea. (366)

T F   8.   Migration rates do not affect the global population. (366)

T F   9.   It is difficult for demographers to forecast population growth. (368)

T F   10.   The primary factor that influences a country's growth rate is the age distribution and sex ratio of its population. (368)

T F   11.   The Industrial Revolution was responsible for the significant growth in the number of large cities. (370)

T F   12.   The process of urban areas turning into metropolises, and metropolises developing into megalopolises is unique to the United States. (371)

T F   13.   In the United States today, the fastest growing cities are in the South and West. (372)

T F   14.   The concentric-zone model is based on the idea that cities expand radially from their central business district. (374)

T F   15.   The multiple-nuclei model is the most accurate model of urban growth. (374)

T F   16.   Louis Wirth saw the city as alienating, because kinship and neighborhood, the bedrock of social control and social solidarity, were undermined. (376)

T F   17.   According to Herbert Gans, the author of *The Urban Villagers*, people in cities are always alienated because they lack a sense of community. (376)

T F   18.   Sports teams often engender community identification in urban areas. (378)

T F   19.   When banks engage in the practice of redlining the quality of life in neighborhoods generally improves. (380)

T F   20.   Although the intention behind enterprise zones is good, the result is often failure. (382)

FILL-IN QUESTIONS

1.   _____ is the study of the size, composition, growth, and distribution of human populations. (358)

2.   A pattern of growth in which numbers double during approximately equal intervals, thus accelerating in the latter stages is the _____. (359)

3.   A(n) _____ is a graphic representation of a population, divided into age and sex. (365)

4.   The _____ refers to the number of children that the average woman bears. (366)

5.   The difference between the number of people moving into an area and the number of people moving out of the area per 1,000 population is the _____. (366)

6.   The basic demographic equation is *growth* = _____ - _____ + _____. (368)

7.   A demographic condition in which women bear only enough children to reproduce the population is referred to as _____. (369)

8.   _____ refers to masses of people moving to cities and to these cities having a growing influence in society. (370)

9.   An overlapping area consisting of at least two metropolises and their many suburbs is a _____. (371)

10.   As Americans migrate and businesses move, _____ have developed near intersections of major highways. (373)

11.   The displacement of the poor by the relatively affluent, who renovate the former's homes is _____. (373)

12.   _____ is the relationship between people and their environment. (373)

13.   _____ is a place people identify with, where they feel a sense of belonging. (376)

14.   Using a newspaper to shield ourselves from others and to indicate our inaccessibility is one example of the _____. (378)
15.   The policy of _____ involves the rehabilitation of rundown areas in a city, with the result that the poor who live there are displaced. (382)

MATCH THESE SOCIAL SCIENTISTS WITH THEIR CONTRIBUTIONS

___1. Thomas Malthus   a. *theorem on population growth*
___2. Ernest Burgess   b. *human ecology*
___3. Herbert Gans   c. *concentric-zone model*
___4. Homer Hoyt   d. *urban villagers*
___5. Robert Park   e. *sector model*

ESSAY QUESTIONS

1.   State the positions of the New Malthusians and the Anti-Malthusians and discuss which view you think is more accurate, based on the information provided about each position.

2.   Analyze why it is so difficult to stem population growth in the Least Industrialized Nations.

3.   Discuss whether or not cities are impersonal *Gesellschafts* or communal *Gemeinschafts*.

"DOWN-TO-EARTH SOCIOLOGY"

1.   After reading about the changing racial/ethnic make-up of the U.S. population on page 367, think about how will institutions like schools, government, hospitals and churches will have to change as our population becomes more diverse. What do you think, should the U.S. government cut off immigration in order to slow the transformation of our population?
2.   Why is the practice described in "Killing Little Girls: An Ancient and Thriving Practice" (p. 369) common in certain cultures and not others? How does it reflect deep-rooted sexism? What social, economic or political changes would help to eliminate this practice?
3.   How do the images painted in "Urbanization in the Least Industrialized Nations," on page 375, compare with your own "picture" of these countries? Do the lives of people in the Least Industrialized Nations have any bearing on your life?
4.   What impact will the growth of gated communities (p. 379) have on our society? In what ways will it further the growing gaps between rich and poor? Will these new developments really "solve" the problems plaguing urban areas? Why or why not?

CHAPTER 15
SOCIAL CHANGE: TECHNOLOGY, SOCIAL MOVEMENTS AND THE ENVIRONMENT

CHAPTER SUMMARY

- Social change, the alteration of culture and society over time, is a vital part of social life. Social change has included four social revolutions, as well as a change from *Gemeinschaft* to *Gesellschaft* societies, capitalism and industrialization, modernization, and global stratification. Ethnic conflicts and social movements indicate cutting edges of social change.

- William Ogburn identified technology as the basis for social change. The processes of social change are innovation, discovery, and diffusion. Cultural lag refers to the symbolic culture lagging behind changes in technology.

- Technology is a driving force in social change, and it can shape an entire society. This is evident when the impact that the computer have had on American society is analyzed. The information superhighway is likely to perpetuate social inequalities both nationally and globally.

- Theories of social change include: evolutionary theories, cyclical theories, and conflict theories.

- Social movements involve a large number of people who are organized to promote or resist social change. Depending on whether their target is individuals or society and whether the amount of change desired is partial or complete, social movements can be classified as alterative, redemptive, reformative, or transformative.

- Because the mass media are the gatekeepers for social movements, their favorable or unfavorable coverage greatly affects a social movement and tactics are chosen with the media in mind.

- Social movements go through distinct stages: initial unrest, mobilization, organization, institutionalization, and finally decline.

- Social change has often had a negative impact on the natural environment. As a result of industrialization, today we face such problems as acid rain, global warming, and the greenhouse effect. Because of the location of polluting factories and hazardous waste sites, environmental problems have a greater impact on minorities and the poor.

- Environmental problems are worldwide, brought about by industrial production and urbanization, the pressures of population growth, and inadequate environmental regulation. The world is facing a basic conflict between the lust for profits through the exploitation of the earth's resources and the need to produce a sustainable environment.

- In response, a worldwide environmental movement has emerged, which seeks to restore a healthy environment for the world's people. The solutions to environmental problems range from education, legislation, and political activism to ecosabotage, sabotaging the efforts of people thought to be legally harming the environment.

- Environmental sociologists attempt to study the relationship between humans and the environment. At the same time, environmental sociologists are generally also environmental activists.

LEARNING OBJECTIVES

As you read Chapter 15, use these learning objectives to organize your notes. After completing your reading, briefly state an answer to each of the objectives, and review the text pages in parentheses.

1. Define social change and describe the four major social revolutions. (388-389)
2. Describe *Gemeinschaft* and *Gesellschaft* societies, explain the relationship between capitalism and Protestantism and social change, and explain the relationship between these forces and

modernization. (389-391)

3.   Identify the shifts in the global map and discuss the threats to the global map. (391)
4.   Explain evolutionary, cyclical, and conflict theories of social change, and note the advantages and disadvantages of each. (392)
5.   Identify and define Ogburn's three processes of social change, and explain what is meant by "cultural lag." (393)
6.   Discuss how the different types of technology have produced social change. (394)
7.   Discuss the impact of computers on our society, including both the advances that computers have made and the concerns that we have about them. (394-397)
8.   Describe the impact of computers on national and global stratification. (397-398)
9.   State the major reasons why social movements exist and compare and contrast proactive and reactive social movements. (398-400)
10.   List the four types of social movements. (400)
11.   Define propaganda and discuss the role of the mass media in social movements. (400-402)
12.   Identify the five stages that social movements go through as they grow and mature. (402-403)
13.   Describe the environmental problems facing the world today, noting differences between the Most Industrialized, the Industrializing, and the Least Industrialized Nations. State ways in which capitalism may have contributed to these problems. (405-407)
14.   Discuss the goals and activities of the environmental movement. (408)
15.   List the assumptions of environmental sociology. (408)
16.   Describe some of the actions which would be necessary to reach the goal of harmony between technology and the environment. (408-410)

CHAPTER OUTLINE

I.	**How Social Change Transforms Society**	
	A.	Social change is a shift in the characteristics of culture and societies over time.
	B.	There have been four social revolutions: (1) the domestication of plants and animals, from which pastoral and horticultural societies arose; (2) the invention of the plow, leading to agricultural societies; (3) the industrial revolution; and (4) the information revolution, resulting in postindustrial societies.
	C.	The shift from agricultural to industrial economic activity was accompanied by a change from *Gemeinschaft* (daily life centers on intimate and personal relationships) to *Gesellschaft* (people have fleeting, impersonal relationships) societies.
	D.	Karl Marx identified capitalism as the basic reason behind the breakup of feudal (agricultural) societies. Max Weber saw religion as the core reason for the development of capitalism: as a result of the Reformation, Protestants no longer felt assured that they were saved by virtue of church membership and concluded that God would show visible favor to the elect.
	E.	Modernization (the change from agricultural to industrial societies) produces sweeping changes in societies. Modern societies are larger, more urbanized, and subject to faster change. They stress formal education and the future and are less religiously oriented. They have smaller families, lower rates of infant mortality, and higher life expectancy; they have higher incomes and more material possessions.
		1. When technology from the industrialized world is brought into traditional societies, the impact on society is evident, as demonstrated by introduction of medicine.

2.   The export of Western medicine to the Least Industrialized Nations reduced death rates but did not affect high birth rates. Rapidly increasing populations strain the resources of the Least Industrialized Nations, leading to widespread hunger and starvation, and the mass migration to cities and to the Most Industrialized Nations.

F.   Already in the 16th century today's global divisions had begun to emerge. As capitalism developed, the industrialized nations exploited the resources of those nations that did not industrialize.

    1.   Dependency theory asserts that because the Least Industrialized Nations have become dependent on the Most Industrialized Nations, they are unable to develop their own resources.

    2.   The world's industrial giants (the United States, Canada, Great Britain, France, Germany, Italy, and Japan--the G7) have decided how they will share the world's markets; by regulating global economic and industrial policy they guarantee their own dominance, including continued access to cheap raw materials from the Least Industrialized Nations.

G.   The resurgence of ethnic conflicts, for example the conflict in Bosnia, threatens the global map as conceived by the G7.

II.   Theories and Processes of Social Change

A.   Evolutionary theories are unilinear or multilinear.

    1.   Unilinear theories assume that all societies follow the same path, evolving from simple to complex through uniform sequences.

    2.   Multilinear theories assume that different routes can lead to a similar stage of development, thus, societies need not pass through the same sequence of stages to become industrialized.

    3.   Both unilinear and multilinear theories assume the idea that societies progress toward a higher state. These theories are now being discredited; because of the crises in Western culture today, these assumptions have been cast aside and evolutionary theories have been rejected.

B.   Cyclical theories examine great civilizations, not a particular society; they presume that societies are like organisms, they are born, reach adolescence, grow old, and die.

    1.   Toynbee proposed that at first a civilization is able to meet challenges, yet when it has become an empire, the ruling elite loses its capacity to keep the masses in line "by charm rather than by force," and the fabric of society is ripped apart.

    2.   Oswald Spengler proposed that Western civilization was on the wane; some analysts think the crisis in Western civilization may indicate he was right.

C.   Marx's conflict theory viewed social change as a dialectical precess, in which a thesis (the status quo) contains its own antithesis (opposition), and the resulting struggle between the thesis and its antithesis leads to a new state or synthesis. Thus, the history of a society is a series of confrontations in which each ruling group creates the seeds of its own destruction (e.g., capitalism sets workers and capitalists on a collision course).

D.   William Ogburn identified three processes of social change: (1) inventions, which can be either material (computers) or social (capitalism); (2) discovery, which is a new way of seeing things; and (3) diffusion, which is the spread of an invention, discovery, or idea from one area to another. Ogburn coined the term cultural lag to describe the situation in which some elements of a culture adapt to an invention or discovery more rapidly than others.

III. **How Technology Changes Society**
  A. Technology refer to both the tools, items used to accomplish tasks, and to the skills or procedures to make and use those tools. The chief characteristic of postindustrial societies is technology that extends our abilities to analyze information, to communicate, and to travel.
    1. These new technologies allow us to probe space and other planets, to communicate instantaneously anywhere on the globe, to travel great distances in a shorter period of time, and to store, retrieve, and analyze vast amounts of information.
    2. Technology changes a people's way of life.
  B. The computer, with its capacity to improve the quality of life, is an example. Currently, it is changing medicine, education, and the workplace.
    1. Although computers can outperform doctors in diagnosis, physicians will resist challenges to their expertise and patients will resist the human touch.
    2. The computer is transforming education and producing a technology gap between rich and poor schools.
    3. The computer is altering the way work in organized, the nature of work relationships, and even the location of work. It also makes possible increased surveillance of workers and depersonalization.
  C. With computers the world is linked by almost instantaneous communication, national boundaries now mean nothing, and information is not contained.
    1. The term information superhighway carries the idea of information traveling at a high rate of speed around the world.
    2. The implications of the information superhighway are enormous; on a national level a new dimension of existing inequality could emerge--the information "have-nots" among inner-city and rural residents. On an international level the question is "who will control the information superhighway?" If the Most Industrialized Nations control the information superhighway the Least Industrialized Nations will be destined to a perpetual pauper status.

IV. **Social Movements as a Source of Social Change**
  A. Social movements consist of large numbers of people, who, through deliberate and sustained efforts, organize to promote or resist social change. At the heart of social movements lie grievances and dissatisfactions.
    1. Proactive social movements promote social change because a current condition of society is intolerable. In contrast, reactive social movements resist changing conditions in society which they perceive as threatening.
    2. To further their goals, people often develop social movement organizations. An example of a proactive social movement is the National Organization of Women (NOW); an example of reactive social movements is the Ku Klux Klan (KKK).
    3. Mayer Zald suggests that a cultural crisis can give birth to a wave of social movements. According to Zald, when a society's institutions fail to keep up with social changes, many people's needs go unfulfilled, massive unrest follows, and social movements come into being to bridge the gap.
  B. David Aberle classified social movements into four broad categories according to the type and amount of social change they seek.
    1. Two types seek to change people but differ in terms of the amount of change desired: alterative social movements seek to alter only particular aspects of people (e.g., the Women's Christian Temperance Union); while redemptive social

movements seek to change people totally (e.g., a religious social movement such as fundamental Christianity that stresses conversion).

    2.   Two types seek to change society but also differ in terms of the amount of change desired: reformative social movements seek to reform only one part of society (e.g., animal rights or the environment); transformative social movements seek to change the social order itself and to replace it with their own version of the ideal society (e.g., revolutions in the American colonies, France, Russia, and Cuba).

C.   Leaders of social movements try to manipulate the media in order to influence public opinion about some issue.

    1.   Propaganda is a key to understanding social movements. Propaganda simply means the presentation of information in an attempt to influence people.

    2.   The mass media play a critical role in social movements. They have become, in effect, the gatekeepers to social movements. If those who control and work in the mass media are sympathetic to a "cause," it will receive sympathetic treatment. If the social movement goes against their own biases, it will either be ignored or receive unfavorable treatment.

D.   Social movements have a life course, that is, they go through five stages as they grow and mature.

    1.   Unrest and agitation grow because people are upset about some social condition; at this stage leaders emerge who verbalize people's feelings

    2.   Leaders mobilize a relatively large number of people who demand that something be done about the problem; charismatic leaders emerge during this stage.

    3.   An organization emerges with a division of labor with leadership that makes policy decisions and a rank and file that actively supports the movement.

    4.   Institutionalization occurs as the movement becomes bureaucratized and leadership passes to career officials who may care more about their position in the organization than about the movement itself.

    5.   The organization declines, but there may be a possibility of resurgence. Some movements cease to exist; others become reinvigorated with new leadership from within or from coming into conflict with other social movements fighting for the opposite side of the issue, (e. g., social movements relating to abortion).

V.   The Growth Machine versus the Earth

A.   Globalization of capitalism is responsible for today's environmental decay.

    1.   The faster-paced economic production caused by the Industrialized Nations pushing for economic growth, the Industrializing Nations playing catch-up, and the Least Industrialized Nations trying to enter to competition means faster-paced destruction of our environment.

    2.   The ecological message is incompatible with an economic message.

B.   Industrialization, while viewed as good for the nation's welfare, has led to a major assault on the environment.

    1.   Industrial growth came at a high cost to the natural environment.

    2.   Many of today's problems--ozone layer depletion, acid rain, the greenhouse effect, and global warming--are linked to our dependence on fossil fuels.

    3.   There is an abundant source of natural energy that would provide low-cost power and therefore help to raise the living standards of human across the globe. Better technology is needed to harness this energy supply. From a conflict perspective, such abundant sources of energy present a threat to the energy monopoly ruled by

multinationals. We cannot expect the practical development and widespread use of alternative sources of power until the multinationals have cornered the market on the technology that will harness them.

    4.   Racial minorities and the poor are disproportionately exposed to air pollution, hazardous waste, pesticides and the like. To deal with this issue a new specialty known as environmental poverty law is developing.

C.   Environmental degradation is also a problem in the Industrializing and Least Industrialized Nations.

    1.   The rush to compete globally, the lack of funds to purchase expensive pollution controls, and few anti-pollution laws have all produced environmental problems in the Industrializing Nations.

    2.   Pollution was treated as a state secret in the former Soviet Union. With protest stifled, no environmental protection laws to inhibit pollution, and production quotas to be met, environmental pollution was rampant. Pollution is so severe that the life expectancy of Russians has dropped.

    3.   The combined pressures of population growth and almost nonexistent environmental regulations destine the Least Industrialized Nations to be the earth's major source of pollution. Some companies in the Most Industrialized Nations use the Least Industrialized Nations as dumping sites for hazardous wastes; they build facilities to produce chemicals no longer tolerated in their own countries.

    4.   The consequences for humanity of the destruction of the tropical rain forests are unknown. With rain forests disappearing at a rate of 2500 acres every hour, it is estimated that 10,000 species are becoming extinct every year.

D.   Concern about the world's environmental problems has produced a worldwide social movement.

    1.   In some countries, the environment has become a major issue in local and national elections (e.g., Germany, Great Britain, and Switzerland).

    2.   This movement generally seeks solutions in education, legislation, and political activism. However, some choose a more radical course, using extreme tactics to try to gain support.

E.   Environmental sociology examines the relationship between human societies and the environment. Its basic assumptions include: (1) the physical environment is a significant variable in sociological investigation; (2) humans are but one species among many that are dependent on the environment; (3) because of intricate feedbacks to nature, human actions have many unintended consequences; (4) the world is finite, so there are potential physical limits to economic growth; (5) economic expansion requires increased extraction of resources from the environment; (6) increased extraction of resources leads to ecological problems; (7) these ecological problems place restrictions on economic expansion; and (8) the state creates environmental problems by trying to create conditions for the profitable accumulation of capital.

F.   If we are to have a world that is worth passing on to the coming generations, we must seek harmony between technology and the natural environment. As a parallel to development of technologies, we must develop a greater awareness of their harmful effects on the planet, systems of control giving more weight to reducing technologies' harm to the environment than to lowering costs, and mechanisms to enforce rules for the production, use, and disposal of technology.

KEY TERMS

After studying the chapter, review each of the following terms.

acid rain: rain containing sulfuric and nitric acid; the result of burning fossil fuels (406)

alterative social movement: a social movement that seeks to alter only particular aspects of people (400)

cultural lag: William Ogburn's term for human behavior lagging behind technological innovation (393)

dialectical process: a view of history and power in which each arrangement, or thesis, contains contradictions, or antitheses, which must be resolved; the new arrangement, or synthesis, contains its own contradictions, and so on (392)

diffusion: the spread of invention or discovery from one area to another; identified by William Ogburn as a major process of social change (393)

discovery: a new way of seeing reality; identified by William Ogburn as a major process of social change (393)

environmental sociology: a subdiscipline of sociology that examines how human activities affect the physical environment and how the physical environment affects human activities (408)

global warming: an increase in the earth's temperature due to the greenhouse effect (406)

greenhouse effect: the buildup of carbon dioxide in the earth's atmosphere that allows light to enter but inhibits the release of heat; believed to cause global warming (406)

ideal type: a composite of characteristics based on many specific examples; "ideal" in this case means a description of abstracted characteristics, not what one desires to exist (390)

invention: the combination of existing elements and materials to form new ones; identified by William Ogburn as a major process of social change (393)

modernization: the transformation of traditional societies into industrial societies (390)

postmodern society: another term for postindustrial society (394)

proactive social movement: a social movement that promotes social change (399)

propaganda: in its broad sense, the presentation of information in the attempt to influence people; in its narrow sense, one-sided information used to try to influence people (400)

public opinion: how people think about some issue (400)

reactive social movement: a social movement that resists social change (399)

redemptive social movement: a social movement that seeks to change people totally (400)

reformative social movement: a social movement that seeks to reform some specific aspect of society (400)

resource mobilization: a stage that social movements succeed or fail based on their ability to mobilize resources such as time, money, and people's skills (402)

social change: the alteration of culture and societies over time (388)

social movement: large numbers of people who organize to promote or resist social change (398)

social movement organization: an organization developed to further the goals of a social movement (399)

sustainable environment: a world system in which we use our physical environment to meet the needs of humanity without destroying our environment (405)

technology: often defined as the applications of science, but can be thought of as tools, items used to accomplish tasks, along with the skills or procedures to make and use those tools (394)

transformative social movement: a social movement that seeks to change society totally (400)

KEY PEOPLE

Review the major theoretical contributions or research findings of these people.

David Aberle: Aberle classified social movements into four types: alterative, redemptive, reformative and transformation based on the amount of intended change and the target of the change. (400)

Jacques Ellul: This French sociologist warned that technology is destroying traditional values and producing a monolithic world culture in which variety is mere appearance. (398)

Alfred & Elizabeth Lee: These sociologists found that propaganda relies on seven basic techniques, which they labeled "tricks of the trade." (401)

Karl Marx: Marx analyzed the emergence of capitalism and developed the theory of dialectical materialism.(390, 392)

John McCarthy and Mayer Zald: These sociologists investigated the resource mobilization of social movements and found that, although there may be a group of angry and agitated people, without this mobilization they will never become a social movement. (402)

Lewis Henry Morgan: Morgan's theory of social development once dominated Western thought. He suggested that societies pass through three stages: savagery, barbarism, and civilization. (392)

William Ogburn: Ogburn identified three processes of social change: invention, discovery, and diffusion. He also coined the term "cultural lag" to describe a situation in which some elements of culture adapt to an invention or discovery more rapidly than others. (393)

Neil Postman: Postman investigated the impact of advancing technology on social life. (398)

Oswald Spengler: Spengler wrote *The Decline of the West* in which he proposed that Western civilization was declining. (392)

Arnold Toynbee: This historian suggest that each time a civilization successfully meets a challenge, oppositional forces are set up. Eventually, the oppositional forces are set loose, and the fabric of society is ripped apart. (392)

Max Weber: Weber argued that capitalism grew out of the Protestant Reformation. (390)

Mayer Zald: In analyzing social movements, Zald suggested that they were like a rolling sea, hitting society like a wave. (399)

SELF-TEST

After completing this self-test, check your answers against the Answer Key beginning on page 274 of this Study Guide and against the text on page(s) indicated in parentheses.

MULTIPLE CHOICE QUESTIONS

1. A shift in the characteristics of culture and society over time is: (388)
   a. social transformation.
   b. social metamorphose.
   c. social alternation.
   d. social change.

2. Paid work, contracts, and especially money are all characteristic of: (389-390)
   a. farming societies.
   b. *Gemeinschaft.*
   c. *Gesellschaft.*
   d. capitalism.

3. Max Weber identified _____ as the core reason for the development of capitalism. (390)
    a. religion
    b. industrialization
    c. politics
    d. None of the above.

4. The Least Industrialized Nations have become reliant on the Most Industrialized Nations and they are unable to develop their own resources according to: (391)
    a. dependency theory.
    b. capitalist exploitation theory.
    c. evolutionary theory.
    d. multilinear evolution theory.

5. Which of the following does the author of the text identify as a threat to the global map that was drawn up by the G7? (391)
    a. stricter environmental controls in the Least Industrialized Nations.
    b. stiffer tariff regulation world-wide.
    c. resurgence of ethnic conflicts.
    d. ecosabotage.

6. _____ theories assume that all societies follow the same path, evolving from simple to complex through uniform sequences. (392)
    a. Cyclical
    b. Uniformity
    c. Unilinear evolution
    d. Multilinear evolution

7. The assumption that civilizations are born, pass through a youthful period in order to reach maturity, and then decline and die is central to _____ theories. (392)
    a. unilinear
    b. multilinear
    c. cyclical
    d. conflict

8. The history of a society is a series of confrontations in which each ruling group creates the seeds of its own destruction, according to: (392)
    a. Karl Marx.
    b. William Ogburn.
    c. Pitirim Sorokin.
    d. Max Weber.

9. The idea of citizenship is an example of: (393)
    a. invention.
    b. discovery.
    c. diffusion.
    d. innovation.

10.   The situation in which some elements of a culture adapt to an invention or discovery more rapidly than others is: (393)
    a.   cultural downtime.
    b.   cultural lag.
    c.   cultural delay.
    d.   cultural drag.

11.   Technology refers to: (394)
    a.   artificial means of extending human abilities.
    b.   tools as simple as a comb as well as those as complicated as a computer.
    c.   the skills or procedures to make and use tools.
    d.   All of the above.

12.   A recent development in the medical field allows doctors, with the use of a stethoscope, to check the hearts and lungs of patients who are hundreds of miles away. This is refereed to as: (396)
    a.   managed care.
    b.   computer-assisted diagnosis.
    c.   remote-site care.
    d.   telemedicine.

13.   The increasing integration of computers into education is likely to: (396)
    a.   reduce social inequalities.
    b.   perpetuate social inequalities.
    c.   increase social inequalities.
    d.   have no impact of social inequalities.

14.   Which of the following aspects of the workplace has <u>not</u> been transformed by computers? (396-397)
    a.   the way in which salaries/pay scales are calculated
    b.   the way in which work is done
    c.   the location where work is carried out
    d.   the nature of social relationships in the workplace

15.   The National Organization of Women is an example of a _____ while the Stop-ERA is an example of _____. (399)
    a.   reactive social movement/proactive social movement
    b.   redemptive social movement/reactive social movement
    c.   proactive social movement/reactive social movement
    d.   proactive social movement/alternative social movement

16.   Social movements that seek to change people totally are: (400)
    a.   alterative social movements.
    b.   redemptive social movements.
    c.   reformative social movements.
    d.   transformative social movements.

17. A social movement that seeks to change society totally is a(n): (400)
    a. alternative social movement.
    b. redemptive social movement.
    c. reformative social movement.
    d. transformative social movement.

18. How people think about some issue is: (400)
    a. irrelevant to most social scientists.
    b. public opinion.
    c. propaganda.
    d. mass-society theory.

19. Advertising is: (401)
    a. a type of propaganda.
    b. an organized attempt to manipulate public opinion.
    c. a one-sided presentation of information that distorts reality.
    d. All of the above.

20. Which of the fine points of propaganda identified by Alfred and Elizabeth Lee would include surrounding the product, candidate, or policy with phrases that arouse positive feelings? (401)
    a. name calling
    b. glittering generality
    c. testimonials
    d. bandwagon

21. Raising money, recruiting people with needed skills, acquiring equipment, and gaining the attention of the media are all part of the process of: (402)
    a. organization building.
    b. bureaucratization.
    c. resource mobilization.
    d. organizational decline.

22. According to conflict theorists, what stands in the way of developing alternative sources of power? (406)
    a. lack of necessary technology
    b. multinationals' need to control technology in order to make profits
    c. unwillingness of consumers to adapt to alternatives
    d. limited access to alternatives

23. Which groups in U.S. society are disproportionately exposed to environmental hazards? (406)
    a. office workers and factory workers
    b. racial minorities and the poor
    c. farm workers and lumberjacks
    d. racial and ethnic groups

24.   The major source of pollution in the future is likely to be: (407)
        a.   the Least Industrialized Nations.
        b.   the Industrializing Nations.
        c.   the Most Industrialized Nations.
        d.   another planet.

25.   Environmental sociology examines: (408)
        a.   how the physical environment affects human activities.
        b.   how human activities affect the physical environment.
        c.   the unintended consequences of human actions.
        d.   All of the above.

TRUE-FALSE QUESTIONS

T F   1.   The rapid social change that the world is currently experiencing is a random event. (388)
T F   2.   Modernization is the change from agricultural to industrial societies. (390)
T F   3.   The resurgence of ethnic conflicts in Europe, North and South America, Africa, and Asia do not really threaten the global map that has been carefully partitioned by the world's industrial giants. (391)
T F   4.   Unilinear evolutionary theories assume that all societies follow the same path. (392)
T F   5.   Cyclical theories assume that civilizations are like organisms. (392)
T F   6.   According to Max Weber, the history of a society is a series of confrontations in which each ruling group sows the seeds of its own destruction. (392)
T F   7.   Invention, discovery, and diffusion are Ogburn's three processes of social change. (393)
T F   8.   Technology usually changes first, followed by culture. (393)
T F   9.   The new technologies of postmodern societies extend our abilities to analyze information, communicate, and travel. (394)
T F   10.   Doctors are likely to support the increased use of computers in medical diagnosis because their output is more accurate than anything a doctor could achieve. (396)
T F   11.   The use of computers in education will significantly reduce existing social inequalities between school districts. (396)
T F   12.   All social movements seek to change society. (399)
T F   13.   The Women's Christian Temperance Union is an example of an alterative social movement. (400)
T F   14.   The environmental movement is an example of a transformative social movement. (400)
T F   15.   Propaganda and advertising are defined quite differently from one another. (401)
T F   16.   In the final stage of a social movement, decline is certain. (403)
T F   17.   There is a strong consensus among scientists that the greenhouse effect is a very serious threat to our natural environment. (406)
T F   18.   The lack of environmental protection laws in the Least Industrialized Nations has contributed to their becoming dumping grounds for hazardous wastes. (407)
T F   19.   Environmental sociology examines the relationship between human societies and the environment. (408)
T F   20.   According to environmental sociologists, governments are not to blame for environmental problems because they actively set limits on the conditions for the profitable accumulation of capital. (408)

FILL-IN QUESTIONS

1.   The transformation of agricultural societies into industrial societies is the outcome of
      _____. (390)
2.   An _____ is a composite of characteristics based on many specific examples. (390)
3.   Karl Marx viewed history as a _____, in which each stage of history contains the sees
      of its own destruction. (392)
4.   The combination of existing elements and materials to form new ones results in _____.
      (393)
5.   Societies change as a result of _____, which reflects a new way of seeing reality. (393)
6.   William Ogburn used the term _____ to describe human behavior that lags behind
      technological innovations. (393)
7.   The world-wide electronic network is referred to as the _____, which conveys the
      idea of information traveling at high rates of speed between homes, schools and businesses around
      the globe. (397)
8.   Broadly speaking, a _____ consists of large numbers of people who organize to
      promote or resist social change. (398)
9.   Alcoholics Anonymous would be an example of a _____ social movement. (399)
10.   The presentation of information in an attempt to influence people is _____. (400)
11.   _____ is created when sulfur dioxide and nitrogen oxide, released as a result of
      burning fossil fuels, react with moisture in the air. (406)
12.   We will have achieved a _____ when we are able to use our physical environment to
      meet the needs of humanity without destroying our environment. (405)
13.   The _____, the buildup of carbon dioxide in the earth's atmosphere that allows light
      to enter but inhibits the release of heat, is believed to cause _____. (406)
14.   _____ examines how human activities affect the physical environment and how the
      physical environment affects human activities. (408)
15.   The use of extreme tactics to try to arouse indignation among the public and force the government
      to take action to protect our natural environment is referred to as _____. (409)

MATCH THESE SOCIAL SCIENTISTS WITH THEIR CONTRIBUTIONS

___1. Karl Marx   a. *compared social movements to a rolling sea*
___2. David Aberle   b. *religion led to the development of capitalism*
___3. William Ogburn   c. *capitalism produces alienation of workers*
___4. Max Weber   d. *the fine art of propaganda*
___5. Oswald Spengler   e. *warned that technology is destroying traditional values*
___6. Jacques Ellul   f. *cyclical theory predicting the decline of Western civilization*
___7. Lewis Morgan   g. *three processes of cultural innovation*
___8. Mayer Zald   h. *three stage theory of social evolution*
___9. Neil Postman   I. *recognized as an opponent of technology*
__10. Al. & Eliza. Lee   j. *classified social movements by type and amount of social change*

ESSAY QUESTIONS
1.   Choose a particular technology--the automobile or the computer--and discuss the impact that it has
      had on U.S. society.
2.   Discuss Ogburn's three processes of social change and provide examples to illustrate each.

3.   Discuss the role that global stratification plays in the worldwide environmental problems.

"DOWN-TO-EARTH SOCIOLOGY"

1.   Why do you think that opposition to technology--such as the Luddites or the Unabomber--appears stronger at some points in history and weaker at other points (p. 398)? What was it about early 19th century England and late 20th century United States that could produce such opposition?

2.   What was your reaction to the Million-Man March (p. 399)? Were you aware that it occurred? Did you attend, or know someone who did attend? In what ways can it be seen as a continuation of the civil rights movement?

3.   After reading "Tricks of the Trade: The Fine Art of Propaganda" on page 401, listen carefully to politicians and leaders of social movements who advocate a particular idea. Are they using some of the techniques described? If yes, which ones?

4.   Read "Which Side of the Barricades? Prochoice and Prolife as a Social Movement" on page 403. Do you agree with the author that no issue divides Americans as abortion does? How does each side see this issue? Why does the author say that there is no way to reconcile the opposing views? In what ways are these social movements different from others? How do you feel about this issue?

5.   After reading about the destruction of the rain forest on page 407, why do you think the West is becoming more concerned about the loss of tribal knowledge? Do you think "cultural ignorance" is a valid defense for crimes committed against groups with diverse cultural backgrounds? Why or why not?

6.   Do you think "Ecosabotage," as described on page 409, is ever justified? Why or why not? Do you think radical acts can do more harm than good? Do they alienate people who support the movement, rather than unite them?

CHAPTER-BY-CHAPTER ANSWER KEY

▲▼CHAPTER 1 -- THE SOCIOLOGICAL PERSPECTIVE

ANSWERS FOR THE MULTIPLE-CHOICE QUESTIONS

1. c   A society is defined as a group of people who share a culture or territory. (5)
2. c   Income, education, gender and race all reflect a person's social location. (5)
3. b   According to the sociological perspective, human behavior is shaped by external forces, that become internalized through the process of socialization. (5)
4. d   Positivism is the application of the scientific approach to the social world. (5)
5. a   Herbert Spencer first stated the principle of "the survival of the fittest;" however, it often is attributed to Charles Darwin. (6)
6. b   The proletariat is the large group of workers who are exploited by the small group of capitalists who own the means of production, according to Karl Marx. (6)
7. a   Durkheim believed that social factors--patterns of behavior that characterize a social group-- explain many types of behavior, including suicide rates. (8)
8. c   Max Weber disagreed with Karl Marx about the central force responsible for social change; he believed religion, rather than economic factors, was critical for social change. (8)
9. c   Harriet Martineau was an early sociologist who studied social life in both England and the United States; she published a book entitled *Society in America*. (9)
10. b   W.E.B. Du Bois was an early U.S. sociologist who studied race relations. (10)
11. c   It is applied sociology that focuses on using sociology to solve problems. (12)
12. b   Symbolic interactionists study the symbols that people use to establish meaning and communicate with one another. (14)
13. c   In explaining the high U.S. divorce rate, the symbolic interaction perspective would focus on explanations such as emotional satisfaction, the meaning of children, and the meaning of parenthood. (14-15)
14. a   According to Robert Merton, an action intended to help a system's equilibrium is a manifest function. (16)
15. d   Industrialization and urbanization have undermined the traditional purposed of the family, according to theorists using functional analysis. (16)
16. c   The idea that conflict is inherent in all relations that have authority was first asserted by Ralf Dahrendorf. (17)
17. b   Conflict theorists might explain the high rate of divorce by looking at society's basic inequalities between males and females. (7-18)
18. d   Since each theoretical perspective provides a different, often contrasting, picture of our world, no theory encompasses all of reality. By putting the contributions of each perspective and level of analysis together, we gain a more comprehensive picture of social life. (19)
19. d   "All of the above" is correct. Sociologists believe that research is necessary because common sense ideas may or may not be true; they want to move beyond guesswork; and researchers want to know what really is going on. (19)
20. c   Eight steps are involved in scientific research. (20-22)
21. a   A relationship between or among variables is predicted by a hypothesis. (20)
22. b   Reliability refers to the extent to which data produce consistent results. (21)

23. a Mean, median, and mode are ways to measure "average." (23)
24. a Ethnomethodology is the study of how people use background assumptions to make sense of life and, thus, is a part of symbolic interactionism. Surveys, unobtrusive measures, and secondary analysis are research methods for gathering data. (23-27)
25. c A sample is defined as the individuals intended to represent the population to be studied. (23)
26. d By becoming involved in the social group he is observing, George has chosen to do participant observation. (26)
27. c The analysis of data already collected by other researchers is secondary analysis. (26)
28. b In an experiment, the control group is not exposed to the independent variable in the study. (27)
29. d "All of the above" is correct. Research ethics require openness; that a researcher not falsify results or plagiarize someone else's work; and that research subjects should not be harmed by the research. (28)
30. a The purpose of basic or pure sociological research is to make discoveries about life in human groups, not to make changes in those groups. On the other hand, applied and clinical sociology are more involved in suggesting or bringing about social change. (30)

ANSWERS FOR TRUE-FALSE QUESTIONS

1. *True* (4)
2. *False*. Sociologists focus on external influences (people's experiences) instead of internal mechanisms, such as instincts. (5)
3. *True* (5)
4. *True* (6)
5. *True* (7)
6. *True* (7)
7. *False*. Although Marx stood firmly behind revolution as the only way for the proletariat to gain control of society, he did not develop the political system called communism, which was a later application of his ideas. (7)
8. *True* (8)
9. *False*. Weber agreed with much of what Marx wrote, but he strongly disagreed that economics is the central force in social change. Weber saw religion as playing that role. (9)
10. *True* (9)
11. *True* (10)
12. *True* (14)
13. *False*. Functionalists believe that both industrialization and urbanization have undermined many of the family's traditional purposes. (16)
14. *False*. Conflict theorists like Ralf Dahrendorf see conflict in all authority relationships. (17)
15. *True* (18)
16. *False*. Research often does not confirm common sense. The application of research methods takes us beyond common sense and allows us to penetrate surface realities so we can better understand social life. (19)
17. *True*. (20)
18. *True*. (21)
19. *True*. (21)
20. *True*. (23)
21. *False*. In survey research, it is always desirable for respondents to express their own ideas. (24)

22. *True.* (24)
23. *False.* Secondary analysis and use of documents are not the same thing. The data used in secondary analysis is gathered by other researchers while documents may be anything from diaries to police records. (26-27)
24. *False.* In an experiment, the experimental group is exposed to the independent variable in the study. The control group is not exposed to the independent variable. (27)
25. *False.* It is not always unethical to observe people's behavior when they are unaware they are being studied. Yet there are certain times when the issue of ethics should be raised. (28)

ANSWERS FOR THE FILL-IN QUESTIONS.

1. The SOCIOLOGICAL PERSPECTIVE stresses the social contexts in which people are immersed and which influence their lives. (5)
2. The use of objective systematic observation to test theories is SCIENTIFIC METHOD. (5)
3. The idea of applying the scientific method to the social world is POSITIVISM. (5)
4. Durkheim used the term SOCIAL INTEGRATION to refer to the degree to which people are tied to their social group. (8)
5. Sociology that is used to solve social problems--from the micro level of family relationships to the macro level of war and pollution is APPLIED SOCIOLOGY. (12)
6. CLINICAL SOCIOLOGY is a type of applied sociology in which sociologists become directly involved in bringing about social change. (12)
7. A THEORY is a general statement about how some parts of the world fit together and how they work. (13)
8. The theoretical perspective in which society is viewed as composed of symbols that people use to establish meaning, develop their views of the world, and communicate with one another is SYMBOLIC INTERACTIONISM. (14)
9. FUNCTIONAL analysis is a theoretical framework in which society is viewed as composed of various parts, each with a function that contributes to society's equilibrium. (15)
10. Karl Marx believed that the key to all human history is class struggle between the BOURGEOISIE, a small group of capitalists who own the means to produce wealth, and the PROLETARIAT, the mass of workers who are exploited by the capitalists. (17)
11. Power that people consider legitimate is known as AUTHORITY. (17)
12. MACRO-LEVEL analysis examines large-scale patterns of society, while MICRO-LEVEL analysis examines small-scale patterns of society. (18)
13. Hypotheses need OPERATIONAL DEFINITIONS -- precise ways to measure variables. (20)
14. RELIABILITY is the extent to which data produce consistent results. (21)
15. The six research methods are: (1) SURVEYS, (2) SECONDARY ANALYSIS, (3) DOCUMENTS, (4) PARTICIPANT OBSERVATION, (5) EXPERIMENTS, and (6) UNOBTRUSIVE MEASURES. (22-28)
16. RAPPORT is a feeling of trust between researchers and subjects. (26)
17. To conduct an experiment, the researcher has two groups: (1) EXPERIMENTAL GROUP and (2) CONTROL GROUP. (21)
18. Research ETHICS require openness, honesty, and truth. (28)
19. BASIC (OR PURE) sociology makes discoveries about life in human groups, not to make changes in those groups. (30)
20. Max Weber argued that sociology should be VALUE FREE, by which he meant that sociologists' personal beliefs about what is good or worthwhile should not affect his or her

research. (30)

ANSWERS TO THE MATCHING QUESTIONS

1. c   August Comte: *proposed the use of positivism*
2. a   Herbert Spencer: *coined the phrase "the survival of the fittest"*
3. f   Karl Marx: *believed the key to human history was class struggle*
4. g   C. Wright Mills: *encouraged the use of the sociological perspective*
5. d   Emile Durkheim: *stressed how individual behavior is shaped by social factors*
6. h   Harriet Martineau: *published **Society in America** and translated Comte's work into English*
7. I   Mario Brajuha: *refused to turn over notes on his research on restaurant work*
8. b   W.E.B. Du Bois: *was an early African American sociologist*
9. e   Max Weber: *believed religion was a central force in social change*
10. l   Rik Scarce: *imprisoned by 159 days on contempt charges*
11. j   Robert K. Merton: *used the terms **functions** and **dysfunctions***
12. k   Laud Humphreys: *his research reflected questionable ethics*

GUIDELINES FOR ANSWERING THE ESSAY QUESTIONS

1.   *Explain what the sociological perspective encompasses and then, using that perspective, discuss the forces that shaped the discipline of sociology.*

There are two parts to this question. First, you are asked to define the sociological perspective. As you define this, you would want to mention the idea of social location, perhaps by bringing into your essay C. Wright Mills' observations on the connection between biography and history (pp. 4-5). The second part of the essay is to discuss the forces that shaped sociology and its early followers. What you are being asked is to think about what was going on in the social world in the early 19th century that might have led to the birth of this new discipline. Referring back to book, you would want to identify three: (1) the Industrial Revolution; (2) the American and French revolutions; and (3) the emergence of the scientific method. You would conclude by discussing how each of the early sociologists -- Auguste Comte, Herbert Spencer, Karl Marx, Emile Durkheim, and Max Weber -- were influenced by these broader forces in making a contribution to sociology (pp. 5-8). You could also bring into the discussion some of the material on sexism in early sociology, noting that the ideas about the appropriate role for women in society functioned to exclude women like Harriet Martineau from the discipline (pp. 8-9), or you could talk about the emergence of sociology in North America (pp. 9-13).

2.   *Explain each of the theoretical perspectives that are used in sociology and describe how a sociologist affiliated with one of another of the perspectives might undertake a study of gangs. Discuss how all three can be used in research.*

There are three major perspectives in sociology: symbolic interactionism, functional analysis, and conflict theory. Your first step is to explain the essential nature of each perspective and then to propose a research topic that would be consistent with the perspective. For example, symbolic interactionism focuses on the symbols that people use to establish meaning, develop their views of the world, and communicate with one another; a symbolic interactionist would want to find out what meaning gangs and gang membership have for individuals who belong to them as well as those who live in communities in which gangs operate (pp. 14-15). Functional analysis, which tries to identify the functions of a particular social pattern, would choose to study what contributions gangs make within the fabric of social life as well as the dysfunctions of gangs (pp. 15-17). Finally, a conflict theorist would study the competition for scarce resources among gangs and between gangs and the larger society because he or she is interested in struggles over power and control within social groups (pp. 17-18).

You would conclude by noting that each perspective provides an answer to an important question about the social order and by combining them you arrive at a more complete picture. (pp. 18-19).

3.	*Choose a topic and explain how you would go through the different steps in the research model.*
In order to answer this question, you must select a topic and then develop this from the beginning to the end of the research process, identifying all eight steps and explaining what tasks are carried out each step of the way. Your answer should make reference to variables, hypothesis, operational definitions, the different research methods, validity and reliability, different ways of analyzing the data, and replication (pp. 20-28).

4.	*Explain why ethical guidelines necessary in social science research.*
Ethical guidelines are necessary for several reasons. First and foremost, the researcher is working with human subjects; there must be guidelines to protect these subjects from any undue physical or psychological harm. Secondly, the research is only valid and reliable if the subjects have honestly and accurately provided information to the researcher. For this reason, they must have confidence in the researcher and the research process; guidelines assure subjects that their identities will remain anonymous and their information will be confidential. Finally, an essential aspect of research is that it be shared with others in the research community as well as members of the wider society. Guidelines regarding falsification and plagiarism guarantee that all research will be carefully scrutinized, thereby assuring its validity and reliability (pp. 28-29).

▲▼CHAPTER 2 -- CULTURE

ANSWERS FOR MULTIPLE CHOICE QUESTIONS

1.	b	Sociologists refer to a group's ways of thinking and doing, including language and other forms of interaction as nonmaterial culture. (37)
2.	d	Material culture includes weapons and machines, eating utensils, jewelry, hairstyles, and clothing; thus all of the above is correct. (37)
3.	a	All of the statements are true regarding culture except "people generally are aware of the effects of their own culture." (37)
4.	d	The disorientation that people experience when they come into contact with a fundamentally different culture and can no longer depend on their taken-for-granted assumptions about life is known as cultural shock. (37)
5.	c	An American who thinks bullfighting is barbarian is demonstrating ethnocentrism. (37)
6.	d	Gestures can lead to misunderstandings and embarrassment. (40)
7.	a	It is possible for human experience to be cumulative and for people to share memories because of language. (41-42)
8.	c	The sociological theory that language itself creates a particular way of thinking and perceiving is known as the Sapir-Whorf hypothesis. (43)
9.	b	Sanctions can be either positive or negative. (44)
10.	d	Norms that are not strictly enforced are folkways. (44)
11.	a	Mores are essential to our core values and require conformity. (44)
12.	d	Subcultures are a world within a world; are the values and related behaviors or a group that distinguish its members from the larger culture; and include ethnic groups. Therefore, all of the above are correct. (45)
13.	c	Sociologically speaking, heavy metal adherents who glorify Satanism, hatred, cruelty, and sexism are examples of countercultures. (45)

14. a   A pluralistic society is made up of many different groups. (46)
15. a   Value contradictions occur when a value, such as the one that stresses group superiority, comes into direct conflict with other values, such as democracy and equality. (48)
16. b   Ideal culture is the ideal values and norms of a people, the goals held out for them. (50)
17. c   In our society, the custom is for the school year to be nine months long, with students having a three-month summer break so that they would be free to help their parents with critical farming tasks. Today, with the invention of highly productive farm machinery, children's labor is no longer needed, and yet the school years remains unchanged. This pattern would an example of cultural lag. (52)
18. a   Copying aspects of another group's culture is cultural diffusion. (52)
19. d   According to technological determinists, machines have become an independent force that is out of human control. (51)
20. d   The Golden Arches of McDonald's in Tokyo, Paris, and London are examples of cultural leveling. (53)

ANSWERS FOR TRUE-FALSE QUESTIONS

1.   *False.* Most people usually do not question the basic assumptions of their daily lives because culture provides a taken-for-granted orientation to life. We assume our own culture is normal or natural, when in fact it is learned. (37)
2.   *True* (38)
3.   *True* (40)
4.   *True* (41)
5.   *False.* Humans could not plan future events without language to convey meanings of past, present, and future points in time. (42)
6.   *True* (44)
7.   *False.* One group's folkways may be another group's mores. (44)
8.   *True* (45)
9.   *True* (47)
10. *True* (48)
11. *True* (48)
12. *False.* Concern for the environment has not always been a core value in U.S. society. It is one of the emergent values that is now increasing in importance. (49)
13. *True* (49)
14. *False.* Ideal culture refers to the values, norms, and goals of a group; real culture refers to the norms and values that a group actually follows. (50)
15. *False.* Technology can refer to tools, but it also includes the skills and procedures necessary to make and use these tools. (50)
16. *False.* New technologies is a term that refers to technologies that have a major impact on human life. (50)
17. *True.* (51)
18. *True.* (52)
19. *True* (52)
20. *True* (53)

ANSWERS FOR FILL-IN QUESTIONS

1. The material objects that distinguish a group of people, such as their art, buildings, weapons, utensils, machines, hairstyles, clothing, and jewelry are known as MATERIAL CULTURE; their ways of thinking and doing are NONMATERIAL CULTURE. (37)
2. The disorientation that people experience when they come in contact with a fundamentally different culture and can no longer depend on their taken-for-granted assumptions about life is CULTURE SHOCK. (37)
3. The tendency to use our own group's way of doing things as a yardstick for judging others is known as ETHNOCENTRISM. (37)
4. A SYMBOL is something to which people attach meaning and then use to communicate with others. (39)
5. The ways in which people use their bodies to communicate with one another are GESTURES. (40)
6. LANGUAGE is a system of symbols that can be combined in an infinite number of ways and can represent not only objects but also abstract thought. (41)
7. VALUES are ideas of what is desirable in life. (41)
8. The expectations or rules or behavior that develop out of values are referred to as NORMS. (44)
9. A TABOO is a norm so strongly ingrained that even the thought of its violation is greeted with revulsion. (44)
10. The United States is a PLURALISTIC society, meaning that it is made up of many different groups. (46)
11. VALUE CLUSTERS are a series of interrelated values that together form a larger whole. (48)
12. Sociologists call the norms and values that people actually follow REAL CULTURE. (49)
13. William Ogburn used the term CULTURAL LAG to refer to a situation in which nonmaterial culture takes a period of time to adjust to changes in the material culture. (52)
14. Air travel and rapid communications have contributed to CULTURAL DIFFUSION. (52)
15. When Western industrial culture is imported and diffused into the Least Industrialized Nations, the process is called CULTURAL LEVELING. (53)

ANSWERS TO THE MATCHING QUESTIONS

1. d   Edward Sapir and Benjamin Whorf: *stated that language shapes reality*
2. g   Robin Williams: *noted core values in U.S. society*
3. b   Marshall McLuhan: *coined the term a "global village"*
4. a   William Ogburn: *coined the term "cultural lag"*
5. f   Robert Edgerton: *critiqued the cultural relativism approach*
6. e   JoEllen Shiverly: *studied Anglos' and Native Americans' views of westerns*
7. h   William Sumner: *developed the concept of ethnocentrism*
8. c   Jacques Ellul: *claimed that technology now dominates civilization*

GUIDELINES FOR ANSWERING THE ESSAY QUESTIONS

1.   *Explain cultural relativism and discuss both the advantages and disadvantages of practicing it.* Your would begin your essay by defining cultural relativism and explaining that it developed in reaction to ethnocentrism. The primary advantage of this approach to looking at other cultures is that we are able to appreciate another way of life without making judgements, thereby reducing the possibilities for conflict between cultures. The primary disadvantage is that it can be used to justify any

cultural practice and especially those that endanger people's health, happiness, and survival. You could conclude with a reference to Robert Edgerton's proposed "quality of life" scale. (pp. 38-39).

2.   *Consider the degree to which the real culture of the United States falls short of the ideal culture. Provide concrete examples to support your essay.*
Your first step is to define what real and ideal culture mean. Then you would want to refer to the core values that are identified in the text as reflective of the ideal culture and discuss the ways in which Americans fall far short of upholding these values in their everyday lives. An interesting example of the difference between ideal and real culture would be the increasing value we place on leisure, and yet we are working more hours than ever before, or the value we place on physical fitness and yet we are more obese and less physically fit that ever (pp. 45-50)

3.   *Evaluate what is gained and what is lost as technology advances in society.*
One way to frame a response to this would be to identify a specific technology that has had a significant impact on our society and then to discuss both the gains and losses. You might want to refer to some of the ideas that are in the "Sociology and New Technology" box on page 51 concerning loss of freedom and creativity as well as the potential for greater understanding among people around the globe.

▲▼CHAPTER 3 -- SOCIALIZATION

ANSWERS FOR MULTIPLE CHOICE QUESTIONS

1. a   From the case of Isabelle, we can conclude that humans have no natural language. (57)
2. c   Research by H. M. Skeels and H. B. Dye demonstrated that human contact, regardless of the intelligence level of the caregiver, was significant in the development of intelligence among young, institutionalized children. (58-60)
3. d   "None of the above" is the correct response because studies of rhesus monkeys isolated for six or more months demonstrated that the monkeys were not able to adjust to monkey life, did not instinctively know how to enter into "monkey interaction" with other monkeys and were rejected by other monkeys. (60)
4. d   The term "looking-glass self" was coined by Charles H. Cooley. (61)
5. b   This statement "we move beyond the looking-glass self as we mature" is incorrect. All of the other statements are correct: the development of self is an ongoing, lifelong process; the process of the looking-glass self applies to old age; and the self is always in process. (61)
6. c   According to Mead's theory, children pretend to take the roles or specific people--such as the Lone Ranger, Supergirl, or Batman--during the play stage. (62)
7. a   To George Mead, the "I" is the self as subject. (62)
8. b   According to Jean Piaget, children develop the ability to use symbols during the preoperational stage. (63)
9. c   Freud's term for a balancing force between the inborn drives for self-gratification and the demands of society is the ego. (64)
10. c   According to this chapter, society sets up effective controls over our behavior by socializing us into emotions. (65)
11. b   The ways in which society sets children onto different courses for life purely because they are male or female is called gender socialization. (65)
12. a   We begin the lifelong process of defining ourselves as female or male in the family. (65)
13. d   Psychologists Susan Goldberg and Michael Lewis observed mothers with their six-month-old infants in a laboratory setting and concluded that the mothers unconsciously rewarded

daughters for being passive and dependent. (65-66)

14. c According to Melvin Kohn, middle-class parents focus on developing their children's curiosity, self-expression, and self-control. (68)

15. b Kohn found that the type of job the parent performed affected the pattern of childrearing; working-class parents employed in jobs characterized by individual autonomy were more likely to follow a middle-class pattern than a working-class one. (68)

16. d "All of the above" is the correct response. Participation in religious services teaches us beliefs about the hereafter; ideas about dress, and speech and manners appropriate for formal occasions. (68)

17. d According to researchers, poor children and children from dysfunctional families seem to benefit most from day care. (69)

18. c A person's musical preferences, clothing styles, and dating standards typically are most influenced by one's peers. (69)

19. b When we work part-time during our school years, we are learning aspects of occupational roles before we are actually expected to fill those roles. This process is called anticipatory socialization. (69)

20. b The process of learning new norms, values and attitudes or behaviors when placed in new life situations is referred to as resocialization. (70)

21. d Resocialization occurs when a person takes a new job, joins a cult, or goes to boot camp. (70)

22. c Total institutions are places in which people are cut off from the rest of society and are almost totally controlled by the officials who run the place. "All of the above" is an incorrect response because the term was coined by Erving Goffman, not Harold Garfinkel, and these institutions exist in democracies as well as in societies with totalitarian governments. (71)

23. b As a consequence of the Industrial Revolution, which produced new surpluses along with an increased demand for education, a new stage of the life course was invented--adolescence. (73)

24. b As woman's role in U.S. society has changed in the past few decades, women have come to believe that they can "have it all"--a career, a marriage and a family. In the middle years, many women face challenges as they try to reconcile the often conflicting demands of multiple social roles. (74)

25. c It is our self that provides each of us with the uniquely individual experience of socialization within the framework of society. Each of us acts on our environment, influencing the experiences we will have. (75)

ANSWERS FOR TRUE-FALSE QUESTIONS

1. *False.* Studies of institutionalized children demonstrate that some of the characteristics that we take for granted as being "human" traits result not from basic instincts but rather from early close relations with other humans. (58)

2. *False.* Because humans are not monkeys, we must always be careful about extrapolating from animal studies to human behavior. (60)

3. *True.* (61)

4. *True.* (62)

5. *True.* (63)

6. *False.* Socialization has a great deal to do with how we feel. Because different individuals' socialization differs, they will actually experience different emotions. (64-65)

7. *True.* (65)

8. *True.* (66)

9.   *False*. Melvin Kohn found that the main concern of middle-class parents was not their children's outward conformity but, rather, they focused on developing their children's curiosity, self-expression, and self-control. Working-class parents, on the other hand, did emphasize their children's outward conformity. (68)
10.   *True*. (68)
11.   *False*. Research shows that children from poor or dysfunctional families appear to benefit, although much depends on the quality of day care. (69)
12.   *True*. (69)
13.   *True*. (69)
14.   *True*. (69)
15.   *False*. Resocialization does not always require learning a radically different perspective; it usually only modifies existing orientations to life. (70)
16.   *True*. (71)
17.   *True*. (73)
18.   *True*. (74)
19.   *True*. (75)
20.   *False*. Sociologists do not think of people as little robots; they recognize that the self is dynamic and that people are actively involved in the social construction of the self. (75)

ANSWERS FOR FILL-IN QUESTIONS

1.   The entire human environment, including direct contact with others, is the SOCIAL ENVIRONMENT. (58)
2.   SOCIALIZATION is the process by which people learn the characteristics of their group--the attitudes, values, and actions thought appropriate for them. (61)
3.   Charles H. Cooley coined the term LOOKING-GLASS SELF to describe the process by which a sense of self develops. (61)
4.   According to George Herbert Mead, the development of the self through role-taking goes through three stages: (1) IMITATION; (2) PLAY; and (3) GAMES. (62)
5.   SIGNIFICANT OTHER is the term used to describe someone, such as a parent and/or a sibling, who plays a major role in our social development. (62)
6.   The idea that personality consists of the id, ego, and superego was developed by SIGMUND FREUD. (64)
7.   The different ways in which a society sets children onto different courses for life because they are male or female is GENDER SOCIALIZATION. (65)
8.   AGENTS OF SOCIALIZATION include the family, religion, day care, schools, peers, and the workplace. (68)
9.   PEER GROUPS are groups of individuals roughly the same age linked by common interests. (69)
10.   The process of learning new norms, values, attitudes, and behaviors to match new life situations is RESOCIALIZATION. (70)
11.   Resocialization often takes place in TOTAL INSTITUTIONS such as boot camps, prisons, and concentration camps. (71)
12.   DEGRADATION CEREMONY is a term coined by Harold Garfinkel to describe an attempt to remake the self by stripping away an individual's self-identity and stamping a new identity in its place. (71)
13.   The first stage in the life course, which takes place between birth and age twelve, is referred to

by sociologists as <u>CHILDHOOD</u>. (72)

14.   The stage of the life course which poses a special challenge for U.S. women is <u>THE EARLY MIDDLE YEARS</u>. (74)

15.   People in the later middle years are sometimes called the <u>SANDWICH GENERATION</u> because they are often caught between providing care for their elderly parents while they are still raising their own children. (74)

ANSWERS TO MATCH THESE SOCIAL SCIENTISTS WITH THEIR CONTRIBUTIONS

1. e   Melvin Kohn: *found social class differences in child rearing*
2. d   Erving Goffman: *studied total institutions*
3. c   George Herbert Mead: *coined the term "generalized other"*
4. a   Charles H. Cooley: *coined the term "looking-glass self"*
5. g   Jean Piaget: *discovered that there are four stages in cognitive development*
6. b   Harry and Margaret Harlow: *conducted studies of isolated rhesus monkeys*
7. f   Sigmund Freud: *asserted that human behavior is based on unconscious drives*
8. h   Philippe Ariès: *analyzed images of childhood in the Middle Ages*

GUIDELINES FOR ANSWERING THE ESSAY QUESTIONS

1.   *Explain what is necessary in order for us to develop into full human beings.*
You might want to be begin by stating that in order for us to become full human beings we need language and intimate social connections to others. You could draw on the information presented in the previous chapter as to what language enables us to do -- grasp relationships to others, think in terms of a shared past and future, and make shared plans. Our knowledge of language, and our ability to use it, develops out of social interaction, as the evidence of those children raised in isolation demonstrates. Furthermore, we develop a sense of ourselves and we learn how to get along with others only through close personal experiences with others. The theories of Cooley and Mead provide us with an framework for understanding this process and the experience of Genie and the children raised in institutionalized settings confirms the importance of this contact (pp. 41-43, 57-66).

2.   *Why do sociologists argue that socialization is a process and not a product?*
Sociologists would argue that socialization is a process rather than a product because there is not end to socialization. It begins at birth and continues throughout one's life, whenever you take on a new role. Cooley was the first to note that we are continually modifying our sense of self depending on our reading of others reactions to us (p. 61). Researchers have identified an series of stages through which we pass as we age; at each stage we are confronted by new demands and new challenges that need to be mastered (pp. 71-75).

3.   *After reading this chapter, how would you answer the question "Are We Prisoners of Socialization?"*
From reading this chapter and learning more about socialization you have hopefully learned that the self is dynamic, interacting with the social environment and being affected by it and it turn affecting it. We are involved in constructing our sense of self as active players rather than passive recipients (p. 75).

▲▼CHAPTER 4 -- SOCIAL STRUCTURE AND SOCIAL INTERACTION

ANSWERS FOR MULTIPLE CHOICE QUESTIONS

1. a   Microsociology places the focus on social interaction. Responses b, c, and d all describe macrosociology. (80)
2. c   Sociologists who study social class and how groups are related to one another are using macrosociology. (80)
3. b   Sociologists believe that people learn certain behaviors and attitudes because of their place in the social structure; in other words, whether they are privileged, deprived, or somewhere in between will affect their behavior and their attitudes. (81)
4. c   Culture is the social inheritance, learned from other people. (82)
5. a   One of the chief components of the social structure which strongly influences people's attitudes, ideas, and behavior is social class. (82-83)
6. d   Income, education, and occupational prestige all define one's social class. (82)
7. d   A person is simultaneously a daughter, a lawyer, a wife, and a mother; all of these together represent her status set. (83)
8. a   One's race, sex, and the social class of his or her parents are examples of ascribed statuses. (83)
9. c   The incorrect statement is: Status symbols are always positive signs or people would not wear them. Some social statuses are negative, and therefore, so are their status symbols (e.g.. prison clothing issued to inmates). (84)
10. b   A master status is one that cuts across the other statuses that a person holds. (84)
11. a   Status inconsistency is most likely to occur when a contradiction or mismatch between statuses exists. An example would be a wealthy African-American doctor who is denied membership in a prestigious country club. (84)
12. d   The behaviors, obligations, and privileges attached to statuses are called roles. (85)
13. b   Sociologically, roles are significant because they lay out what behaviors and attitudes are expected by society. (85)
14. b   A group is defined as people who regularly and consciously interact with one another. (85)
15. c   Religion, politics, education, and the military are examples of social institutions. (86)
16. c   The simplest societies are the hunting and gathering societies. (87)
17. a   Of all types of societies, the most egalitarian is the hunting and gathering society. (87)
18. b   Pastoral societies are based on the pasturing of animals. (87)
19. d   "All of the above" is correct. The domestication revolution led to the human group becoming larger, the creation of a food surplus, and a more specialized division of labor. (87)
20. c   A society based on large-scale agriculture, dependent on plows drawn by animals, is known as an agricultural society. (88)
21. c   In agricultural societies, social inequality became more extensive than that found in earlier societies. (88)
22. a   Postindustrial society is based on information, services, and high technology. (89)
23. d   All of the above is correct. Organic solidarity refers to a society with a highly specialized division of labor; whose members who are interdependent on one another; and with a high degree of impersonal relationships. (90)
24. c   Personal space might be a research topic for a sociologist using symbolic interactionism. (92)
25. c   The Thomas theorem is based on symbolic interactionism. (98)

ANSWERS FOR TRUE-FALSE QUESTIONS

1. *False*. Social structure has a large impact on the typical individual because it gives direction to and establishes limits on a person's behavior. (81)
2. *True*. (82-83)
3. *False*. Social class is a large number of people with similar amounts of income and education who work at jobs that are roughly comparable in prestige. Social status refers to the social position that a person occupies (mother, teacher, daughter, or wife). Thus, sociologists use the two terms quite differently. (82-83)
4. *True*. (83)
5. *True*. (84)
6. *True*. (85)
7. *False*. Sociologists have identified at least nine basic social institutions in modern societies. (86)
8. *True*. (87)
9. *False*. The simplest societies are called hunting-and-gathering societies. (87)
10. *False*. It was not hunting-and-gathering societies, but rather agricultural societies that were recognized as the "dawn of civilization" because things popularly known as "culture," such as philosophy, art, literature, and architecture, emerged during this time. (87)
11. *True*. (87)
12. *False*. Industrial societies were brought about by the invention of the steam engine. (88)
13. *False*. The United States was the first country to have more than 50 percent of its work force employed in service industries. (89)
14. *False*. According to Durkheim, with industrialization the basis for social cohesion shifts from the mechanical solidarity that characterizes agricultural societies to organic solidarity. (90)
15. *False*. It is *Gesellschaft* society, not *Gemeinschaft* society, that is characterized by impersonal, short-term relationships. (90)
16. *True*. (92)
17. *True*. (93)
18. *False*. Role strain, not role conflict, is defined as a conflict someone feels within a role. Role conflict is when the expectations of one role are incompatible with those of another role. (93)
19. *False*. Studied nonobservance, not impression management, is a face-saving technique in which people give the impression that they are unaware of a flaw in someone's performance. Impression management describes people's efforts to control the impressions that others receive of them. (93)
20. *False*. Symbolic interactionists do not assume that reality has an independent existence, and people must deal with it. They believe that people define their own reality and then live within those definitions. (96)

ANSWERS FOR FILL-IN QUESTIONS

1. MACROSOCIOLOGY investigates such things as social class and how groups are related to one another. (80)
2. The level of sociological analysis used by symbolic interactionists is MICROSOCIOLOGY. (80)
3. STATUS SYMBOLS are signs used to identify a status. (84)
4. Sociologists refer to the condition in which a person ranks high on some dimensions of social class but low on others as STATUS INCONSISTENCY. (84)
5. The simplest societies are called HUNTING-AND-GATHERING societies. (87)
6. A society based on information, services, and high technology is called the

POSTINDUSTRIAL society. (89)

7.   The degree to which members of a group or society feel united by shared values and other social bonds is referred to as SOCIAL COHESION. (90)

8.   Durkheim referred to a collective consciousness that people experience due to performing the same or similar tasks as MECHANICAL SOLIDARITY. (90)

9.   Ferdinand Tönnies used the term *GESELLSCHAFT* to refer to societies dominated by impersonal relationships, individual accomplishments, and self-interest. (90)

10.   Erving Goffman used the term IMPRESSION MANAGEMENT to describe people's efforts to control the impressions that others receive of them. (93)

11.   ROLE CONFLICT occurs when the expectations of one role are incompatible with those of another role. (93)

12.   Sometimes the same role has conflicting expectations built into it, which is known as ROLE CONFLICT. (93)

13.   Goffman called the techniques that we use to try and salvage a performance that is going bad as FACE-SAVING BEHAVIOR. (93-94)

14.   The THOMAS THEOREM states, "If people define situations as real, they are real in their consequences." (96)

15.   What people define as real because of their background assumptions and life experiences is the SOCIAL CONSTRUCTION OF REALITY. (96)

ANSWERS TO MATCH THESE SOCIAL SCIENTISTS WITH THEIR CONTRIBUTIONS

1. b   Emile Durkheim: *wrote about mechanical/organic solidarity*
2. a   Ferdinand Tönnies: *described **Gemeinschaft** and **Gesellschaft** societies*
3. e   Edward Hall: *studied the concept of personal space*
4. c   Erving Goffman: *analyzed everyday life in terms of dramaturgy*
5. f   W. I. Thomas: *wrote the theorem about the nature of social reality*
6. d   Harold Garfinkel: *founder of ethnomethodology*

GUIDELINES FOR ANSWERING THE ESSAY QUESTIONS

1.   *Choose a research topic and discuss how you approach this topic using both macrosociological and microsociological approaches.*
The way to answer this question is to first think of a topic -- I've chosen the topic of labor unions. Remember that the macrosociological level focuses on the broad features of society (p. 81). So from this level, I might research the role that unions play within the economy of the political system, what types of workers are organized into unions, the level of union organization among workers, or the level of union activity. Shifting to a microsociological level of analysis, I would want to look at what happens within unions or between unions and management in terms of social interaction (p. 92). From this perspective, I might want to investigate the behavior of union members and leaders at a union meeting, or the behavior of union and management negotiators at a bargaining session. By combining both perspectives, I have achieved a much broader understanding of the role of unions within society.

2.   *Today we see many examples of people wanting to re-create a simpler way of life. Using Tönnies' framework, analyze this tendency.*
You would want to begin by describing Tönnies' framework of *Gemeinschaft* and *Gesellschaft*, and discussing the characteristics of each. Using these concepts, you would indicate that individuals' seek for community reflects a rejection of the ever-increasing impersonality and formality of modern

society. In their actions, people are trying to re-create a social world where everyone knows each other within the context of intimate groups. Some sociologists have used the term "pseudo-*Gemeinschaft*" to describe the attractiveness of the past -- people building colonial homes and decorating them with antiques. (pp. 90-91)

3.   *Assume that you have been asked to give a presentation to your sociology class on Goffman's dramaturgy approach. Describe what information you would want to include in such a presentation.* You could begin by explaining how Goffman saw life as a drama that was acted out on a stage. This would lead you to making a distinction between front stage and back stage (p. 93). You might even want to provide some examples -- for instance, you are presenting on a front stage, but you practiced for this presentation in your bedroom without any audience. An important contribution of Goffman's was his insights into impression management, so you would want to explain what that is and how it involves the use of three different types of sign-vehicles -- social setting, appearance, and manner (pp. 93). Finally, you could conclude with his concept of teamwork, especially as it relates to face-saving behavior (p. 94). And remember to include examples of all of these concepts as you proceed.

▲▼CHAPTER 5 -- SOCIAL GROUPS AND FORMAL ORGANIZATIONS

ANSWERS FOR MULTIPLE CHOICE QUESTIONS

1. d   People who have something in common and who believe that what they have in common is significant are called a group. (104)
2. a   Primary groups are essential to an individual's psychological well-being. (104)
3. d   "All of the above" is correct. Secondary groups have members who are likely to interact on the basis of specific roles; are characteristic of industrial societies; and are essential to the functioning of contemporary societies. (104-105)
4. d   "All of the above" is correct. Voluntary associations are groups made up of volunteers who organize on the basis of some mutual interest. They include political parties, unions, professional associations, and churches, and they have been an important part of American life. (105)
5. c   The tendency for organizations to be dominated by a small, self-perpetuating elite is called the iron law of oligarchy. (106)
6. b   Groups which provide a sense of identification or belonging are referred to as in-groups. (106)
7. c   The groups we use as a standard to evaluate ourselves are reference groups. (107)
8. a   Sociologically speaking, the social ties radiating outward from the self, that link people together are social networks. (108)
9. a   Sociologists refer to the process of consciously using or cultivating networks for some gain as networking. (108)
10. b   This choice is not a characteristic of bureaucracy because this type of organizational structure has a hierarchy with assignments flowing downward and accountability flowing upward. (110-111)
11. c   Goal displacement occurs when an organization achieves its original goals and then adopts new goals. (111)
12. c   The term "rationalization of society" was coined by Max Weber. (112)
13. c   George Ritzer used the term "the McDonaldization of society" to refer to the increasing rationalization of daily living. (113)

14. b   We usually refer to the "correct procedures" of bureaucracies as red tape. (112)

15. b   A feeling of separation from work and work environments is referred to as alienation (112)

16. d   "All of the above" is correct because workers resist alienation by forming primary groups, praising each other and expressing sympathy when something goes wrong, and putting pictures and personal items in their work areas. (114)

17. a   According to Rosabeth Moss Kanter, in a large corporation the corporate culture creates a self-fulfilling prophecy that affects an individual's corporate fate. (114)

18. b   In the corporation, lifetime security is taken for granted in Japan. (115)

19. c   As the Japanese economy was hit by the worldwide recessions in the 1990s, it became apparent that only employees of major corporations--representing only about one-third of the workforce--were protected by lifetime job security. Many workers found themselves without employment as companies scrambled to remain competitive in tough economic times. (116)

20. c   Small groups can be either primary or secondary groups. (117)

21. d   "All of the above" is correct. Dyads are the most intense or intimate of human groups; require continuing active participation and commitment of both members; and are the most unstable of social groups. (117)

22. c   An expressive leader increases harmony and minimizes conflict in a group. (119)

23. d   "All of the above" is correct. According to sociologists, leaders tend to have certain characteristics which may include: they are seen as strongly representing the group's values; they tend to be taller and are judged better-looking than others; and where they sit in a group. (120)

24. b   In the Asch experiments, about 25 percent always gave the correct answer, even when that meant going against the sentiments of the groups. (121)

25. c   The Milgram experiment demonstrates how strongly people are influenced by authority. (122)

ANSWERS FOR TRUE-FALSE QUESTIONS

1.   *False.* Members of secondary, not primary, groups are likely to interact on the basis of specific roles. (104)

2.   False. Voluntary associations are a special type of secondary group. (105)

3.   *True.* (105)

4.   *True.* (106)

5.   *False.* Rather than disappearing, tensions between in-groups and out-groups are heightened in socially diverse societies. (106)

6.   *True.* (107)

7.   *False.* A person does not have to belong to a group to use that group as a reference group. (107)

8.   *False.* Networks tend to perpetuate social inequality because some people's networks are more important than others and because most jobs are secured through social networks. (108)

9.   *True.* (108)

10. *False.* Electronic communities, whose members communicate over the Internet, are groups in the sociological sense even though their members are not involved in face-to-face interactions. They still interact with one another and think of themselves as belonging together. (108)

11. *True.* (110-111)

12. *True.* (111)

13. *False.* Bureaucracies are not likely to disappear as our dominant form of social organization in the near future because they generally are effective in getting the job done. Most people spend

their working lives in such organizational environments. (112)

14. *True.* (112)
15. *False.* It is difficult for workers to prevent becoming alienated because of the nature of the organizational environment in which they work. According to Marx, alienation occurs because workers are cut off from the product of their own labor, which results in estrangement not only from the products but from their whole work environment. (114)
16. *True.* (115)
17. *True.* (118)
18. *False.* Sociologically speaking, a leader does not have to be officially appointed or elected to be the "leader." A leader is someone who influences the behaviors of others. (119)
19. *False.* The study concluded that the democratic leader got the best results. (120)
20. *False.* To study conformity the Asch experiment used cards with lines on them. To study obedience to authority the Milgram experiment used fake electrical shocks. (122-123)

ANSWERS FOR FILL-IN QUESTIONS

1. People who have similar characteristics make up a <u>CATEGORY</u>. (104)
2. A <u>SECONDARY</u> group is characterized by relatively temporary, more anonymous, formal, and impersonal relationships. (104)
3. A group made up of volunteers who have organized on the basis of some mutual interest is called a(n) <u>VOLUNTARY ASSOCIATION</u>. (105)
4. <u>THE IRON LAW OF OLIGARCHY</u> refers to the tendency of formal organizations to be dominated by a small, self-perpetuating elite. (106)
5. <u>IN-GROUPS</u> provide a sense of identification or belonging while producing feelings of antagonisms towards <u>OUT-GROUPS</u>. (106)
6. The groups we use as standards to evaluate ourselves are <u>REFERENCE GROUPS</u>. (107)
7. The social ties radiating outward from the self, that link people together are known as <u>SOCIAL NETWORKS</u>. (108)
8. <u>GOAL DISPLACEMENT</u> occurs when new goals are adopted by an organization to replace previous goals which may have been fulfilled. (111)
9. The phrase <u>THE RATIONALIZATION OF SOCIETY</u> refers to the increasing influence of bureaucracies in society. (112)
10. <u>ALIENATION</u> is a feeling of powerlessness and normlessness; the experience of being cut off from the product of one's labor. (112)
11. The smallest possible group is a(n) <u>DYAD</u>. (117)
12. A <u>COALITION</u> is formed when some members of a group align themselves against other members. (119)
13. Someone who influences the behavior of others is a(n) <u>LEADER</u>. (119)
14. An individual who tries to keep the group moving toward its goals is a(n) <u>INSTRUMENTAL</u> leader. An individual who increases harmony and minimizes conflict is a(n) <u>EXPRESSIVE</u> leader. (119)
15. <u>GROUPTHINK</u> is a narrowing of thought by a group of people, which results in overconfidence and tunnel vision. (121)

ANSWERS TO MATCH THESE SOCIAL SCIENTISTS WITH THEIR CONTRIBUTIONS

1. e   Irving Janis: *groupthink*

2. c   Georg Simmel: *dyads*
3. d   Robert Michels: *the iron law of oligarchy*
4. b   Stanley Milgram: *obedience to authority*
5. f   Solomon Asch: *conformity to peer pressure*
6. a   Charles H. Cooley: *primary group*

GUIDELINES FOR ANSWERING THE ESSAY QUESTIONS

1.   *Define the iron law of oligarchy and discuss why this problem occurs in voluntary associations.*
You would begin by explaining that the iron law of oligarchy is the tendency within organizations for
the leadership to become self-perpetuating (p. 105-106). Although this problem occurs in all types of
organizations, it is particularly evident in voluntary associations. A major reason for this is because the
membership varies in its degree of commitment to and involvement in the organization. Turnover is
high, so that members come and go, but the leadership stays on (p. 106)
2.   *Identify the advantages and disadvantages of bureaucracy and discuss some of the ways in
which the problems can be addressed.*
You must begin with the characteristics of bureaucracy and think about what benefits they provide to
large-scale organizations and how they can also create problems (pp. 110-111). For example, you
could point out that one of the features of bureaucracy is a hierarchy of authority and a division of
labor; in large organizations which have many members and many tasks to accomplish, dividing
authority and work up and assigning a specific level of authority and a specific task to each person
assures that the work is coordinated and gets done. You might also point out however, that when a
person is assigned only one task and has limited authority, it is possible that alienation will result (p.
112). You would want to do the same for other aspects of bureaucracies--the impersonality, written
rules, and written records help to organize people and coordinate activities, but they also produce
enormous red tape (p. 112). You could also touch on the problem of goal displacement (p.111).
Finally, you would conclude with some discussion about how people resist the negative side of
bureaucracy by forming primary groups and staking a claim to individuality (p. 114).
3.   *Explain the three different leadership styles and suggest reasons why the democratic leader is
the best style of leader for most situations.*
You would want to begin by identifying the three styles of leadership and listing the characteristics of
each. Then you should evaluate how characteristics of a democratic leader like holding group
discussions, outlining the steps necessary to reach the goals, suggesting alternatives, and allowing the
group members to work at their own pace all contributed to the outcomes like greater friendliness,
group-mindedness, and mutual respect, and ability to work without supervision. Finally, consider why
the those qualities and outcomes were just to be the best (pp. 119-120).

▲▼ ANSWERS FOR CHAPTER 6 -- DEVIANCE AND SOCIAL CONTROL

ANSWERS FOR MULTIPLE CHOICE QUESTIONS

1. b   In sociology, the term deviance refers to all violations of social rules. (130)
2. d   "All of the above" is the correct answer. Because norms lay out the basic guidelines for how
        we play our roles and how we interact with others, they represent the foundation for social life,
        creating predictability, and allowing for social order. (131)

3. c   Erving Goffman used the term sigma to refer to attributes, such as blindness, deafness, physical deformities and obesity, that society uses to discredit people. (131)

4. c   Frowns, gossip, and crossing people off guest lists are examples of negative sanctions. (132)

5. c   The sociological perspective attempts to understand deviance in terms of factors that lie outside the individual. They assume that there is something in the individual's environment that is influencing him or her to become deviant. (133)

6. c   Differential association theory is based on the symbolic interactionist perspective. (134)

7. c   The idea that two control systems--inner controls made up of internalized morality and outer controls represented by your network of friends and family who influence you not to deviate--work against our pushes and pulls toward deviance is called control theory. (135)

8. c   All of the following are ways of neutralizing deviance: appeal to higher loyalties, denial of responsibility, and denial of injury and of a victim. Denial of deviant labels is not one of the ways of neutralizing such behavior. (135-136)

9. b   William Chambliss's study of the Saints and the Roughnecks suggests that people often live up to the labels that a community gives them. (136-137)

10. d   "All of the above" is correct. William Chambliss states that all of these are factors which influence whether or not people will be seen as deviant: social class, the visibility of offenders, and their styles of interaction. (136)

11. a   According to the functionalist perspective, deviance promotes social unity and social change. (139)

12. d   Recidivism is not one of the responses to anomie identified by Merton. (140)

13. b   According to Merton's strain theory, people who drop out of the pursuit of success by abusing alcohol or drugs are retreatists. (140)

14. d   The illegitimate opportunity structures theory is based on the functionalist perspective. (141)

15. b   Contrary to what many people believe, the motive for joining a gang was not to escape a broken home or to find a substitute family or to prove one's masculinity. After studying a number of street gangs in different cities around the U.S. for more than ten years, Martín Sánchez Jankowski concluded that young men joined a gang because it was seen as an economic alternative to the dead-end jobs held by parents. (141-142)

16. c   Crimes committed by people of respectable and high social status in the course of their occupations are called white-collar crime. (142)

17. d   "All of the above" is correct. The criminal justice system is made up of the police, the courts, and the prisons. (143)

18. d   "All of the above" is correct. The marginal working class includes people with few skills, who hold low-paying, part-time, seasonal jobs, and who are the most desperate members of the working class. (143)

19. b   According to Henslin, a severe problem associated with the policy of imprisonment is the rate of recidivism. (145)

20. d   The purpose of deterrence is to create fear in others, with the idea that they will not commit the crimes. (145)

21. a   Halfway houses are community facilities where ex-prisoners supervise aspects of their lives. (145)

22. c   Rehabilitation switches the focus from punishing offenders to resocializing them so that they can become conforming citizens. (146)

23. b   Incapacitation removes offenders from "normal" society, taking them "off the streets." (147)

24. c   The medicalization of deviance refers to viewing deviance as a medical matter. (147)

25. c   Thomas Szasz was critical of the approach of medicalizing deviance, arguing that such

conditions are neither mental nor illnesses, but simply problem behaviors, produced because some people fail to cope very well with the challenges of everyday life. (148)

ANSWERS FOR TRUE-FALSE QUESTIONS

1. *True.* (130)
2. *False.* What is deviant to some is not deviant to others. This principle holds true within a society as well as across cultures. Thus, acts perfectly acceptable in one culture may be considered deviant in another culture. (130)
3. *True.* (134)
4. *True.* (135)
5. *True.* (135)
6. *False.* Some people and groups do embrace deviance and want to be labeled with a deviant identity. Examples include teenagers who make certain that their clothing, music, and hairstyles are outside adult norms, and outlaw bikers. (136)
7. *True.* (136)
8. *True.* (137)
9. *True.* (139)
10. *False.* According to strain theory, everyone does not have an equal chance to get ahead in society because of structural factors in the society which may deny them access to the approved ways of achieving cultural goals. (140)
11. *False.* Not all of Merton's modes of adaptation involve illegal behavior. One mode is conformity. Behavior arising out of such modes as ritualism or retreatism may not be in violation of the law. (140)
12. *True.* (141)
13. *False.* In his study of gangs, Martín Sánchez Jankowski found that as many gang members came from intact homes as came from broken homes. (141)
14. *False.* White-collar crime often is more costly than street crime. Examples include the plundering of the U.S. savings and loan industry and other "crimes in the suites." (142)
15. *False.* Conflict theorists believe that the criminal justice system functions for the well-being of the capitalist class. (143)
16. *False.* According to conflict theorists, most of those who are imprisoned in the United States come from the *marginal* working class. (144)
17. *True.* (145)
18. *False.* The purpose of retribution is to right a wrong by making offenders suffer or pay back what they have stolen. The purpose of deterrence is to create fear so that others won't break the law. (145)
19. *True.* (147)
20. *True.* (148)

ANSWERS FOR FILL-IN QUESTIONS

1. <u>DEVIANCE</u> is the violation of rules or norms. (130)
2. <u>CRIME</u> is the violation of norms that are written into law. (131)
3. Erving Goffman used the term <u>STIGMA</u> to refer to attributes that discredit people. (131)
4. <u>SOCIAL ORDER</u> is a group's usual and customary social arrangements, on which its members depend and on which they base their lives. (131)
5. <u>NEGATIVE SANCTIONS</u> range from mild, informal reactions such as frowns to formal prison sentences or even capital punishment. (132)
6. Inborn tendencies towards deviances such as juvenile delinquency and crime are called <u>GENETIC PREDISPOSITIONS</u>. (133)
7. Crimes such as mugging, rape and burglary are referred to as <u>STREET CRIME</u>. (133)
8. The term differential association was coined by <u>EDWIN SUTHERLAND</u>. (134)
9. By influencing a person to stay away from crime, friends, family, and the police are all examples of <u>OUTER CONTROL</u> system. (135)
10. When a deviant reacts by saying "Who are *you* to talk?" he/she is practicing one of the <u>TECHNIQUES OF NEUTRALIZATION</u>. (135)
11. Strain theory is based on the idea that large number of people are socialized into desiring <u>CULTURAL GOALS</u> (the legitimate objects held out to everyone) but many do not have access to <u>INSTITUTIONALIZED MEANS</u> in order to achieve those goals. (140)
12. Embezzlers, robbers, and con artists are all examples of what Robert Merton called <u>INNOVATORS</u>. (140)
13. The most desperate members of the working class, who have few skills, little job security, and are often unemployed, are referred to as the <u>MARGINAL WORKING CLASS</u>. (143)
14. The <u>RECIDIVISM RATE</u> refers to the proportion of people who are rearrested. (145)
15. Creating fear so people will refrain from committing a deviant act is the goal of <u>DETERRENCE</u>. (145)

ANSWERS TO MATCH THESE SOCIAL SCIENTISTS WITH THEIR CONTRIBUTIONS

1. c   Edwin Sutherland: *white collar crime*
2. a   Robert Merton: *strain theory*
3. f   Erving Goffman: *importance of stigma*
4. h   Thomas Szasz: *myth of mental illness*
5. d   Emile Durkheim: *functions of deviance*
6. e   William Chambliss: *effects of labeling*
7. g   Gresham Sykes and David Matza: *techniques of neutralization*
8. b   Walter Reckless: *control theory*

GUIDELINES FOR ANSWERING THE ESSAY QUESTIONS

1.   *Discuss how the different sociological perspectives could be combined in order to provide a more complete picture of deviance.*
You would begin by identifying the strengths of each perspective--symbolic interactionism focuses on group membership and interaction within and between groups (pp. 133-137), functionalism focuses on how deviance is a part of the social order (pp. 139-142), and conflict theory focuses on how social inequality impacts on definitions of and reactions to acts of deviance (pp. 143-147). An example of

combining perspectives is reflected in the work of William Chambliss on the Saints and the Roughnecks; he looked at patterns of inequality and different interaction styles to explain the different treatment the two groups received (pp. 136-137). Another example would be Cloward and Ohlin's work on illegitimate opportunity structures; they added the concept of social class inequality to the notion of the strain between institutionalized means and cultural goals to explain patterns of lower class deviance (pp. 141-142).

2. *In light of the difference explanations for deviance, evaluate the effectiveness of the various reactions to deviance.*

In answering this question, you would want to think first about the role of stigma and sanctions in maintaining social control (pp. 131-132). Then discuss the purpose or goal of different reactions to crime (pp.145-147). Consider whether of not the goal will effectively address the deviance, given what different sociologists have said about deviance. Consider this question: Would imprisonment be effective against someone embraces the deviant label (p. 136)?

3. *Explain what the author means when he says that "homelessness and mental illness are reciprocal."*

You might begin by talking about Thomas Szasz's ideas about mental illness (p. 147). Then consider the following questions: In what ways could homelessness produce behaviors that are viewed as problematic in our society? Likewise, why would the mentally ill be a higher risk of becoming homeless? What role does stigma play here?

▲▼ ANSWERS FOR CHAPTER 7 -- SOCIAL STRATIFICATION IN GLOBAL PERSPECTIVE

ANSWERS FOR MULTIPLE CHOICE QUESTIONS

1. b   The division of people into layers according to their relative power, property, and prestige is social stratification. (154)
2. b   Slavery is a form of social stratification in which some people own other people. (155)
3. a   Initially in antiquity, violation of the law, debt, and war and conquest were all ways in which a society justified the enslavement of individuals. It was only later, in the United States, that racism became a justification for the enslavement of Africans. (155)
4. d   "All of the above" is correct. In the United States the colonists initially tried to enslave Native Americans; when this practice proved to be unworkable, they turned to Africa for a supply of slave labor. An ideology of racism justified these actions by asserting that the slaves were inferior, and perhaps not even fully human. Slavery became inheritable because if one's parents were slaves, the child also was considered to be a slave. (156)
5. b   Caste systems practice endogamy, marriage within the group, and prohibit intermarriage. (156)
6. c   India is the best example of a caste system, although industrialization and other global factors are contributing to the gradual demise of that system. (156)
7. a   Class systems are characterized by social mobility--either upward or downward. (158)
8. b   Marx concluded that social class depends on the means of production. (159)
9. a   According to Max Weber, social class is determined by one's property, prestige, and power. (159)
10. d   The functionalist view of social stratification was developed by Kingsley Davis and Wilbert Moore. (160)
11. c   Of the criticisms listed, the only one that Tumin did not voice what the idea the functionalists

considered that stratification is the same everywhere and at all points in history; his critique included the fact that the functionalists do not provide an adequate method for measuring the social importance of the position; they assume that social stratification is beneficial to everyone, which it is not; and they view society as a meritocracy in which positions are awarded on the basis of merit, when in reality other factors such as income and gender influence one's placement in the system of stratification. (161)

12. a   A form or social stratification in which all positions are awarded on the basis of merit is called a meritocratic system. (161)

13. b   According to conflict theorists, the basis of stratification is conflict over limited resources. (161)

14. d   Gaetano Mosca argued that every society will be stratified by power. (161)

15. d   "All of the above" is correct. The key to maintaining national stratification is having control over ideas and information, social networks, and technology. (162-163)

16. c   The British perpetuate their class system from one generation to the next by education. (164)

17. c   The system of stratification in the former Soviet Union was based on membership in the Communist Party; within the party there was also stratification, with most members at the bottom, some bureaucrats in the middle, and a small elite at the top. (164)

18. a   The United States, Canada, Great Britain, and France are examples of the Most Industrialized Nations. (165)

19. a   Most people in the Least Industrialized World live on less than $1,000 a year. (168)

20. b   Colonialism occurs when a more powerful nation first invades and subdues a less powerful nation, and then establishes a controlling force to exploit the labor and natural resources of the defeated nation. (168)

21. d   According to Wallerstein these groups of interconnected nations exist: core nations--which are rich and powerful; nations on the semiperiphery which have become highly dependent on trade with core nations; nations on the periphery which sell cash crops to the core nations; and the external area--including most of Africa and Asia--which have been left out of the development of capitalism and had few, if any, economic connections with the core nations. (170)

22. b   Banana republics are Central American countries that developed a single cash crop for export to the United States, thereby becoming economically dependent upon the U.S. (171)

23. c   John Kenneth Galbraith used the culture of poverty theory to analyze global stratification. (171)

24. a   Multinational corporations are companies that operate across many national boundaries. According to the text, they do not always exploit the Least Industrialized Nations directly, but they do not benefit the Least Industrialized Nations as much as they do the Most Industrialized Nations. (172-173)

25. c   According to Henslin, control of technology is a key to the continued global dominance by the Most Industrialized Nations. (173)

ANSWERS FOR TRUE-FALSE QUESTIONS

1.   *True.* (154)

3.   *True.* (155)

3.   *False.* Historically, slavery was based on defeat in battle, a criminal act, or a debt, but not some supposedly inherently inferior status such as race. (155)

4.   *True.* (156)

5.   *True.* (156)

6.   *False.* While India may be the best known example of a caste system, it is by no means the

only one. The system of segregation that was established in this country after the Civil War, as well as the system of apartheid that existed in South Africa, represent examples of a caste system based on race. (156)

7. *True.* (159)
8. *True.* (159)
9. *False.* Max Weber disagreed sharply with Karl Marx, arguing instead that class standing was a combination of power, prestige, and property. (159)
10. *False.* Functionalists believe that society offers greater rewards for its more responsible, demanding, and accountable positions because society works better if its most qualified people hold its most important positions. From this standpoint, unique abilities would not be more important than the type of position held by the individual. (160)
11. *True.* (161)
12. *False.* Gerhard Lenski felt that the functional view of stratification was most appropriate when studying societies that did not accumulate wealth. (162)
13. *False.* In maintaining stratification, the elite finds the control of ideas more effective than brute force. (162)
14. *True.* (162)
15. *False.* While Lenin and Trotsky led the Russian Revolution that resulted in the creation of the Soviet Union, a classless society never existed; instead, a system of stratification based on membership in the Community Party was established. (164)
16. *True.* (165)
17. *True.* (170)
18. *True.* (170)
19. *False.* Most sociologists find imperialism, world systems and dependency theory preferable to an explanation based on the culture of poverty. (171)
20. *True.* (171)

ANSWERS FOR FILL-IN QUESTIONS

1. SOCIAL STRATIFICATION is a system in which people are divided into layers according to their relative power, property, and prestige. (154)
2. A form of social stratification in which some people own other people is SLAVERY. (155)
3. A CASTE system is a form of social stratification in which individual status is determined by birth and is lifelong. (156)
4. Caste societies use the practice of ENDOGAMY to make certain that boundaries between castes remain firm. (156)
5. According to Marx, the tools, factories, land, and investment capital used to produce wealth is THE MEANS OF PRODUCTION. (158)
6. According to Marx, the awareness of a common identity based on one's position in the means of production is CLASS CONSCIOUSNESS. (159)
7. Karl Marx's term for the mistaken identification of workers with the interests of capitalists was FALSE CONSCIOUSNESS. (159)
8. If stratification was truly organized as the functionalists describe it, society would be a MERITOCRACY, with positions awarded on the basis of merit. (161)
9. The DIVINE RIGHT OF KINGS is the idea that the king's authority comes directly from God. (162)
10. COLONIALISM is the process in which one nation takes over another nation, usually for the

purpose of exploiting its labor and natural resources. (168)
11. World system theory was developed by <u>IMMANUEL WALLERSTEIN</u>. (170)
12. <u>GLOBALIZATION</u> is the extensive interconnections among world nations resulting from the expansion of capitalism. (170)
13. <u>CULTURE OF POVERTY</u> is a culture that perpetuates poverty from one generation to the next. (171)
14. <u>NEOCOLONIALISM</u> is the political and economic dominance of the Least Industrialized Nations by the Most Industrialized Nations. (171)
15. Companies that operate across many national boundaries are <u>MULTINATIONAL CORPORATIONS</u>. (172)

<u>ANSWERS TO MATCH THESE SOCIAL SCIENTISTS WITH THEIR CONTRIBUTIONS</u>

1. d   Karl Marx: *false consciousness*
2. e   Kingsley Davis and Wilbert Moore: *the functionalist view on stratification*
3. f   Gaetano Mosca: *forerunner of the conflict view on stratification*
4. a   Immanuel Wallerstein: *world system theory*
5. g   Michael Harrington: *neocolonialism*
6. c   John Kenneth Galbraith: *stressed the culture of poverty*
7. h   Max Weber: *class based on property, prestige and power*
8. b   Melvin Tumin: *criticism of the functionalist view on stratification*

<u>GUIDELINES FOR ANSWERING THE ESSAY QUESTIONS</u>
1. *Compare and contrast Marx's theory of stratification with Weber's theory. Discuss why Weber's is more widely accepted by sociologists.*
Your first task is to summarize these two perspectives, pointing out the similarities as well as the differences between the two (pp. 158-159) Then you would want to consider the advantages offered by Weber's theory. You could mention that Weber's concept of property (or wealth) was broadened to include *control* over decision-making as well as ownership; that prestige and power can both be based on factors other than wealth; that the three dimensions are interrelated but can, and do, operate independently. Your conclusion should be that Weber's theory offers sociologists a more complete framework for understanding and analyzing systems of stratification.
2. *Consider why ideology is a more effective way of maintaining stratification than brute force.*
You should begin by considering why it is even necessary to "maintain stratification." On the surface, the idea that some people get more than other people should produce widespread instability--after all, isn't it natural for those without to want to do whatever they can to take some away from those with? However, this doesn't often happen because the elites have a number of methods for maintaining stratification, ranging from ideology to force. Without question, the most effective is ideology. Once a system of beliefs develop and people accept the idea in their minds that a particular system of stratification is right or just, then they will go along the status quo. (pp. 162-163)
3. *In the 1960s most former colonies around the globe won their political independence. Since that time the position of these countries has remained largely unchanged within the global system of stratification. Provide some explanation as to why political independence alone was not enough to alter their status.*
In order to answer this question you need to review the different explanations as to what forces led to the initial system of global stratification. Three of the four theories presented in your book focus on *economic* forces -- the only one that does not is the culture of poverty explanation (pp. 168-171). So

the initial system of global stratification was based on economic relationships. Even after these countries won their political independence, they were still intimately linked together in economic terms. Therefore, the explanation as to why so little has changed continues to be economic. To explain this, you would want to refer to neocolonialism, the development of multinational corporations, and the role of technology (pp. 171-173).

▲▼ ANSWERS FOR CHAPTER 8 -- SOCIAL CLASS IN THE UNITED STATES

ANSWERS FOR MULTIPLE CHOICE QUESTIONS

1. c According to your text, most sociologists agree with Max Weber that social class is best defined by employing three dimensions of social class. (178)
2. d It is safe to say that in the United States wealth is highly concentrated, with the top one percent of U.S. families worth more than the bottom 90 percent. (178)
3. c According to economist Paul Samuelson, if an income pyramid were made out of a child's blocks, most U.S. residents would be near the bottom of the pyramid. (178)
4. a The term "power elite" was coined by C. Wright Mills. (181)
5. b Hellinger and Judd refer to this ideology about popular participation in making important governmental decisions through the election of representatives to government as the democratic facade; this ideology effectively conceals the real source of power in the U.S. (181)
6. c It is true that the most prestigious jobs pay more, require more education, and offer greater autonomy. However, they do not necessarily require special talent or skills. (182)
7. a Capitalists, petty bourgeoisie, managers, and workers are the four classes in U.S. society, according to Erik Wright. (184)
8. c Capitalist, upper-middle, lower-middle, working class, working poor, and underclass are the six classes in the United States, according to Dennis Gilbert and Joseph Kahl. (184-187)
9. b According to Gilbert and Kahl, people who have made fortunes in entertainment or sports would be in the new money category. (1886)
10. b All of the following are characteristics of the working class: most are employed in relatively unskilled blue-collar and white-collar jobs; most hope to get ahead by achieving seniority on the job; and about thirty percent of the population belong to this class. However, most have not attended college for one or two years. (186)
11. c According to your text, the typical mechanic in a Ford dealership would be in the working class. (187)
12. d The correct answer is "d." In most cases, choice of mate, politics, and even sickness and health are affected by one's social class. (188)
13. a People in the working class are more likely to be liberal on economic issues and conservative on social issues. (188)
14. c Relative to those above them on the social class ladder, members of the lower class experience more stress in daily life. Those higher up have more resources for coping with stress--they can afford vacations and psychiatrists and counselors; their class position gives them greater control over their lives. (189)
15. d A homeless person whose father was a physician has experienced downward mobility. (191)
16. b As computers have been integrated into the workplace, opportunities for white-collar employment have expanded. Many blue-collar workers switched into white-collar jobs as a

result. This type of upward mobility is the result of changes in employment opportunities and is referred to as structural mobility. (191)

17. a As compared with their fathers, about one-half of U.S. men have a higher status. (192)

18. c Higginbotham and Weber studied women professionals from working class backgrounds and found parental encouragement for postponing marriage and getting an education. (192)

19. c The official measure of poverty calculated to include those whose incomes equal less than three times a low-cost food budget is the poverty line. (193)

20. d Divorce, births to unmarried women, and the fact that female workers are paid lower wages all contribute to the feminization of poverty. (196)

21. b In the U.S., the poor are most likely to be racial minorities, children and women. The elderly are less likely to be poor because of programs such as Social Security and Medicare. (196)

22. b According to U.S. Senator Daniel Moynihan, the increase in the rate of child poverty is due to the breakdown of the U.S. family. As the rate of divorce and the rate of childbirth outside of marriage have both increased, the result has been an increase in the number of female-headed households whose children are being raised in poverty. (197)

23. d The correct answer is the culture of poverty, a theory that assumes that the values and behaviors of the poor make them fundamentally different from other people and that these factors are largely responsible for their poverty. (196)

24. b Approximately one-quarter of the U.S. population is or has been poor for at least one year. (198)

25. d "All of the above" is correct. The Horatio Alger myth is beneficial to society, according to the functionalists, because it shifts the blame for failure away from the social system and onto the shoulders of the individual, thereby reducing pressures on the system. It also motivates people to try harder to succeed because "anything is possible." (201)

ANSWERS FOR TRUE-FALSE QUESTIONS

1.   *False.* Most sociologists accept Weber's views on social class, using the components of wealth, power and prestige in studying social class. (178)

2.   *False.* Wealth and income are not the same; wealth includes both property and income. (178)

3.   *True.* (178)

4.   *True.* (180)

5.   *False.* Occupational prestige rankings are very consistent across countries and over time. (182)

6.   *False.* Most U.S. residents are highly conscious of prestige. (183)

7.   *True.* (183)

8.   *True.* (185)

9.   *False.* The upper-middle class, not the capitalist class, is the one most shaped by education. (186)

10. *True.* (187)

11. *True.* (186-187)

12. *False.* Children of the capitalist class have a narrower field of eligible mates than do children of any other social class because this class places such emphasis on family tradition. (188)

13. *False.* Divorce is more common among the lower social classes, given their more difficult life. (188)

14. *True.* (190)

15. *True.* (191)

16. *True.* (192)

17. *True*. (192)
18. *False*. The poverty rate among the rural poor is higher than the national average. This group is less likely than the non-rural poor to be on welfare and to live in single-parent households, are more likely than the non-rural poor to have low skills and less education. (194)
19. *True*. (198)
20. *True*. (198)

ANSWERS FOR FILL-IN QUESTIONS

1.   According to Max Weber, the three dimensions of social class are: (1) WEALTH; (2) POWER; and (3) PRESTIGE. (178)
2.   PROPERTY, which encompasses buildings, land, cars, stocks, and bank accounts, is a form of wealth. (178)
3.   Money received as wages, rents, interest, royalties, or proceeds from a business is INCOME. (178)
4.   According to C. Wright Mills, the POWER ELITE makes the big decisions in U.S. society. (181)
5.   A person is considered to be STATUS INCONSISTENT if he or she ranks high on some dimensions of social class and low on others. (183)
6.   According to Erik Wright, a position in the class structure that generates conflicting interests is CONTRADICTORY CLASS LOCATION. (184)
7.   According to Gilbert and Kahl, the capitalist class can be divided into two groups: (1) OLD MONEY and (2) NEW MONEY. (185)
8.   The UNDERCLASS consists of a small group of people for whom poverty persists year after year and across generations. (187)
9.   UPWARD MOBILITY is movement up the social class ladder. (191)
10. Movement up or down the social class ladder that is attributed to changes in the structure of society, not to individual efforts, is STRUCTURAL MOBILITY. (191)
11. The official measure of poverty is referred to as THE POVERTY LINE. (193)
12. THE FEMINIZATION OF POVERTY is a trend whereby most poor families in the U.S. are headed by women. (196)
13. That the poor have values and beliefs that set them apart from the rest of society is the main argument of the CULTURE OF POVERTY theory. (296)
14. Foregoing something in the present in hope of achieving greater gains in the future is DEFERRED GRATIFICATION. (199)
15. The HORATIO ALGER MYTH is the belief that anyone can get ahead if only he or she tries hard enough. (201)

ANSWERS TO MATCH THESE SOCIAL SCIENTISTS WITH THEIR CONTRIBUTIONS

1. c   Gerhard Lenski: *status inconsistency*
2. b   C. Wright Mills: *power elite*
3. e   Erik Wright: *updated Marx's model*
4. h   Dennis Gilbert and Joseph Kahl: *updated Weber's model*
5. d   William Domhoff: *continued the tradition of C. Wright Mills*
6. f   Elliot Liebow: *street corner men in Washington, D.C.*
7. a   Daniel J. Moyniyhan: *poverty and the breakdown of the U.S. family*

8. g   Oscar Lewis: *culture of poverty*

GUIDELINES FOR ANSWERING THE ESSAY QUESTIONS

1.   *Explain why status inconsistency is often related to political radicalism.*
You will first want to define what status inconsistency is and then talk about Lenski's notion that we try to promote our highest status in our interactions with others, while others want to relate to us in terms of our lowest status. You might also discuss how those who are status inconsistent react by rejects others' claims to higher status, as the research by Ray Gold demonstrated. The consequence of all of this can be frustration which can lead to radical politics. You might want to explore how such radicalism could be left of center, as in the example provided in the textbook, but it does not have to be. (p. 183)
2.   *Discuss why you think women have been largely ignored in studies of mobility.*
You would want to point out that most studies of mobility have focused on occupational mobility. Until quite recently, most women did not have continuous occupational careers because of the nature of traditional gender roles. They derived their status from their fathers and their husbands. Therefore, in studies of intergenerational mobility, they were excluded because they did not have work histories that spanned their lifetime. As women's roles have changed, so has researchers awareness of them as research subjects. Also, because of structural changes in the economy, employment opportunities for women have opened up; this reflects structural mobility. You could point out the work by Higginbotham and Weber (p. 192).
3.   *Describe which groups are a greatest risk of poverty and then suggest ways in which poverty can be reduced by targeting these populations.*
You would want to begin by identifying those groups that are greater risk -- the rural poor, minorities, the undereducated, female heads of household, and children (pp. 194-196). You would then discuss specific ideas you have for overcoming some of the conditions that place these groups at greater risk; some possible programs would be improvements in education, including more funding for college and technical training, increases in minimum wage, increased number of jobs that pay a living wage, and more aggressive enforcement of anti-discrimination laws.

▲▼ ANSWERS FOR CHAPTER 9 -- INEQUALITIES OF RACE AND ETHNICITY

ANSWERS FOR MULTIPLE CHOICE QUESTIONS

1. b   Race is inherited physical characteristics that distinguish one group from another. (206)
2. a   A minority group is discriminated against because of physical or cultural differences. (214)
3. a   The dominant group in a society almost always considers its position to be due to its own innate superiority. (209)
4. b   Minority groups are created through the expansion of political boundaries and the voluntary and involuntary movement of people from one society to another. They do not emerge simply because they may represent a minority of the population; in fact, a group's status as a minority is not dependent on its size at all. (210)
5. d   Size of the ethnic group, power of the ethnic group, experiences with discrimination, as well as appearance are all factors that influences the sense of ethnic identity. The factor that is not related to the sense of ethnic identity is education. (210)

6. b   Activities that range from trying to trace one's family line to preserving the food, language and holidays are considered ethnic work. (211)

7. c   Prejudice and discrimination appear to characterize every society. (211)

8. d   "All of the above" is correct. Prejudice is an attitude, it may be positive or negative, and it often is the basis for discrimination. (211)

9. a   The negative treatment of one person by another on the basis of that person's characteristics is referred to as individual discrimination. (213)

10. d   As compared with a white baby, an African American baby has twice the chance of dying in infancy. (215)

11. a   The idea that prejudice is the result of frustration was suggested by John Dollard. (215)

12. c   An experiment conducted by Muzafer and Carolyn Serif demonstrated that prejudice is functional and shaped by the social environment. They first created a competitive environment between cabins within a summer camp setting and then found that strong in-groups formed within only a few days and lifelong friends, who were now competing against one another, were demonstrating a strong mutual dislike. (216)

13. d   "All of the above" is correct. According to conflict theorists, prejudice benefits capitalists by splitting workers along racial or ethnic lines; contributes to the exploitation of workers by producing a split-labor market; and is a factor in keeping workers from demanding higher wages and better working conditions. (216-217)

14. a   The term used by conflict theorists for the unemployed who can be put to work during times of high production and then discarded when no longer needed is reserve labor force. (217)

15. c   Symbolic interactionists stress that prejudiced people learn their prejudices in interaction with others. (217)

16. d   "All of the above" is correct. Genocide occurred when Hitler attempted to destroy all Jews. Genocide is the systematic annihilation of a race or ethnic group, and it often requires the cooperation of ordinary citizens. (217-219)

17. b   When a minority is expelled from a country or from a particular area of a country, the process is called direct population transfer. (219)

18. c   A society's policy of exploiting a minority group, using social institutions to deny the minority access to the society's full benefits, is referred to as internal colonialism. (220)

19. b   The process of being absorbed into the mainstream culture is assimilation. (220)

20. b   Following the passage of the Civil Rights Act in 1964 and the Voting Rights Act in 1965, many African Americans experienced rising expectations about improved social, economic and political conditions. Frustration over the pace of change led to urban riots in the late 1960s. (223)

21. b   According to William Wilson, social class--not race--is the major determinant of the quality of life for African Americans in the United States today. (225)

22. a   According to your text, Latinos are distinguished from other ethnic minorities in the United States by the Spanish language. (226)

23. b   Today, the fastest-growing minority in the U.S. is Asian Americans, whose numbers have doubled in just the past ten years. (228)

24. d   Of all American minorities, the worst off are Native Americans. (230)

25. d   "All of the above" is the correct answer. The backlash currently directed against immigrants is due to concerns that immigrants will undermine social institutions and contribute to social decay; anxiety that immigrants will take jobs away from native workers; and fears that immigrants will gain political power at the expense of other groups. (232)

ANSWERS FOR TRUE-FALSE QUESTIONS

1.   *False*. The notion of a "pure" race exists is a myth. Thus, no societies have a "pure race." (207)
2.   *False*. Race is physical characteristics; ethnicity is cultural. (209)
3.   *True*. (209)
4.   *False*. Sociologically speaking, size is not an important defining characteristics of minority group status. Being singled out for unequal treatment and objects of collective discrimination are. (209)
5.   *True*. (209)
6.   *True*. (209)
7.   *False*. After the United States defeated Mexico in war and annexed the Southwest, the Mexicans living there were transformed from the dominant group into a minority group. (209)
8.   *False*. In order to understand discrimination in the United States it is necessary to explain the patterns of institutional discrimination. (213)
9.   *True*. (214)
10. *True*. (215)
11. *True*. (215-216)
12. *True*. (216)
13. *False*. Conflict theorists, not functionalists, focus on the role of the capitalist class in exploiting racism and ethnic inequalities. (216)
14. *True*. (217)
15. *True*. (219)
16. *True*. (220)
17. *False*. African Americans continue to lag behind whites with respect to politics, economics, and education. There is only one African American U.S. Senator, African Americans average only 60 percent of white income, have more unemployment and poverty, and only 14 percent graduate from college. (223-224)
18. *True*. (227)
19. *True*. (228)
20. *True*. (229-232)

ANSWERS FOR FILL-IN QUESTIONS

1.   RACE is inherited physical characteristics that distinguish one group from another. (206)
2.   The systematic annihilation or attempted annihilation of a race or ethnic group is GENOCIDE. (207)
3.   Activities designed to discover, enhance, or maintain ethnic and racial identity are called ETHNIC WORK. (211)
4.   RACISM is discrimination on the basis of race. (211)
5.   INSTITUTIONAL discrimination is the negative treatment of a minority group that is built into a society's institutions. (214)
6.   Theodor Adorno's term for people who are prejudiced and rank high on scales of conformity, intolerance, insecurity, respect for authority, and submissiveness to superiors is THE AUTHORITARIAN PERSONALITY. (216)
7.   FUNCTIONAL theorists believe that prejudice can be both functional and dysfunctional. (216)
8.   Split-labor market is used by CONFLICT theorists to explain how the racial and ethnic strife

can be used to pit workers against one another. (216)

9.   The term used to describe the unemployed who can be put to work during times of high production and then discarded when no longer needed is THE RESERVE LABOR FORCE. (217)

10.   SELECTIVE PERCEPTION is the ability to see certain points but remain blind to others. (217)

11.   The types of population transfer are: (1) DIRECT and (2) INDIRECT. (219)

12.   The policy of forced expulsion and genocide is referred to as ETHNIC CLEANSING. (219)

13.   ASSIMILATION is the process of being absorbed into the mainstream culture. (220)

14.   In the period immediately following passage of the Civil Rights Act, many African Americans experienced RISING EXPECTATIONS, a belief that better conditions were in sight. (223)

15.   Emphasizing the common elements that run through Native American cultures in the attempt to develop a self-identity that goes beyond the tribe is the goal of PAN-INDIANISM. (231)

ANSWERS TO MATCH THESE SOCIAL SCIENTISTS WITH THEIR CONTRIBUTIONS

1. d   Theodor Adorno: *identified the authoritarian personality type*
2. f   Ashley Doane: *identified four factors that affect an individual's sense of ethnic identity*
3. g   John Dollard: *suggested that prejudice is the result of frustration*
4. j   Raphael Ezekiel: *studied racism in neo-Nazis and the KKK organizations*
5. i   Louis Wirth: *offered a sociological definition of minority group*
6. h   Eugene Hartley: *prejudice against one group leads to prejudice against other groups*
7. a   Donald Muir: *measured racial attitudes of white students*
8. b   William Wilson: *argues that class is more important than race in explaining inequality*
9. e   Charles Willie: *argues that race is still an important criterion for discrimination*
10. c   Bobo & Kluegel: *prejudice varies by age and education*

GUIDELINES FOR ANSWERING THE ESSAY QUESTIONS

1.   *Explain what the author means when he says that race is both a myth and a reality.*
You would begin by defining the concept of race (p. 206). Then you would move on to talking about the myth of race -- how there is no universal agreement as to how many races there are and how a system of racial classification is more a reflection of the society in which one lives than any underlying biological bases (p. 206-207). At the same time, race is a reality -- in terms of people's subjective feelings about race and the superiority of some, and the inferiority of other, races. You should bring Thomas's observations into the essay -- if people believe something is real, then it is real in its consequences (p. 208-209).

2.   *Explore how both psychological and sociological theories can be used together to gain a deeper understanding of prejudice and discrimination.*
Your essay should discuss how psychological theories provide us with a deeper understanding of individual behavior, while sociological theories provide insights into the societal framework of prejudice and discrimination. You could discuss the work of Theodor Adorno on the authoritarian personality or Dollard's work on individual frustration and the role of scapegoats (p. 215). But without an understanding of the social environment, this work is incomplete. Bridging the two perspectives is symbolic interactionism and the analysis of the role of labels, selective perception, and the self-fulfilling prophecy in maintaining prejudice (pp. 217). But you should also include in your essay some reference to the functionalist analysis and the work of Muzafer and Carolyn Sherif as well as the conflict theorists and how the capitalist class exploits racial and ethnic strife to retain power and control in society (pp. 216-217).

3.   *Using the experiences of different racial and ethnic groups in the U.S., identify and discuss the*

six patterns of intergroup relations.
The book identifies six different types of intergroup relations--genocide, population transfer, internal colonialism, segregation, assimilation, and multiculturalism (pp. 217-220). You could begin by mentioning how these are arranged along a continuum from rejection and inhumanity to acceptance and humanity. Then, as you define each pattern, bring into your discussion an example, or examples, from the history of the U.S. (refer to pp. 220-231). For example, in discussing genocide you could mention the treatment of Native Americans by the U.S. military; in discussing internal colonialism you could mention the economic exploitation of Latino farmworkers. An example of assimilation would be the experiences of European immigrants.

▲▼ ANSWERS FOR CHAPTER 10 -- INEQUALITIES OF GENDER AND AGE

ANSWERS FOR MULTIPLE CHOICE QUESTIONS

1. d   "All of the above" is correct. Gender stratification cuts across all aspects of social life and represents a primary division between people. The term refers to men's and women's unequal access to power, prestige, and property on the basis of their sex. (240)

2. b   The term "sex" refers to the biological characteristics that distinguish females and males. (240)

3. c   According to sociologists, if biology were the principal factor in human behavior, around the world we would find women to be one sort of person and men another. (241)

4. d   The reason women's work was traditionally accorded little prestige was because women were not seen as risking their lives for the group; men were seen as risking their lives whenever they hunted animals or waged war, so their work was accorded more prestige. (243)

5. d   "All of the above" is correct. Patriarchy is a society in which men dominate women. Patriarchy has existed throughout most of history, and it is universal. (243)

6. b   Feminism is the view that gender stratification is wrong and should by resisted by both men and women. (244)

7. c   Gender inequality in education is perpetuated because students are still tracked into different academic disciplines based on their sex. (245)

8. b   The continuing increase in the proportion of women in the workforce since the 1960s is referred to as the "quiet revolution" because the changes have been gradual, while the implications, in terms of consumer patterns, relations at work, self-concepts, and relationships with significant others, are profound. (247)

9. c   The pay gap between men and women is found in both jobs require little education and those that require a lot. (249)

10. b   What keeps women from breaking through the glass ceiling is not a lack of self-confidence, educational credentials, or the burden of childcare responsibilities. Rather, women are often "detoured" away from the core positions which serve as springboards to executive positions. Seen as more suited for jobs that provide "support," such as public relations and human services, women do not get the corporate experience required for top management. (251)

11. a   The use of a person's position to force unwanted sexual demands on someone is referred to as sexual harassment. (252)

12. c   Sexual harassment involves a person in authority, usually a male, who uses that position to force unwanted sexual actions on a subordinate, usually a female. (252)

13. d   Date rape is not an isolated event; it is more likely to happen after a couple has dated for a

period of time rather than on the first few dates; and most date rapes go unreported. (253-254)

14. c Women are reluctant to get involved in politics because the demands of political life are in conflict with the demands of their roles as wives and mothers. (256)

15. c Increased female participation in decision-making processes of social institutions is most likely going to result in breaking down the stereotypes that lock both males and females into traditional gender activities. (256)

16. b The Abkhasians are an interesting example regarding age because they live such long lives. (258)

17. c The principle that attitudes towards the aged are rooted in society and therefore differ from one social group to another is referred to as the social construction of aging. (258)

18. d The increase in life expectancy in industrialized nations is due to improvements in sanitation, developments in medicine, and the control of deadly childhood diseases. (258)

19. b The process by which older persons make up an increasing proportion of the United States population is referred to as the "graying of America." (259)

20. c Prior to industrialization, old people in U.S. society were viewed in a positive light, seen as wise and virtuous. In a time when many died before reaching old age, those who survived were listened to for advise about how to live a long life; they provided guidance on how to live a good life; and they were seen as knowledgeable about work skills. (261)

21. b Some researchers believe that the process of disengagement actually begins during middle age. (262)

22. a The belief that satisfaction during old age is related to a person's level and quality of activity is called activity theory. (263)

23. b Conflict theorists believe that retirement benefits reflect competition among interest groups. (264)

24. b The dependency ratio refers to the number of workers it takes to pay one person's Social Security. (265)

25. b Trends in poverty over the past 30 years indicate that the percentage of elderly who are poor has decreased. At the same time, the percentage of children living in poverty has increased. Some argue that the young have suffered at the expense of the old, a view that is challenged by conflict theorists such as Meredith Minkler and Ann Robertson. (265)

ANSWERS FOR TRUE-FALSE QUESTIONS

1. *False.* Sex refers to biological characteristics that distinguish females and males. Gender refers to social characteristics that a society considers proper for its males and females. (240)

2. *True.* (241)

3. *False.* Women are considered to be a minority group, but not because there are fewer women than men in the United States. They are considered to be a minority group because they are discriminated against--economically, in education, in politics, and in everyday life--on the basis of physical characteristics. (242)

4. *True.* (243)

5. *True.* (243)

6. *True.* (244)

7. *False.* While it is true that women outnumber men on college campuses today, it is not true that they earn less than one-half of all bachelor's degrees. Rather, they earn 55 percent of all bachelor's degrees. (245)

8. *True.* (246)

9. *True.* (247)
10. *False.* The pay gap in men's and women's earnings is due as much to discrimination on the basis of gender as to any other factor such as type of job or educational levels. Research by Fuller and Schoenberger found that women just starting their careers were hired at salaries 11 percent below those of men just starting out, even when their grades and internship experiences were superior. The gap grew over the years. (250)
11. *False.* It is men, not women, employed in non-traditional occupations, who are finding new opportunities for advancement and higher pay; sociologist Christine Williams refers to this phenomenon as the glass escalator. (252)
12. *True.* (252)
13. *False.* Females are much more likely than males to be victims of violence. (252)
14. *True.* (255)
15. *True.* (256)
16. *False.* Among the Abkhasian retirement is unknown and unthinkable; even the very old continue to work, averaging about 4 hours daily. (258)
17. *False.* The United States is not alone in the "graying" trend. All industrialized nations are graying because industrialization brings health measures that allow a larger proportion of a population to reach an advanced age. (258)
18. *True.* (258)
19. *True.* (265)
20. *False.* Conflict theorists Minkler and Robertson caution against this interpretation of the trends. They argue that increasing expenditures for one group does not automatically result in a reduction in resources to another group; rather, the pattern of spending is a reflection of government decision-making. Framing the issue in terms of gains and losses simply leads to divisions among groups. (265)

ANSWERS FOR FILL-IN QUESTIONS

1. SEX refers to biological characteristics that distinguish females and males, consisting of primary and secondary sex characteristics. (240)
2. Around the world, GENDER is the primary division between people. (240)
3. Frederick Engels proposed that PATRIARCHY developed with the origin of private property. (243)
4. Patriarchy was attributed to warfare and physical strength by anthropologist MARVIN HARRIS. (243)
5. FEMINISM is the philosophy that gender stratification is wrong and should be resisted. (244)
6. The GLASS CEILING prevents women from advancing to top executive positions. (251)
7. Men in non-traditional jobs often ride the GLASS ESCALATOR to more desirable work assignments, higher-level positions, and larger salaries. (252)
8. FEMALE CIRCUMCISION is a particular form of violence directed exclusively against women. (254)
9. The process by which older persons make up an increasing proportion of the United States population is called THE GRAYING OF AMERICA. (259)
10. The maximum length of life is referred to as the AGE SPAN. (260)
11. AGEISM is the discrimination against people because of their age. (261)
12. People who are born at roughly the same time and who pass through the life course together are considered a(n) AGE COHORT. (262)

13.   The belief that society prevents disruption by having the elderly vacate their positions of responsibility is <u>DISENGAGEMENT THEORY</u>. (262)

14.   <u>ACTIVITY</u> theory asserts that satisfaction during old age is related to a person's level and quality of activity. (263)

15.   The number of workers it takes to pay one person's Social Security is a <u>DEPENDENCY RATIO</u>. (265)

ANSWERS TO MATCH THESE SOCIAL SCIENTISTS WITH THEIR CONTRIBUTIONS

1. h   Janet Chafetz: *studied the second wave of feminism in the 1960s*
2. g   Alice Rossi: *women are better prepared biologically for "mothering" than are men*
3. a   Christine Williams: *men in non-traditional occupations often experience a glass escalator*
4. e   Sue Fisher: *documented physicians' practice of recommending unnecessary surgery*
5. b   Felice Schwartz: *founder of Catalyst*
6. f   Robert Butler: *coined "ageism" to refer to prejudice or discrimination based on age*
7. I   Dorothy Jerrome: *criticized disengagement theory for its implicit bias against the old*
8. d   Cumming & Henry: *developed disengagement theory*
9. c   Robertson & Minkler: *found no evidence that the elderly gained at children's expense*
10. j   Charles Hart: *anthropological study of the Tiwi tribe*

GUIDELINES FOR ANSWERING THE ESSAY QUESTIONS

1.   *Summarize the sociobiology argument concerning behavioral differences between men and women. Explain which position most closely reflects your own -- biological, sociological, or sociobiological.*

You would want to begin by stating how sociologists and biologists each explain the basis for differences in gendered behavior and then discuss how sociobiology tries to bridge the gulf between these two disciplines' views (pp. 240-241). In discussing sociobiology you could refer to Alice Rossi's suggestion concerning the biological basis for mothering and the connection between biological predispositions and cultural norms (pp. 241). As further evidence of the relationship between biology and social forces, you could discuss the two studies cited in the text -- the case of the young boy whose sex was changed and the study of Vietnam veterans (pp. 241-242). Your final task would be to state which view you think is most consistent with what you have learned about gender inequality and explain why.

2.   *Compare and contrast the two waves of the feminist movement in this country by identifying the forces that contributed to both waves.*

You could begin by noting that both waves of the feminist movement were committed to ending gender stratification and both met with strong opposition from both males and females. In both cases, there were two different branches that emerged -- a liberal and a conservative branch, and within theses branches there were radical wings. The major difference between the two had to do with goals. The first wave was characterized by rather narrow goals -- the movement focused on winning the vote for women -- while the second wave was broader and wanted to address issues ranging from changing work roles to changing policies on violence against women (pp. 244-245).

3.   *Choose one of the three different perspectives and discuss how that perspective approaches the subject of aging. Consider both the strengths and the weaknesses of the perspective you choose.*

In this question you have the option of writing about symbolic interactionism, functionalism, or conflict theory. If you choose symbolic interactionism (pp. 260-262), you would want to talk the concept of "ageism," the role of the media in defining images, and how the labels change over time. In particular, you could discuss how these labels changed with industrialization and how they are once again changing with the advent of a postindustrial society. The strengths of this perspective is that it provides us with insights into the social nature of a biological process; a weakness would be that it does not consider the conflict that may surround the labeling process.

If you choose to write about functionalism, remember that this perspective focuses on how the different parts of society work together (pp. 262-263). The two theories associated with this perspective are disengagement theory and activity theory. Strengths might be the focus on adjustment and the smooth transitioning from one generation to the next. Weaknesses are tied to the theories; disengagement theory overlooks the possibility that the elderly disengage from one set of roles (work-related) but may engage in another set of roles (friendship), while activity theory does not identify the key variables that underlie people's activities.

Finally, if you choose conflict theory, you would want to focus on the conflict that is generated between different age groups in society as they compete for scarce resources (pp. 263-266). As an example you would want to discuss the controversy over social security--from its birth to the present time. A strength of this perspective is that it provides us with an understanding of why the elderly have reduced the level of poverty over time; a weakness might be that it tends to emphasis conflict to the extent that cooperation between generations is overlooked.

▲▼ ANSWERS FOR CHAPTER 11 -- POLITICS AND THE ECONOMY

ANSWERS FOR MULTIPLE CHOICE QUESTIONS

1. d   "All of the above" is correct. Power was defined by Max Weber; is the ability to carry out one's will in spite of resistance from others; and it is an inevitable part of everyday life. (272)
2. c   According to Weber, the state claims a monopoly on legitimate force or violence. (273)
3. d   "All of the above" is correct. Traditional authority is the hallmark of preliterate groups; it is based on custom; and it was identified by Max Weber. (273)
4. c   The least stable type of authority is the charismatic. (275)
5. d   None of the above is correct. Democracy first occurred in Athens, not the United States. Democracy is a system of government in which authority derives from the people, not from elected officials. Democracy was practiced in Athens two thousand years ago, so it is not a modern idea. (275)
6. b   An individual who seizes power and imposes his will onto the people is a dictator. (276)
7. c   A form of government that exerts almost total control is a totalitarian regime. (276)
8. b   Studies of voting patterns in the United States show that voting varies by age, race/ethnicity, education, employment, and income. (278)
9. b   Today in the United States, approximately two out of every five eligible voters do not vote for the President of the United States; this low voter turnout reflects both alienation (the feeling that voting will not affect your life one way or another) and apathy (the feeling that your vote won't make a difference anyway). (279)
10. d   "All of the above" is correct. Lobbyists are people paid to influence legislation on behalf of their clients; are employed by special-interest groups; and are a major force in American politics. (280)
11. d   "All of the above" is correct. Functionalists believe that any one group is prevented from gaining control of the government because of the existence of pluralism, the use of checks and

balances, and the presence of many interest groups to which politicians must pay attention. (281)

12. c   According to conflict theorists, the ruling class is made up of people whose backgrounds and orientations to life are so similar that they automatically share the same goals. (282)

13. c   Hunting and gathering societies are characterized by a subsistence economy. (283)

14. d   "All of the above" is correct. Industrial economies are based on fuel-powered machines, created a tremendous, and emerged following the invention of the steam engine. (283)

15. b   Workers who package fish, process copper into electrical wire, and turn trees into lumber and paper are in the secondary sector. (284)

16. d   All of the above is correct. Postindustrial economies are characterized by a large surplus of goods; extensive trade among nations; and a "global village." (285)

17. b   Since 1970 the buy power of the American worker's pay check has worsened. (286)

18. d   Private ownership of the means of production is an essential feature of capitalism. (287)

19. d   The term "welfare capitalism" refers to a system in which private individuals own the businesses and pursue profits, but they do so within a system of laws designed to protect the welfare of the population. This is the kind of capitalism that now exists in the United States. (288)

20. b   An economic system characterized by the public ownership of the means of production, central planning, and the distribution of goods without a profit motive is socialism. (288)

21. d   Socialism views profits as immoral; socialists argue that because an item's value represents the work that goes into it, profit is an amount withheld from workers. (289)

22. c   Unemployment compensation, subsidized housing, welfare, minimum wage, and Social Security are all examples of socialist practices that are now part of U.S. society. (290)

23. c   The joint ownership of a business enterprise, whose liabilities and obligations are separate from those of its owners, is a corporation. (290)

24. c   The elite who sit on the boards of directors of not just one but several companies are referred to as interlocking directorates. (291)

25. b   The sociological significance of multinational corporations is that increasingly they have become detached from the interests and values of their country of origin. They owe allegiance not to any nation but only to profits and market shares. (292)

ANSWERS FOR TRUE-FALSE QUESTIONS

1.   *True.* (272)
2.   *False.* Authority, not coercion, refers to legitimate power. (272)
3.   *True.* As societies industrialize, traditional authority is undermined; however, it never totally dies out. Parental authority provides an excellent example. (273)
4.   *True.* (273)
5.   *True.* (275)
6.   *True.* (276)
7.   *True.* (276)
8.   *False.* The idea of universal citizenship caught on very slowly in the United States. (276)
9.   *False.* Employment and income do affect the probability that people will vote. (278)
10.   *False.* Most political action committees do not represent broad social interests but rather, stand for narrow financial concerns, such as the dairy, oil, banking, and construction industries. (280)
11.   *True.* (281)

12.   *False.* Conflict theorists do not believe that the ruling class is a group that meets together and agrees on specific matters. Rather, it consists of people whose backgrounds and orientations to life are so similar that they automatically share the same goals. (282)
13.   *False.* Pastoral and horticultural societies, not hunting and gathering societies, were the first economies to have a surplus. (283)
14.   *True.* (283)
15.   *False.* Postindustrial economy is based on information processing and providing services. (284)
16.   *True.* (286)
17.   *True.* (288)
18.   *True.* (289)
19.   *False.* According to convergence theory, as nations industrialize they will become more similar to one another. However, rather than adopting the traits of one type of economic system or another, they will reflect a hybrid or mixed economy, combining elements of both. (290)
20.   *True.* (290)

ANSWERS FOR FILL-IN QUESTIONS

1.   STATE, synonymous with government, is the source of legitimate violence in society. (273)
2.   TRADITIONAL AUTHORITY is authority based on custom. (273)
3.   Bureaucratic authority is also called RATIONAL-LEGAL AUTHORITY. (273)
4.   An independent city whose power radiates outward, bringing the adjacent area under its rule is a CITY-STATE. (275)
5.   DIRECT DEMOCRACY is a form of democracy in which the eligible voters meet together to discuss issues and make their decisions. (276)
6.   The concept that birth and residence in a country impart basic rights is known as CITIZENSHIP. (276)
7.   A form of government that exerts almost total control over the people is TOTALITARIANISM. (276)
8.   VOTER APATHY refers to indifference and inaction on the part of individuals or groups with respect to the political process. (278)
9.   POWER ELITE refers to the top people in leading corporations, the most powerful generals and admirals of the armed forces, and certain elite politicians. (281)
10.   ECONOMY is the term for a system of distribution of goods and services. (283)
11.   Barry Bluestone and Bennett Harrison use the expression "THE GREAT AMERICAN U-TURN" to refer to the net decline in the wages and standard of living of U.S. workers. (286)
12.   A type of economic system in which market forces operate without interference from the government would be LAISSEZ-FAIRE CAPITALISM. (288)
13.   The view that as capitalist and socialist economic systems each adopt features of the other, a hybrid (or mixed) economic system may emerge is CONVERGENCE THEORY. (290)
14.   The refusal of a corporation's stockholders to rubber-stamp decisions made by its managers is referred to as STOCKHOLDERS' REVOLT. (291)
15.   When individuals serve on the board of directors of several companies simultaneously, the result is the emergence of INTERLOCKING DIRECTORATES. (291)

ANSWERS TO MATCH THESE SOCIAL SCIENTISTS WITH THEIR CONTRIBUTIONS

1. f   Daniel Bell: *identified the characteristics of postindustrial societies*

2. h   Peter Berger: *violence is the foundation of the political order*
3. e   Michael Useem: *studied the activities of the "inner circle"*
4. c   Willaim Domhoff: *ruling class*
5. b   Thorstein Veblen: *created the term "conspicuous consumption"*
6. g   C. Wright Mills: *power elite*
7. d   Max Weber: *three types of authority*
8. a   William Form: *supported convergence theory*

GUIDELINES FOR ANSWERING THE ESSAY QUESTIONS
1.   *Discuss the three sources of authority and the issues related to the transfer of authority.*

Max Weber identified three different sources of authority in society--traditional, rational-legal, and charismatic (pp. 273-275). You would begin your essay by defining each of these types of authority and discussing the social conditions associated with the exercise of each type. To show the professor that you understand each type, you should include some examples to illustrate your discussion. The final part of the essay is to discuss how authority is transferred from one leader to the next (p. 275). With traditional authority that are both customs and rules and with rational-legal there are clearly written procedures. Charismatic authority poses the greatest challenge since it is based on extraordinary or outstanding qualities of an individual; for this reason, it is extremely difficult to pass that authority on. Recognizing this, some charismatic leaders will name a successor, while others will create an organization and establish procedures. The latter is referred to as the "routinization of authority."

2.   *Discuss the system of democracy found in the U.S and consider how some of the problems associated with our system -- voter apathy and the power of political action committees -- are related to our system of government.*

For this essay you would want to point out that the system is democratic, which means that the ultimate power resides in the people (p. 275), but that it is a representative rather than direct democracy, which means that citizens vote for representatives who actually make the decisions rather than the citizens themselves voting on each decision; you might want to add some discussion as to why it became a representative government (p. 276). Ours has a "winner-takes-all" orientation, which discourages the formation of third parties. Additionally, both parties fall around the center of the political continuum, avoiding an extreme political positions, and party control over individual members is weak, so that elected officials will often vote against the party on certain issues (p. 276). Finally, to run for public office is costly, which means that candidates have to raise enormous sums of money in order to compete.

Having laid out the general characteristics of our system, you would want to consider how voter apathy, the power of political action committees, and the concentration of power are related to the specific features of the U.S. system. First, you might want to talk about how the winner-takes-all arrangement encourages the development of centrist parties which are forced to appeal to the middle of the voting population in order to receive the majority of the votes; because of this, many people come to feel that the political parties are too superficial and do not really represent their ideas or interests, so they decide to sit out the elections (pp. 278-279). The second problem -- power of PACs -- is also related to the particular feature of winner-takes-all systems. With so much riding on elections, candidates are pressured into spending excessive amounts of money in order to get their name and their message out to the voters. The cash requirements provide a perfect opportunity for PACs to donate and thereby influence not only the outcomes of elections but the voting behavior of the elected candidate (p. 280).

3.   *Discuss the advantages and disadvantages of both capitalism and socialism as ideologies and as*

economic systems.

This is a difficult question to answer because it is laden with social values. In this country we have been taught that capitalism is good and socialism is bad. Nevertheless, you should try to approach this from as objective a position as possible. You would want to begin by discussing the advantages and disadvantages of capitalism. For advantages you could mention the idea of private ownership and the pursuit of profits, the motivation among workers to work hard, and the vast array of goods that are available in the marketplace. Among the disadvantages you could note the possibility for monopoly, the creation of constant discontent through advertizing, and the violation of certain basic human right like freedom from poverty. Turning to socialism, you could not that advantages include production for the general welfare rather than individual enrichment and the distribution of goods and services according to need rather than ability to pay. Critics point out that socialism violates basic human rights such as individual freedom of decision and opportunity (pp. 287-290).

▲▼ ANSWERS FOR CHAPTER 12

ANSWERS FOR MULTIPLE CHOICE QUESTIONS

1. a   Polyandry is a marriage in which a woman has more than one husband. (298)
2. d   None of the above is correct; family of orientation is the one in which a person grows up. (299)
3. b   Endogamy is the practice of marrying within one's own group. (299)
4. a   In a matrilineal system descent is figured only on the mother's side. (300)
5. b   According to functionalists, the family serves certain essential functions in all societies. (300)
6. d   All of the above is correct. The incest taboo is rules specifying the degrees of kinship that prohibit sex or marriage; helps families avoid role confusion; and facilitates the socialization of children. (300-301)
7. b   According to Arlie Hochschild, men use four different strategies of resistance to avoid doing housework: waiting it out (not volunteering, thereby forcing their wives to ask for help); playing dumb (doing chores incompetently so they will not be asked again); needs reduction (reducing his need for services thereby forcing the wife to step in because of her greater need to see that his needs were being met); and substitute offerings (showing appreciation for the great job his wife was doing balancing the demands of work and family). The one she does not identify is purchasing services. (303-304)
8. c   According to researchers, if a husband's earnings are relatively close to those of his wife's, then he is more likely to do his share of the housework. If his earnings are less, then he is less likely to do his share. (302)
9. b   Most people in the U.S. consider romantic love to be the single most important factor in marriage. (304)
10. c   The tendency of people with similar characteristics to marry one another is homogamy. (306)
11. b   In her interviews with 75 couples, Lillian Rubin found that the social class of the parents was important in explaining how couples adjust to the arrival of children. The average working class couple began a family less than a year after marriage; they did not have the financial resources, nor were they even adjusted to marital roles before the baby arrived. In contrast, the average middle class couple waited two years before having their first child; the longer time allowed them to accumulate some financial resources and to adjust to each other before having to assume parent roles. (307)
12. a   A recent national survey found that 23 percent of children in two-parent households were being

cared for by their fathers. (307)

13. a The empty nest syndrome is not a reality for most parents. (309)
14. b Women are more likely than men to face problems adjusting to widowhood because they live longer than men on the average and they are more likely to have married older men. (309)
15. c According to your text, a major concern of upper class African-American families is how to maintain family lineage. (309)
16. d All of the above is correct. Machismo, an emphasis on male strength and dominance, distinguishes Latino families from other groups; and is seen in some Chicano families where the husband-father plays a strong role in his family. (310)
17. b The most significant issue facing Native-American families today is whether to follow traditional values or assimilate. (311)
18. b The primary source of stress for one-parent families is poverty. (312)
19. d All of the above is correct. Children from single-parent families are more likely to drop out of school, become delinquent, and be poor as adults. (312)
20. c A family whose members were once part of other families is known as a blended family. (313)
21. d All of the above is correct. Cohabitation, the condition of living together as an unmarried couple, has increased about eight times in just 25 years; it has occurred before about half of all couples marry. (314)
22. c The "sandwich generation" refers to people who find themselves responsible for the care of their own children and their aging parents simultaneously. (315)
23. b Serial fatherhood is the term used to describe a current pattern of parenting. When a man and a woman divorce, the man continues to have a relationship with his children from that marriage only until he forms a new relationship with another woman; he then is involved in parenting any children from that subsequent relationship, foregoing continued contact with children from the previous relationship. As he ends and begins new relationships with women, he also ends and begins new relationships with the children attached to that relationship. Consequently, he has a series of relationships with different children over his lifetime. (319)
24. d Today, the average divorced woman will wait about five years to remarry. (320)
25. b According to Murray Straus, gender inequality underlies much marital violence. Given the sexist structure of our society, some men end up thinking that they are superior and have a right to force their will on their wives. (321)

ANSWERS FOR TRUE-FALSE QUESTIONS

1. *False.* Households are people who live together in the same housing unit; families consist of two or more people who consider themselves related by blood, marriage or adoption. (299)
2. *False.* The incest taboo, which prohibits sex and marriage among certain relatives, is an example of exogamy, not endogamy. (299)
3. *True.* (300)
4. *True.* (303)
5. *False.* According to Arlie Hochschild, one of the strategies used by some husbands to resist doing housework is "substitute offerings"--expressing appreciation to the wife for her being so organized that she can handle both work for wages and the second shift at home--when, instead, it would be better if he actually shared the work with her. (304)
6. *False.* Of all categories of husbands, those who earn less than their wives do the least housework. Sociologists explain this pattern in terms of gender role; because men are expected to earn more than women, when a man does not he feels threatened and tries to avoid any kind

of activity, especially housework, that would further undermine his masculinity. (303)

7.   *True.* (306)
8.   *False.* The birth of a child usually decreases the level of marital satisfaction. (306)
9.   *True.* (307)
10.   *True.* (308)
11.   *True.* (308)
12.   False. Researchers have found that most husbands and wives do not experience the empty nest when their last child leaves home. Often just the opposite occurs because the couple now has more time and money to use at their own discretion. (309)
13.   *True.* (310)
14.   *False.* Marriage between homosexuals is not legal in any state; however, some gay churches conduct marriage ceremonies which are not recognized in the eyes of the law. (313)
15.   *True.* (314)
16.   *False.* Among industrialized nations, the United States ranks in the middle one-third in terms of the rate of births to unmarried women. (315)
17.   *True.* (318)
18.   *False.* The pattern is for contact to be high during the first 1-2 years following the divorce and then decline rapidly. (319)
19.   *True.* (320)
20.   *True.* (322)

ANSWERS FOR FILL-IN QUESTIONS

1.   A marriage in which a man has more than one wife is <u>POLYGYNY</u>. (298)
2.   A <u>HOUSEHOLD</u> consists of all people who occupy the same housing unit. (299)
3.   A(n) <u>NUCLEAR FAMILY</u> is a family consisting of a husband, wife, and child(ren). (299)
4.   The family you grow up in is called your <u>FAMILY OF ORIENTATION</u>. (299)
5.   A social group's approval arrangement for mating, usually marked by a ritual ceremony of some sort, is <u>MARRIAGE</u>. (299)
6.   <u>EXOGAMY</u> is the practice of marrying outside one's group. (299)
7.   Those societies in which descent is only counted on the father's side are <u>PATRILINEAL</u>. (300)
8.   Female control of a society or group is a(n) <u>MATRIARCHY</u>. (300)
9.   Feelings of erotic attraction, accompanied by an idealization of the other, is the definition of <u>ROMANTIC LOVE</u>. (304)
10.   <u>HOMOGAMY</u> is the tendency of people with similar characteristics to get married. (306)
11.   A married couple's domestic situation after the last child has left home is sometimes referred to as the <u>EMPTY NEST</u>. (309)
12.   An emphasis on male strength and dominance is <u>MACHISMO</u>. (310)
13.   A <u>BLENDED FAMILY</u> is one whose members were once part of other families. (313)
14.   The term sociologists use to describe adults who are living together in a sexual relationship without being married is <u>COHABITATION</u>. (314)
15.   The pattern of divorced fathers living with, supporting, and playing an active fathering role with the children of the woman with whom they are currently involved is known as <u>SERIAL FATHERHOOD</u>. (319)

ANSWERS TO MATCH THESE SOCIAL SCIENTISTS WITH THEIR CONTRIBUTIONS

1. b   Blumstein & Schwartz:*studied household issues of same-sex couples*
2. f   Dutton & Aron: *studied the relationship between danger and sexual arousal*
3. h   Andrew Cherlin: *noted lack of norms regarding remarriage*
4. a   Lauer & Lauer: *factors associated with successful marriages*
5. e   Kathleen Gerson: *identified reasons why couples choose to be child-free*
6. j   Arlie Hochschild: *identified the second shift*
7. i   Melvin Kohn: *studied social class differences in child-rearing*
8. c   Lillian Rubin: *found that women's satisfaction increased after last child moved out*
9. d   Diana Russell: *studied incest victims*
10.g   Bob Suzuki: *identified distinctive characteristics of Asian American families*

GUIDELINES FOR ANSWERING THE ESSAY QUESTIONS

1.   *Explore why it is so difficult to answer the question "What is a family, anyway?"*
        This question is posed at the very beginning of the chapter and then proceeds to answer the question throughout the chapter, as the author talks about the vast diversity of family forms. The most direct way to answer this question would be to talk about the global variations in family structure, bringing into the discussion information about monogamy vs. polygamy, nuclear vs. extended families, different systems of descent and inheritance, different systems of authority, and different practices of mate selection (298-300). From there you could go on to talk about some of the different types of families that are found within the U.S. today (pp. 309-313). You would conclude by noting that despite all the variations, all of these families have one thing in common -- they consist of two or more people who consider themselves related by blood, marriage, or adoption (p. 299).

2.   *Identify the stages in the family life cycle, discussing what tasks are accomplished in each stage and what event marks that transition from one stage to the next.*
        You will want to discuss each of the several stages in sequence: love and courtship, marriage, childbirth, child rearing, and the family in later life--including mention of the empty nest and widowhood (pp.304-309). For each stage, you should include the work that takes place as well as the events that mark the beginning and end of that stage. For example, the first stage is love and courtship. In our culture, this involves romantic love -- individuals being sexually attracted to one another and idealizing the other. There are two components--one is emotion, related to feelings of sexual attraction, and the other is cognitive, attaching labels to our feelings. The stage begins with our meeting and being attracted to another person, and ends when we decide to get engaged to be married.

3.   *Discuss the impact that divorce has on family members -- men, women and children.*
You would want to discuss each family role separately--children, wives and husbands. In your response, be sure to talk about the research on the impact on children, especially the long-term impact, including a loss of connection to parents and difficulties forming intimate relations (pp. 318-319); you might also mention the factors that are associated with positive adjustments (p. 319). For spouses, there is anger, depression and anxiety following a divorce, but each also experiences unique problems related to their gender. For women, there is often a decrease in the standard of living, although the impact varies by social class. For men, there is a loss of connection to their children and the possible development of a series of families (pp. 319-320).

▲▼ ANSWERS FOR CHAPTER 13 -- EDUCATION AND RELIGION

ANSWERS FOR MULTIPLE CHOICE QUESTIONS

1. a   The use of diplomas and degrees to determine who is eligible for jobs, even though the diploma or degree may be irrelevant to the actual work is known as a credential society. (328)
2. b   In Japan, college admission is based on making a high score on a national test. (329)
3. b   The function of education that sorts people into a society's various positions is social placement. (332)
4. a   From a conflict perspective, the real purpose of education is to perpetuate existing social inequalities. (332)
5. c   The hidden curriculum is based on the conflict perspective. (333)
6. c   Public schools are largely supported by local property taxes. (334)
7. c   Teacher expectations and face-to-face interactions are of interest to symbolic interaction theorists. (335)
8. d   Research by George Farkas focused on how teacher expectations affect students' grades. (335)
9. b   During the past twenty to thirty years, combined scores on tests such as the SAT have declined. (336)
10. c   High school graduates who have difficulty with basic reading and math are known as functional illiterates. (337)
11. d   Providing a safe learning environment, setting higher expectations, and increasing parental involvement have all been proposed as solutions to the problems of U.S. education. Eliminating the hidden curriculum has not been suggested as a solution. (337)
12. c   Durkheim used the word church in an unusual way to refer to a group of believers organized around a set of beliefs and practices regarding the sacred. (340)
13. a   The following are functions of religion: instilling the value of patriotism; spearheading social change; and providing guidelines for daily life. Encouraging wars for holy causes is a dysfunction of religion. (340-341)
14. c   War and religious persecution are dysfunctions of religion. (341)
15. c   Religion is the opium of the people according to some conflict theorists. (343)
16. d   All of the above is correct. These are all examples of the use of religion to legitimize social inequalities: the divine right of kings; a declaration that the Pharaoh or Emperor is god or divine; and the defense of slavery as being God's will. (344)
17. a   Weber believed that religion held the key to modernization. (344)
18. d   None of the above is correct. The spirit of capitalism is the desire to accumulate capital as a duty --not to spend it, but as an end in itself. It is not the desire to accumulate capital in order to spend it and show others how one "has it made." Nor is it Marx's term for the driving force in the exploitation of workers or the ideal of a highly moral life, hard work, industriousness, and frugality (which is the Protestant ethic). (344)
19. d   All of the above is correct. A cult is a new religion with few followers; has teachings and practices which put it at odds with the dominant culture; and often is at odds with other religions. (345-347)
20. c   Although larger than a cult, a sect may still feel substantial hostility from society. (347)
21. d   All of the above is correct. Churches are highly bureaucratized; have more sedate worship services; and gain new members from within, from children born to existing members. (347)
22. a   A "brand name" within a major religion is a denomination. (347)
23. a   Church membership is highest in the South and Midwest. (348)
24. c   Fundamentalist churches teach that the Bible is literally true and that salvation comes only through a personal relationship with Jesus Christ. (350)
25. d   All of the above is correct. Questions that science cannot answer include: is there a God? what is the purpose of life? and what happens when a person dies? (352)

ANSWERS FOR TRUE-FALSE QUESTIONS

1. *True.* (328)
2. *False.* In Japanese schools the value of cooperation rather than competition is stressed. (329)
3. *False.* In Post-Soviet Russia, private, religious, and foreign-run schools are allowed to operate. (330)
4. *False.* Despite the fact that Egyptian education is free at all levels. children of the wealthy are more likely to get an education. (330)
5. *True.* (330)
6. *False.* American schools encourage, rather than discourage, individualism and although teamwork is encouraged, individuals are singled out for praise when the team does well. (331)
7. *True.* (331)
8. *False.* Functional theorists believe that social placement is helpful, not harmful, to society because the process helps insure that the "best" people will acquire a good education and subsequently perform the most needed tasks of society. (332)
9. *False.* Conflict theorists, not functionalists, emphasize the hidden curriculum in their analysis of American education. (333)
10. *True.* (334)
11. *False.* Research by Ray Rist concluded that the child's journey through school was preordained by the eighth day, not the end of the first year, of kindergarten. (335)
12. *False.* According to Farkas's research females and Asian Americans got higher grades because they communicated to teachers through their demeanor and behavior that they were interested in what the teacher was teaching; they fit the teacher's idea of what a good student should be. (335)
13. *True.* (337)
14. *False.* The goal of the sociological study of religion is to analyze the relationship between society and religion and to gain insight into the role that religion plays in people's lives. It is not to determine which religions are most effective in peoples' lives. (339)
15. *True.* (340)
16. *True.* (341)
17. *False.* The term "born again" is a term used by some Protestants to describe people who have undergone a life-transforming religious experience. (343)
18. *True.* (344)
19. *False.* Max Weber wrote <u>The Protestant Ethic and the Spirit of Capitalism</u>. (344)
20. *True.* (346)
21. *False.* The terms ecclesia and state religion mean the same thing, not church and state religion. (347)
22. *True.* (347)
23. *True.* (347)
24. *False.* The racial segregation observed in church membership is based on social custom. (349)
25. *True.* (350)

ANSWERS FOR FILL-IN QUESTIONS

1. Using diplomas and degrees to determine who is eligible for jobs, even though the diploma or degree may be irrelevant to the actual work, is characteristic of <u>CREDENTIAL SOCIETY</u>. (328)

2.   MANIFEST FUNCTIONS are the intended consequences of people's actions designed to help some part of the social system. (330)

3.   The function of MAINSTREAMING is intended to help people become part of the mainstream of society. (331)

4.   The process by which education opens and closes doors of opportunity for individuals in a society is the GATEKEEPING function of education. (332)

5.   Many U.S. schools practice TRACKING, the sorting of students into different educational programs based on their real or perceived abilities. (332)

6.   The unwritten goals of schools, such as teaching obedience to authority and conformity to cultural norms, is referred to as HIDDEN CURRICULUM. (333)

7.   A high school graduate who has difficulty with basic reading and math is FUNCTIONALLY ILLITERATE. (337)

8.   Durkheim's term for common elements of everyday life was PROFANE. (340)

9.   Answering questions about ultimate meaning, providing emotional comfort, and social solidarity are FUNCTIONS of religion. (340)

10.   For Muslims, the crescent moon and star, for Jews the Star of David, and for Christians the cross, all are examples of RELIGIOUS SYMBOLS. (342)

11.   COSMOLOGY is teachings or ideas that provide a unified picture of the world. (343)

12.   According to conflict theorists, religion is the OPIUM OF THE MASSES. (343)

13.   THE PROTESTANT ETHIC is Weber's term to describe the ideal of a highly moral life, hard work, industriousness, and frugality. (345)

14.   A(n) CHARISMATIC LEADER is someone who exerts extraordinary appeal to a group of followers. (346)

15.   SECULARIZATION OF RELIGION is the replacement of a religion's "otherworldly" concerns with concerns about "this world." (352)

ANSWERS TO MATCH THESE SOCIAL SCIENTISTS WITH THEIR CONTRIBUTIONS

1. c   Randall Collins: *credential society*
2. f   Ray Rist: *expectations of kindergarten teachers*
3. g   George Farkas: *teacher expectations in grading students*
4. b   Talcott Parsons: *the gatekeeping function of education*
5. d   Emile Durkheim: *The Elementary Forms of the Religious Life*
6. h   Max Weber: *The Protestant Ethic and the Spirit of Capitalism*
7. e   Karl Marx: *"religion is the opium of the people"*
8. a   Ernest Troeltsch: *cult-sect-church-ecclesia typology*

GUIDELINES FOR ANSWERING THE ESSAY QUESTIONS

2.   *Select one of the three perspectives and design a research project to test the claims of that perspective about the nature of education.*
In order to answer this question you must first choose one of the three perspectives. For example, you might choose the conflict perspective and decide to do a research project on the relationship between ethnicity and individual educational achievement and goals. Your research will involve an analysis of student choices of curricula, their grades, retention rates, and graduation from a large racially/ethnically diverse high school. You have access to student records and you collect data on students in one class as this class moves through the high school. You will compare white students'

records to those of African-American and Hispanic students in order to test whether the conflict theorists are correct in their assertion that the educational system reproduces the students' class background.

3.   *In discussing solutions to educational problems, the author suggests that one direction in which schools should go is towards setting higher educational standards. Both the research by James Coleman and Thomas Hoffer, and the success of Jaime Escalante, support this. Discuss social factors that might explain why such a proposal has not been widely adopted by public schools across the country.*

In answering this question you will want to focus on obstacles to implementation. You could refer to some of the research on teacher expectations and student tracking to illustrate the status quo in the majority of schools (p. 335). The conflict theorists have pointed out the ways in which our system of education perpetuating social inequalities, and Rist's research on how teachers use social class as a basis for tracking students fits with this perspective. The result of tracking is that it creates a self-fulfilling prophecy; students limit their abilities. Finally, as the experience of Jaime Escalante demonstrated, it was only after he changed the system of instruction that student attitudes and performance changed (p. 338-339).

1.   *Assume that you have been asked to make a presentation about religion to a group of people who have absolutely no idea what religion is. Prepare a speech in which you define religion and explain why it exists.*

For this question, your first task is to explain what religion is. To do this you might want to refer to Durkheim's work on the elementary forms of religious life (pp. 339-340), talking about the differences between the sacred and profane, the presence of beliefs, practices, and a moral community. Once you've done this you next task is to discuss why religion exists. Here you could talk about either the functionalist perspective or the conflict perspective or both. If you choose to focus only on the functionalist view, you would want to talk about how religion meets basic human needs (pp. 340-341); you might also want to refer to the symbolic interactionist views on community (pp. 342-343). If you want to focus only on conflict theory, or add that to your discussion of functionalism, you would want to talk about how, for Marx, religion is like a drug that helps the oppressed forget about their exploitation at the hands of the capitalists (pp. 343-344). Furthermore, conflict theorists point out that capitalists use religion legitimate social inequalities and maintain the status quo.

▲▼ ANSWERS FOR CHAPTER 14 -- POPULATION AND URBANIZATION

ANSWERS FOR MULTIPLE CHOICE QUESTIONS

1. b   The proposition that the population grows geometrically while food supply increases arithmetically is known as the Malthus theorem. (358)

2. d   According to the New Malthusians, the world's population is following an exponential growth curve, which means that after doubling during approximately equal intervals of time, the world's population growth suddenly accelerates. (359)

3. d   None of the above is correct. Anti-Malthusians do not believe that people will blindly reproduce until there is no room left on earth, or that it is possible to project the world's current population growth into the indefinite future. They believe that most people do use intelligence and rational planning when it comes to having children. (360-361)

4. b   The three-stage historical process of population growth is the demographic transition. (360)

5. c   The process by which a country's population becomes smaller because its birth rate and immigration are too low to replace those who die and emigrate is population shrinkage. (361)

6. c   According to the Anti-Malthusians, starvation is due to a mismatch between where the greatest supply of food is and where the greatest demand for it is. Those areas of the world where populations are growing at a slow rate also produce an oversupply of food, while those areas of the world that are growing at a fast rate are not able to produce enough food. (362)

7. d   All of the above is correct. People in the Least Industrialized Nations have so many children because parenthood provides status, children are considered to be an economic asset, and the community encourages people to have children. (364)

8. c   Demographers use population pyramids to describe the age and sex distribution of a nation. (365)

9. a   Factors that influence population growth (fertility, mortality, and net migration) are demographic variables. (366)

10. a   The annual number of deaths per 1,000 population is the crude death rate. (366)

11. d   All of the above is correct. The factors pushing someone to emigrate include poverty, lack of religious and political freedoms, and political persecution. (367)

12. a   According to your text, it is difficult to forecast population growth because of government programs that impact on fertility. (368)

13. b   The key to the origin of cities is more efficient agriculture; the production of surplus agricultural produces enables some people to stop producing food for themselves and, instead, gather in cities to spend time in other pursuits. (370)

14. d   Urbanization is when an increasing proportion of a population lives in cities. (370)

15. b   The area in Florida between Miami, Orlando, and Tampa is considered a megalopolis. (371)

16. d   All of the above is correct. Edge cities consist of a cluster of shopping malls, hotels, office parks, and residential areas near the intersection of major highways; they overlap political boundaries and include parts of several cities or towns; and they provide a sense of place to whose living there. (373)

17. c   Gentrification is the movement of middle-class people into rundown areas of a city. (373)

18. c   The model which is based on the idea that land use in cities is based on several centers, such as a clustering of restaurants or automobile dealerships is the multiple-nuclei model. (374)

19. d   As the number of low-income neighborhood residents increases, they begin to spill over into adjacent middle-class neighborhoods. The consequences is that the middle class begins to move out, thereby expanding the sector of low-income housing. Sociologists refer to this as invasion-succession cycle. (374)

20. a   The different models of urban growth have been criticized because they do not adequately explain urban growth in the Least Industrialized Nations. In these countries, the wealthy often claim the inner city, while the poor settle around the fringes. (374)

21. b   *Gesellschaft* societies are characterized by secondary, impersonal relationships; the end result of this can be alienation. (376)

22. d   All of the above is correct. According to Gans's typology, the trapped includes downwardly mobile persons, elderly persons, and alcoholics and drug addicts. (377-378)

23. c   The Kitty Genovese case in an example of alienation. (378)

24. b   Suburbanization is the movement from the city to the suburbs. (380)

25. a   In many urban neighborhoods, as the tax base began to erode and services decline, banks adopted policies of refusing to make loans for housing or business. This practices is called redlining. (380)

ANSWERS FOR TRUE-FALSE QUESTIONS

1. *False*. Thomas Malthus not a sociologist at the University of Chicago in the 1920s. He was an English economist who lived from 1766 to 1834. (358)
2. *True*. (359)
3. *False*. There are three stages, not four, in the process of demographic transition. (360)
4. *False*. The major reason why people in the Least Industrialized Nations have so many children is not necessarily because they do not know how to prevent conception. The reason is more sociological in nature, including the status which is conferred on parents for producing children, as well as the need for children to take care of a person when she or he is old. (364)
5. *False*. Population pyramids represent a population, divided into age and sex--but not race. (365)
6. *True*. (366)
7. *False*. The fertility rate and fecundity are different terms that express different ideas. The fertility rate is the number of children the average woman bears, while fecundity is the number of children a woman is capable of bearing; fecundity is significantly higher than the fertility rate. (366)
8. *True*. (366)
9. *True*. (368)
10. *False*. The primary factor that influences a country's growth rate is the rate of industrialization; in every country that industrializes, the growth rate declines. (368)
11. *True*. (3370)
12. *False*. The process of urban areas turning into metropolises, and metropolises developing into megalopolises is not unique to the United States, but is a worldwide phenomenon. (371)
13. *True*. (372)
14. *True*. (374)
15. *False*. No one model is considered to be the most accurate because different cities develop and grow in different ways, especially if there are certain kinds of natural barriers such as rivers or mountains. (374)
16. *True*. (376)
17. *False*. Herbert Gans, the author of *The Urban Villagers*, found that people living in large cities created a sense of community through their involvement in extensive social networks, thereby avoiding feelings of alienation. (376)
18. *True*. (378)
19. *False*. When banks engage in the practice of redlining the quality of life in neighborhoods generally deteriorated. (380)
20. *True*. (382)

ANSWERS FOR FILL-IN QUESTIONS

1. <u>DEMOGRAPHY</u> is the study of the size, composition, growth, and distribution of human populations. (358)
2. A pattern of growth in which numbers double during approximately equal intervals, thus accelerating in the latter stages is the <u>EXPONENTIAL GROWTH CURVE</u>. (359)
3. A(n) <u>POPULATION PYRAMID</u> is a graphic representation of a population, divided into age and sex. (365)
4. The <u>FERTILITY RATE</u> refers to the number of children that the average woman bears. (366)

5. The difference between the number of people moving into an area and the number of people moving out of the area per 1,000 population is the <u>NET MIGRATION RATE</u>. (366)
6. The basic demographic equation is *growth* = <u>*BIRTHS*</u> - <u>*DEATHS*</u> +<u>*MIGRATION*</u>. (368)
7. A demographic condition in which women bear only enough children to reproduce the population is referred to as <u>ZERO POPULATION GROWTH</u>. (369)
8. <u>URBANIZATION</u> refers to masses of people moving to cities and to these cities having a growing influence in society. (370)
9. An overlapping area consisting of at least two metropolises and their many suburbs is a <u>MEGALOPOLIS</u>. (371)
10. As Americans migrate and businesses move, <u>EDGE CITIES</u> have developed near intersections of major highways. (373)
11. The displacement of the poor by the relatively affluent, who renovate the former's homes is <u>GENTRIFICATION</u>. (373)
12. <u>HUMAN ECOLOGY</u> is the relationship between people and their environment. (376)
13. <u>COMMUNITY</u> is a place people identify with, where they feel a sense of belonging. (376)
14. Using a newspaper to shield ourselves from others and to indicate our inaccessibility is one example of the <u>NORM OF NONINVOLVEMENT</u>. (378)
15. The policy of <u>URBAN RENEWAL</u> involves the rehabilitation of rundown areas in a city, with the result that the poor who live there are displaced. (382)

ANSWERS TO MATCH THESE SOCIAL SCIENTISTS WITH THEIR CONTRIBUTIONS

1. a   Thomas Malthus: *theorem on population growth*
2. c   Ernest Burgess: *concentric-zone model*
3. d   Herbert Gans: *urban villagers*
4. e   Homer Hoyt: *sector model*
5. b   Robert Park: *human ecology*

GUIDELINES FOR ANSWERING THE ESSAY QUESTIONS

1.   *State the positions of the New Malthusians and the Anti-Malthusians and discuss which view you think is more accurate, based on the information provided about each position.*
        The author outlines both sides positions on pages 358 through 362. You should begin this essay by summarizing each side's arguments. For the New Malthusians you would want to include the idea of the exponential growth curve, while for the Anti-Malthusians you would want to refer to the concepts of the demographic transition and population shrinkage. For both you would want to include some of the facts--that world population growth does seem to reflect the exponential growth curve (New Malthusians), while the Least Industrialized Nations reflect the second stage of the demographic transition and the population of European countries is shrinking (Anti-Malthusians). Finally, you need to draw conclusions about which view you think is more accurate.

2.   *Analyze why it is so difficult to stem population growth in the Least Industrialized Nations.*
        There are several reasons why it is so difficult to convince people living in the Least Industrialized Nations to have fewer children. The textbook provides some discussion of this issue on page 364. You would want to consider what functions children play in their parents' lives and in the life of the community--conferring status on their parents, representing an economic asset to their parents, and reinforcing community views. Additionally, as the conflict theorists point out, women are oppressed by the men in all aspects their lives, even reproduction; because there is often a cultural

emphasis on male virility, men want to father many children, to show the community that they are truly masculine.

3.   *Discuss whether or not cities are impersonal Gesellschafts or communal Gemeinschafts.*
For this essay you would want to refer to the work of Louis Wirth and Herbert Gans. Wirth talked about the breakup of kinship and neighborhoods with the growth of cities; the result was alienation (p. 376). On the other hand, Gans found evidence of villages embedded within urban landscapes, which provided people with a sense of community (pp. 376-377). In particular, he discusses the "ethnic villagers."   If you decide to argue for the impersonality of urban life, you should also include some discussion of the norm of noninvolvement and the diffusion of responsibility (p. 378). If you choose to talk about communities within cities, then you should refer to how people create intimacy by personalizing their environment, developing attachments to sports teams, objects, and even city locations (p. 378).

▲▼ ANSWERS FOR CHAPTER 15 -- SOCIAL CHANGE

ANSWERS FOR MULTIPLE CHOICE QUESTIONS

1. d   The shift in the characteristics of culture and society over time is social change. (388)
2. c   Paid work, contracts, and especially money is characteristic of *Gesellschaft*. (389-390)
3. a   Max Weber identified religion as the core reason for the development of capitalism. (390)
4. a   The Least Industrialized Nations have become dependent on the Most Industrialized Nations and they are unable to develop their own resources according to dependency theory. (391)
5. c   The current resurgence of ethnic conflicts, particularly in Bosnia, threatens the global map drawn up by the G7. (391)
6. c   Unilinear evolution theories assume that all societies follow the same path, evolving from simple to complex through uniform sequences. (392)
7. c   The assumption that civilizations are born, pass through a youthful period in order to reach maturity, and then decline and die is central to cyclical theories. (392)
8. a   The history of a society is a series of confrontations in which each ruling group creates the seeds of its own destruction, according to Karl Marx. (392)
9. c   According to William Ogburn, the idea of citizenship is an example of diffusion. (393)
10. b   The situation in which some elements of a culture adapt to an invention or discovery more rapidly than others is cultural lag. (393)
11. d   "All of the above" is the correct choice. Technology refers to tools as simple as a comb as well as those as complicated as a computer and the skills or procedures to make and use those tools. Apart from these specific meanings, technology refers to artificial means of extending human abilities. (394)
12. d   A recent development in the medical field allows doctors, with the use of a stethoscope, to check the hearts and lungs of patients who are hundreds of miles away. This is refereed to as telemedicine. (396)
13. b   The increasing integration of computers into education is likely to perpetuate social inequalities because rich school districts will be able to afford the new technology while poor school districts will not. (396)
14. a   Computers have transformed the way in which work is done, the location where work is carried out, and even the nature of social relationships in the workplace. What computers have not affected is the way in which salaries/pay scales are calculated. (396-397)

15. c The National Organization of Women is an example of a **proactive social movement** while the Stop-ERA is an example of **reactive social movement**. (399)

16. b Social movements that seek to change people totally are redemptive social movements. (400)

17. d A social movement that seeks to change society totally is a transformative social movement. (400)

18. b How people think about some issue is public opinion. (400)

19. d All of the above is correct. Advertising is a type of propaganda, an organized attempt to manipulate public opinion, and a one-sided presentation of information that distorts reality. (401)

20. b The fine point of propaganda identified by Alfred and Elizabeth Lee that would include surrounding the product, candidate, or policy with phrases that arouse positive feelings is "glittering generality." For example, calling a candidate a "*real* Democrat" or a supporter of "individualism" is so general that it is meaningless, but the audience believes that it has learned something very specific about the individual. (401)

21. c Raising money, recruiting people with needed skills, acquiring equipment, and gaining the attention of the media are all part of the process of resource mobilization. (402)

22. b According to conflict theorists, the multinationals' need to control technology in order to make profits stands in the way of developing alternative sources of power; once they have cornered the market on the technology that will harness the alternative energy sources, and can continue to make huge profits, then alternatives will be developed. (406)

23. b Racial minorities and the poor are disproportionately exposed to environmental hazards. (406)

24. c The major source of pollution is likely to become the Least Industrialized Nations. (407)

25. d "All of the above" is correct. Environmental sociology examines how the physical environment affects human activities; how human activities affect the physical environment; and the unintended consequences of human actions. (408)

ANSWERS FOR TRUE-FALSE QUESTIONS

1. *False*. The rapid social change that the world is currently experiencing is not a random event. It is the result or fundamental forces unleashed many years ago. (388)

2. *True*. (390)

3. *False*. The resurgence of ethnic conflicts in Europe, North and South America, Africa, and Asia does threaten the global map that has been carefully partitioned by the world's industrial giants; of special concern is the continued economic and political stability in countries that provide the essential raw materials for the G7's industrial machine. (391)

4. *True*. (392)

5. *True*. (392)

6. *False*. It was not Max Weber but rather Karl Marx who believed that the history of a society is a series of confrontations in which each ruling group sows the seeds of its own destruction. (392)

7. *True*. (393)

8. *True*. (393)

9. *True*. (394)

10. *False*. Doctors are not likely to support the increased use of computers in medical diagnosis even when the computers do a more accurate job than the doctor could achieve. They view computers as a fundamental challenge to their medical expertise. (396)

11. *False*. The use of computers in education is likely to perpetuate, rather than decrease, the social

inequality between school districts, because poor districts will not be able to afford the hardware. (396)

12. *False*. Not all social movements seek to change society; some seek to change people. (399)
13. *True*. (400)
14. *False*. The environmental movement is an example of a reformative, not a transformative, social movement. (400)
15. *False*. Propaganda and advertising are not quite different from one another. In essence, advertising is a type of propaganda because it fits both the broad and the narrow definition of propaganda perfectly. (400-401)
16. *False*. In the final stage of a social movement, decline is not always certain. Sometimes an emerging group with the same goals and new leadership will take over the "cause." (403)
17. *False*. There is not a strong consensus among scientists that the greenhouse effect is a very serious threat to our natural environment; some scientists even doubt its existence. (406)
18. *True*. (407)
19. *True*. (408)
20. *False*. According to environmental sociologists, governments are often to blame for environmental problems because they try to create conditions for the profitable accumulation of capital. (408)

ANSWERS FOR FILL-IN QUESTIONS

1. The transformation of agricultural societies into industrial societies is the outcome of MODERNIZATION. (390)
2. An IDEAL TYPE is a composite of characteristics based on many specific examples. (390)
3. Karl Marx viewed history as a DIALECTICAL PROCESS, in which each stage of history contains the sees of its own destruction. (392)
4. The combination of existing elements and materials to form new ones results in INVENTION. (393)
5. Societies change as a result of DISCOVERY, which reflects a new way of seeing reality. (393)
6. William Ogburn used the term CULTURAL LAG to describe human behavior that lags behind technological innovations. (393)
7. The world-wide electronic network is referred to as the INFORMATION SUPERHIGHWAY, which conveys the idea of information traveling at high rates of speed between homes, schools and businesses around the globe. (397)
8. Broadly speaking, a SOCIAL MOVEMENT consists of large numbers of people who organize to promote or resist social change. (398)
9. Alcoholics Anonymous would be an example of a ALTERATIVE social movement. (399)
10. The presentation of information in an attempt to influence people is PROPAGANDA. (400)
11. ACID RAIN is created when sulfur dioxide and nitrogen oxide, released as a result of burning fossil fuels, react with moisture in the air. (406)
12. We will have achieved a SUSTAINABLE ENVIRONMENT when we are able to use our physical environment to meet the needs of humanity without destroying our environment. (405)
13. The GREENHOUSE EFFECT, the buildup of carbon dioxide in the earth's atmosphere that allows light to enter but inhibits the release of heat, is believed to cause GLOBAL WARMING. (406)
14. ENVIRONMENTAL SOCIOLOGY examines how human activities affect the physical environment and how the physical environment affects human activities. (408)

15.   The use of extreme tactics to try to arouse indignation among the public and force the government to take action to protect our natural environment is referred to as ECOSABOTAGE. (409)

ANSWERS TO MATCH THESE SOCIAL SCIENTISTS WITH THEIR CONTRIBUTIONS

1. c   Karl Marx: *capitalism produces alienation of workers*
2. j   David Aberle: *classified social movements by type and amount of social change*
3. g   William Ogburn: *three processes of cultural innovation*
4. b   Max Weber: *religion led to the development of capitalism*
5. f   Oswald Spengler: *cyclical theory predicting the decline of Western civilization*
6. e   Jacques Ellul: *warned that technology is destroying traditional values*
7. h   Lewis Morgan: *three stage theory of social evolution*
8. a   Mayer Zald: *compared social movements to a rolling sea*
9. i   Neil Postman: *recognized as an opponent of technology*
10. d   Al. & Eliza. Lee: *the fine art of propaganda*

GUIDELINES FOR ANSWERING THE ESSAY QUESTIONS

1.   *Choose a particular technology--you can use the automobile or the computer--and discuss the impact that it has had on U.S. society.*
        The author discusses how technology is more than just the tools we use; it also includes the skills and procedures needed to make and use those tools (p. 394). As you talk about a particular tool -- the automobile or the computer for instance -- think about the skills and procedures that we have adopted to enable us to effectively use this tool. Then discuss how one particular technology impacts on different aspects of social life. The book provides information on how computers have altered the way medicine is practiced, the delivery of education, and the conduct of work (pp. 395-396). In your essay you can bring in information Henslin provides or you can talk about another kind of technology -- the automobile, the airplane, the telephone, or the television.

2.   *Discuss Ogburn's three processes of social change and provide examples to illustrate each.*
        This is a fairly straightforward essay question. What you need to do is to discuss each of Ogburn's processes -- invention, discovery, and diffusion -- and provide examples for each (pp. 393-394).

3.   *Discuss the role that global stratification plays in the worldwide environmental problems.*
        For this essay you would want to first divide the world into three camps -- the Most Industrialized Nations, the Industrializing Nations, and the Least Industrialized Nations and then discuss the type of environmental problems, and the source of those problems, within each of the worlds of industrialization (pp. 405-407). You would also want to talk about how these three worlds are inter-connected when it comes to environmental problems; pollution and environmental degradation does not stop at national boundaries.

GLOSSARY OF WORDS TO KNOW

A

aberration: something that deviates from norms

abject poverty: greatest degree of most miserable poverty

adherents: people who argue in favor of something

albeit: although

alleviate: make less painful

aloof: reserved or indifferent

amenable: able to be influenced

amniocentesis: a surgical procedure in which a needle in inserted into the uterus of a pregnant woman and a small amount of amniotic fluid is extracted and analyzed in order to detect birth defects as well as the sex of the fetus

amorphous: not having a definite shape or structure

apparatus: equipment

arable: suitable for cultivation

arbitrary: making distinctions that may be incorrect

armchair philosophy: to speculate about the nature things without ever doing scientific research

assembly-line worker: someone employed in a factory, whose work involves doing the same task over and over again

astride: on top of

avengers: people who get satisfaction from punishing a wrongdoer

B

backlash: a strong negative reaction to a recent political or social development

bag lady: a street woman who carries her belongings in bag

bag of scum: an insulting expression, meaning someone is disgusting

bandied about: passed along without being careful

barrage: a massive amount of information given in a concentrated format

barren: unable to conceive a child

bartered: traded for something else

beamed: smiled with joy

"beamed aboard": to be transported from earth to a spaceship instantly through the use of advanced technology; the phrase gained popularity because of its usage by crew members of the Star Trek's Enterprise

bewilderment: hopeless confusion

bilingual: speaking at least two languages

Black Maria: police wagon

blindfolded: having something placed over the eyes so that a person cannot see

bludgeoned: to hit with heavy impact

bondage: held in chains; slavery

boozers: heavy drinkers of alcoholic beverages

boycott: an organized decision not to dealings with someone, usually in order to express disapproval and to force acceptance of certain conditions

bickering: arguing over trivial matters

bolster: to re-enforce; to give a boost to

bottom line: the essential point

burnout: condition of having become emotionally exhausted by a job, etc.

burros: donkeys

C

Calvinism: one of the early Protestant religious groups whose followers believed that their fate after death was determined before they were even born

cantankerous: bad-tempered

capital gains: gains from selling an asset held for investment

cardinal rule: a basic rule

carjacking: forcing the driver of a car out of the car while it is in motion and then stealing it away from him or her

car pools: an arrangement in which different drivers take turns driving

catcalls: whistles and comments, generally directed at a woman by men

circumvent: get around

clamored: gathered around demanding something

cliques: small, tightly-knit groups

coalesce: come together

cockeyed: slightly crazy; ridiculous

codified: systematically classified

collapsed: broken down, so they no longer are separate

collision course: a situation in which two forces are set to run headlong into one another

collusion: acting together to cause something illegal or wrong to occur

common sense: things everyone should realize

con artists: people who take advantage of others who are easily fooled

concrete: being solid or specific

conjugal rights: rights as a husband or wife

constraints: forced limits

convergence: coming together; the place where that happens

coronation: ceremony proclaiming a person as king or queen

cracks in the seamless surface: the idea that everything is not perfect

credit histories: a written record of an individual's loans from banks and credit companies

crucible: a container capable of withstanding high temperatures, used for melting a substance

cumbersome: awkward

curtsies: bending the knees and slightly bowing in a gesture of respect

czarist Russia: Russia during the time it was ruled by czars (monarch)

D

deaf-mute: a person who is deaf and unable to speak

death squads: military squadrons that engage in the clandestine murder of civilians *debutante balls*: formal dances at which young women from socially prominent families are "presented" to society

deferential behavior: very respectful behavior

defrocked rabbi, priest, or nun: a person who formerly was a priest

deleterious: harmful

demure: modest, shy

deplorable: bad or wretched

despicable: deserving of contempt

detention: being held after school because of misbehavior during school hours

deteriorating: run down; in poor condition

disequilibrium: things not being in balance

disheveled: unkempt; to be in disarray

disjunction: a separation

dissertation: a lengthy paper written in connection with obtaining a doctoral degree

dissociated: to have separated from your previous association with someone or something

distended: inflated

distill: reduce

distortion: being twisted out of shape

divergent: varying from one to another

divine providence: care or guidance coming from God

docksiders: a type of shoe worn by sailors

doctoral: of or relating to work towards a doctorate degree

doting: seeming overly fond of someone

driving a wedge: doing something that would result in a separation

drudgery: work, viewed as a chore or grind

dweebs, dorks, nerds: people regarded as dull

dyed-in-the-wool: holding inflexible opinions

E

e-mail: electronic mail; communicating by using telephone lines to connect to computers

easel: three-legged structure to hold a chart, etc.

ecstatic: very happy

eerily: weirdly, disturbingly

egalitarian: characterized by people having equal rights

electrodes: terminals that conduct electricity

elusive: difficult to grasp

emblazoned: decorated

embodiment: solid example of

enclave: small, almost completely surrounded, areas

encompasses: contains within it

encrusted: coated over with

encumbered: to be burdened by something, or weighed down by something

endemic: native to a particular people or country

engenders: produces or generates

enmeshed: tangled up in

entice: lure or tempt

epileptic seizures: type of physical and mental dysfunctions caused by nervous disorders
erogenous zone: body areas that are sexually stimulating
espouse: to take up and support a cause
estrange: alienated; to break the bonds of loyalty
estrangement: separation between people who formerly were friendly
ethnic stews: a mix of ethnic groups
euphoric: extremely happy
exorbitant: very, very high (as with regard to price)
extols: praises highly
extrapolating: estimating a result based on known values
exuberant: joyful

F

face-saving: preserving a person's respect
Fahrenheit: a scale for measuring temperature
fallout: an chance result of product of something else happening
falsification: changing something to make it appear different
fax: a method of communicating by sending messages between machines that are connected to telephone lines
faze: disturb
felony: serious offense for which people frequently are imprisoned
flagging: drooping
flailing: moving his arms around wildly
flare-ups: sudden outbursts of anger
flesh this out: make this discussion more complete
flock: a large number of people attracted to a leader
floundering: acting in a clumsy or ineffective way
flunkies: servants who obediently obey their superiors
fluttered: flapped, like a bird flaps its wings
flying in the face: not conforming to the expected outcome
food stamps: government-issued stamps that are used by poorer people to purchase food
forefinger: finger closest to the thumb
free-for-all: chaotic situation
freshly minted: newly issued
frugal: being extremely careful with one's money
full-blown: to be fully developed

G

gain the ear of: get access to; are heard by
gangsters: members of a gang of criminals; racketeers
generic sheepskin: degree from a college not having much prestige
gleaned: collected
grievances: complaints

gringo: Latin American slang for Anglo-Americans
gruesome: horrible, disgusting
gunslinging heroes: cowboys in the Wild West who wore guns in holsters and engaged in gun fights
gynecological: relating to the female reproductive system

H

hallmark: a feature or trait that distinguishes something from everything else
hallucinogenic: causing a person to see and hear things that don't exist
haphazard: not kept in a meaningful manner
harnessing: to make use of something
hassle: a troubling situation
hawk: to sell something by calling out in the street
hefty: very large or heavy
heralds: indicates the beginning
heretic: nonbeliever
hesitation: pausing because of uncertainty
hogtied: to be made helpless
Holsteins: a breed of cattle
home economics: a course of study in which activities associated with maintaining a home and family are stressed
honing: making something more effective
hovered: stayed more or less in one place; very slight movement
hybrid: the offspring of two plants of different varieties
hygiene: practices related to cleanliness
hypocrites: people who say one thing, but do another
hypothesis: a statement about the relationship between two phenomenon

I

idyllic: careful or romantic; rustic or pastoral
inalienable rights: rights that may not be taken or traded away
incapacitation: to make ineligible or incapable of performance
incontinent: having to control over one's bladder
indelible: something that cannot be removed; permanent
indigenous: coming from a particular region
indolence: laziness
infrastructure: the underlying foundation or basic structure
ingrained: forming an essential part of one's being
inherent: related to the essential character of something
inherently: involving the essential character of something
innate: existing from birth
inner city: a term applied to poor neighborhoods, usually located adjacent to, or near, the central core of downtown area
innumerable: too many in number to be counted
internalized: make part of your own thinking

internships: supervised work experiences while still a student in preparation for a particular career

interpenetrate: mutual penetration

interrelated: connected in various ways

inveterate conformists: people who always conform to a particular way of doing things

iron-fisted: acting in both a harsh and ruthless manner

irrefutable: unable to be disputed

J

jaywalker: person who crosses streets at improper places

juxtaposing: placing things side by side

K

kibbutz: a type or settlement in Israel

L

landfills: sites where garbage and other wastes are dumped

lap of luxury: living in grand style

laudable: worthy of praise

leeway: a margin of freedom or tolerance that is recognized as acceptable

lethal barrage: a prolonged, deadly burst of gunfire

levy: to impose a fee

light years: a very long period of time

liturgy: religious rite appropriate to some event

load the dice: unfairly influence the outcome

longevity: long lifetime

looking out for number one: putting one's own interests first, focusing on one's own needs or concerns

looking-glass: a mirror

lowest bidder: in an auction or competition for business, the one who quotes the lowest price

M

maimed: disfigured or crippled

mainstream: the dominant direction of activity or influence

makeshift: crude and temporary; a substitute

maladjusted: a person who does not fit in well

malnourished: not fed enough food to be healthy

martyr: person who suffers greatly for a cause

mascot: animal or thing used by a group as a symbol

mecca: a place sought as a goal by many people

menacing: threatening

metamorphosis: process of change in something, as when a caterpillar turns into a butterfly

meted out: carried out the prescribed penalty

microbes: very small organisms, such as germs

microchip: the electronic device on which information and directions are stored in a computer

microcosms: small samples

mind-boggling: an idea or thought that is hard to understand or to comprehend

mired: stuck in something, such as mud

misguided do-gooders: people who get in the way while thinking they are helping

monolingual: speaking only one language

monolithic: characterized by rigid uniformity

mortality: relating to death and death rates

mortgage payments: payments to a back or loan company on a home loan

mucus: slimy substance coming from the nasal passages

mused: thought over (here, I said to myself)

mushroomed: having increased very rapidly

mystique: a combination of mystical ideas and attitudes that develop around something or someone

N

nagged: complained

ne'er-do-wells: people who never do well or right

nostalgic: looking back in time, fondly

O

objectivity: expressing facts without consideration of personal feelings or prejudices

"old boys" network: a term used to refer to the informal social ties that exist among men, growing out of associations formed in college and carried through into the business world

on-line: being connected to a mainframe computer from a remote terminal by means of a modem

on-line services: businesses that provide customers with direct connections to computer networks

on-site: activity that take place on the spot

orphanages: institutions where children without parents are sometimes cared for

outlandish: very strange; bizarre

outpatient services: medical services for which a person is not hospitalized

override: to dominate over; to prevail over

overwhelmingly: many more people do than do not

P

Pacific Rim: a term used to refer to countries whose boundaries are on the Pacific Ocean; it includes countries in both North and South America as well as Asia

paleontologist: one who studies prehistoric life forms

palladium: a silver-white metallic element of the platinum group used as a catalyst

papyrus: a written scroll made of the le

pastoral: relating to the countryside

pathological: diseased

pecking order: social hierarchy based on asserting rank or power

pelvic: area of body where spinal column reaches legs

perks: benefits of a particular position or job

perplexed: confused and concerned

pervade: occur throughout

pervasive: spread throughout

philanthropy: helping mankind, by giving gifts and doing good deeds

picket line: a line formed by protesters, usually marching in front of some building

pinpointing: locating something very specifically

piqued: to stir up an interest in something

pittance: a very small (pitiful) amount

plummeting: rapidly falling aves of a papyrus plant

pluralistic: composed of many different groups

polarizing: reaching opposite extremes

police cruiser: police car

pollsters: people whose job it is to carry out surveys (public opinion polls)

precariously: depending upon known circumstances

precepts: rules of action or conduct

preconceived: formed in advance

predestined: determined beforehand; in the case of Protestantism, this term is used to signify that one's afterlife is determined even before they are born

preliterate: existing prior to the emergence of written language

prep school: school that prepares people for college

prerogatives: special privileges based on status

pristine: being free and clean, untouched

proactive: taking the initiative to make a change

profound: having deep feelings

projects (the): housing developments, owned and managed by the government, in which poorer people live because the rents are low

pyramid: a solid shape that is broad at the base and narrows to a point at the top

R

ramifications: consequences

rampant: spreading rapidly

ravishing: exceptionally attractive

recurring: taking place again and again

reemergence: coming out again

relentless: stubborn, persistent

relinquish: giving something up to someone else

reminiscent: something similar from the past

remittance: payment

remnants: the small parts or portions that are left over

remunerative: providing payment that is profitable

repentance: to feel sorrow or regret

repugnant: offensive to the senses

Resurrection: the belief in the Christian church that Church rose from death and once again lived among mortals *rickety:* not well built, thus dangerous

rigorous: strict, precise

rubber-stamp: approve almost without thinking about it

rudimentary: most simple

ruthless: without mercy, cruel

ruthlessly: to show no mercy

S

sabotage: deliberately damage

saloons: establishments in which alcoholic beverages are sold and consumed

satanism: the worship of Satan

scapegoating: blaming someone else for what is wrong

scowled: facial expression showing contempt or disgust

segregating: setting apart

semidarkness: almost, but not quite, dark

sequence: the order in which things appear

sexual promiscuity: engaging in sex with many persons

shadowed: the act of being watched or, in many cases, followed

share-cropping: a system of farming in which the farmer is provided with credit for seed, tools, living quarters, and food in exchange for working the land. When the crop is harvested, the farmer receives an agreed upon share of the value for the crop minus the credit charges

shoo off the flies: driving flies away by sounds or gestures

shoplift: steal something from a store that is open for business

shorthand: using symbols for words or thoughts

shroud: a cloth which is used to cover the body for burial

siblings: brothers and sisters

sidestepped: gotten around

sidetracked: diverted from the main issue

skateboarders: people who ride small boards on small wheels

skid row: a place where bums hang out

skittering gait: moving along quickly

sleight-of-hand: deceiving, as with magic tricks

smugness: feeling extremely correct about something; very satisfied with yourself

sniveling: falsely displaying a need for sympathy

sojourners: temporary residents; transients

sovereign: being of the most supreme kind

spigot: water faucet or valve

splinter: to split into parts or factions; a group that has split off from the parent organization

split second: a really short period of time

spontaneous: occurring naturally, instead of from ritual; doing something without really thinking

squatter settlements: places where people live without paying any rent or other fees, having claimed a right to the space

squealing: informing on someone to the authorities

stagnated: changing very little

stampeding: rushing wildly, out of control

steered away: discouraged from following a particular course of action *stock options:* the opportunity to acquire shares in a company

stooges: people who play the role of the victim of another's pranks

straitjacket: something that restrains a person

strange tongue: unaccustomed language

striptease: slowly removing clothes to excite someone

Styrofoam cup: a rigid, lightweight cup

subconscious: being aware of something without thinking about it

subjugated: brought under the control of

subpoenaed: required to be produced in connection with legal proceedings

subservient: subordinate

subtle: difficult to distinguish; elusive

subvert: to overturn or overthrow from the foundation

succinct: stated clearly in a very few words

superimposed: placed over something else

supposition: something that is supposed to be true

surreptitiously: secretly, furtively

surveillance: watching specific people or places, as by the police, without being seen

swastikas: a symbol used by the Nazis

sweatshop: a workplace where people work long hours for low pay

swishing: moving through a liquid with a light noise

synonymous: alike in meaning or significance

T

taint: a mark or influences that is contaminating

tallied: counted

temporal: worldly; relating to time rather than space

tenacious: persistence

tenure: lifetime employment security granted to professors and teachers

theologians: individuals who study the works of religious bodies

Thunderbird: a brand of cheap wine

toddler: a very small child

touchdown: scoring points by crossing a goal line in football

town meetings: in an earlier time, meetings of all adults in a town to vote on the business of local government

treadmill: a revolving device on which you walk without getting anywhere

tried-and-true: proven arrangements

tunnel vision: the inability to consider a range of perspectives, preferring to keep attention focused in one direction only

turned ... tricks: engaged in prostitution

tweak the nose: irritate (literally, flick a finger on the nose)

typology: analysis based on symbols or meaning

U

unabashed: obvious, and intended to be so

undergird: support

underscores: to underline, to emphasize or stress the importance of

unflinching: not moving or shrinking away

unkempt: tangled, not combed

unobtrusive: not getting in people's way

urbanization: the movement from rural areas into cities

utterances: statements

V

vagrants: people with no home or job

vegetate: engage in no activities

veil of foliage: an area with a mass of plants and trees that may conceal things

veneer: a thin outer layer

vested: to give someone power or authority to do something

vested interest: a situation in which a person (or organization) has a strong personal commitment to the existing arrangements

vibrant: full of life or activity

virility: a characteristic in which masculinity is associated with being able to impregnate a woman

voice-over: the voice that speaks over the action, for instance in a TV commercial

volatile: unstable, and likely to explode

vulnerability: capable of being wounded

W

weeded out: removed from something more desirable

wheezing: breathing with difficulty; the breathing is often accompanied by a whistling sound

widowhood: being single as a result of spouse's death

willy-nilly: randomly

workaholic: a person addicted to work

wrenching away: painfully removing

"wrong track": to move in the wrong direction

XYZ

yardstick: a standard using in measuring

zap: to use speed or force to impart something

zigzag: a pattern of forward motion followed by backward motion

NOTES

NOTES

NOTES

NOTES

NOTES

NOTES

NOTES